CW00566488

House of Commons

Political and Constitutional Reform Committee

Introducing a statutory register of lobbyists

Second Report of Session 2012–13

Volume I

Volume I: Report, together with formal minutes, oral and written evidence

Additional written evidence is contained in Volume II, available on the Committee website at www.parliament.uk/pcrc

Ordered by the House of Commons to be printed 10 July 2012

HC 153 [incorporating HC 1809-i-v, Session 2010-12]
Published on 13 July 2012
by authority of the House of Commons
London: The Stationery Office Limited
£20.00

The Political and Constitutional Reform Committee

The Political and Constitutional Reform Committee is appointed by the House of Commons to consider political and constitutional reform.

Current membership

Mr Graham Allen MP (*Labour, Nottingham North*) (*Chair*)
Mr Christopher Chope MP (*Conservative, Christchurch*)
Paul Flynn (*Labour, Newport West*)
Sheila Gilmore MP (*Labour, Edinburgh East*)
Andrew Griffiths MP *(Conservative, Burton)*
Fabian Hamilton MP, *(Labour, Leeds North East)*
Simon Hart MP (*Conservative, Camarthen West and South Pembrokeshire*)
Tristram Hunt MP (*Labour, Stoke on Trent Central*)
Mrs Eleanor Laing MP (*Conservative, Epping Forest*)
Mr Andrew Turner MP (*Conservative, Isle of Wight*)
Stephen Williams MP (*Liberal Democrat, Bristol West*)

Powers

The Committee's powers are set out in House of Commons Standing Orders, principally in Temporary Standing Order (Political and Constitutional Reform Committee). These are available on the Internet via http://www.publications.parliament.uk/pa/cm/cmstords.htm.

Publication

The Reports and evidence of the Committee are published by The Stationery Office by Order of the House. All publications of the Committee (including press notices) are on the internet at www.parliament.uk/pcrc. A list of Reports of the Committee in the present Parliament is at the back of this volume.

The Reports of the Committee, the formal minutes relating to that report, oral evidence taken and some or all written evidence are available in a printed volume.

Additional written evidence may be published on the internet only.

Committee staff

The current staff of the Committee are Joanna Dodd (Clerk), Helen Kinghorn (Legal Specialist), Lorna Horton (Inquiry Manager), Louise Glen (Senior Committee Assistant), Jim Lawford, (Committee Assistant) and Jessica Bridges-Palmer (Media Officer).

Contacts

All correspondence should be addressed to the Clerk of the Political and Constitutional Reform Committee, House of Commons, 7 Millbank, London SW1P 3JA. The telephone number for general enquiries is 020 7219 6287; the Committee's email address is pcrc@parliament.uk.

Contents

Summary

The right of citizens to lobby their Government and elected representatives is fundamental to a healthy, vibrant democracy. Lobbying itself comes in many forms, from one individual seeking to influence another, to an organised attempt, by a group of citizens, a company, or the media, to influence legislators by a variety of means.

Lobbyists can provide Government and parliamentarians with beneficial expert information and help refine and improve policy. However, when there are concerns, as published widely in the media of late, that some lobbyists may have undue access and influence over the policy making process it threatens to reduce public confidence in the whole political system.

It has been difficult to ascertain the Government's intent on lobbying regulation from the consultation paper, *Introducing a statutory register of lobbyists*, published on 20 January 2012. The Government's proposals attempt to shed light on whom third-party lobbyists and lobbying firms represent when they meet Ministers. The proposals are limited to third party lobbyists, as the Government has made it very clear that it prefers a limited register of activity to a regulator for the whole industry.

The consultation paper also questions whether the scope of the register should be expanded to include all those who lobby professionally, which could include charities, trade unions, trade associations, think tanks and campaign groups. Many of these groups are already subject to regulations in their own sectors. Charities who wish to lobby must follow strict guidance laid down by the Charity Commission, and trade union activities are regulated by the Certification Office.

Our report looks at the Government's proposals, and examines whether a statutory register of lobbyists would increase transparency about who is lobbying whom. We consider other options for statutory regulation, and finally identify ways in which Government could immediately improve transparency surrounding lobbying, through publishing more details of ministerial meetings, irrespective of the type of statutory register it may eventually decide to implement.

It has been extremely difficult to scrutinise the Government's proposals for introducing a statutory register of lobbyists, as the consultation raises questions regarding the scope, breadth and resources needed if different definitions of lobbying were to be decided upon. Defining the activity of lobbying is fundamental to defining who is a lobbyist. The Government's consultation paper fails to do so.

1 Introduction

1. On 8 February 2010, when he was still the Leader of the Opposition, David Cameron stated that lobbying would be the next big political scandal:

> I'm talking about lobbying—and we all know how it works. The lunches, the hospitality, the quiet word in your ear, the ex-ministers and ex-advisors for hire, helping big business find the right way to get its way. In this party, we believe in competition, not cronyism. We believe in market economics, not crony capitalism. So we must be the party that sorts all this out.[1]

Lobbying: Access and Influence in Whitehall

2. David Cameron's remarks followed a critical report on the lobbying industry: *Lobbying: Access and Influence in Whitehall*, published by the Public Administration Select Committee in January 2009. The report concluded that the current system of self-regulation by three different lobbying industry bodies, the Association of Professional Political Consultants, the Public Relations Consultants Association, and the Chartered Institute of Public Relations, allowed lobbyists to "pick and choose the rules that apply to them in a way that is incompatible with effective self regulation".[2]

3. The report's main recommendations were to:

- establish a single umbrella organisation with both corporate and individual membership, in order to be able to cover all those who are involved in lobbying as a substantial part of their work.

- create a mandatory register of lobbying activity, covering all those outside the public sector involved in accessing and influencing public sector decision makers, which should be managed and enforced by a body independent of both Government and lobbyists.

4. The then Government rejected the Public Administration Select Committee's recommendation for a statutory register of lobbyists, stating that "the Government believes that effective voluntary self-regulation must be the preferred approach". The Government response added that the issue of lobbying would be kept under review "to ensure that progress is made in developing an effective system of voluntary self-regulation".[3]

5. The Coalition's Programme for Government, published in May 2010, contained a commitment to "regulate lobbying through introducing a statutory register of lobbyists and ensuring greater transparency".[4]

---

1 *Rebuilding trust in politics*, 8 February 2010, http://www.conservatives.com/News/Speeches/2010/02/David_Cameron_Rebuilding_trust_in_politics.aspx

2 Public Administration Committee, First Report of Session 2008-09, *Lobbying: Access and Influence in Whitehall*, HC 36, para 57

3 Publication Administration Committee, Eighth Special Report of Session 2008-09, *Lobbying: Access and influence in Whitehall: Government Response to the Committee's First Report of Session 2008–09*, HC1058, para 5

4 HM Government, *The Coalition: our programme for Government*, May 2010, p21

6. In response to the Public Administration Select Committee report, the industry's three self-regulatory bodies set up the UK Public Affairs Council in July 2010. The aim of the Council was to "to offer a system of voluntary regulation to ensure that all those involved in lobbying institutions of government can be governed by a clear set of principles, underpinned by enforceable Codes of Conduct". This involved a voluntary register of lobbyists, first published in March 2011, but not subsequently kept fully up to date. Following the procurement of new IT systems the Council's voluntary register of lobbyists was finally re-launched in February 2012.

7. On 9 December 2011 the Public Relations Consultants Association withdrew from the Council, stating that self-regulation had not been successful, and called on the Government quickly to introduce a statutory register "held by an independent body, to run in parallel with the Codes of Conduct that exist already within the industry".[5]

The Committee's inquiry

8. On 20 January 2012, the Government published its proposals for *Introducing a Statutory Register of Lobbyists*, for consultation. The consultation paper proposes that only third party lobbyists would be required to be on a statutory register; those working in-house would be exempt. Third party lobbyists would be required to sign up to and update a statutory register on a quarterly basis, giving details of the:

- registered address of the company and company number;
- names of the employees engaged in lobbying;
- whether those employees are former Ministers or Senior Civil Servants;
- client lists.

The Government stated that registration "should be no more burdensome than filling out an online form".[6] The Government proposes to make the register publicly searchable, but does not plan to include data on specific meetings between lobbyists and Ministers, arguing that these are already published on Departmental websites. The Government proposes that the register should be "managed and enforced by a body which is independent of the lobbying industry, and of Government,"[7] and be self-funded by the lobbying industry.

9. One of the key issues for consultation was the definition of a lobbyist. The consultation paper defines lobbyists as "those who undertake lobbying activities on behalf of a third party client or whose employees conduct lobbying activities on behalf of a third party client".[8] There is discussion of the usefulness of the Government's definition of a lobbyist in chapter 3. The consultation paper also asks whether in-house lobbyists, be it those in

---

5 E-mail received by Elizabeth France, Chairman of UKPAC, from Francis Ingham, PRCA, 9 December 2011, http://www.publicaffairscouncil.org.uk/en/news/index.cfm/E-mail-received-by-UKPAC-from-Francis-Ingham-of-PRCA

6 HM Government, *Introducing a Statutory Register of Lobbyists*, January 2012, p10

7 HM Government, *Introducing a Statutory Register of Lobbyists*, January 2012, p17

8 HM Government, *Introducing a Statutory Register of Lobbyists*, January 2012, p11

commercial, trade union or charitable organisations, should also be required to register. **We welcome the fact that these proposals have been published for parliamentary scrutiny, as well as for wider consultation.**

10. We launched our inquiry into the Government's proposals for a statutory register on the same day that the consultation paper was published. Our witnesses have included lobbyists, representatives from the lobbying self-regulatory bodies, academic experts, and the Government. We have also sought, and received, evidence from representatives of some of those groups who might be particularly affected by the proposals if the Government's definition of lobbying was broadened, including transparency campaign groups, charities, trade unions, and lawyers. We are grateful as ever to all those who contributed to our inquiry.

11. This report looks first at the nature of the problem. This is followed by a detailed discussion of the Government's proposals and whether they will solve the problem that "when Ministers meet lobbying firms it is not transparent on whose behalf they are lobbying".[9] We also consider whether the Government's proposals will help to improve transparency about lobbying and help rebuild public trust in politics. Next we consider some other options for a statutory register. Finally we look at other measures to improve transparency around who is lobbying whom.

12. As the Public Administration Committee is currently conducting an inquiry into the *Business Appointment Rules*, which will cover the Advisory Committee on Business Appointments (ACoBA) and the 'revolving door' between the civil service and the private sector we will not consider this issue within our report. However, we urge Government to take a joined up approach to lobbying regulations, and urge it to consider any changes to ACoBA alongside potential lobbying regulations.

9 HM Government, *Introducing a Statutory Register of Lobbyists*, January 2012, p9

2 What is the problem?

The perception of undue influence

13. The right of citizens to lobby Government and Parliament, or to engage others to lobby on their behalf, is a fundamental part of a vibrant democracy. However, there is a perception in some quarters that some people have undue access to, and influence over, the policy-making process.

14. The 2009 Public Administration Select Committee report stated that "some of the concerns that exist around improper influence are closely linked to the power of informal networks of friendships and relationships".[10] David Cameron outlined what he believed to be the problem of lobbying in February 2010:

> I believe that secret corporate lobbying, like the expenses scandal, goes to the heart of why people are so fed up with politics. It arouses people's worst fears and suspicions about how our political system works, with money buying power, power fishing for money, and a cosy club at the top making decisions in their own interest".[11]

As Tamasin Cave, campaigner for Spinwatch and the Alliance for Lobbying Transparency told us: "We do not have public scrutiny of who is meeting whom and about what. So we have no way of knowing whether vested interests are having undue influence on policy."[12]

15. Since 2010 there have been a number of media reports surrounding allegations of undue influence. These include

- In March 2010, several then Members of Parliament were recorded expressing a willingness to use their contacts to lobby Government and Parliament, and were subsequently suspended from Parliament for varying periods on the recommendation of the Standards and Privileges Committee.[13]
- In October 2011, the Defence Secretary Liam Fox resigned when it was alleged that he had breached the Ministerial Code. An investigation conducted by the then Cabinet Secretary Sir Gus O'Donnell concluded that Liam Fox had breached the Ministerial Code.
- In December 2011 Bell Pottinger, a lobbying firm, were filmed boasting that they had direct access to the Prime Minister and other senior Ministers.

---

10 Public Administration Committee, First Report of Session 2008-09, *Lobbying: Access and Influence in Whitehall*, HC 36, para 41

11 *Rebuilding trust in politics*, 8 February 2010, http://www.conservatives.com/News/Speeches/2010/02/David_Cameron_Rebuilding_trust_in_politics.aspx

12 Q 57

13 Standards and Privileges Committee, Ninth Report of Session 2009-10, *Sir John Butterfill, Mr Stephen Byers, Ms Patricia Hewitt, Mr Geoff Hoon, Mr Richard Caborn and Mr Adam Ingram*, HC654

- In March 2012, Peter Cruddas, the co-treasurer of the Conservative Party was filmed apparently offering access to the Prime Minister in return for donations. He later resigned.

- In April 2012 it was revealed that Frederic Michel, an in-house lobbyist for News Corporation, had been in regular communication with officials at the Department for Culture, Media and Sport, including sending texts to the Secretary of State Jeremy Hunt, during the consideration of News International's bid for BSkyB. Adam Smith, special adviser to the Secretary of State, resigned.

Newspaper reports alleging close contact between politicians and lobbyists do nothing to reduce the suspicion felt by many ordinary people that large corporations or wealthy individuals have disproportionate influence over political decision making. Greater transparency regarding contacts between Ministers and lobbyists could help reduce this problem.

16. Opinions from witnesses differed about whether the public concern about lobbying was justified. Francis Ingham, Chief Executive of the Public Relations Consultants Association claimed that: "there is unwarranted public concern that there are relationships between the lobbying community and parliamentarians or former parliamentarians or former ministers that is inappropriate".[14] However, Mark Adams, a lobbyist and author of the blog standup4lobbying, stated: "we have to accept our share of the blame for the fact that when lobbyists behave badly—and if there is a lobbyist behaving badly, I am afraid on the whole it means there is a politician behaving badly on the other side—we are to blame for the public perception".[15] In its consultation paper the Government stresses that the aim of a statutory register of lobbyists is to "increase the information available about lobbyists without unduly restricting lobbyists' freedom".[16] **There is a public perception in some quarters that there are inappropriate relationships between Ministers and lobbyists and there is a need for action to address this perception.**

14 Q 193

15 Q 86

16 HM Government, *Introducing a Statutory Register of Lobbyists*, January 2012, p7

3 The Government's proposals

The Government's definition of a lobbyist

17. The Government's consultation paper, *Introducing a statutory register of lobbyists* proposes that a register of lobbyists should include only "those who undertake lobbying activities on behalf of a third party client or whose employees conduct lobbying activities on behalf of a third party client".[17] The Government makes the case that as Ministers already publish details of whom they are meeting there is no need to register in-house lobbyists. However, it claims that "under the current system, when Ministers meet lobbying firms it is not transparent on whose behalf they are lobbying".[18]

18. A majority of our witnesses felt that the Government's definition of a lobbyist was too narrow. Professor Justin Fisher of Brunel University told us "the definition in the Government's proposals is wholly inadequate".[19] Action on Smoking and Health (ASH) added:

> the Government's preference is clearly for a register containing only minimal information about lobbying activities and one that would only apply to a minority of lobbyists, those working for agencies and not......those working in-house or for other types of organisations known as 'think tanks'[20]

Professor Raj Chari, co-author of *Regulating Lobbying: a global comparison*, a comparative analysis of lobbying regulations across the world, told us that the Government's definition of a lobbyist was "pretty narrow from a comparative perspective".[21]

19. Edelman, a public affairs consultancy, also raised concerns that the Government's current definition of lobbyists was ambiguous, stating "the definition of lobbying as proposed includes only direct communications with Government and Parliament. It is unclear whether the act of advising others on such communications would be a registerable activity".[22] The Chartered Institute of Public Relations lamented that the range of questions presented in the consultation paper gave "little or no idea as to the Government's preferred definition".[23]

20. Helen Johnson, Chief Executive of the Association of Professional Political Consultants, told us it was unclear whether only direct representation would be covered by the lobbying register: "as bizarre as it may sound, as the proposals stand currently, it is not clear that the current Chair of the APPC will be required to add herself to this statutory register".[24] Indeed, Mark Adams also told us that he did not believe he would be required

---

17 HM Government, *Introducing a Statutory Register of Lobbyists*, January 2012, p9

18 HM Government, *Introducing a Statutory Register of Lobbyists*, January 2012, p9

19 Q 32

20 Ev w1

21 Q 331

22 Ev w64

23 Ev 108

24 Q 167

to register under the Government's current proposals "because it is about direct interactions on behalf of clients and, on the whole, I don't do that".[25] **We recommend that Government clarify whether its definition of lobbying includes lobbying advice, or only direct representation, to avoid confusion regarding who should, and should not register as a lobbyist if it goes ahead with its proposals.**

21. The consultation paper also asks whether the definition of lobbying should be broadened to include those who seek to influence policy on behalf of trade unions and charities. Nigel Stanley, Head of Policy and Communications for the Trade Union Congress told us that, while they would broadly accept a widening of the definition of lobbying, they felt that it would be unfair for them to be on a register alongside just third party lobbyists. In his oral evidence he stated:

> If it was a list of organisations then, yes, we would be happy to join it. We would be a little resentful, though, if we were singled out as a special category of organisation that needed to be registered when, say, employer organisations—which have a perfectly legitimate role in influencing public policy in the same way that we do, and in many ways are rather analogous—don't have to join that register. I think we would feel a bit cheesed off if that happened.[26]

22. The UK Deans of Science argued that broadening the definition of lobbying would be unfair if it required representative bodies to register alongside professional lobbyists. They stated: "What is of concern to UKDS is that what we consider as legitimate efforts to influence government and any or all political parties could ... put our organisation on a par with professional, paid, lobby companies, thus requiring it to register, possibly pay a registration fee and to be listed alongside those who lobby for a living".[27]

23. Tamasin Cave, transparency campaigner for Spinwatch and the Alliance for Lobbying Transparency, suggested that while defining lobbying was contentious, it had been done before in other countries. She told us: "they've got registers in Australia, Canada, the US and the EU, Germany has one to an extent and Austria is getting one. Nick one of their definitions and we'll start with that".[28]

24. The current definition of lobbying on the UK Public Affairs Council website states that

> Lobbying means, in a professional capacity, attempting to influence, or advising those who wish to influence the UK Government, Parliament, devolved legislatures or administrations, regional or local government or other public bodies on any matter within their competence.[29]

This definition is broader than the Government's definition of lobbying as it includes those who advise others on how to lobby as well as those who lobby directly. However, Elizabeth France, Chair of the Council, told us that the definition, while suitable for a voluntary

---

25 Q 87

26 Q 269

27 Ev w56

28 Q 65

29 Ev 104

register, was not likely to be robust enough for a statutory register. She told us: "It wasn't drafted by parliamentary counsel and, as it stands, it wouldn't be fit simply to slip into a piece of legislation. But the key thing I would want to emphasise is that it defines lobbying, not lobbyists."[30]

25. The Chartered Institute of Public Relations sent us an exhaustive, technical draft definition of lobbying activity prepared by Berwin Leighton Paisner LLP, that has also been submitted to the Government's consultation. **We are not going to endorse any particular definitions of lobbying as the definition may differ depending on the scope of a statutory register. We do not wish to pre-judge the debate. However, we urge the Government carefully to consider all definitions provided to the consultation, as the definition will be key to the success and effectiveness of any future register.**

Third party lobbyists

26. Many of our witnesses felt that the consultation paper lacked evidence to show why a statutory register of third party lobbyists was more necessary than any other kind of lobbying register. The Government's Impact Assessment includes the UK Public Affairs Council's estimate of the possible coverage of a statutory register of all lobbyists, using the Council's definition of lobbying. The data suggest that a register of third party lobbyists would cover around 100 organisations, who between them would have around 1,000 staff engaged in lobbying.

Table 1: estimated number of organisations involved in lobbying

Type of organisation	Number of organisations	Employees engaged in lobbying (total)
Public affairs specialists	100	1000
Companies with in-house staff	60	100
Charities/voluntary sector	40	120
Unions	30	50
Trade associations	25	50
Law practices	20	50
Others		130
Total	275	1500

Source: Impact Assessment, Proposals to introduce a statutory register of lobbyists[31]

27. However, we have some concerns about the accuracy of the data in this table. It was suggested that there may be many more in-house lobbyists than the table shows and that the total number of lobbyists may be greater than 1,500. When giving oral evidence, Lionel Zetter, a lobbyist for APCO Worldwide stated that the three self-regulatory bodies for public relations had almost 10,000 members between them.[32] While it is not uncommon for lobbyists to join more than one professional body, it seems likely that the estimate of 1,500 lobbyists across charities, trade unions, trade associations, law practices, in-house and agency lobbyists could be too low. Evidence provided by Spinwatch suggested that "the

30 Q 112

31 HM Government, *Introducing a statutory register of lobbyists*, Impact Assessment, January 2012

32 Q 20

industry estimates that there are now 3,500-4,000 full-time lobbyists (consultants and in-house) in the UK".[33]

28. The UK Public Affairs Council Register, which contains details of those registered by the Chartered Institute of Public Relations and the Association of Professional Political Consultants, lists 1,387 individual lobbyists for the period 1 December 2011 to 29 February 2012.[34] The Government's impact assessment admits that "although the UK Public Affairs Council ... has held a voluntary register since 2010, registration rates remain low".[35]

In-house lobbyists

29. Under the current proposals, lobbyists working in-house for a range of organisations, from large commercial organisations like Tesco, to trade associations like the Confederation of British Industry, to large charities like Friends of the Earth, would not be required to register as lobbyists. However, if any of these organisations then retained a lobbyist or lobbying firm, they would be listed on the register as a client.

30. The Government's proposals state that there is no need for in-house lobbyists to register as

> the Government already publishes quarterly information about Ministers meetings. Information about which stakeholders are meeting Ministers to put forward their views on policies is therefore already in the public domain. But under the current system, when Ministers meet lobbying firms it is not transparent on whose behalf they are lobbying.[36]

The UK Public Affairs Council stated that "this argument is fundamentally misconceived because it is based on a misapprehension of how public affairs consultancies normally conduct their business".[37] It highlighted that many public affairs consultancies provide mainly monitoring and advice, and that "rarely, if ever, do the services include making representations directly on behalf of the client".[38]

31. The Minister for Political and Constitutional Reform, Mark Harper MP, told us that in-house lobbyists had not been considered for the statutory register as it was clear who they were, when they met Ministers. He added:

> if a minister meets an external organisation, and it is from an in-house lobbyist, we say, 'The minister is meeting a man from Tesco'—just to pick someone at random—and it is clear that you are meeting someone from Tesco. If you say that

33 Ev 99

34 Public Affairs Council register of lobbyists, Retrieved May 15th 2012 http://www.publicaffairscouncil.org.uk/en/search-the-register/index.cfm

35 HM Government, *Introducing a Statutory Register of Lobbyists*,Impact Assessment, November 2011, p5

36 HM Government, *Introducing a Statutory Register of Lobbyists*, January 2012, p9

37 Ev 105

38 Ev 105

> you are meeting someone from a lobbying company, it is not entirely clear. That lobbying company could be acting for any organisation.[39]

However, Unlock Democracy a transparency campaign group, demonstrated that even smaller organisations can lobby Government on a wide array of issues. They stated that unless the topic was disclosed when the meeting was published it would be impossible to know the subject of the discussion:

> Unlock Democracy is currently lobbying the Cabinet Office on a number of different policy areas. If we were to have a meeting with Mark Harper it could be about individual elector registration, House of Lords reform, lobbying, boundary changes, or other democratic reform issues that we may wish the Government to pursue. This would not be apparent just from the fact that he was meeting us.[40]

32. The Minister stated that when a meeting with a Minister or official is disclosed, the topic being discussed is revealed. However, an analysis conducted by *The Independent* in January 2012 concluded that "more than 700 are simply reported as 'introductory' meetings and 350 are described as general 'catch-up' or 'discussion'".[41]

A statutory code of conduct

33. The Government proposes that a statutory register of lobbyists would not require an accompanying statutory code of conduct. The consultation paper states:

> The Government supports the industry's efforts to improve lobbying practice, and to develop a code of conduct that helps lobbyists perform to the highest possible standards. However, it thinks that this is a matter for the industry itself, not for the operator of the register. The register should be a register of activity, not a complete regulator for the industry.[42]

The consultation paper states that a statutory code of conduct is unnecessary because it "would impose costly and unnecessary regulation on the industry, their clients and the Government".[43]

34. Concerns were expressed that a statutory register without an accompanying statutory code of conduct could lead to less regulation of the lobbying industry. Ben Kernighan, Deputy Chief Executive of the National Council for Voluntary Organisations, said of the Government's proposals:

> We think that the Government has missed an opportunity in its proposals in taking a wider look at lobbying, which may have led to a greater increase in public trust and confidence, and there are two key things that we think are missing. One is

---

39 Q 426

40 Ev w57

41 *"Lobbying official turned down reform meetings"*. The Independent, January 2012 http://www.independent.co.uk/news/uk/politics/lobbying-official-turned-down-reform-meetings-6296562.html

42 HM Government, *Introducing a Statutory Register of Lobbyists*, January 2012, p15

43 HM Government, *Introducing a Statutory Register of Lobbyists*, January 2012, p9

setting out clear standards of professional conduct for lobbyists, and the other is making it clear who is lobbying whom.[44]

35. Elizabeth France, Chair of the UK Public Affairs Council, agreed that the lack of a statutory code of conduct could lead to less regulation of lobbying:

> let's assume there is a fee to pay to join the statutory register, and you are a small lobbying firm and you have to decide whether you can afford both to go on the statutory register, which you must go on, and join a professional body that has a professional set of standards and a code of practice you must adhere to. If we are not careful, the second is going to become a luxury and we are going to end up with fewer people. However, an unintended consequence could be that you get fewer people signing up to bodies that have ethical standards and codes of practice."[45]

Mark Ramsdale, a lobbyist and former Secretary to the UK Public Affairs Council, stated: "a register without any adherence to these, or other suitable codes offers a retrograde step for the industry".[46]

36. The Government's proposals have similarities with Australia's register of lobbyists, which came into force on 1 July 2008. The Australian register requires only those who "conduct lobbying activities on behalf of a third party client or whose employees conduct lobbying activities on behalf of a third party client" to be registered.[47] Charitable, religious, non-profit organisations and individuals who lobby the Australian Government are not required to be on the statutory register. Individual lobbyists are required to list their name, their position, whether they are a former public official, and if so, when they ceased to be a public official.[48]

37. However it is important to note that the Australian register also has an accompanying statutory code of conduct. The only sanction for breaching the terms of the code is removal from the register, but Government representatives are not permitted to meet with any lobbyists who are not on the statutory register.

38. Elizabeth France told us that a hybrid model of conduct, where registered lobbyists abide by the code of conduct of their profession, but make it clear which professional body can be contacted if there is an allegation of improper behaviour, could help to ensure that those who lobby could be held to account without a statutory code of conduct:

> one way would be to have a hybrid where the register showed whether a particular entrant on the register was signed up to a code of practice, which code of practice and who enforced it. So if you were a member of the APPC or the CIPR, or perhaps if you were a lawyer regulated by the Solicitors Regulation Authority but you were a public affairs consultant, maybe you could put that on the register and then it

---

44 Q 254

45 Q 121

46 Ev 103

47 Australian Government register of lobbyists , Retrieved 14 June 2012,http://lobbyists.pmc.gov.au/

48 Australian Government register of lobbyists Retrieved 14 June 2012, http://lobbyists.pmc.gov.au/who_register_lobbyists.cfm

> would be clear to people which body was making sure you behaved ethically and held you to account.[49]

39. If the Government is convinced that a statutory code of conduct would be burdensome, a hybrid code of conduct is a viable alternative, as it would make it clear to whom organisations on the register could be held accountable. However, the main disadvantage of a hybrid model would be that organisations on the register would be held accountable to different sets of professional standards. There may be some organisations, such as think tanks, and campaign groups, which might not be members of a professional body that require them to sign up to a code of conduct. **We recommend that Government looks further at the hybrid model for a code of conduct for lobbyists. If Government decides on a hybrid model, it needs to consider what provision it will make for organisations that are not already a member of a professional body with a code of conduct.**

How effective are the Government's proposals?

40. It was suggested that the proposed statutory register was being introduced as an 'easy win' for the Government. Mark Adams, lobbyist and author of the blog standup4lobbying stated of the proposals: "it is a box-ticking exercise to deliver something that the Conservatives agreed with the Liberal Democrats as the price of forming the coalition".[50] Other witnesses raised similar concerns about the Government's motive for a statutory register. Tamasin Cave, campaigner for Spinwatch and the Alliance for Lobbying Transparency, stated that, "the Government have made up a problem to fit the solution that they have".[51] The Whitehouse Consultancy agreed, stating:

> whilst officials have drafted the Consultation Paper in such a way as to appear that many issues are still open for discussion, the fundamental principles (rejection of a Statutory Code, a misplaced trust in UK PAC, a naive respect for industry self-regulation, a narrow definition of lobbying etc) have clearly been decided in advance and in many cases are not sensible."[52]

41. The Government seems to have united both the lobbying industry and transparency campaigners in condemnation of its proposals for a statutory register. Francis Ingham, Chief Executive of the Public Relations Consultants Association, told us "Regarding the document itself, it is a kind of grubby little document really. It has 'compromise' stamped all over it".[53] The Chief Executive of the National Council of Voluntary Organisations, Sir Stuart Etherington, said the Government's plan for a statutory register was "so weak now there's no point us joining it".[54] Justice in Financial Services put their opinion very simply:

---

49 Q 122

50 Q 89

51 Q 6

52 Ev w61

53 Q 221

54 "NCVO changes its mind on 'weak' lobbying register" 29 February 2012, *Civil Society*,http://www.civilsociety.co.uk/governance/news/content/11668/ncvo_changes_its_mind_on_weak_lobbying_register?topic=&print=1

"the proposals in the consultation document *Introducing a statutory register of lobbyists* fail".[55]

42. The advantages of the Government's proposals are that it would be simple to administer, and the narrow definition of a lobbyist makes it clear that only third party lobbyists should be registered. However it is not clear from the Government's current definition of lobbying whether public affairs consultancies who provide advice to clients but do not represent them in meetings with officials or Ministers, would have to be registered. The Government's proposals as they stand would not require any money from the public purse as the Government proposes "that the cost of running the register and the ancillary costs arising from it should be met on a self-funding basis by the lobbying industry".[56]

43. However, the disadvantages of such a system are many. Dr Raj Chari, co-author of *Regulating Lobbying: A global comparison*, stated that countries with lobbying regulations which are characterised as low regulation are "window dressing. It looks good but its effectiveness, in terms of regulating lobbyists, can be considered wanting".[57] As the proposed register will also not require any additional features, such as a requirement to disclose the issues lobbied on, the public would know who had engaged a lobbying firm, but not why. This could cause public disillusionment with the register. Spinwatch stated that: "the Government's proposals for a statutory register of lobbyists are fundamentally flawed, and will deliver little more than the system of voluntary self-regulation that currently exists".[58]

44. Rob McKinnon, the founder and operator of Who's Lobbying, a website that collates and presents data on ministerial meetings, pointed out that according to the Who's Lobbying database, Ministers' meetings with third party lobbyists were a very small percentage of ministerial meetings:

> In the Who's Lobbying database I have almost 8,000 meetings that were declared by departments. Of those, at present only 18 of those meetings included a lobbying firm. That is less than a quarter of a percent of all of the government meetings. In comparison, law firms have twice as many at 34 meetings, which is about 0.4% of government meetings. Organisations that are in Wikipedia's political and economic think-tanks category have had 163 declared meetings with government, which is about 2% of the meetings I have in my database. We can see that in comparison think-tanks have almost 10 times as many meetings with ministers.[59]

45. We also heard from several witnesses that a lack of transparency surrounding third party lobbyists was not a significant enough problem for third party lobbyists to be singled out as the sole signatories to a statutory register. Professor Justin Fisher, of Brunel University, told us "there is no evidence whatsoever that multi-client agencies are a

55 Ev w35

56 HM Government, *Introducing a Statutory Register of Lobbyists*, January 2012, p16

57 Q 335

58 Ev 95

59 Q 337

particular problem. The differentiation between them and lobbying by in-house, charities and so on, such as NGOs, is irrelevant".[60] Dr Raj Chari, told us: "of all lobbyists that are in the UK, what percentage do professional consultancies represent? I don't know the specific data, but in other jurisdictions it would be around 10% to 15%, and that is a very small percentage of all lobbyists".[61]

46. **A statutory register would be likely to solve the problem the Government poses, as it would allow the public to see the clients of lobbying firms. However, we question whether a lack of transparency over third party lobbyists in particular is as great a problem as the Government claims. We consider that the current proposals for a statutory register of lobbyists will do nothing to resolve wider public concerns about a lack of transparency around who is meeting whom.**

47. **The consultation paper is lacking in clear intent from the Government, and only limited evidence is put forward to support its proposals. We conclude that a statutory register which includes only third party lobbyists would do little to improve transparency about who is lobbying whom, as these meetings constitute only a small part of the lobbying industry. The Government's proposals only scratch the surface when it comes to tackling public concern about undue access and influence over the policy making process, and they are unlikely to prevent lobbying from becoming the "next big political scandal".**

48. **We recommend that the Government scrap its proposals for a statutory register of third party lobbyists. It is our view that the proposals in their current form will do nothing to improve transparency and accountability about lobbying. Imposing a statutory register on a small part of the lobbying industry without requiring registrants to sign up to a code of conduct could paradoxically lead to less regulation of the lobbying industry.**

60 Q 19

61 Q 336

4 Other options for a statutory register

49. We do not regard the Government's proposals for a statutory register of lobbyists as fit for purpose. In this chapter we consider some alternative approaches, from no register at all to a highly regulated system such as the US Federal lobbying regulations. The options below are not meant to be an exhaustive list of all the potential forms that lobbying regulation could take, but rather seek to demonstrate the diversity that already exists in lobbying regulations in different jurisdictions.

Option 1: no statutory register

50. The first option would be to have no statutory register of lobbyists. Lobbyist Mark Adams and Professor Justin Fisher, were both unconvinced that a statutory register of lobbyists was necessary, and thought that self-regulation of the industry was still possible. However, Conor McGrath, an academic and public affairs consultant, stated, "the perfect lobbying regulation does not exist anywhere, but some regulation is always better than none".[62]

51. A statutory register that provides no more information than current self-regulatory regimes could have the perverse outcome of reducing regulation of the lobbying industry for the reasons discussed in the previous chapter. The Government's proposals for a statutory register are very narrowly defined, and most likely would not have prevented any of the recent allegations regarding undue influence.

52. **While we are not, generally, in favour of this option we believe that no statutory register is better than what the Government currently proposes.**

Option 2: medium regulation

53. Option 2 encompasses the Government's proposals for a statutory register of third party lobbyists, including disclosure of client lists, and whether or not the lobbyist is a former Minister or senior official, but includes the following additional features:

- a broadened definition of a lobbyist, to include anyone who lobbies professionally in a paid role (thus in-house lobbyists, trade associations, trade unions, think tanks, campaign groups and charities may be required to register);
- disclosure of the issues being lobbied on;
- disclosure of when lobbying services have been provided on a pro bono basis;
- a statutory code of conduct or a hybrid code of conduct (whereby organisations and individuals must indicate that they have signed up to their industry's relevant code of conduct, so it is clear where complaints can be addressed); and
- incorporation of published data on whom Ministers are meeting.

62 Ev w39

54. There would be no requirement of financial disclosure, and the obligation would be on lobbyists to provide the necessary information to an independent body self-funded by the industry from subscription fees. Enforcement mechanisms could be limited to removal from the register. Ministers and officials would only meet with lobbyists who are on the register, although there could be a facility for retrospective registration (up to 28 days after the meeting occurred).

55. The European Transparency Register (covering the European Commission and the Parliament) is a voluntary register of lobbyists. Sanctions can be imposed for providing, or failing to correct, incomplete or inaccurate information in the register or for non-compliance with the code of practice. These sanctions include temporary suspension from the register or removal from it. Removal can lead to the withdrawal of access privileges to the European Parliament, and registration is a prerequisite for meeting with officials. If the Government introduced a compulsory statutory register along these lines, it would considered to be medium regulation.

56. Dr Raj Chari, commenting on the make-up of the European Transparency Register, stated that uptake of the voluntary register had been low despite attempts by the EU institutions to encourage registration:

> If you actually look at the percentage of the in-house lobbyists and trade associations that are registered, that would represent about 50% of all of those that are registered in the Commission's transparency registry. NGOs and think-tanks would represent about 30%, other religious organisations and academic organisations about 10%. Effectively now we know that the uptake of registering professional consultancies in the European Commission has been very low.[63]

57. The advantages of medium regulation are that information on whom lobbyists are lobbying and why would all be on one searchable register, making it easier for the public, and other interested parties to access. Political Lobbying and Media Relations, a public affairs consultancy, stated that "a well-considered, all inclusive, and transparent, statutory register that requires universal membership would be a considerable step forward to restoring the confidence of the general public in the Public Affairs industry".[64] John Hogan, co-author of *Regulating Lobbying: a global comparison,* stated that politicians in countries that had lobbying regulations were in favour of registers as it gave legitimacy to their meetings. He stated: "lobbying legislation, however, places very little responsibility on the politicians themselves to declare with whom they talk. But our research has shown that with a register, politicians themselves are open with whom they have talked".[65]

58. The disadvantages of medium regulation would be that a definition of 'anyone who lobbies professionally' could lead to anomalies where small charities who employ a full time lobbyist would have to register yet activist volunteers of another charity would not. The Institute of Economic Affairs and the Taxpayers Alliance both provided examples of potential loopholes in a medium regulated system. However, the risk that some people

---

63 Q 336

64 Ev w50

65 Ev 118

would seek to act outside the system should not be a deterrent for implementing lobbying regulation, although any definition of lobbying would have to be carefully worded to avoid capturing ordinary citizens within the definition.

59. The Law Society cautioned that if the definition of lobbying were to be broadened then careful consideration would need to be given to a definition that drew a distinction between legal advice and lobbying. John Wotton, the President of the Law Society, told us

> Where one is assisting the client in the client's interactions with the decision maker, which may be an investigating body or a licence-granting body or whatever, then I think that is clearly not within lobbying activity. That is the legal advice and representation area. When one moves into the area of seeking to influence other parties or the legislative process, then that is probably within the area of lobbying. So in the case of a law firm that has a significant activity, let us say, in advising clients on lobbying Parliament on legislation, I think that is lobbying in principle.[66]

60. Nigel Stanley of the Trade Union Congress also raised similar concerns regarding the broadening of a definition of lobbying:

> I can't go round the TUC staff and say, 'They're a lobbyist and they're not a lobbyist'. Anyone who works on policy in the TUC may well meet an MP, meet a minister, meet a special advisor, because on the whole we like to send the people who know what they are talking about to see ministers.[67]

61. It was suggested that the activity of lobbying should be defined first, rather than attempting to define what a lobbyist is. Tamasin Cave of Spinwatch told us: "In terms of defining lobbying, we look at the activity and we define the activity. Whoever is carrying out the activity defined as lobbying is a lobbyist, whether they work for a trade union, in-house, an agency or a charity".[68] Who's Lobbying agreed, adding: "it is the activity that needs to be defined, and then anyone engaged in an activity should be included in the legislation as being required to register".[69] **If it is the activity of lobbying that is defined, rather than what a lobbyist is, then it should be easier to require anyone who is carrying out the defined activity to be registered as a lobbyist.**

62. Another key disadvantage of a medium regulated system would be that if the definition of lobbying were broadened organisations that are already regulated could be subject to even more regulation. Charities and trade unions, who are likely to be caught by an expanded definition of lobbying are already regulated by the Charity Commission and the Certification Office respectively, and must submit detailed accounts which are already searchable online. Ben Kernighan, Deputy Chief Executive of the National Council for Voluntary Organisations, highlighted what he saw as the differences between charities who engage in lobbying and professional lobbyists: charities "are accountable to a board of

66 Q 313

67 Q 255

68 Q 15

69 Q 337

trustees, usually unpaid, they are legally required to act for public benefit, and all but the tiniest bit of them are regulated in their lobbying activity by the Charity Commission".[70]

63. Mr Kernighan explained the extent to which austerity was already squeezing charities' resources:

> we anticipate that about £3 billion of charitable income is going to be reduced between now and the end of the next Parliament because of reductions in public spending, and a large majority of charities are very small organisations. We are concerned about a regulatory burden, both in terms of what that might mean for the time people have to spend, and in terms of costs.[71]

We would not wish to burden any organisations with undue regulation, particularly during the difficult economic climate, and consider that any financial or administrative cost of the register should be minimal. Lionel Zetter, a lobbyist and former President of the Chartered Institute of Public Relations, outlined the costs of belonging to their organisation:"It has 9,500 members, it charges about £200 a year and it makes a very small profit, so it is self-financing."[72] A sum in the region of £200 is not unreasonable for registration and membership of a register, and exemptions could be considered for very small organisations who wish to lobby but could not afford even nominal fees.

Option 3: A highly regulated system

64. Option 3 encompasses the Government's proposals, and the features of medium regulation as outlined in option 2, but includes the following additional features:

- a statutory register run by an independent regulatory body either self-funded by subscriptions or funded by Government;
- financial disclosure of both money made as a lobbyist and the amount spent on lobbying activities in bands of £5,000; and
- stiff penalties for breaches of the rules, including large monetary fines, and possible jail sentences.

Option 3 would be considered to be a highly regulated system. Dr Raj Chari told us: "What distinguishes the high-regulated systems from the medium or the low is that there are full spending disclosures given by the lobbyists."[73]

65. A highly regulated UK system could also include a provision similar to the US 1938 Foreign Agents Registration Act (FARA). The Act requires that all lobbyists working on behalf of foreign governments must declare whom they are working for, how much is being spent on lobbying activity and who is being lobbied. Index on Censorship endorsed a FARA style Act for the UK and stated:

---

70 Q 254

71 Q 280

72 Q 20

73 Q 334

> the lack of transparency in international lobbying can and should be tackled both at source and at destination. Index considers wider consideration is needed of how to promote transparency of lobby organisations based in the UK but lobbying abroad whose activities—or all of whose activities—will not be captured by the UK statutory register".[74]

The Bureau of Investigative Journalism also called for the UK to require lobbyists working on behalf of foreign governments to disclose that activity: "for journalists aiming to scrutinize the lobbying process, a US FARA-type register is most helpful, as it is so comprehensive".[75]

66. Under the US and Canadian federal lobbying regulations, steep fines and prison sentences can be meted out to those who knowingly flout the rules. In Canada knowingly giving false or misleading statements in returns can result in a fine of up to $200,000 or two years' imprisonment, while other contraventions are punishable by a fine of up to $50,000. However, Karen E. Shepherd, Canada's Lobbying Commissioner told us: "no one has ever been charged or convicted of an offence under either the Lobbyists Registration Act, or the Lobbying Act ... Since 2005, twelve cases have been referred to the Royal Canadian Mounted Police".[76]

67. Under the US Lobbying Disclosure Act 1995 and the Honest Leadership and Open Government Act 2007, a civil penalty of up to $200,000 can be levied for failure to "remedy a defective filing within 60 days after notice of such a defect by the Secretary of the Senate or the Clerk of the House of Representatives; or...[to]comply with any other provision of this Act".[77] The Lobbying Disclosure Act states that a lobbyist who "knowingly and corruptly fails to comply with any provision of this Act shall be imprisoned for not more than 5 years or fined".[78]

68. Canada and the US require lobbyists to register only if they spend more than 20% of their time on lobbying activities. In giving evidence Dr Raj Chari stated that lobbying thresholds were often very difficult to assess objectively, and led to suspicions that some lobbyists were underestimating the time they spent on lobbying activity to avoid registration. He told us:

> If you were to follow the Canadian model then avoid things like trying to quantify it in terms of percentage of time. This is also seen in the United States as well: that if you work 20% over six months, then you are required to register. So this threshold of 20% is very contentious.[79]

---

74 Ev w29

75 Ev w7

76 Ev w12

77 Lobbying Disclosure Act 1995, Section 7, Retrieved 14 June 2012 http://www.senate.gov/legislative/Lobbying/Lobby_Disclosure_Act/7_Penalties.htm

78 Lobbying Disclosure Act 1995, Section 7, Retrieved 14 June 2012 http://www.senate.gov/legislative/Lobbying/Lobby_Disclosure_Act/7_Penalties.htm

79 Q 351

John Wotton of the Law Society concurred with this.[80] **We would not consider a simple 20% threshold to be a sensible way to determine whether or not an organisation or an individual should be required to register as a lobbyist.**

69. The advantages of a highly regulated system are that it would be highly transparent, as financial resources and the issues being lobbied on would be disclosed. Dr Raj Chari told us that lobbying registers are "widely consumed, yes. In fact registrars will get third-party complaints all the time about citizens knowing, or I suppose competitors as well, that people are lobbying without having registered, and they will file that third party complaint to a registrar".[81] Karen Shepherd, Canada's Lobbying Commissioner, noted that the Commission's website, which includes the register, is widely used. She stated: "Our website is one of our main outreach tools, and visits to the website are on the rise. More than 110,000 visits were recorded last year, an increase from the 89,000 visits in the previous year".[82]

70. The main disadvantages of such a system are that highly regulated systems are costly to run. When Dr Raj Chari gave evidence to us, he stated that "the disadvantage is that you might have regulatory offices that are highly staffed, which could cost a lot of money to the state".[83] Another key disadvantage is that organisations which lobby but also provide other services may find it difficult to determine exactly how much of their income is derived from lobbying, as would be necessary under a US style system.[84] Mark Boleat, a lobbyist, highlighted that "lobbying is generally not a stand-alone function but rather part of a package of services".[85]

71. **However desirable it may be to have a comprehensive register of lobbying activity with full spending disclosures, the regulator needed to enforce such a register would be likely to be very costly. We do not think it would be appropriate to recommend a highly regulated system as a starting point for statutory registration of the lobbying industry in the current economic climate.**

72. **In our view, medium regulation is the most desirable, and most feasible form of a statutory register, and would certainly be an improvement on the register the Government currently proposes. We recommend that Government implement medium regulation as a starting point for a statutory register of lobbyists.**

---

80 Q 327

81 Q 402

82 Ev w12

83 Q 335

84 Q 255

85 Ev w3

5 Ministerial meetings

73. Regardless of whether the Government introduces a statutory register of lobbyists, a number of relatively simple steps could be implemented quickly which would improve transparency regarding who is lobbying whom. On 29 May 2010, shortly after becoming Prime Minister, David Cameron spoke on the issue of transparency in a Number 10 podcast. He stated:

> So we're going to rip off that cloak of secrecy and extend transparency as far and as wide as possible. By bringing information out into the open, you'll be able to hold government and public services to account...
>
> With a whole army of effective armchair auditors looking over the books, ministers in this government are not going to be able to get away with all the waste, the expensive vanity projects and pointless schemes that we've had in the past...
>
> We saw what happened with MPs' expenses once they were put online, out in the open. No one will ever be so free and easy with public money again.
>
> But it's not just about efficiency and saving money. I also think transparency can help us to re-build trust in our politics. One of the reasons people don't trust politicians is because they think we've always got something to hide.[86]

74. The consultation paper states that

> the Government does not propose that any information on meetings should be included in a register. Details of meetings between Ministers and third parties are already published regularly, and the Government feels the provision of duplicate information in a statutory register of lobbyists is unnecessary.[87]

However, the Confederation of British Industry stated: "we agree that information should not be duplicated but are concerned that the Government's argument is undermined by the way this information is currently presented in practice".[88] We heard evidence from witnesses that Departments were not releasing details of ministerial meetings in a timely or efficient manner. Francis Ingham, Chief Executive of the Public Relations Consultants Association, concurred with this view, stating:

> Ministerial diaries could be improved considerably; they are frequently late or inaccurate. I think transparency cuts both ways and it would be a good thing for ministerial private offices to be a bit more open about who they meet, as well as the demand for lobbyists to be more open about what they do as well.[89]

86 Text of David Cameron'spodcast on transparency, 29 May 2010, http://www.number10.gov.uk/news/pms-podcast-on-transparency/

87 HM Government, *Introducing a Statutory Register of Lobbyists*, January 2012, p14

88 Ev w8

89 Q 245

75. The Minister, Mark Harper, talking about meetings with third party lobbyists, stated "the Minister may know—in fact, will know—but the outside world will not, and that is the gap we were trying to close in our proposals".[90] Central Lobby Consultants a public affairs firm, told us that it would be extremely rare for them to meet Ministers without the client being present.[91] **If the Government is adamant that the problem which needs to be solved is that people do not know the clients of third party lobbyists, the Government could simply disclose whom the lobbying firm is representing when the detail of the meeting is published.**

Timeliness

76. Who's Lobbying, a website that collates and presents data on ministerial meetings, told us that there were issues with the way that ministerial meetings were currently being disclosed by Government Departments. Departments had last published meeting reports for the period July to September 2011, and in some cases the public had to wait up to eight months for departments to publish reports, which, Who's Lobbying stated, "is a denial of transparency in a way".[92]

77. Section 8.14 of the Ministerial Code states that:

> Ministers meet many people and organisations and consider a wide range of views as part of the formulation of Government policy. Departments will publish, at least quarterly, details of Ministers' external meetings.[93]

We wrote to the Cabinet Secretary, Jeremy Heywood, asking for confirmation that ministerial meetings should be published quarterly. The response stated that "the Government's commitment is to publish this information on a quarterly basis".[94] The Cabinet Secretary added: "I do agree that this information should be published as quickly as practically possible, and I have asked Departments to continue to work to speed up the process".[95] When we asked the Minister about the timeliness of disclosures of ministerial meetings, he replied "one of the things that slows it down is checking what is published, so the more you publish, the more it has to be checked".[96]

78. However Rob McKinnon of Who's Lobbying pointed out that many Departments managed to update social media on a monthly, or even weekly basis:

> many government departments now have a photo publishing account on a website called flickr.com, and they are regularly publishing information in quite a timely fashion there. Here is an example from the No. 10 stream. I am holding here a photograph of a meeting David Cameron had in May 2010. In the same month that

90 Q 404

91 Ev w10

92 Q 329

93 HM Government, *The Ministerial Code*, May 2010, Section 8.14.

94 Ev 135

95 Ev 135

96 Q 453

photo was published on flickr.com, and then we had to wait until October 2010 before the report of that meeting was published as part of the regular ministerial meeting reports from the departments."[97]

If Government can publish photos of meetings within a month it should not take up to eight months to publish lists of meetings with outside stakeholders. We recommend that Departments publish details of ministerial meetings no more than a month after the month in which the meeting occurred.

The format of meeting data

79. We heard from Who's Lobbying that ministerial meetings were not currently published in a consistent format, which made collating and analysing the data difficult. Rob McKinnon told us: "there are over 24 department websites you need to visit to find this information. Currently, it has been published in over 150 different files. If you had a researcher trying to collate this information, it might take them days just to collate the activity of a single organisation right now if the Who's Lobbying website was not there."[98]

80. When we put this point to the Minister, he stated that data on whom Ministers and officials were meeting were "pretty straightforwardly published in the two different file types".[99] The majority of files on ministerial meetings are published in either PDF, or CSV format, which are machine readable. However a quick trawl of Government Department websites also found data on ministerial meetings published in Word on the Business Innovation and Skills website, and Rich Text Format on the Department for Culture, Media and Sport website.[100] **The more Government publishes data in consistent file formats the easier it will be for 'armchair auditors' to analyse the data and hold Government to account for its decisions. We recommend that the Cabinet Office publish a ministerial and official meeting template in a specific machine readable format for all Departments to adhere to when publishing details of ministerial meetings.**

Level of detail in meeting disclosures

81. Additionally, Departments are providing only very basic details of the meetings. As Who's Lobbying told us, "the current Government meeting reports do not provide a date. They only provide the month of the meeting, so it makes it very hard to do further analysis".[101] When we put this to the Minister, he told us that "this Government are being far more transparent than any previous Government have been in terms of publishing the details of ministerial meetings, who Ministers are meeting, when those meetings are with external organisations, and the purpose of those meetings".[102]

97 Q 376

98 Ev 121

99 Q 450

100 Who Ministers are meeting, www.number10.gov.uk, retrieved 14 June 2012, http://www.number10.gov.uk/transparency/who-ministers-are-meeting/

101 Ev 121

102 Q 410

82. However, a comparison between details of the Secretary of State for Energy and Climate Change's meetings published under the previous Government and this Government reveals that ministerial meetings declared under the previous Government routinely showed the date of the meeting, while now only the month of the meeting is declared. Our decision to use the Department for Energy and Climate Change as a comparative example stems from the fact that they retain records of ministerial meetings from the previous Government on their website, when many other Departments have not. We consider such transparency to be positive.

Department of Energy and Climate Change, Quarterly information 1 July – 30 Sept 2011, Meetings with External Organsiations (including meetings with newspaper and other media proprietors, editors and senior executives,) Secretary of State for Energy and Climate Change		
Date of Meeting	**Name of External Organisation**	**Purpose of Meeting**
July 11	Mainstream Renewable Power; Dong Energy, EDP Renovaveis, Enevo Wind UK	To discuss energy and climate change issues
July 11	Ovo energy; Good Energy, Cooperative Energy; First Utility, Cornwall Energy, Ecotricity	To discuss energy and climate change issues
July 11	CBI	To discuss energy and climate change issues

Department for Energy and Climate Change[103]

Department of Energy and Climate Change, 1 October 2009 to 31 December 2009 Secretary of State for Energy and Climate Change		
Date of Meeting	**Name of Organisation**	**Purpose of Meeting**
1 Oct 2009	Smith School of Enterprise and the Environment	Climate change
8 Oct 2009	Green Alliance, E.ON, RWE, Npower, Scottish Power, Scottish & Southern Energy, Greenpeace & European Climate Foundation	Climate Change and Energy Issues
8 Oct 2009	BA & Virgin Atlantic Airways	Environment
22 Oct 2009	RWE Npower	Energy Issues
22 Oct 2009	Green Alliance	Climate change and energy issues
28 Oct 2009	National Federation of	Climate Change

103 Department of Energy and Climate Change, Secretary of State external meetings, July-September 2011http://www.decc.gov.uk/assets/decc/11/access-information/4999-huhne-external-meetings-jul-sep.pdf

	Women's Institute	
4 Nov 2008	WWF, Greenpeace, ActionAid, Oxfam & Friends of the Earth	Climate change and energy issues

Department for Energy and Climate Change[104]

83. We understand that there needs to be a 'safe space' where officials can give Ministers full and frank advice regarding policy proposals and policy development. However, stating the date a meeting took place could help improve transparency surrounding lobbying and improve public confidence without violating this 'safe space'. For example if a Department announces a policy that would be favourable to a particular sector at the beginning of a month, then has meetings with lobbying organisations associated with that same sector later in the same month, the way that the meeting is currently declared could lead some to believe that there had been undue influence because it would not be clear whether the meetings had taken place before or after the policy announcement. **If the specific date of a meeting were declared there would be less scope for unfounded allegations of undue influence. We strongly recommend that Departments publish the date and topic of a meeting with Ministers and officials.**

84. The Minister told us: "we already publish not just the fact of meetings and who Ministers are meeting, but the purpose of the meeting, which therefore gives an indication of the topics being discussed".[105] However, the term 'general discussion' appears to be the most used phrase when departments are describing the purpose of the meeting, which does not, by itself, give any indication of the topic being discussed. **General terms such as 'introductory' and 'catch-up' are too vague to be listed as the topic of a meeting. We recommend that the Government publish the specific topic of the meeting, unless there are immediate security concerns preventing disclosure.**

85. Rob McKinnon of Who's Lobbying, stated that he had found many variations of company names, including acronyms, in the lists of disclosed ministerial meetings, which could make it difficult to collate the lobbying activity of particular companies. He told us:

> almost 30% of the organisations that are declared in government meetings have been put into reports with a variant of their name, which makes it very difficult to collate their activity by organisation. I would strongly recommend any proposal by the Government require that any time a legal entity is mentioned, if it is a company, that the company number be provided, if it is a charity, that the charity number be provided, And if it is registered in a different jurisdiction, that the jurisdiction and the registration number in that jurisdiction be provided.[106]

The practice of requiring a company number and trading name of an organisation to be listed on the lobbying register is already a feature of the Australian lobbying regulations. The Government does propose that lobbyists be required to register their company

104 Department of Energy and Climate Change, Secretary of State external meetings, October-December 2009, http://www.decc.gov.uk/assets/decc/accesstoinformation/1_20100329130625_e_@@_coreturnsmeetingsoutsideinterestsedmiliband.pdf

105 Q 414

106 Q 371

number and registered address. This is a sensible proposal that we think should also be used when publishing data about whom Ministers are meeting.

86. **We recommend that the Government provide the company or charity number of any organisation Ministers meet. This would ensure that even if a company is listed under an acronym, or a trading name, its identity can be verified. Companies and charities will be aware of this information and it should provide no undue burden to require them to give this information to Departments when meetings occur.**

A central government portal

87. The Government may wish to take heed of the website Who's Lobbying, which uploads details of all ministerial meetings, Select Committee hearings and publicly available details of lobbyists. We are concerned that such a valuable source of information on who is meeting with Ministers, officials and appearing before parliamentary Committees is reliant on the goodwill of a software developer uploading the information in his spare time. If Mr McKinnon decided to discontinue the Who's Lobbying project there would no longer be a single website with a free, publicly searchable way of ascertaining how many meetings an organisation had with Government, although the information would still be released individually by Departments. This would be a blow for transparency regarding whom Ministers and senior public officials are meeting.

88. We note that Government has recently been trialling a single Government domain, with ten Government Departments keeping the site up to date at the same time as managing their existing websites.[107] The results of this trial have not yet been published, but given the experience of Mr McKinnon, it should not be particularly costly or time consuming to put this data in one place, particularly if Government moves to a standardised format for disclosing who is meeting Ministers. **We recommend that the Government publish details of ministerial meetings on one website. The experience of the Who's Lobbying project suggests that it is possible to do so.**

---

107 Inside Government Beta, www.gov.uk https://www.gov.uk/government

6 Conclusion

89. **In conclusion, we are not convinced that the Government's current proposals for introducing a statutory register of lobbyists will do much to increase the transparency of lobbying activity in the UK. The Government's definition of a lobbyist is considered to be too narrow and potentially unworkable by lobbyists, academics, charities and transparency campaigners alike.**

90. **We call on the Government to scrap its current proposals for a statutory register and implement a system of medium regulation. A system of medium regulation would include all those who lobby professionally, in a paid role, and would require lobbyists to disclose the issues they are lobbying Government on. In our view, this would improve transparency about lobbying, and help to reduce public concerns about undue influence.**

91. **We believe that there is much the Government can do immediately to improve transparency around who is lobbying whom, through enhanced disclosure of ministerial meetings. We recommend that the Government:**

- **publish information about ministerial meetings no more than a month after the month in which the meeting occurred;**
- **standardize the format of meeting data, with a view to publishing all ministerial and official meetings on one website, rather than on 24 different Government websites;**
- **improve the level of detail in meeting disclosures, so that the actual topic of a meeting is disclosed, rather than obscure terms like 'general discussion'; and**
- **publish, where applicable, the company or charity number of any organisation that meets with Ministers or officials, so that the identity of the organisation can be properly verified.**

Conclusions and recommendations

1. We welcome the fact that these proposals have been published for parliamentary scrutiny, as well as for wider consultation. (Paragraph 9)

2. There is a public perception in some quarters that there are inappropriate relationships between Ministers and lobbyists and there is a need for action to address this perception. (Paragraph 16)

3. We recommend that Government clarify whether its definition of lobbying includes lobbying advice, or only direct representation, to avoid confusion regarding who should, and should not register as a lobbyist if it goes ahead with its proposals. (Paragraph 20)

4. We are not going to endorse any particular definitions of lobbying as the definition may differ depending on the scope of a statutory register. We do not wish to pre-judge the debate. However, we urge the Government carefully to consider all definitions provided to the consultation, as the definition will be key to the success and effectiveness of any future register. (Paragraph 25)

5. We recommend that Government looks further at the hybrid model for a code of conduct for lobbyists. If Government decides on a hybrid model, it needs to consider what provision it will make for organisations that are not already a member of a professional body with a code of conduct. (Paragraph 39)

6. A statutory register would be likely to solve the problem the Government poses, as it would allow the public to see the clients of lobbying firms. However, we question whether a lack of transparency over third party lobbyists in particular is as great a problem as the Government claims. We consider that the current proposals for a statutory register of lobbyists will do nothing to resolve wider public concerns about a lack of transparency around who is meeting whom. (Paragraph 46)

7. The consultation paper is lacking in clear intent from the Government, and only limited evidence is put forward to support its proposals. We conclude that a statutory register which includes only third party lobbyists would do little to improve transparency about who is lobbying whom, as these meetings constitute only a small part of the lobbying industry. The Government's proposals only scratch the surface when it comes to tackling public concern about undue access and influence over the policy making process, and they are unlikely to prevent lobbying from becoming the "next big political scandal". (Paragraph 47)

8. We recommend that the Government scrap its proposals for a statutory register of third party lobbyists. It is our view that the proposals in their current form will do nothing to improve transparency and accountability about lobbying. Imposing a statutory register on a small part of the lobbying industry without requiring registrants to sign up to a code of conduct could paradoxically lead to less regulation of the lobbying industry. (Paragraph 48)

9. While we are not, generally, in favour of this option we believe that no statutory register is better than what the Government currently proposes. (Paragraph 52)

10. If it is the activity of lobbying that is defined, rather than what a lobbyist is, then it should be easier to require anyone who is carrying out the defined activity to be registered as a lobbyist. (Paragraph 61)

11. We would not consider a simple 20% threshold to be a sensible way to determine whether or not an organisation or an individual should be required to register as a lobbyist. (Paragraph 68)

12. However desirable it may be to have a comprehensive register of lobbying activity with full spending disclosures, the regulator needed to enforce such a register would be likely to be very costly. We do not think it would be appropriate to recommend a highly regulated system as a starting point for statutory registration of the lobbying industry in the current economic climate. (Paragraph 71)

13. In our view, medium regulation is the most desirable, and most feasible form of a statutory register, and would certainly be an improvement on the register the Government currently proposes. We recommend that Government implement medium regulation as a starting point for a statutory register of lobbyists. (Paragraph 72)

14. If the Government is adamant that the problem which needs to be solved is that people do not know the clients of third party lobbyists, the Government could simply disclose whom the lobbying firm is representing when the detail of the meeting is published. (Paragraph 75)

15. If Government can publish photos of meetings within a month it should not take up to eight months to publish lists of meetings with outside stakeholders. We recommend that Departments publish details of ministerial meetings no more than a month after the month in which the meeting occurred. (Paragraph 78)

16. The more Government publishes data in consistent file formats the easier it will be for 'armchair auditors' to analyse the data and hold Government to account for its decisions. We recommend that the Cabinet Office publish a ministerial and official meeting template in a specific machine readable format for all Departments to adhere to when publishing details of ministerial meetings. (Paragraph 80)

17. If the specific date of a meeting were declared there would be less scope for unfounded allegations of undue influence. We strongly recommend that Departments publish the date and topic of a meeting with Ministers and officials. (Paragraph 83)

18. However, the term 'general discussion' appears to be the most used phrase when departments are describing the purpose of the meeting, which does not, by itself, give any indication of the topic being discussed. General terms such as 'introductory' and 'catch-up' are too vague to be listed as the topic of a meeting. We recommend that the Government publish the specific topic of the meeting, unless there are immediate security concerns preventing disclosure. (Paragraph 84)

19. We recommend that the Government provide the company or charity number of any organisation Ministers meet. This would ensure that even if a company is listed under an acronym, or a trading name, its identity can be verified. Companies and charities will be aware of this information and it should provide no undue burden to require them to give this information to Departments when meetings occur. (Paragraph 86)

20. We recommend that the Government publish details of ministerial meetings on one website. The experience of the Who's Lobbying project suggests that it is possible to do so. (Paragraph 88)

21. In conclusion, we are not convinced that the Government's current proposals for introducing a statutory register of lobbyists will do much to increase the transparency of lobbying activity in the UK. The Government's definition of a lobbyist is considered to be too narrow and potentially unworkable by lobbyists, academics, charities and transparency campaigners alike. (Paragraph 89)

22. We call on the Government to scrap its current proposals for a statutory register and implement a system of medium regulation. A system of medium regulation would include all those who lobby professionally, in a paid role, and would require lobbyists to disclose the issues they are lobbying Government on. In our view, this would improve transparency about lobbying, and help to reduce public concerns about undue influence. (Paragraph 90)

23. We believe that there is much the Government can do immediately to improve transparency around who is lobbying whom, through enhanced disclosure of ministerial meetings. We recommend that the Government:

publish information about ministerial meetings no more than a month after the month in which the meeting occurred;

standardize the format of meeting data, with a view to publishing all ministerial and official meetings on one website, rather than on 24 different Government websites;

improve the level of detail in meeting disclosures, so that the actual topic of a meeting is disclosed, rather than obscure terms like 'general discussion'; and

publish, where applicable, the company or charity number of any organisation that meets with Ministers or officials, so that the identity of the organisation can be properly verified. (Paragraph 91)

Formal Minutes

Tuesday 10 July 2012

Members present:

Mr Graham Allen, in the Chair

Mr Christopher Chope
Fabian Hamilton
Mr Andrew Turner

Draft Report (*Introducing a statutory register of lobbyists*), proposed by the Chair, brought up and read.

Ordered, That the draft Report be read a second time, paragraph by paragraph.

Paragraphs 1 to 91 read and agreed to.

Summary agreed to.

Resolved, That the Report be the Second Report of the Committee to the House.

Ordered, That the Chair make the Report to the House.

Ordered, That embargoed copies of the Report be made available, in accordance with the provisions of Standing Order No. 134.

Written evidence was ordered to be reported to the House for printing with the Report (previously reported and ordered to be published on 1 and 8 March, 19 April in the previous Parliamentary Session, and 17 May).

[Adjourned till Thursday 12 July at 9.40 am

Witnesses

List of printed written evidence

List of additional written evidence

(published in Volume II on the Committee's website www.parliament.uk/pcrc)

List of Reports from the Committee during the current Parliament

The reference number of the Government's response to each Report is printed in brackets after the HC printing number.

Session 2010–12

First Report	Parliamentary Voting System and Constituencies Bill	HC 422
Second Report	Fixed-term Parliaments Bill	HC 436 (Cm 7951)
Third Report	Parliamentary Voting System and Constituencies Bill	HC 437 (Cm 7997)
Fourth Report	Lessons from the process of Government formation after the 2010 General Election	HC 528 (HC 866)
Fifth Report	Voting by convicted prisoners: Summary of evidence	HC 776
Sixth Report	Constitutional implications of the Cabinet Manual	HC 734 (Cm 8213)
Seventh Report	Seminar on the House of Lords: Outcomes	HC 961
Eighth Report	Parliament's role in conflict decisions	HC 923 (HC 1477)
Ninth Report	Parliament's role in conflict decisions: Government Response to the Committee's Eighth Report of Session 2010-12	HC 1477 (HC 1673)
Tenth Report	Individual Electoral Registration and Electoral Administration	HC 1463
Eleventh Report	Rules of Royal Succession	HC 1615
Twelfth Report	Parliament's role in conflict decisions—further Government Response: Government Response to the Committee's Ninth Report of Session 2010-12	HC 1673
Thirteenth Report	Political party finance	HC 1763

Session 2012–13

First Report	Recall of MPs	HC 373

Oral evidence

Taken before the Political and Constitutional Reform Committee on Thursday 2 February 2012

Members present:

Mr Graham Allen (Chair)

Mr Christopher Chope
Paul Flynn
Sheila Gilmore
Andrew Griffiths
Fabian Hamilton
Simon Hart
Tristram Hunt
Mrs Eleanor Laing
Mr Andrew Turner

Examination of Witnesses

Witnesses: **Tamasin Cave**, SpinWatch and the Alliance for Lobbying Transparency, **Justin Fisher**, Professor of Political Science, Brunel University, and **Lionel Zetter**, Lobbyist and author of "Lobbying: the Art of Political Persuasion", gave evidence.

Q1 Chair: Welcome, witnesses and colleagues to this evidence session on the introduction of a statutory register of lobbyists. It is very kind of you to spare the time to come along this morning and give us the benefit of your views. What I normally do is ask people whether they want to make a short opening statement just to set the framework. Lionel?

Lionel Zetter: Thank you, Chairman. I should like to make a short opening statement. As you may or may not know, I am the author of a book called "Lobbying: the art of political persuasion". I train on public affairs for the CIPR, the PRCA and various commercial trainers. I am a former president of the CIPR and a former chairman of the Government Affairs Group.

I shall briefly declare my interests. I am still a board member of the CIPR and a director of the Enterprise Forum. I am the proprietor of Zetter's Political Services and vice-president of Public Affairs Asia. I am also retained in the capacity of senior counsel by APCO, a global communications agency with a strong public affairs offering, who are members of the APPC and the PRCA. However, I emphasise that I am giving evidence in my own capacity and not on behalf of any of these organisations.

Q2 Chair: Is there anything you want to say in terms of lobbying?

Lionel Zetter: On lobbying, the Cabinet Office proposals are widely welcomed by the industry. We think that they are proportionate. We recognise that all the political parties are committed to bringing into being a statutory register. We have no problem with that. The only areas of discussion are who and what should be included on that register. Obviously, I have views on that, and I have been fed views by various trade and professional bodies. I am happy to elaborate, but I think that it will come up during the course of discussions.

Justin Fisher: Just some background: I was specialist adviser on the Public Administration Select Committee inquiry into lobbying and subsequently was involved in the initial stages of the establishment of UKPAC. In my professional life, I am Professor of Political Science at Brunel university and run a master's course in public affairs and lobbying for students who want to go into the industry. The university has had a long relationship with the industry.

I would like to ask the Committee to consider the purpose of the Government's proposals. There are five pertinent points. On the proposed transparency, it is very difficult to argue against the idea of transparency, but this proposal provides only partial transparency because it covers only multi-client agencies. If the Government's proposals were to go no further—and that would be a mistake—a practical solution might be to combine this register with the existing data on meetings with ministers because, as things stand, the proposals would mean that any interested party would have to search around in a number of different registers.

Secondly, if the purpose of all this is the avoidance of inappropriate behaviour, a register would not do that. It is a very minor step. If you are looking to clean up lobbying—that is not necessarily to imply that there is a problem—a register is not the way to do that.

Thirdly, if it is a process of trying to improve public confidence, regulation and/or a register will not guarantee this. It is very important to note—this is not an argument against transparency—that, when data are published by such as is proposed through a register, this does not guarantee that these data will be used in a misleading manner by people who either do not understand the data or people who have malicious intent.

For example, there is a website up at the moment called "Whoslobbying", which gathers together data of meetings with ministers. Vanity meant that I had a look for myself on the register, and I discovered that I was apparently a lobbyist after having appeared in front of this Committee, giving evidence about the Parliamentary Voting System and Constituencies Bill in July 2010. That is an example of data being used badly. We also had the example from the publication of political donations, whereby there was nothing wrong with transparency, but people can use the data inappropriately.

Fourthly, you need to consider whether or not statutory regulation of this industry is better than self-regulation. My view is that UKPAC has failed as a self-regulator, but I still think that self-regulation can work. There must be some oversight of the industry, but it needs to look afresh at how it does this.

Finally, I have a plea that mirrors other aspects of areas of political regulation: we must resist the temptation to regulate the life out of general political activity. It is important to remember that standards are what matter, not ticking boxes. That is a very important point. What is proposed here is the minimal action to improve public confidence and general standards.

Tamasin Cave: I am Tamasin Cave. I work for a not-for-profit company called SpinWatch, which investigates the PR and lobbying industry. In 2007, we established a group called the Alliance for Lobbying Transparency, which is a coalition of charities and unions that are concerned about what we see as the growing influence of professional lobbying on public policy making. We think this reflects a growing public concern about the activities of lobbyists.

On the proposals—we have waited nearly two years for these—I am going to quote Mark Adams: I think they are "shameful". He described them as the worst consultation paper he had seen in 20 years. I agree with him. I would like to try to explain what I think—

Chair: Who said that?

Tamasin Cave: Mark Adams—he is a lobbyist. I was going to quote an unnamed lobbyist, but he is in the room, so I thought I would mention his name.

By way of trying to explain what I think has happened, I would like to quote Elizabeth France, who is the chairperson of UKPAC. She said, back in January 2011, that the industry's approach to this was to persuade the Government that what they need to do is embrace UKPAC's register "with a statutory hug". And that is broadly what they have done. That therefore explains this consultation paper. It is seeking to justify that position, which is why it is incredibly unbalanced. It is nonsensical in places, and I think it is deliberately misleading in others.

It is safe to say that the Cabinet Office does not get transparency in lobbying. This has been demonstrated amply by the fact that it has repeatedly sought to block the release of information under the FOI Act on its dealings with lobbyists, without any irony whatsoever. We now know that the Minister gave the nod for his officials to meet UKPAC on "a monthly basis", while at the same time saying it would be inappropriate to meet with transparency campaigners. This was before the official in charge of drafting the register made her views on transparency campaigners known in a fairly ill-judged tweet. In summary, this is bad policy making from a Department that has no interest in bringing greater transparency to lobbying.

Q3 Paul Flynn: Good morning, Tamasin and gentlemen. Here we go again. Do you think that what the Government are proposing is a fair and reasonable way forward?

Lionel Zetter: I think it is a very good starting point; I think it is only that. There has been a progression of regulation of lobbying going from the individual trade and professional bodies regulating their own members, to forming the umbrella body of UKPAC to, as I said, the three main political parties deciding that a statutory register was the way forward. I think they are right. On the other hand, I think a limitation on the proposals is that it encompasses probably less than 20% of the people who lobby. The problem with that is very straightforward.

I have to declare an interest—I have already done so—in that I work for a multi-client agency. Before that I was a freelance public affairs consultant. I have never worked in-house, but the majority of lobbyists work in-house.

If you restrict the proposals simply to multi-client agencies—people who lobby on behalf of third-party advocates—a number of things will flow from that. First, you will not have a sufficient base to fund a register properly. The problem with that was very straightforward, as far as I was concerned.

Q4 Paul Flynn: Why should it cost a lot to fund a register? The proposal from PASC was mainly to draw on what existed in diaries and so on. It is virtually nil cost in order to acquire transparency. Where is the great cost going to be in the Government's proposal?

Lionel Zetter: You might think that that would be the case, and you might possibly be right. First, you obviously have to have officials overseeing this. We have the Chairman, Elizabeth France, who is paid very modestly—but nevertheless it is a fee—for her efforts. The main problem has been with IT. The three organisations tried to do this on the cheap, and it was a catastrophic failure.

Q5 Paul Flynn: May I ask the others? I have several questions I want to ask.

Justin Fisher: It is a move forward inasmuch as it is a change from the status quo. I reiterate that it is a tiny step. My own view is that the proposals in the PASC report were more sensible and more encompassing, even if, on occasion, the report was—I think—excessively hostile to the industry. I come back to the question: what is the point of all this? What is the point of a register? It seems to me that one could make a case for a register—

Paul Flynn: May I interrupt you? Sorry about this. We have been on this. The report from PASC last time went way beyond your advice. I think it is fair to say that it went beyond the evidence, in a way. No smoking gun was found. After the report became public, smoking guns appeared everywhere, especially the sting in the House of Lords, where certain Lords were accused of pimping for various bodies that they were on.

Chair: Let's look at what we can do in the future. I do not want to go back over the report that is not the property of this Committee.

Justin Fisher: I agree. My framing of the question in terms of the PASC report was that I thought that in general, that represented a more sensible set of proposals. I go back to the question: what is the point of a register if it is simply an exercise in box-ticking, which is all that is included here? I echo Lionel's point that it covers only a very small part of the

industry. It is a small step forward, and there is a longer road to travel.
Paul Flynn: Tamasin?
Tamasin Cave: Paul, could you repeat your question?

Q6 Paul Flynn: Just your general response to the Government's report. Is it adequate?
Tamasin Cave: Oh no, it is completely inadequate. There are two very central flaws to it. Quite deliberately, the Government have made up a problem to fit the solution that they have. The problem that they say—this seems to be key to the consultation—
Chair: Is that a quote from Whitehall?
Tamasin Cave: I am going to quote the Minister. He says that ministers already have to say whom they meet. If they have met outside organisations, they say that they have met those organisations, so that is transparent. The gap is that if ministers meet a lobbying company, they know they have met it, but if people do not know who its clients are, they do not know whom it is representing. That is the gap that the Minister says he has sought to address with his proposals. This is a problem that does not exist. Justin mentioned the website, Whoslobbying.com, which has done a good job of collating ministerial meeting logs. It has managed to crunch the data, and of the 5,114 meetings with outside interests that ministers have logged, 10 were with agencies.
Chair: Sorry, 10 are with agencies?
Tamasin Cave: Ten are with agencies, so if Mark Harper is saying that the problem that exists is that there is no transparency about whom agencies are representing, he is talking about setting up a register to address the lack of transparency in 10 meetings. Of those 10, five also declare the clients alongside the agency. So we are talking about five ministerial meetings. This is according to the problem that he has identified in the proposals. It is difficult to know how to tackle it. It is wholly inadequate for that central reason.

Q7 Paul Flynn: You said many times, Mr Zetter, that the key to lobbying is not who you know, but what you know. On your website, I find a photograph of you with Boris Johnson, a photograph of you with Siân Lloyd, a photograph of you with Michael Howard and a photograph of you with Nick de Bois and David Burrowes. Who you know is on your website, but precious little of what you know is. Is this a classic case of commandment 1 of the lobbying industry, which is to say one thing and do another?
Lionel Zetter: I take your point. I must have a look at my website. It really is about what you know: which minister is responsible for which particular area, who is his or her special adviser and who is the civil servant who has day-to-day charge of your particular issue. So few lobbying companies are listed on the current register because the best advocate is the client. They are the ones who know more about the subject. They are much more passionate about it. We can hopefully help them arrange the meetings. We can brief them in advance, but they are the people who have to put forward the case.

Q8 Paul Flynn: You stood for Parliament last time.
Lionel Zetter: The time before.

Q9 Paul Flynn: What sort of metamorphosis would you undertake if you went from lobbyist to MP, as many of your fellow lobbyists have done and are now in Parliament? How should they change?
Lionel Zetter: Their focus needs to change completely. When you are a lobbyist—

Q10 Paul Flynn: Do you think that they should still be taking money from lobbyists and be employed by them?
Lionel Zetter: No, of course not. That would be against all rules and regulations.
Paul Flynn: They shouldn't be an MP.
Chair: Paul, wait a second. Ask a question and then let the witness answer the question.
Lionel Zetter: Members of Parliament are perfectly entitled to have outside interests and I think they should have outside interests, otherwise they get caught up in this Westminster bubble and have no idea what is happening in the world at large. So, no, they should not be taking money from lobbyists. The rules and regulations, as they currently stand, prohibit that.

Q11 Paul Flynn: What advice would you give lobbyists on influencing MPs for business questions, which will happen in the next hour?
Lionel Zetter: We would approach MPs with a constituency interest. You do not just randomly pick out MPs and seek to brief them. You raise what is occurring in their constituencies. For example, if there was an opportunity to bring in more work for BAE and India, you press that. I sought to represent Edmonton and I did not succeed. In Edmonton, there is a whole range of light industry, which suffers many of the problems of manufacturing industry in the United Kingdom.

Q12 Paul Flynn: That is what an MP does anyway. It is part of the core job of an MP to represent, for which he or she is paid a salary. Would you think it quite improper for any MP to take any interest or receive any favours that would be seen to be entirely commercial and not connected with his constituency?
Lionel Zetter: I do not believe that for one moment, no. As I have said, I think that MPs need outside interests to keep them in touch with the real world. This is a country with a struggling economy. The people who get us out of that trough will be British business. The more interaction there is between British business, MPs, ministers, civil servants and special advisers, the better.

Q13 Paul Flynn: If we get a case where Parliament and government are lobbied to settle contracts that are four times the going rate on the market, but it happens to be British or European rather than American, do you regard that as being successful, in spite of the fact that it is a huge burden on the public purse? We can give examples, such as the two aircraft carriers that we will now be landed with. Billions has been wasted on that contract. Was that the result of successful lobbying, because of the strong British interest?

Lionel Zetter: No, I suspect that it was a result of who was Prime Minister at the time and who were the Government at the time and where they needed to generate jobs and therefore votes.

Q14 Paul Flynn: I'm not getting involved or disagreeing on this particular point, but this is a characteristic of all governments for the past 50 years: contracts are settled for constituency nationalism, British nationalism or European nationalism. Do you not see the point that lobbying distorts those decisions and that it exists to give further advantages to the already advantaged? You serve the client—
Chair: Okay, we've had the question. Lionel, can we have an answer please?
Lionel Zetter: I strongly disagree. I think lobbying informs the decisions of ministers. It makes sure they take into account not just the headline price of a contract, but what the implications are for employment, for skills and for jobs locally. You have to look at these decisions in the round. If it was just about the money, it would be very straightforward and we would be out of business. But it is not. It is about all the other things that go with it.

Q15 Simon Hart: May we go back a couple of steps? Up until this meeting, I thought I might be a former lobbyist, but I am not really certain whether I am or not. Perhaps that remains to be discovered. I have to say, by way of an opening remark, as the newest MP around this table—I think—that I welcome the input and persuasive efforts of lobbyists in the broader sense, whether they are multi-client agencies or not. Where is the evidence—I don't want an opinion—that there is massive public concern about the activity of multi-client agency lobbyists as opposed to lobbyists in what we might describe as the broader sense?
I represented a membership organisation that lobbied, and indeed a charity that lobbied. We thought we lobbied—perhaps we did not; perhaps we just persuaded. Where is the evidence that separates those two elements of the persuaders who come in here?
Tamasin Cave: There is no evidence. The Government make a distinction, but we certainly do not. In terms of defining lobbying, we look at the activity and we define the activity. Whoever is carrying out the activity defined as lobbying is a lobbyist, whether they work for a trade union, in-house, an agency or a charity. I am a lobbyist. I work for a non-profit company. I do not think there is a distinction. Public concern is largely with in-house lobbyists. On the work that we have been doing, I have not gone out and found it. People have found me. There is opposition, and the Government's NHS reforms and planning reforms are two key concerns at the moment. There are accusations about the lobbyists or the industry—whether it is private health care or property developers—having their fingerprints all over the policies.
People are very concerned about the undue influence that commercial interests are having on policies. They are coming to me and saying, "Do you know anything about this? Can we find out about lobbying by the private health care industry or by the private insurance industry?" We know that we are facing an unseen army of private health care lobbyists, but there is no information whatever on these people, so what you have is a very skewed national debate framed in terms of patient choice and empowering doctors, when we know that there is millions of pounds-worth of lobbying by companies that at one stage were spending $1m lobbying against Obama's health reforms.

Q16 Simon Hart: My point is that there is lobbying by all sorts of people about things such as health reform. Some lobbying is done by multi-client agency organisations and some happens to be done by small groups of patients or GPs based in constituencies. We are talking about introducing a statutory register of lobbyists. We are uncertain what that is going to achieve, but more importantly, I think we should introduce anything that is statutory only on the basis of an overwhelming public need based on evidence. But you say there is no evidence.
Tamasin Cave: No. There is no evidence that people are more concerned about agency lobbyists as opposed to in-house lobbyists.

Q17 Simon Hart: Where is the evidence about lobbying?
Tamasin Cave: There is a lot of interest. You only have to read the newspapers.
Simon Hart: There may be evidence—
Chair: Simon, let the witness answer the question.
Simon Hart: It's catching.

Q18 Chair: We have an arrangement here. Members restrain themselves on their own opinions and try to establish certain facts from the witnesses, and the witnesses answer the questions put briefly and succinctly by the members of this Committee. It's your turn, Tamasin. Where's the evidence?
Tamasin Cave: I would say there is massive evidence. We have talked about various scandals that have happened since PASC did their report, whether it is Laws, Stephen Byers and his "cab for hire" remarks, Geoff Hoon or Patricia Hewitt. We have had the Bell Pottingers boasting that there is no problem getting messages through to No. 10. We had the Adam Werritty/Liam Fox affair, which I don't think anyone has really got to the bottom of. You must be aware of public concern about things like NHS and planning reforms. There is a big public campaign against them, as there is with many other policies. That is as it should be, but people are focusing—a lot of editorials have led with "This has lobbyist fingerprints all over it," whether it is property developers, private health care or whatever.
Sufficient evidence is out there of public concern. You can go back to official reports, such as the Power inquiry, six years ago. A lot of evidence was taken from people, which showed that they had big concerns about vested interests and lobbying.

Q19 Simon Hart: We have not heard from anyone else on the panel about that point, but that is my fault, not yours. Would Adam Werritty have been caught by the Government proposals? I suspect not, but that is only my opinion.

Finally, if there were a register—I'm not against one as such—would it address the so-called evidence, if you don't mind me describing it as that? You have come up with a lot of examples, but, as a virgin MP, I have yet to receive a single representation from a single member of the public on this topic.
Tamasin Cave: It is very difficult to prove cause and effect in lobbying. We know, for example, that Eric Pickles had a dinner at the Savoy with the chief executive of an airport operator. The application went through 10 days later. He said he never spoke with the man, but he did not declare the meeting because it was held in a private rather than a ministerial capacity. People will read that and think that perhaps something has gone on, but we don't know. Unless you are at that meeting and are party to those conversations, you have no idea.
Justin Fisher: Let me reiterate, there is no evidence whatsoever that multi-client agencies are a particular problem. The differentiation between them and lobbying by in-house, charities and so on, such as NGOs, is irrelevant. Why the Government have seen fit to delineate is beyond me.
To pick up on a point that you made, Simon. Public opinion in itself is not a reason to act. A friend of mine who is a university professor once said to me, "People get upset about everything." And he is right. "What are you against?"; "What have you got?". That is not to say that we should dismiss public opinion, of course, but you have to be very careful about using it as a guide to policy making. If you look at comparable areas, such as regulation of party finance, for example, you could pass the most extensive piece of legislation in the world and people would still be fed up, upset and suspicious. It is very difficult, and you should be very careful about that path.
The fact that no one has complained to you is, frankly, irrelevant. If it needs to be done as a preventive measure, that is the most appropriate thing to do. It is not about whether someone has written you a letter.
Chair: Simon, do you want to come back on that?
Simon Hart: Not now; maybe later.

Q20 Mr Turner: What are the costs of running your organisations?
Lionel Zetter: Are you referring to the UK Public Affairs Council?
Mr Turner: Whatever you are representing.
Lionel Zetter: As I said, I am representing no one but myself, but to give you a brief overview, the CIPR is a chartered institute that has been around for 60 years. It has 9,500 members, it charges about £200 a year and it makes a very small profit, so it is self-financing. The PRCA is a trade association representing consultancies, both public affairs and PR. It has several hundred members, it is highly profitable and, again, it pays its own way and pays for its own overheads. The APPC represents purely public affairs consultancies. It has about 65 members, which covers the majority of the industries. It levies on its own members a fee according to their size. Again, it employs a part-time member of staff and it covers its own costs.
The three bodies formed the UK Public Affairs Council, which had three non-executive members, headed by Elizabeth France, and four industry representatives. It therefore had overheads in terms of paying those three individuals and trying to bring together the three existing registers. Some people might think that that is a simple exercise; the Government realise that it is never a simple exercise. It spent, I believe, about £60,000 a year—paid equally by the three representative bodies—and that was simply not enough. The scale of the IT problem defeated it in the first instance. It has now appointed a new IT company, with more experience in this field. That will probably cost more money, but it is confident that the fully functioning register will be up by the end of this month. But it has taken a lot of money to get to that point.

Q21 Mr Turner: Professor Fisher, same question—the cost of whatever it is you are representing here.
Justin Fisher: I represent the university.

Q22 Mr Turner: So there is nothing related to this which does not come from the university?
Justin Fisher: Sorry, I do not follow the question.

Q23 Mr Turner: I am trying to work out how much money is spent, from your representations.
Justin Fisher: None whatsoever. I am here, one assumes, because of some expertise.
Tamasin Cave: We are grant funded. We have various different projects, but the work on lobbying transparency is funded by a three-year fund from the Joseph Rowntree Charitable Trust of £90,000 over three years.

Q24 Mr Turner: Thank you very much. Can I go, in a sense, from the other end? If I am a Member of Parliament and somebody comes to my surgery and complains about one issue, I take it that that is not lobbying. Does anyone disagree with that?
Tamasin Cave: I would say it was lobbying. In the broadest terms, lobbying is what I do when I write to my MP to complain about whatever or in support of something. In terms of defining lobbying for the register, we define it as professional lobbying activity, which means that you are explicitly paid to lobby.

Q25 Mr Turner: So you are paid?
Tamasin Cave: You are paid.

Q26 Mr Turner: What if you are Zac Goldsmith, and he puts a lot of money behind one of his campaigns, which he does from his own money. He is very wealthy.
Tamasin Cave: He would be funding a campaign group and that campaign group, if it was sufficiently big enough as a charitable organisation that it triggered registration, should be registered as a lobbying organisation.

Q27 Mr Turner: I am asking you: does this count, for your purposes, as lobbying or does it not?
Tamasin Cave: Yes. I would say that the charity or the campaign group that he is funding should, if it is engaged in lobbying, be registered and it should probably declare its funders.

Q28 Mr Turner: But he is not going to get any money out of it.
Tamasin Cave: He will not, personally, but if it is engaged in lobbying activities—

Q29 Mr Turner: I am trying to find out what lobbying means in this context.
Tamasin Cave: Lobbying we define as an activity. It is not a handing over of money; we define lobbying as contacts. As Lionel described it, it is facilitating and arranging contacts with public officials and communicating with officials. So you define the lobbying activity, and then anybody who undertakes that activity for money would be required to register.

Q30 Mr Turner: Sorry, but are you saying that he does not need to earn money for this purpose? He is wealthy.
Tamasin Cave: Oh, I see—he is not paid. No, I do not think it would capture that—

Q31 Mr Turner: Right. But someone who comes from outside the constituency, so long as it doesn't involve earning money, is free to approach me as a Member of Parliament, but not as a Member of Parliament for that constituency.
Tamasin Cave: We don't want to restrict people's right to petition their MP or any other Member of Parliament, or a civil servant for that matter. So there would be no restrictions. What we think there should be is a sensible threshold. But if you are, what most people would think of as a paid professional lobbyist—whether that is working for a charity, a trade union, an agency or Tesco's—you should be registered, and everybody else should be exempt.

Q32 Mr Turner: Do you, Mr Zetter and Professor Fisher, agree with that?
Justin Fisher: I think so. You are absolutely right to draw our attention to the difficulties in the definition. That is terrifically important. That is something certainly that has been wrestled with in the past to see who or what is captured by any self-regulation or statutory register. I return to my opening statement: if you try to regulate the life out of politics, there is a danger that you capture perfectly innocent activity and almost prevent people from doing it. I think that there is a real danger there. You are absolutely right to draw it to our attention. There is an element of common sense about this, and Tamasin's ideas would fall under that category of common sense. There are issues of definition, and they need to be considered very, very carefully. The definition in the Government's proposals is wholly inadequate. On balance, the UKPAC definition—for all UKPAC's ills—that it came up with was probably broadly speaking a workable one.

Q33 Mr Turner: Somebody who lives in my constituency runs a lobbying firm, in the broad sense of the word. He also comes and visits me quite a number of times on perfectly normal parliamentary, local issues. Where does the line exist—that he is paid for some things, but not paid for others? How do you know what?
Lionel Zetter: I would say that it is for that individual to make it very plain in what capacity he is approaching you, whether as a local resident, whether as an unpaid representative of a local pressure group or whether on behalf of a client for whom he or she is paid. They need to be very, very clear about that.

Q34 Mr Turner: Sorry, this is the point. You are saying that he would have to make it clear that he was coming to see me as a Member of Parliament on a matter that might be serious and confidential, and which I would not wish to be released.
Lionel Zetter: You raise a very interesting point. There is obviously a strong imperative for confidentiality, whether somebody is approaching their doctor or their MP. As long as the individual makes it plain who he is representing and as long as his company is a member of one of the three organisations I have mentioned, you could have a look to see who he is representing, but I don't think that there is any proposal—as far as I am aware—that the details of meetings are to be disclosed, whether it is with a minister or with an MP. There is such a thing as constituent confidentiality and there is also such a thing as commercial confidentiality, and they are both very important principles that need to be maintained.

Q35 Fabian Hamilton: May I put this to you? Having registers, having lists and having legislation is completely irrelevant. A framework of anti-corruption legislation, which we have in this country, complete and open transparency, freedom of information that actually works and a genuine free press are the things we need to ensure that lobbying does not corrupt and that it is free, fair and open. In other words, the Adam Werritty issue and some of the issues that you raised, Tamasin, have been exposed by media that are determined to ensure that we do not have this sort of corruption. Isn't that all we need? Registers can be perverted and can be used for specific ends, as you have pointed out, but an open and free press combined with transparency and freedom of information—in other words, openly registering everything properly—is the important thing. Those are the criteria that will ensure that lobbying does not become a corrupt practice. Discuss.
Tamasin Cave: You mentioned the Adam Werritty thing as exposed, and various other things. *The Daily Telegraph* has done a really good job of highlighting some of the lobbying on the planning reforms. I'll give you one example. We did some work, looking at the NHS reforms. Using the Freedom of Information Act, we found that discussions were being brokered by McKinsey, between the German private hospital company and the Department of Health, over the takeover of the management of public NHS hospitals in London.
It took a long time to get that story out through FOI. If we had had a public register of lobbyists, we might have seen that that German private hospital company was approaching the Department of Health over its reform agenda. We would have seen that it was part of the game. The fact that I managed to find that one particular case suddenly gave people an insight into things that were happening under the reforms.

We work on a budget of 30 grand a year. I can tell you that, despite the fact that the newspapers do a very good job, there is not much investigative money floating around to do work like that. Having a public register and being able to see some of the players that are involved in lobbying has the power to change the nature of the debate. You would be able to see who is influencing policy, and I don't think you can rely on the newspapers to do that.

Q36 Fabian Hamilton: On that point, you are arguing for the freedom of information legislation to work better rather than for a register. The fact that it took you so much time and effort to get that information tells me that the FOI legislation is not working properly and people are not abiding by its spirit.

Tamasin Cave: It is partly that, but it is also partly the fact that I don't work in the national press; I am a campaigner. There are a lot of good people who are doing investigative work, but not many. This is one story out of how many hundreds of thousands out there that we do not know about? There is not a sufficient check and, as you say, the freedom of information laws are not working at the moment, as our case with the Cabinet Office shows.

Justin Fisher: I don't think transparency is enough. You highlight the Adam Werritty case. That episode illustrates the fact that by the time these things come to light, it is too late. The transparency provided a salacious story, but it was one unholy mess, and there is no evidence that the transparency that currently exists would necessarily deliver appropriate behaviour—people holding back from engaging in questionable activity.

What is really required is some sort of preventive measure. This is why I have a concern about relying solely on things like a statutory register, because that provides a maximum on the standards of behaviour rather than a minimum. The register is a bit of a red herring. An effective form of regulation—preferably self-regulation for the industry—would be better. That would set a minimum behaviour standard; a register would set a maximum standard. The general principle is that we have an interest in improving conduct in political life rather than simply ticking boxes, which, effectively, is what a register is.

Q37 Fabian Hamilton: Isn't what you've just said a criticism of the fact that there was not sufficient transparency? Once that story came to light, it was clear that the Minister should have registered or at least told civil servants of the interest of Mr Werritty.

Justin Fisher: My argument is not against transparency. It would be very difficult to argue against transparency—in whose interest would it be? My point is that that alone is not enough. The level of transparency will not necessarily deter people from acting unethically. The key thing is whether they tick the box in terms of registration, not whether they perform their duties in an open way.

Take the case of Bell Pottinger. I am not sure that a register would prevent informal communications between an agency and No. 10. In some ways, it is a kind of very small sticking plaster over a potentially large wound. I am not arguing that there is necessarily a large wound, but you see my point.

Lionel Zetter: As I said at the beginning, the majority of people in the public affairs industry, such as it is, are in favour of a statutory register. The reason for that is I think because most of us already belong to a voluntary register, but there really will never be universality without some element of compulsion. I find that strange, coming from my mouth.

One thing that the three bodies and the one umbrella body that I mentioned do is that we all operate our own codes of practice. The UK Public Affairs Council put together a generic code of practice. It is pretty well mom and apple pie, and it lists the things that are probably covered, as you say, by anti-bribery legislation elsewhere. Nevertheless, it is worth stating the way in which people should behave, just like it is worth being transparent about who we are and whom we represent.

I have always maintained that, just as important as any rules and regulations, there should be a culture of compliance, so that people in the industry ought to be squirming slightly when our colleagues are caught out on camera being a little boastful and vainglorious. There is a temptation for all of us, in privacy, to take that route. When large fees are involved, obviously there is a temptation to slightly exaggerate your reach and influence. Those things are very hard to legislate against. It is more about the culture and about saying, "Yes, of course we have influence, but our influence extends very narrowly to, first, the strengths, validity and power of the policy arguments that we propose, and secondly, the case of the people we are representing." Those are the two things that matter: the policy and the client. We are merely facilitators. We have no influence in and of ourselves, and when we claim to do so, which from time to time we all do, yes, we all ought to be slapped down.

Q38 Fabian Hamilton: Yet you receive a fee for bringing the two together.

Lionel Zetter: We do indeed. I think we save everybody's time. We save the company or the client, whoever they are, from knocking on the wrong door. We save the Ministers' time because they are not being badgered with meetings with people over areas of which they have no control whatsoever. Very often, the advice to clients is, "Don't even bother with the Minister. There is a civil servant whose job it is to oversee your area of activity. They have been doing it for years, and they know the subject inside out. If you think there is a problem, that is the person you need to meet." Yes, we are paid for doing that.

Justin Fisher: I want to come in on a point that Lionel made. I would generally concur with Lionel's points, but just so that the Committee is clear regarding codes of conduct I should tell you that one of the significant problems with the existing set-up of UKPAC is that it does not cover a significant proportion of the industry. A large proportion of the in-house industry is not covered. None of the charities are covered. That is entirely because of the way in which UKPAC was established, and I am happy to return to that point later. The idea that it covers the

industry and represents the industry as a whole is very wide of the mark.
Chair: Paul, is your question a quick one on this particular point?

Q39 Paul Flynn: Very quickly, do you not all agree with what the Prime Minister said: that lobbying is going to be the next major scandal, that we have a crisis of democracy in this country with the collapse of faith in politicians and the political system, and that we must have a puritanical form of regulation and transparency in lobbying to avoid that future scandal?
Lionel Zetter: Generally, I try not to gainsay the Prime Minister, but I think he is entirely wrong on this one. When I appeared in front of your previous committee, I think I referred to the fact that MPs' expenses were going to be a problem. I think I would now predict that the problem going forward would be party funding. I think lobbying is always there, or thereabouts, but it is never a really big issue, and there hasn't been a really big genuine scandal for decades.
Justin Fisher: "Crisis" is a big word. I suspect there is a vulnerability to this happening, and I think we should be on the lookout for it, in the way we should be on the lookout for potential problems in other areas. I wouldn't single lobbying out, but I do think that as things currently stand there is a risk.
Tamasin Cave: The Prime Minister said it was the next big scandal waiting to happen, but he also underlined why this is crucial, because I think you said that there are billions of pounds-worth of government contracts at stake here, and that is true. We only have to look at something like the NHS IT contract, which is widely seen now as a disaster, which was heavily lobbied for in the first instance, was badly designed, and then cost us a lot of money. It is contracts like that that really need to have a balanced approach.

Q40 Fabian Hamilton: Can I just move this on to all-party parliamentary groups? There are so many in this place, I think it is almost impossible to count them. There is a very clever and sensible system of registration, and part of that registration process is that you not only meet certain criteria about officers and membership, but declare openly who the secretarial support services are provided by, and if there is any commercial involvement. I am sure all of us in this room chair, or are officers of, some of these all-party groups. There are significant commercial interests involved. For example, one group that I chair, to do with prison health, involves a pharmaceutical company, the British Liver Trust, various other bodies, prison reform groups and so on. We have deliberately spread it. My point is this, though: in spite of the careful system of registration, which is very tightly followed, do you think it is adequate, or is the all-party parliamentary group system another way of commercial interests infiltrating and lobbying MPs and peers?
Justin Fisher: Almost certainly, it is a way.

Q41 Fabian Hamilton: Is that positive or negative?
Justin Fisher: I think it is a positive thing that there are such things: MPs coming together with a shared interest and engaging with the outside world. I echo Lionel's earlier points that it is important for MPs to have regular interaction with various interests, in order not only to hear arguments but also to be better informed. There are dangers, but I think it would be hugely regrettable if that sort of interaction was either over-regulated or phased out, because of concerns about possible outcomes. One would hope—and I am on record as speaking up for MPs as being good people, and underpaid, I should add, but in general very good people—
Chair: Take a few more minutes.
Justin Fisher: I have to say I think the reaction in the wake of expenses, both inside and outside Parliament, was excessive; but one would hope that the standards that MPs display in every other aspect of life are on show in the all-party groups. Yes, there is a danger, but I am not sure it is a particular danger.
Tamasin Cave: I think it's fact, actually: it is widely seen that they are a route to lobbying. Somebody told me the other day—I am going to get the details wrong, so I will not give details—that company X was sponsoring a particular sport APPG: no known interest in that particular sport, but because of a particular politician who was on that APPG. So it is definitely the case that they are seen as routes to lobbying, but I think you bring up quite an important point: we have rules for parliamentarians and ministers, and various people, and they have just introduced new register of interest rules, which Peter Mandelson seems to be getting round—but the rules are always tightened up for parliamentarians. In the meantime, we have scandal after scandal, and the entire lobbying industry is left unregulated. This has happened over years and years. You can keep tightening up—it is good to keep revising rules, if the situation changes, for parliamentarians—but I thought that we had recognised that maybe it was time to turn our attention to an unregulated industry and that that was where transparency was needed. I do not think it is going to be sufficient to keep tightening up the rules for parliamentarians and for Parliament.
Lionel Zetter: I think APPGs serve a very valuable function. You can have only so many Select Committees, and only so many MPs sitting on them. If you have a Health Committee, it has to look at the big picture. All-party groups can look at conditions which are quite small, quite discrete and restricted to a small number of sufferers. They can help small countries become more known and understood. They can do many things to broaden the knowledge between individual patient groups, industries, countries and parliamentarians. Parliamentarians do not have to join these groups; they have to officially sign up. The names of the first 20 members are published. Any money that is paid towards them or any funding in either goods or service is declared. The last time I went through the register, a handful of them received funding of tens of thousands. The vast majority get by on a shoestring and operate at almost zero cost to the taxpayer, and I think they perform a very valuable function.

Q42 Fabian Hamilton: I assume you would draw a distinction between organisations such as the National

Council for Palliative Care, which services the all-party group on hospice and palliative care, and, say, one of the pharmaceutical companies.
Justin Fisher: Why?

Q43 Fabian Hamilton: Would you draw a distinction between them?
Justin Fisher: No. This is what has got in the way of good debate about lobbying—the idea that there are good lobbyists and bad lobbyists. Lobbying is lobbying, regardless of whether it is conducted by a charity or by a business.
Tamasin Cave: When it comes to charities and, for that matter, trade unions, there is a degree of transparency about what we are lobbying for. Trade unions will put it on banners, and we cannot tell enough people about what we are doing. In the case of companies, if a pharmaceutical company that wants to access a certain politician and has particular issues—whether on employment, tax, NICE, regulation or whatever it is—there is not a great deal of transparency about what it is lobbying for. There is a distinction there in that there is a serious lack of transparency.

Q44 Fabian Hamilton: Fuller transparency would help everybody?
Tamasin Cave: Yes.

Q45 Mrs Laing: What is the difference between lobbying and campaigning?
Lionel Zetter: It is one of definition. A lot of lobbying is simply about developing policy and making sure that that policy is brought to the attention of key opinion formers and key decision makers, so it is a fairly discreet, but not secretive, activity. Campaigning is much more what Tamasin referred to earlier—taking to the streets and waving banners. Generally, as a lobbyist, you try to conduct the client's affairs in a manner that does not make a lot of waves, does not take up a lot of time and does not stir up any kind of furore. It is talking to civil servants, talking to special advisers and looking to influence and inform them. If you fail in that activity, that is when you have to go to the media to get a campaign going or even take to the streets to bring something to the attention of Government. Generally speaking, they are just different stages of the same process.

Q46 Mrs Laing: Do you agree with that definition, Professor Fisher?
Justin Fisher: By and large. There are levels of specificity, inasmuch as campaigning would almost certainly be much more broad, whereas lobbying might seek to change a particularly small clause in a proposed piece of legislation or something like that. I also think one can differentiate. It goes back to an earlier point that Mr Turner made about how we define such things and the extent to which a transaction is involved, either through a multi-client agency or if people are employed by a charity or an in-house organisation to work on a particular issue. One would look at campaigning and treat that much more in terms of voluntary groups or political parties that may be coming together. It is imprecise. It is a very good question, but levels of specificity would be where I would focus.
Tamasin Cave: I am not sure that I agree with that entirely. At the moment, the NHS campaigners seem to be fighting over a couple of amendments, which is pretty specific. I agree that the engagement with the public is a key part of it. I draw attention to the fact that, with certain lobbying campaigns, it is a deliberate strategy to keep things out of the press and the public domain.
A while ago, there was a case study on the CIPR website about a particular campaign against the pesticides tax. It was being run by the pesticides industry, by a company called Hill and Knowlton, I think. Their campaign strategy says that it was a deliberate intention to keep it out of the national press because they did not want to raise it among green groups. They did not want to catch the attention of environmental groups, and this is explicit in their campaign strategy. What they did want to do was engage with the trade press because they needed the farmers to lobby on their behalf. The use of the media is a very deliberate, covert tactic and technique in the lobbying industry.

Q47 Mrs Laing: Not in campaigning?
Tamasin Cave: No. In campaigning, we are much more public facing. We do not have an awful lot of interest in keeping things secret, because a lot is about public engagement.

Q48 Mrs Laing: Is there a value judgment of whether something is inherently good or not inherently good, as to whether it is a campaign or a lobby?
Tamasin Cave: No.

Q49 Mrs Laing: Because you think that a particular charity is acting for the public good, that is campaigning not lobbying?
Tamasin Cave: No, I'm not saying that. The nature of most campaign groups is that they are public facing, but it can be a deliberate tactic of the lobbyists to keep things out of the press.

Q50 Mrs Laing: Thank you. It doesn't matter that you can't answer my question, it puts the subject before the Committee.
Is there an inherent assumption that, if ministers or indeed MPs, civil servants or anyone else involved in the decision-making process on a particular issue meet a lobbyist, those ministers or other decision makers will be influenced by that lobbyist?
It looks like I will get, a "No, no, no" for that one. That would be good.
Lionel Zetter: Hopefully, they would. If the case being put forward was valid, and it was put forward in a coherent fashion, then, yes, the idea is that they would be influenced. Equally, they would be subject to a counter lobby by the other side. The whole point about lobbying is that there are at least two sides to every argument—often more—and it is only through lobbying that all these issues come to light and all these other arguments are tested by MPs and ministers who are there because their judgment is trusted. At

the end of the day, it is your judgment that counts, not ours. It is yours.
Justin Fisher: It's a very important point. There is absolutely no guarantee that having access leads to impact. The example I always give to my students is that I can meet my vice chancellor whenever I like, but there is absolutely no guarantee that he will take me seriously. One can meet whoever one likes, but there is no guarantee that it will lead to anything in particular.
Tamasin Cave: I don't think it is the case that necessarily there will be influence, but you would then have to have the counter argument. I come back to a case study—I am using it not because I am involved, but because it is a very good case study—of the Cabinet Office's approach to this particular issue. It granted privileged access to the industry, whereby ministers sanctioned monthly meetings with UKPAC, but explicitly wrote to me to say that it would be inappropriate to meet me before the consultation was published. Therefore, it isn't getting any information from me and it isn't getting a counter argument put to it. With many, many policies, you will have disproportionate access given to industry compared with, say, environmental groups. The figures on the planning reforms bear that out.

Q51 Mrs Laing: I'm reluctant to go down that road any further, because I think that Ms Cave is trying to plead her own case here. I do not think that that is a good idea in front of our Committee. That is not what we are here for. There must be plenty of other examples.
I should perhaps take the question a step further. Is it not to be assumed, therefore, that every minister or other decision-maker meets one set of people and someone who is acting responsibly in their decision-making process would automatically meet people who are putting the case from all sides of an issue? You all said that it is of course not to be assumed that a minister will be influenced by meeting a particular lobbyist. You all suggested that the matter would be examined from all sides of the issue.
Justin Fisher: I am not sure that that follows. My point was that you cannot guarantee that access leads to influence. I am not sure that it follows from that that you should assume that all decision makers would look at all sides of an argument equally. Having said that, there are many people who would probably feel that they should have an input into a decision being made. Some of them are credible and some of them are not. You cannot blame decision makers for being selective on from whom they receive evidence. That is not to cast aspersions at all on Tamasin's organisation, but A. N. Other organisation could well write to the Cabinet Office and say that it wants to have some input but there is simply not enough room in the diary, because the Cabinet Office has no idea who these people are. I would dispute your logic that one flows from the other.

Q52 Mrs Laing: I am only asking the question. Ms Cave said in her remarks at the beginning of this meeting—if I can ask Ms Cave first and then ask Mr Zetter and Professor Fisher to comment on it—that the Government's consultation paper does not answer the problem, but answers a different question. So, what is the problem?
Tamasin Cave: The problem is that we have no public scrutiny of who is lobbying who and for what in this country. We could increase government accountability by improving public scrutiny of lobbying. This proposal, as it stands, will not do that. They have identified a problem that does not exist and applied a solution to that, which is the point I made earlier.

Q53 Mrs Laing: Would you perhaps like to state it more clearly?
Tamasin Cave: Certainly. Mark Harper said on the "World at One" that the problem that they were seeking to address with these proposals was the lack of transparency of ministerial meetings. He said that when ministers meet a company, it is very clear who they are meeting and everyone knows what that is about, whereas if they meet an agency, it is not always clear which clients the agency is representing. That is what we seek to address with these proposals. That is what he told the "World at One". It is all backed up in the consultation paper that that is the problem that they are seeking to address with this. Having used data from whoslobbying.com, we have done the figures. Of the 5,144 meetings that have been logged by ministers since May 2010, about 10 are with multi-client agencies.

Q54 Mrs Laing: I recall that you said that earlier, but what is the problem?
Tamasin Cave: There is no problem. The problem that Mark Harper is seeking to address, which is a lack of transparency with regard to multi-client agencies—he cites ministerial meetings—is not a problem. Does that make sense?

Q55 Mrs Laing: But what is the problem?
Tamasin Cave: The problem is this lack of transparency within the whole of the lobbying industry. Three quarters of the lobbying industry is in-house lobbyists and a quarter is agencies. Those are industry figures, although if you look at the Government's consultation paper, they have put the ratio at less than one in-house lobbyist to two agency lobbyists. I do not know where they have got their figures from, but they say that there are 1,000 agency lobbyists in this country and 320 in-house.

Q56 Mrs Laing: Sorry. We do not seem to be getting there. What is the problem? How is democracy being harmed by the current situation? That is not a rhetorical question; it is an absolutely straight question: what is the problem?
Tamasin Cave: The problem is, I would argue, that we have growing public concern—I would say that it is very high—about undue influence and access afforded to lobbyists. So there is public concern that government are listening to lobbyists more than they listen to the general public. That is the easiest way of putting it. In terms of a particular policy, whether it is the planning regulations, changes to planning law, NHS reforms, particular contracts or whatever, there

is public concern that there are vested interests at work here.

Q57 Mrs Laing: I want to get this very clear. You are asserting that the problem is that ministers give undue attention to lobbyists rather than to people in general who bring issues to them.
Tamasin Cave: I am saying that the democratic process is being subverted by a £2 billion professional lobbying industry. May I quote David Cameron? He says, "Lobbying is perfectly reasonable…when it's open and transparent, when people know who is meeting who, for what reason and with what outcome." We do not have that at the moment. We do not have public scrutiny of who is meeting whom and about what. So we have no way of knowing whether vested interests are having undue influence on policy.

Q58 Mrs Laing: Thank you. Can I ask Professor Fisher if he thinks that that is the problem?
Justin Fisher: In the broadest terms, the general principle is that transparency has been applied to most areas of political life and lobbying is one area that is a particular exception. If you are saying, "What is the problem for democracy as such?" that would be my general response. But there is also a problem for the industry. The concerns about some of the sharp practices that have been engaged in tarnishes all lobbyists. That, in a sense, is the problem. In the aftermath of the PASC inquiry, we had a round table in the Palace of Westminster and many of the charitable people there, who were lobbyists, were saying that they would welcome regulation because when somebody behaves badly in the commercial sector, their work subsequently gets tarnished. If there is a big problem, it is a big problem for the industry; the whole thing gets dragged down because of a few bad apples.
Lionel Zetter: I firmly believe that lobbying enhances the democratic process. In a mature democracy like the United Kingdom, we make sure that all sides of the argument are put. We also level the playing field. When a party is in opposition, it is, as we are all aware, stripped of its civil servants. It has no paid-for special advisers, the money does not flow and it is short of resources. If we lobbyists do not get what we want from the Government, we go to the Opposition and say, "Have you thought of asking this? Have you thought of tabling this Bill? What about this EDM?" So we level the playing field.
If there is a problem, it is not with democracy; it is with our image. That is what we tried to address with the UK Public Affairs Council. We did half the job. In order to do the other half, we need a bit of help from the Government. I am not talking about money; I am talking about the compulsion that will lead to universality and bring everybody under the same rules in the same tent. We can then go forward from there. But at the moment it is we at the core, who have always engaged, belonged to professional bodies and declared our interests, who are at a disadvantage. So we are saying to the Government, "Help us out here. Let's bring everybody within that tent." That, I am afraid, means a statutory register.
Mrs Laing: Thank you.

Q59 Chair: Members of Parliament are meant to represent everybody, whether they are constituents or people with broader interests. Is it not a reflection on the position of Members of Parliament in politics that there is a paid lobbying industry? Should Parliament and Members of Parliament not be looking to themselves to beef up their own capability, so that they can more effectively represent all sorts of views in all sorts of ways to Parliament? Would paid lobbyists then be out of a job?
Justin Fisher: I do not see that that follows at all, not least because you would not have the time to do that, with all the various and complex things that MPs must consider. One of the benefits of lobbying is that it provides information to generalists and can lead, on occasions, to better-informed policy. To answer your question, that probably should be the case, but it would be impossible to achieve, simply because you don't have the time.
Tamasin Cave: I agree, but despite the fact that you have a very important job, a lot of decisions are taken by civil servants. If I were a lobbyist—
Mr Chope: You are.
Tamasin Cave: Thank you. I have to remind myself—if I were a regulated lobbyist. You target civil servants, as is the case with this policy.

Q60 Chair: Lionel, I think I know what your answer will be.
Lionel Zetter: I probably should have declared that I am a local councillor in Enfield. I spend a lot of my time dealing with pretty micro issues, from dog mess to pavements and so on, but we are also confronted with planning issues. Even as councillors, we have to take a judgment about whether we look at the half dozen people who are living round a development, who will be inconvenienced and whose property value may be damaged by a proposal, or whether we look at the bigger picture and say, "We need jobs. We need a new school. We need a waste processing plant." We have to balance that. Even as councillors, we are lobbied, so we have some idea of what that is all about.
But would you have time to do that? I don't need to tell you that different Members of Parliament have different priorities depending on what constituency they represent. For some, the social worker aspect is the priority. You are acting as super-councillors, stepping in where the councillors cannot resolve the issues. For others, it really is about green belt, property values or industry. If you have time to do them all—absolutely fantastic, but you are on Select Committees, all-party groups and you have your constituency work. If we can make your life easier going forward, I am happy to help.

Q61 Chair: I am sometimes irritated by organisations that approach me through lobbying companies. If people have passion and care for their subject, they can get hold of me straight away. I don't need the facilitation or oil of a middleman or middlewoman.
Justin Fisher: But that is often not the reason why they use a lobbying company. It is a question of

expertise and how best to put a case across. That is why you hire a solicitor to help you buy a house.

Chair: I may have similar views about lawyers, but I better not—

Lionel Zetter: Ones I'd share.

Tamasin Cave: I have nothing to add.

Q62 Mr Chope: Your last line of questioning, Chairman, has been very instructive. Basically, everyone in the professional lobbying industry has a vested interest in trying to minimise the influence of MPs in the public's view. Many's the time that a company in my constituency would be much better off coming and speaking to me than spending a lot of money going to a professional lobbying organisation. Now, in order to give professional lobbying more credibility, you set up your register. You will be really excited if we can waste more parliamentary time setting up a statutory register, because you think that it will turn your industry into a profession and that everyone will give you more credibility, and you will be able to demand higher fees as a result.

This is a complete charade, isn't it? Isn't that exemplified by the introductory memorandum that Tamasin gave us from Spinwatch. In the first paragraph, she says, "We established the Alliance for Lobbying Transparency (ALT)", which is a coalition of NGOs and unions, many of which are lobby groups, "including"—I am being selective—"Friends of the Earth." She says that they are "concerned about the growing influence of lobbying on policy-making in the UK." Friends of the Earth is one of the most prolific lobbyists of Members of Parliament and of government—so much so that, in my experience, it purports to get signatures on postcards when quite often the people whose signatures are on those postcards deny any knowledge of ever having signed them, but let us leave that on one side.

Surely, it is arguable that the great success of the last Government in getting the Climate Change Act through Parliament with, I think, only five of us voting against the Third Reading—right across the whole of Parliament—was the very successful result of a big, single issue pressure group, which put pressure on MPs and ultimately on the Government to do something that in the long term is costing ordinary energy consumers in this country a fortune, because they are having to pay extra for the regulatory costs of that climate change legislation.

So when Tamasin says that SpinWatch is engaged in this, would it not be fairer to say that SpinWatch is concerned about the counter-commercial lobbyists—the ones that may be countering the effectiveness of the groups which she represents?

Chair: Can I start, Tamasin, with Lionel on the first point about Members of Parliament and lobbyists, and then come to Tamasin and to Justin at the end?

Lionel Zetter: Putting it in terms which, I hope, you would appreciate, Mr Chope, if we were not doing a reasonable job, companies and organisations would not hire us. If we were not reasonably effective, MPs and ministers would not see us. At the moment, there is no sign of that. It is not a huge industry in the UK, but it has grown steadily, which seems to indicate that there is a need.

You talk about the profession. Yes, you are absolutely right. You are a barrister. Lots of lobbyists would like to see themselves in that same legal category; we are not. We really are not of that calibre, but we are seeking to become more professional, to be better trained and to be more ethical. I hope those efforts are appreciated by politicians, by the media and by Spinwatch. A lot of us are passionate about politics. Quite a few of us have tried to get into politics. We are failed politicians, if you like—we are failed politicians and we want to be lawyers, so we are caught between the two. Hopefully, we do a good job: that is why people hire us and that is why people see us.

Tamasin Cave: We are the first to admit that we are all—most of us—lobbying groups. Friends of the Earth definitely is, and I am a lobbyist. I would like to be as transparent as I can be about the lobbying that we do, but you are right. A group such as Friends of the Earth is particularly interesting, because it has come up against the disparity in influence, access and resources—crucially—when it is facing, for example, the energy industry.

One of the things that we think should be on the register—we have not really discussed the details of the register—is financial disclosure, just to show the massive disparity in financial resources of industry and Greenpeace or Friends of the Earth. Yes, they have a very high media profile and a very active membership who will write to MPs, but they are dwarfed by the scale of the energy industry lobby. It should be in the public domain that there are significantly more dollars being spent by the oil companies, for example, than by Friends of the Earth, to influence politics.

Q63 Mr Chope: If what you have just described is a problem, how is a statutory register going to sort it out?

Tamasin Cave: Well, if you had it in the public domain, for example, that Friends of the Earth had registered that it has six in-house lobbyists—I do not know how big its team is—and that it was lobbying on this particular piece of legislation, that it had approached whichever department it was and that it was spending this much money on it, that would be captured on a register. Then you have the one from BP, and it will say that BP has an in-house team of this, that it is lobbying on this and this, that it has approached this department and that it is spending this much on it. That is what the American register shows you, and you can see, for example, the massive disparity between people who were pro-Obama's health care reforms and the industry that was opposed to them. That then changes the nature of the debate, because you can see both sides; you do not have this invisible army and a very public campaigning side. Then you can actually start to talk about the issues.

Justin Fisher: I am not sure I follow the purpose of the question. If it is to argue about whether or not lobbying has any impact at all and is a waste of money, I eagerly await the Committee's inquiry into the homeopathy industry. People will spend money on all sorts of things that may or may not work, so in a sense that is irrelevant.

Should they professionalise? What is the argument against professionalisation? An industry exists, and there is a desire among some in the industry, but not all, to raise standards, so that the legitimate work that goes on for businesses, charities and so on to promote their case is not seen as automatically tawdry, which is the way it is presented.

I cannot speak for SpinWatch and who they support—I am nothing to do with them. I am here as an independent person. I cannot speak for SpinWatch, but in a sense, if it does not work, who cares? I do not see the problem.

Q64 Mr Chope: The problem is that what we are talking about is spending parliamentary time putting another piece of regulatory legislation on the statute book. Certainly, some of us sitting around this table would say, "Before you do that, you have to prove that it is going to be worth doing."

Justin Fisher: No. I go back to the answer that I gave to Eleanor. There has been a general move towards greater transparency in political life. This is an activity of political life that thus far has not been subject to the same level of transparency that we see elsewhere. Broadly speaking, I think the arguments in favour of transparency have been accepted. We have moved on a lot in the last 15 years on that issue.

Q65 Mr Chope: May I ask a question about definitions? From some of the discussion earlier, you would describe a lawyer who writes to an MP on behalf of a constituent who has an immigration issue as a lobbyist, because that is a person who is being paid to act on behalf of a client and is communicating directly with a Member of Parliament, or perhaps with a department. You could get all sorts of professionals, such as accountants, coming into that category. Are you thinking that all those people will be included in the register?

Justin Fisher: There is a distinction to be made. The example you give would be someone who is acting on a point of law rather than putting across a particular policy argument. There is a key distinction there.

Tamasin Cave: There would be important exemptions. A constituent writing to an MP, whether via a third party or not, should be exempt. That should be private between an MP and their constituent.

On the issue of definition, when you talk to campaigners in the States, who have been doing this for 20 years, they say that definition was a big sticking point for them there. Yet the guy who writes *Public Affairs News*, the lobbyist trade magazine, wrote an editorial the other day saying, "Look guys. They've passed definition and they've got registers in Australia, Canada, the US and the EU—Germany has one to an extent and Austria is getting one. Nick one of their definitions and we'll start with that." They have workable definitions around the world. It can be made to work.

Q66 Sheila Gilmore: That leads quite neatly into what I was going to ask about. What is the experience elsewhere? It is significant that although the US has apparently the most extensive process of registration and transparency, many people would probably say that it has one of the most effective lobbied legislatures going. We know that more money went into lobbying against Obama's health care than for it, but that did not necessarily affect in any sense the outcome of that process. Is there any evidence from these other countries that their systems have worked? What have they done? How have they improved the situation?

Justin Fisher: Barely, is the honest response to that. As a model for comparing regulation, the United States is always a poor comparator in my view, not least because it goes down the path of trying to regulate everything that moves—you have to declare having a cup of coffee with someone and so on. If you are asking whether there is a successful regulatory system in other parts of the world, the honest answer to that question is no. Some appear to work more effectively than others—Canada and possibly some of the reforms in Australia—but to be perfectly honest, few countries do it. As I recall from the PASC inquiry, there was recognition that you could not simply take regulation in another country in this area and just put it in the British context. There is no good evidence that it works elsewhere.

Tamasin Cave: Works in what sense? The register is not trying to stop lobbying; it is trying to increase Government accountability, transparency in the process, and public trust in decision making. It is not trying to stop it. In terms of raising the level of debate around lobbying and public understanding of the lobbying industry, in the States that has had a positive effect. They know the scale of their industry. They know that the financial services industry in the last decade has spent \$5.1 billion lobbying Washington; they know that, and they can then factor that into debates about what we do next and bank lobbying now. We cannot have those debates in this country because it is often painted as some sort of cottage industry here, but it is not: it is a £2 billion industry. You have Washington, Brussels and then London. It is a significant industry that we know nothing about.

Lionel Zetter: I would dearly love to know where that £2 billion figure comes from.

Tamasin Cave: The Hansard Society.

Lionel Zetter: It is a bizarre notion. If you add up the turnover of all the members of the APPC and the PRCA, it would not come to anything like £2 billion. I wish it did.

We are not a cottage industry, but we are a small industry in the UK, and likely to remain so for one very good reason. In the United States, it is perfectly possible to buy influence because getting elected in the US, as I am sure you all know, is a very expensive business. If you want to get elected to the House, it will cost you \$15 million to \$20 million; if you want to get to the Senate, it will probably cost you \$50 million. If you want to be the Prime Minister, it could cost you between half a billion and a billion. Money talks in America.

Chair: President.

Lionel Zetter: Yes, if you want to be President. The reason why it talks is because they have advertising: you can buy advertising, and that is really expensive. Whereas in this country, political parties—as you know better than me—will spend £25 million on the entire election, if I want to stand for a no-hope seat in north London, it will cost me £10,000. That is the scale. Money does not talk in politics in the UK. It does in America.

I go back to my earlier point: we are not relying on rules and regulations to keep us honest. We do rely on the free press, but we also rely within ourselves on this culture of compliance. If people do not get caught out, we do not say, "Oh, bad luck," or, "Oh, well done. That was quite a neat trick you nearly pulled off." We say, "That is really not helpful." We are all trying to bring about a culture of compliance that means we help each other to promote the image of the industry and we can go forward. A statutory register is a good foundation on which to build.

Q67 Sheila Gilmore: Are there any examples of statutory registers?

Lionel Zetter: I quite like the European Parliament one, and for a very good reason. Like many people in this room, I am perhaps not the biggest fan of the European Union, but their register works. I shall tell you why I think it works: there is a stick and a carrot. If you are a lobbyist, and you come in and out of this place two or three times a day, it can get very cold out there and you are searched by the same person wearing the same gear that you were wearing the last time you came in. It is a pain for us, and it is also not cost-effective for the security of the House. In Europe, if you sign up to a register, you get issued with a pass and that means that you can go in and out at will, but it clearly labels you as a lobbyist. Like at party conference, everyone knows who you are and who you are representing. The carrot in Europe is that you get one of the passes and, if you misbehave, it gets taken away, which is a massive inconvenience, so it is a real incentive to behave properly. That is something that I would like to be considered. I very much doubt that it will be, but most systems work better when there is not just compulsion, but reward.

Tamasin Cave: The register is not there for the convenience of lobbyists. It is good that it makes your lives easier, but the last time I looked at the Brussels lobbying register, there was not one law firm on it. It has serious omissions, because it is voluntary.

Lionel Zetter: It is currently voluntary.

Q68 Andrew Griffiths: Just a brief question to start. Tamasin—this may have already been covered, so forgive me colleagues—you said that there was growing public concern about lobbying and the operation of lobbyists. I see stories in the newspaper about lobbying. We all want to see greater transparency about how this process operates, but have you got any quantitative evidence that it is a concern of the public? Has any survey been done? I must admit that, on the doorstep in Burton, no one has ever said to me that their No. 1 concern is the transparency of lobbying.

Tamasin Cave: No, they won't, but they might tell you that they do not like what is happening in the NHS and will ask why that is happening.

Q69 Andrew Griffiths: That is not the same thing, is it? We all have concerns about government policy in one shape or form, but that is not related in any way, shape or form to the lobbying process.

Chair: Tamasin, evidence please.

Tamasin Cave: There is evidence that concern about NHS reforms is directed at undue influence, improper access and vested interests at work.

Q70 Andrew Griffiths: What is that evidence?

Tamasin Cave: I speak to a lot of people and they are very concerned about this. I am sorry, that is anecdotal.

May I return to your original question?

Q71 Andrew Griffiths: Just to answer my question, is there any quantitative evidence at all that the public are concerned about this?

Tamasin Cave: Well, moving from the NHS to the planning reforms, if you take *The Daily Telegraph's* coverage—let's suggest that it reflects a public concern—it has been uncovering and exposing that sort of lobbying, whether it is a donor's club for the Conservatives that is run by a property developer or the industry.

Q72 Andrew Griffiths: That is a newspaper story. That is no evidence that this is a concern of the general public.

Tamasin Cave: There are surveys—I am afraid that I do not have them in front of me—such as the one done in 2004. Then we had the Power inquiry and I think that the Conservatives did a recent one in 2008, all of which point towards the fact that there is public concern about vested interests having undue influence on policy. I will just draw your attention to what David Cameron said—

Q73 Andrew Griffiths: Can you share those with the Committee?

Tamasin Cave: I can certainly send them to you. I am sorry I don't have them here.

Q74 Chair: Justin, do you have information that is historical or current from polling organisations or any other source that suggests that this is a matter, not of concern, but, as two questioners have said, of public concern?

Justin Fisher: There are no data of which I am aware. There may be isolated surveys, although, to be honest, I would take anything that was in the Power inquiry with a huge tub of salt. Even if there is an individual survey, that could indicate growing concern. You weren't in the room at the time, Mr Griffiths, but I return to the point I made earlier that the presence or absence of public concern is a red herring. It is whether or not it is an appropriate thing to do in terms of the prevention of future problems in political life.

Chair: I will ask you separately for your evidence about the tub of salt. I suggest that Tamasin drops us a note, if you want to research this, and address the concerns that have been raised by a couple of Members about the public view.

Q75 Andrew Griffiths: On the question earlier about people being contacted on behalf of constituents, I was contacted by a lawyer acting on behalf of a constituent who was concerned. The constituent owned a car park and they were concerned about the implications of the Government's proposals on clamping and regulation on clamping. Is that lobbying? That is question one.

Secondly, the proposal is that in order to register there will be a signing-on fee, if you like, and then a yearly registration. Do you have any views about the level at which that should be set, and do you have any concerns about whether that might prevent smaller organisations from being able to take part in the lobbying process?

Lionel Zetter: Very much so, yes. That is the problem with the UK Public Affairs Council—that only a small proportion of the industry has joined in, which means that it cannot properly bear the overheads that are necessary. Running a register for 300 people is the same as running it for 3,000, more or less, so it did not have the resources. If we charge too much, that would scare people off. The way to avoid charging too much is to spread the load as wide as possible.

In terms of what you would pay, I pay £140 a year to belong to the NUJ and £200 a year to belong to the CIPR. Those kinds of figures should not be scary if you are serious about your profession. If it were firms paying, there would certainly be an argument to vary the fee according to the head count, so that smaller firms—one-man bands, two-man bands—were not squeezed out. The current proposals would be especially unfair on freelance public affairs consultants, of which I used to be one, because they simply do not have the means to bear the same kind of costs as a small, medium or large agency.

I keep coming back to the point that universality is the key. Unfortunately, we are never going to get near that unless the Government, in one form or another—whether that is primary legislation, a clause in an existing Bill or an SI—tell us we have to.

As for the point about lawyers, they are regulated by the Law Society and the Bar Council. There is no question, usually, about their behaviour. Obviously, from time to time, lawyers misbehave, like any other profession, but there are sanctions to deal with that. When they stray into lobbying, potentially that could be a problem, which goes back to the definition. If they are spending the majority of their time, half their time or a sizeable proportion of their time lobbying, then there is definitely an argument. If they happen to be a lawyer who happens to represent a client who happens to have a planning issue and they lobby on their behalf, I do not think that brings them into the tent. If it becomes an everyday occurrence, that is different.

Justin Fisher: I am slightly puzzled about the Government's proposal to set up a statutory register and pass on the cost to someone else. The thinking on that seems to me to be slightly illogical. None the less, it equally seems to me that if you wish to practise in a particular area, and you wish to be considered as professional, there are costs associated with that. You may be a one-man band dentist, but you still have to register with the British Dental Association and so on and so forth, although the remuneration for dentists is, I suspect, rather higher than it is for public affairs professionals.

To go back to your example, I echo Lionel's point, but I also think that it is important that, when thinking about the general principles, you do not get bogged down in the "What if?" questions. Those obviously need to be considered in detail, and no definition will be 100% watertight. But that does not mean that the exercise should not be attempted, if it were deemed appropriate.

Tamasin Cave: I think you mentioned charities. Charities should definitely be on this. The National Council for Voluntary Organisations is likely to be on board, as long as it does not affect the very small charities, which brings me on to the discussion about the funding of it. I do not think that it is like dentistry. I do not think that this is an activity like pulling teeth. If we talk about lobbying as a democratic right, and we do not want any barriers to people engaging in the activity of lobbying—which we certainly do not—there cannot be a financial barrier to people actually behaving transparently as a lobbyist.

They are always saying that it should be applied to professional lobbyists, but in the case of, say, a large charity that is campaigning on something, there should not be a barrier—whether it is a £250 CIPR registration fee—to show that they are lobbying. This must be government-funded. I refer back to my earlier point, which was David Cameron saying that there are billions of pounds-worth of government contracts at stake here. The potential savings in terms of better policy making, better procurement decisions and things like that mean that it would pay for itself very quickly.

Chair: I ask colleagues who want to come back to ask very quick, clear, specific questions, and perhaps witnesses could be brief, too, so that we can get everyone in before 12 o'clock.

Q76 Simon Hart: You mentioned, Tamasin, that charities should be included. You also referred to financial disclosure without explaining what exactly that meant. You also commented on there being a sensible threshold. Having been involved in a lobbying charity, how can you assure me that the interests would be protected, particularly when that charity actually used members to lobby constituency MPs in their constituency? How can we be protected from your proposals, whatever they are?

Tamasin Cave: Protected in what sense? Protected from declaring?

Q77 Simon Hart: No, not protected from declaring, but protected from actually having an inordinate cost and bureaucracy to deal with, and protected from donors being concerned about their perfectly reasonable private donations being made public. I need some further explanation of what you consider a sensible threshold for a small charity to become a big charity in your eyes.

Tamasin Cave: We put the threshold probably too low. We have been in discussion with the NCVO about where the threshold should be. It is often the case that a chief executive of a charity will undertake some lobbying activity, but if they have a full-time public affairs person or a full-time lobbyist, should that be the trigger for registration? Grass-roots lobbying is another case. I don't think that petitioning your members to petition MPs should necessarily be included.

Q78 Fabian Hamilton: Professor Fisher, earlier you said that there is no distinction between good lobbyists and bad lobbyists; there are just lobbyists. I put this to you. Surely there are those who lobby because they believe that there is a public interest in changing the law or influencing MPs, and those who lobby because they want to sell a product and make a profit for their company. Would you not draw that distinction?
Justin Fisher: No. Charities employ people to work on their behalf, often who have no interest whatever in the aims of the charity—marketing officers, public affairs officials. It is irrelevant whether it is a charity or a business.

Q79 Fabian Hamilton: But their aims are not to sell a product to make a profit, their aims are to improve the world we live in.
Justin Fisher: No. Improve the world from their point of view. The distinction is a meaningless one.
Tamasin Cave: Lobbying is a tactical investment by a company, and a stat from the States says that, for every dollar spent on lobbying, a company can expect $100 return, at least. So there is a reason why they do it, which is different from charities.

Q80 Mr Turner: It used to be, didn't it, that charities were not allowed to campaign and non-charities were. Is that a possible division in the future?
Lionel Zetter: I fear that distinction has gone, Mr Turner. Now the Charity Commission allows charities to campaign. There is no distinction between a charity and a pressure group or an action group.
Chair: I shall call it quits there. It has been a fascinating session. Members have not only had full rein in their questions, they have come back again. We could go on for another hour at least, I am sure. Thank you all very much indeed. Lionel, Justin, Tamasin, you have been extremely helpful. Feel free to send in further opinions and information, should you wish. Thank you.

Thursday 1 March 2012

Members present:

Mr Graham Allen (Chair)

Mr Christopher Chope
Sheila Gilmore
Andrew Griffiths
Fabian Hamilton
Simon Hart
Tristram Hunt
Mr Andrew Turner
Stephen Williams

Examination of Witnesses

Witnesses: **Mark Adams OBE**, standup4lobbying, and **Mark Ramsdale**, gave evidence.

Q81 Chair: Thank you for your time this morning, and for helping us on our continuing inquiry on lobbying. I wonder whether you would like to take a little time to open up with some introductory remarks.

Mark Ramsdale: Sure. Good morning. My name is Mark Ramsdale. I am an independent public affairs practitioner, otherwise known as a lobbyist.

Firstly, as someone who is both a lobbyist and who has worked on this issue, I would like to thank the Committee for the opportunity to speak today. I have worked in and around Westminster and Whitehall for over 10 years now, including as a researcher for a Member of Parliament. I have been acting as an independent consultant, providing a range of public affairs services to clients since 2008, operating as a limited company since April 2010.

I have worked in various guises for the Chartered Institute of PR, the Public Relations Consultants Association and other bodies. Between July 2010 and December 2011, I was Executive Secretary to the UK Public Affairs Council, an organisation that, among other things, provides a voluntary register of lobbyists. However, I would like to make clear that I am speaking entirely in my own capacity today; any views are my own and not necessarily those of existing or previous clients or employers. I would also like to declare that I have a parliamentary pass, sponsored by Lord Smith of Leigh. I use that in relation to my duties as the Secretariat to the Parliamentary Rugby League Group.

In terms of the Government's consultation, I think the vast majority in the public affairs industry—certainly those that I have spoken to, anyway—welcome the Cabinet Office consultation. It provides a focus to enable us to make clear that we are committed to transparency. However, I don't think that it addresses issues such as parallel regulation or sanctions for transgression from codes of conduct. I also have concerns over registering those that operate in multi-client agencies and the tendency, I feel, to overlook non-commercial bodies, but of course I would be more than happy to provide further thoughts on that.

Mark Adams: Thank you, Chairman. I might begin by saying Dydd Gwl Dewi hapus—happy St David's Day. Chairman, I am proud to call myself a professional lobbyist. My trade is advising my clients on how to present their case to government as effectively as possible, just as a barrister's trade is to present their client's case in court as effectively as possible. I am the Chairman of the Professional Lobbying Company and also the self-appointed Director of the campaign group standup4lobbying—although with permission, Chairman, I will give my evidence sitting down.

I am proud of what I do. I believe I offer my clients a valuable professional service. Unlike Tim Collins of Bell Pottinger, I do not have the Foreign Secretary's mobile telephone number, but I don't believe I need it to do my job well. I also believe in a broader, socially responsible approach to my profession. I regularly undertake pro bono work for good causes and look to give back in other ways. I have just assisted voluntarily this morning with a citizenship course at a local school, Grey Coat Hospital—a school that I know is well known to you, Chairman.

I believe in strong and effective regulation of lobbying and have been involved in trying to build such regulation throughout my lobbying career. I was heavily involved in the formation of the UK Public Affairs Council. In my view, it is purely an empirical matter whether self-regulation works better than statutory regulation or not. I have seen no proposals for statutory regulation that work better, in my view, than the current system of self-regulation, either in the Government's current consultation paper or elsewhere.

As I understand it, the concern about lobbyists is that they can have undue influence over the political process, either because politicians have a too cosy relationship with lobbyists or because they are too easily swayed by slick arguments by lobbyists. That in a nutshell seems to be the concern. As we have a representative cross-section of Members of Parliament in this room, perhaps we should begin by establishing whether any of you feel you have a too cosy relationship with lobbyists or are too easily swayed by the slick arguments we use.

Chair: We will leave that question open, Mark, as we progress. No doubt colleagues will wish to answer that in their own way.

Q82 Tristram Hunt: Could I begin by asking where, in a sense, self-regulation went wrong? For those of us looking at this, it seems a bit "People's Front of Judea" territory in terms of the divisions within the UK lobbying sector. Why do so many of your colleagues think that self-regulation hasn't worked and there is an argument for statutory regulation, and why you think those divisions exist within the UK lobbying firmament?

Mark Adams: Let me answer that question very directly by saying that, of course, I recognise that there are issues of concern that arise within the lobbying profession. For me that doesn't mean self-regulation has failed. Crime still exists, but no one says that therefore the police have failed and they should be replaced. So bad things will happen and bad things will continue to happen—we shouldn't kid ourselves—if we have a system of statutory regulation. It won't be the ultimate panacea.

So I don't accept the argument that self-regulation has failed. Currently, there is an ongoing investigation into claims made in *The Independent* newspaper against Bell Pottinger, using existing self-regulatory machinery. Any one of us in this room could have raised a complaint against Bell Pottinger on the basis of those stories. Only one person in this room did, which is me; I am currently pursuing that complaint under the existing self-regulatory machinery, because I believe self-regulation works.

If you ask Tim Bell whether he believes self-regulation is working, well, I think he can see the potential damage that under a self-regulatory regime, that story having come into the public domain, has delivered. I am not convinced that the damage to Bell Pottinger's reputation that may flow from this would be any different at all if there were this statutory register.

Mark Ramsdale: I would certainly endorse Mark's comments about self-regulation not having failed. I think there is a regulatory regime out there. The issue is about the proportion of the industry that views self-regulation as a means for transparency and ethical behaviour.

One of the things that we need to make the case for, in terms of self-regulation, is that more people need to be involved in some form of regulatory regime. There are three industry bodies that exist that have codes of conduct and can authorise sanctions against anyone that might transgress them, but any regime is only as good as the volume of people or organisations that it covers.

The one thing that a statutory register would allow is blanket coverage. There will still be a few people—a few organisations—that don't want to register, for whatever reason. They may view a definition as one of the arguments for not doing so, but if you get a very large proportion of an industry either in a self-regulatory regime or under a statutory regime, I think you are starting to deal with the issue.

Q83 Tristram Hunt: Leaving aside the politics of this and the attractiveness of doing this, is the attempt at statutory regulation in many senses a product of your own industry's internal divisions and weaknesses, because if there was one unified body with one voice rather than three, who seem to be scrapping quite a bit, you would not necessarily be entering this place?

Mark Adams: As someone who has been a member of all three bodies, I have incorporated a new company, and as soon as my new company joins the APPC and the PRCA I will be once again a member of all three. Generally, competition is supposed to be a good thing in life. It is very easy to explain; it takes about 30 seconds to explain that the three bodies have distinct roles but they came together. I was heavily involved in the unified body, the United Kingdom Public Affairs Council, and you will hear from the Chairman of that Council after us. It is an illustration of the fact that the profession recognised the issue years ago. Well before the Public Administration Select Committee in the last Parliament got into the issue, we had started the work of pulling together the three bodies into the Public Affairs Council.

Q84 Tristram Hunt: Then do you think the decision of some to leave was a real mistake?

Mark Adams: Individual members of the organisations will have to answer for themselves. I have been very clear throughout that there should be a unified body. But I have been critical. I helped set it up, but I withdrew from it at the foundation and I have gone on record to express two serious concerns I have about the operation of the UK Public Affairs Council, which I am happy to set out. That is why I have not been involved in it. So others—the PRCA—clearly do have concerns and they have now withdrawn.

Q85 Tristram Hunt: Finally, in terms of the statutory register, one of the big complaints—particularly from SpinWatch and others—was that you are basically not accounting for the in-house lobbying capacity, and if that is something like BP or BAE or even the Church of England, there is a big gulf there. Is that your critique as well?

Mark Adams: It is. One of the oddities of the consultation paper—because hopefully I have had a very healthy debate regularly with Tamasin Cave of the Alliance for Lobbying Transparency—is the Government has been able to unite both the ALT on one side and vast parts of the industry on the other in arguing that the Government have this wrong.

The Government seem to be saying, "Well, we must be doing something right because they both disagree with us". That to me is a sign of them doing something wrong. I have gone on record again to describe this consultation paper as shameful, and that is still my position. In my view, they completely miss the basic point that if you are going to have a statutory register of lobbyists, then what is a lobbyist? It is someone who lobbies, and anyone who lobbies, in my view, therefore should be on a statutory register of lobbyists.

If you have a statutory register for something else, call it something else and create it. But if it is a statutory register of lobbyists, then those who lobby in a professional capacity—I agree we keep out of it people who are doing it on a voluntary basis, constituents lobbying their MPs, of course—everybody who does it on a professional basis should be on that statutory register if there is going to be a statutory register.

Mark Ramsdale: I would certainly agree with that. The one thing that I took from the Cabinet Office consultation that I was in agreement with—and this is from the impact assessment—was that the purpose of a statutory register will be to increase transparency by making available to the public and decision-makers, and so on, authoritative and easily accessible information about who is lobbying.

If you are talking about transparency, the whole point of it is that it needs to be comprehensive. It has to cover in-house lobbyists—those that are independent, such as myself and Mark, as well as those who are providing services for commercial bodies, trade unions, religious groups, as you mentioned, and even pro bono work. What it should not include are those that are lobbying on a constituency issue, and therein lies the issue.

I understand the Cabinet Office argument that it bridges the gap between the likes of the commercial bodies you mentioned that are lobbying, because we know who they are and broadly what they are lobbying on, but we don't necessarily know who the agency is representing in a particular meeting. I understand that, but I would also endorse what Mark said—that a register of lobbyists needs to cover all lobbyists. If you are a lobbyist, you lobby irrespective of the issue, and there is no "good cause" clause either. It is all about function and the activity.

Q86 Simon Hart: Can we go back a bit, because I do not understand what the problem is, and I do not understand what David Cameron means when he says this is the next big scandal? Before we talk about registers—who is on them and who is not on them and what they might mean and whether this is a code of practice—what is the problem that we are trying to resolve, and what is the public clamour that apparently exists, but which I haven't yet heard, about this industry? Can somebody at least start me there?

Mark Adams: Yes. That is a very important question. I agree with you wholeheartedly. When the consultation paper came out, I turned with interest to the impact assessment because that is one of the questions that the Government is required to answer—"Why is Government intervention necessary?"—and this is the answer. I am quoting from it: "However, where lobbying is opaque, this creates a market failure caused by imperfect information that can undermine public confidence in the decision-making process and its results". So that is very clear, isn't it?

I trained as an economist the first time round; I understand what market failure means. This is written by someone who doesn't understand what market failure means and presumably thought that if they throw some jargon into a sentence, we will all be convinced by it. I am not. I also agree with your point about, where is the public clamour? On the whole, my friends are reasonably intelligent people—not all of them, and I won't name the ones I think aren't—but when I talk about my job and say, "I am a lobbyist", most of them look puzzled.

Tamasin Cave quotes evidence from a recent opinion poll, taken immediately after the Adam Werritty issue, that 53%—I think she says—expressed the view that lobbyists have too much influence over the political system. For me, that is an empirical issue. Do they or don't they? We should do an academic study to look at it. If I heard that 53% of the public thought the moon was made out of cheese, that wouldn't lead me blindly to think that the moon must be made out of cheese; it would make me realise that opinion polls are of limited value.

Of course opinion polls are important, but opinion polls about empirical issues just tell you how well informed the public are about that empirical issue. It doesn't tell you anything else, and that is important. We are to blame in the lobbying profession, and that is why I created standup4lobbying. I am afraid politicians are to blame as well. We have to accept our share of the blame for the fact that when lobbyists behave badly—and if there is a lobbyist behaving badly, I am afraid on the whole it means there is a politician behaving badly on the other side—we are to blame for the public perception.

Q87 Simon Hart: I am asking you some stupid questions on purpose because I simply don't get it. What is a "lobbyist behaving badly"? Adam Werritty wasn't a lobbyist; he wouldn't be on any register as proposed by the Government anyway, so in my opinion we can't use people like Werritty as an example because he falls outside the proposal. I was in an organisation that attempted to persuade, inform and educate, and all those other expressions lobbyists use. As an MP, I rather like lobbyists; I like to be lobbied, and I am one of these people that fit into the "not enough lobbying" category because I find it a helpful experience to get outside expertise. But what is this bad behaviour we are talking about, because nobody has got there yet?

Mark Adams: Mr Hart, I should say that I disagree with Sir Gus O'Donnell in his report when he said that Adam Werritty was not a lobbyist, because I think that goes to the heart. I mean, what on earth was he doing there on behalf of his clients? What is undoubted is he was a friend of the Defence Secretary. He had clients who were paying him because of his ability to influence the Defence Secretary and to take the Defence Secretary where those clients wanted him to be. In my book, that makes him a lobbyist. So I disagreed with Gus O'Donnell's report when it said that he wasn't a lobbyist. Any register that is going to be effective—frankly, if it doesn't catch that kind of behaviour, then that rather illustrates that it is not achieving.

But I agree. As things stand at the moment, it is doubtful whether I personally would have to be on this statutory register of lobbyists, bizarrely, as it is currently defined, because it is about direct interactions on behalf of clients and, on the whole, I don't do that. My clients are the ones who interact with MPs, interact with ministers and interact with civil servants. I advise them on how to do it. That in my book still makes me a lobbyist, and in the profession's definition of a lobbyist. That is why I register because I am caught by our profession's definition of lobbying. But arguably, I am not going to be caught by the Government's definition of a lobbyist, and in my view that illustrates in a nutshell how ridiculous these proposals are.

Chair: Let me just bring Mark in.

Mark Ramsdale: Yes. Again I would say that I agree with Mark; the current definition within the Cabinet Office about third-party agencies would mean that I would not necessarily need to register.

In terms of good and bad lobbying, without going into specific examples, I think there are three codes of conduct that exist for lobbyists, be they organisational or individual. If you want to look at anything that might transgress from that, there are your examples of bad practice. I also agree that the best lobbyists themselves are the clients. They put the arguments forward far more passionately, more concisely and certainly more enthusiastically than an independent lobbyist might. Our job is to help facilitate meetings, to understand the system and to help them put their case forward as best they can. On the other side of an argument, there will be another lobbying group or an individual organisation doing the same thing. Ultimately, the Member of Parliament decides.

Q88 Simon Hart: I accept absolutely what you said. There was a question earlier on, when we were trying to define what was bad lobbying and what was the cause of the alleged public concern, and one of the expressions that one or other of you used was a relationship that might be described as "too cosy". I want to explore that a little bit more, because I don't know what "too cosy" is.

When I was attempting to do what you now do, I found that, yes, of course you could get access to ministers, but invariably the Civil Service wall was a pretty good one, and that if my lot went in to see a minister, somebody representing an alternative view was almost certainly waiting outside in order to follow. I think we overlook the fact, do we not, that there is quite a lot of protection within the political system against dodgy lobbying, whatever dodgy lobbying is.

Mark Adams: An example I have to give: as it happens, I used to play golf regularly with Gus O'Donnell and I would say to clients, "What do you expect me to do? Is it just as he is about to take his putt on the 14th green that I am supposed to say, 'Before you take your putt, I have a client who needs help' and he says, 'Mark, leave it with me, let's get back the golf'." Of course it doesn't work like that and it is a nonsense to suggest it does. If it did work like that—if that really was how it worked—would it be me at fault for trying to exercise that influence or would it be Sir Gus O'Donnell, the Head of the Civil Service, at fault for going along with it?

In my view, if there is that kind of corrupt influence, let's root those public servants out of public life. Let's deal with the corruption at its source in public life. Don't come after private individuals like me—well, not like me because I don't believe it works like that, but those who do think it works like that and try to take advantage of corrupt public officials. They are not the people it should be aimed at. It should be aimed at rooting out corruption in public life. In my view, if there is a problem that should be the real target and the real solution to it.

Mark Ramsdale: I think you're alluding to the Civil Service Code of Conduct and Ministerial Code of Conduct. The bit that is missing is the other part of the democratic process, which is those that are lobbying professionally. There are codes of conduct; the fact is that it is not statutory at the moment. But again, I play rugby with Members of Parliament. I think if I tried to talk to them about anything in particular on the field at the bottom of a ruck, they would quite quickly tell me that that was not appropriate.

When I do have to talk to them I usually write a letter, so that I have something on record, so that they are aware that I am doing this in a formal capacity, and they will take a decision based on the argument I put forward. I know that of all the Members of Parliament that I know, and I would expect that right across all 650 Members.

Q89 Simon Hart: One last question to both of you. Do you think that what is happening is that the Government is deciding to do the least it possibly can manage in order to say that it has ticked the box marked "Statutory registered office", and this is just a token gesture in the direction of those who are rather keen on this measure?

Mark Ramsdale: The difficulty is the definition, actually. I know that greater minds than mine have spent a lot of time thinking about this, other legislative bodies similarly have spent a lot of time on that. I don't necessarily think it is the easiest route that the Cabinet Office has taken. Certainly, from the criticism that the consultation has faced, it would have been easier to have perhaps taken a different set of opinions before putting this particular consultation out.

What I would say is that they are listening to what has been said, and certainly the industry, and those that I have spoken to, seem to be of one mind that transparency is best suited to this industry. Also, regulation would provide the opportunity for them to demonstrate that they are not bad guys at all and are behaving appropriately in the same way Members of Parliament do.

Mark Adams: Mr Hart, the short answer to your question is yes. The slightly longer answer is that it was a proposal originally in the Liberal Democrat election manifesto. The Liberal Democrats typically write their election manifesto in the knowledge that they won't ever have to implement any of their proposals. Because of the way the election turned out, we have a coalition Government in which, inevitably, the coalition agreement had to give way on some things.

In my cynical view, I think the Conservatives looked at this and thought, "Well, this is something that we can give way on. It is not too damaging. It doesn't make much sense". Now it is in the coalition agreement, I am 99% certain we will get it. Does that mean it is right? Of course not. Does it make it sensible? Of course not. Yes, it is a box-ticking exercise to deliver something that the Conservatives agreed with the Liberal Democrats as the price of forming the coalition.

Q90 Mr Chope: So say all of us, but I go back to Simon's point and what the evidence is. If there is a problem, it is a problem that can be sorted out through transparency on the part of people who are being lobbied rather than by trying to register the lobbyists, and since we can't define lobbyists, it seems as though the Government is trying to pander to public opinion, which suggests that lobbying or lobbyists are a bad thing. But can I ask you, first of all, at the beginning one of you described yourself as "a public affairs

practitioner, otherwise known as a lobbyist". I thought there was a distinction between a public affairs practitioner and a lobbyist. Can you explain?
Mark Ramsdale: Certainly. Public affairs practice is more broad than lobbying. Lobbying certainly includes the rhetoric that you put forward when trying to influence a decision. Public affairs practice includes things like monitoring, understanding where a bill might be in Parliament, being expert in what a particular government department is doing, knowing who appropriate officials are, special advisers, and so on and a ministerial brief.

It also includes understanding which committees, parliamentary groups and constituency MPs have a particular interest in that issue. Thereafter, lobbying will take place and you will talk to those Members of Parliament, that minister, that special adviser, about the issue, but I would certainly say that public affairs practice encompasses lobbying. Lobbying is a small part of practice. When you say "public affairs practitioner", it is easier to say "lobbyist", and it is certainly more transparent.
Mark Adams: Mr Chairman, I want to disagree with what Mr Ramsdale has just said. I am terribly afraid that I am going to get a reputation for being very cynical about matters generally. I think "public affairs practitioner" was something that lobbyists started to call themselves when the word "lobbying" got itself a bad name. I am dedicating the latter stage of my career to trying to rebuild the reputation of lobbying because I think it is an honourable profession. That is why I call my campaign standup4lobbying, and I hope at some stage in the future public affairs practitioners, whatever that means, will stop calling themselves that and use the name that it should say on the tin, "lobbying", because that is certainly what they are doing in the tin.

I would like to pick up briefly, though, on the bit you said at the start about surely the best thing to do being to just get those on the inside to be transparent. I put that to the Minister responsible—and if you do call him before this Committee, I hope you will do as well. I said, "If it is about understanding who lobbyists are representing when they meet ministers, why not just require that to be declared at the start of the meeting and put it on the record? That seems a very sensible solution". His answer to that was, "It is not just meetings with ministers we are interested in. It is meetings with Members of Parliament". It is a perfectly fair point, and he is saying, "We in government have no control over what MPs do; therefore, we are going after the lobbyists. We are going to come at it from the other side".

It seems to me that a more sensible approach would have been to enter into discussions with the House authorities to see if the House authorities would agree. I agree that the Government can't impose its will on Parliament in that way, but the House authorities might like to consider it. It may be a recommendation that the Committee might like to consider. If there is a need for greater transparency, why not make it a requirement on MPs that they are more transparent about the meetings they hold, rather than me, a private citizen, having to publish information of what I get up to as part of, essentially, my private business life?

Q91 Mr Chope: Did the Minister in this response extend lobbying into the area where you have lobbying of the public? If lobbying of MPs is pernicious and needs to be controlled, surely lobbying of the public—for example, when people who are trying to promote wind power or renewables have a deep financial interest in the promotion of that cause, they are lobbying the public. The public don't realise that so-called environmental groups are actually in it for the money, for themselves or for their clients. How is that going to be controlled?
Mark Adams: Mr Chope, I am very pleased to report that the Minister didn't suggest extending it into that area. I think it is worrying enough when governments try to regulate the people who are lobbying them. The Government and you people around this table—you are supposed to listen to us. We are supposed to make our representations and you weigh them up. That is your duty, to weigh them up.

The idea that governments start regulating how we go about lobbying you, to me is a deeply, deeply worrying development in a democracy; I can hardly believe that of a Conservative-led government. At the end of Margaret Thatcher's reign 20 years ago, the idea that a Conservative-led government would be seriously considering restrictions on the freedom of the press, and restrictions on the right to lobby, would have been unbelievable. But that is exactly what we have from a Conservative-led government now, and I find that astonishing.
Mark Ramsdale: Again, I was going to talk about how the best lobbyists out there are the newspapers—the fact that they can have huge sway over Members of Parliament by influencing the general public. I think campaign legislation exists already. Certainly there are rules about campaigning, being honest and forthright with members of the public, and there is a sense that transparency right across the piece is required and that lobbying is just one part of the democratic process. Essentially, that needs to be brought up to the same levels of transparency.

Q92 Mr Chope: So why are we doing this at all? Do you agree that this is an area where the Government is talking about more regulation when we don't need any more regulation at all?
Mark Ramsdale: It is talking about less regulation, because it is only talking about having a statutory register of consultancy bodies. The self-regulatory element of the UK Public Affairs Council, for example, which brings together the codes of conduct and rules on transgressions and sanctions against those that transgress, is more stringent that the Cabinet Office proposals. They would be best served by listening to those in the industry and others, those that are critical, because we come together on this with greater transparency and more regulation.

Q93 Mr Chope: Let me distinguish between what you might describe as self-regulation, which is a private matter, and government legislative regulation, under which the Government is supposedly committed to reduce regulation and interference in our lives. Yet this seems to be going completely in the opposite direction.

Mark Ramsdale: I don't see the reason why it couldn't say there must be a regulatory body out there that is self-funding, and it is within the Secretary of State's gift to award the regulatory regime to that body at no cost to the taxpayer.

Q94 Mr Chope: But in a sense, for those who participate in the game of cricket, you could describe the rules as self-regulation but we wouldn't say that the rules of cricket are part of a regulatory burden. This is a private thing. As lobbyists, if you want to regulate yourselves and set up your own rulebook and then introduce your own private sanctions that people comply with, then that is a matter for you. It is nothing to do with the Government or with the state or with statute and legislation.

Mark Ramsdale: I agree. As a cricket fan, I am disheartened when players do transgress from those rules. Thankfully they are being taken to task, and I think self-regulation within this industry could do exactly the same thing.

Mark Adams: That is a very important question, because I said at the start that I believe in effective regulation of lobbying. I just believe it should be self-regulation and I think that is because we can offer a better professional service to our clients by being effectively regulated, so our clients can see that we behave in a certain professional way.

Something is deeply worrying—the more I read about this consultation paper, the more worried I get. For example, the way that the Government have disapplied the moratorium on new domestic regulation for micro-businesses that it announced in a fanfare for a three-year period, and it says, "As a significant proportion of the lobbying industry is made up of sole operators and micro-businesses, the Government has disapplied the moratorium to these proposals". I used to work in government on SME policy, and 98% of businesses in all walks of life are small businesses. So if it can be disapplied in this case, that fanfare three-year moratorium, frankly, isn't worth the paper that the Chancellor's speech was written on at that particular party conference.

Mr Chope: Thank you very much for making that point.

Q95 Mr Turner: I must say that I feel a sense of disagreement with Christopher Chope, which is unusual for me, because he was talking about people in general. I don't think it is people in general. You know the lady who used to run *The Sun*, I have forgotten her name.

Chair: Rebekah Wade.

Mr Turner: Thank you, yes. It appears she has been given a horse to look after by the Metropolitan Police. I am trying to work out whether anyone is lobbying. I realise it is not the Government's intention that they should control the Metropolitan Police's lobbyists, but would she be the sort of person who should be covered?

Mark Adams: Mr Turner, I am tempted to quote the Minister himself in an event that I attended that he spoke at yesterday, when he said, "Lord Leveson is looking at matters like that and is much better qualified than I to come to a conclusion". That is how I feel on this. There clearly are very important issues to do with the relationship between the media and public bodies. Clearly the media, in my view, do lobby, so there is an overlap in these proposals, but I think I have enough to worry about in thinking about the lobbying profession not to concern myself too much about the way the media is operating, mindful that someone much cleverer than I, in the shape of Lord Leveson, is looking into those matters.

Mark Ramsdale: I have nothing more to add on that. I think that is a very good point.

Q96 Mr Turner: You are saying that she is being dealt with by someone else?

Mark Adams: What I am saying is that Lord Leveson's inquiry is obviously looking into the relationship between the media and public bodies—and, indeed, between the media and society more generally. I would expect the proposals to come out of that to cover the issues that you are concerned about. However it takes this consultation forward, I wouldn't be expecting the Government to concern itself with a matter like that.

Q97 Mr Turner: No. But what I am trying to work out is what is lobbying. I suppose I am following Simon Hart's case, but what is lobbying? Does it include—

Mark Adams: On one level it is very, very simple and then the complexity, as very often in life, is how you then apply that very, very simple definition.

In my view, lobbying is an attempt, directly or indirectly, to influence public policy as set by public bodies, be they European Union bodies, national governments, the Welsh Assembly, the Scottish Parliament, or indeed local councils. All that is within the definition of "lobbying", and I say it very explicitly, directly or indirectly. So clearly, the media have a role to play within that. After all, what did *The Sun* headline very famously say the day after the 1992 election? They clearly thought they were lobbying.

Clearly therefore, any proposals that are dealing with lobbyists need to be mindful of the role of the media in that. Frankly, what I am saying is that I think the issues thrown up by the media are more serious. They are clearly more serious. What are we talking about in terms of the so-called lobbying scandals? We are talking about one or two naive—in my view—lobbyists, who have made a bit ridiculous and unsubstantiated claims to undercover journalists. In the case of the media, we are talking about people who have hacked into the voicemail of a murdered teenager. The scale of the problem is massively different. I have no interest myself in straying into that very complex area—a very important and, in my view, much more serious area that is being dealt with very effectively by the Leveson inquiry.

Q98 Mr Turner: But you have illustrated how she was lobbied.

Mark Adams: Whatever the specifics of that case are, the media in general is an important part of the lobbying world.

Mark Ramsdale: Yes. I agree with that. The issue of the definition is fundamental to anything that we are trying to achieve. I endorse Mark's comments.

The UK Public Affairs Council definition—and you can argue that, having worked for the UK Public Affairs Council, I would endorse this—is "Lobbying means, in a professional capacity, attempting to influence, or advising those who wish to influence, the UK Government, Parliament, the devolved legislatures or administrations, regional or local government or other public bodies on any matter within their competence".

Within that, newspapers would be caught or certainly those working for newspapers would be caught. They would become in-house lobbyists, but I think there are things around newspapers and media, and so on, that Lord Leveson is looking at that are best suited to that inquiry and on campaigning, for example, as well. That is best suited there. If we are talking about those that are lobbying as we understand it—we know when we see it. That is the issue. We understand a lobbyist when we see one. But when you try to write it down and include exemptions about constituents who have an absolute fundamental right to lobby, then it gets difficult, particularly in the statutory regime where it has to be enforceable.

Q99 Chair: If I can just draw us back from horses and cricket, back towards golf and rugby league. Mark Ramsdale, why can't Members of Parliament who are interested in a particular subject use their own resources and their staff resources and club together and, if they really are interested in a particular subject, organise themselves to be a parliamentary group? Why do they need your good offices to do that?

Mark Ramsdale: I think it is purely this: Members of Parliament like to serve their constituents. Parliamentary groups bring together Members of Parliament from all sides from both Houses on a particular issue. It would be inappropriate to use public money to work on an issue that they may be personally interested in, or based on their constituency. It is appropriate that parliamentary groups exist to facilitate the opportunity for outside bodies to come together to discuss issues that, perhaps, a select committee or a debate can't achieve under the auspices of either House.

Q100 Chair: Isn't it very appropriate that Members of Parliament use the public resources in order to pursue issues of importance and interest? It may well be that in this instance rugby league is a very significant issue for many Members of Parliament. It has economic consequences as well. Is that not undermined by Members saying, "Well, we will leave the organisation of this all-party group to someone who is, firstly, not a Member of Parliament and, secondly, is a professional lobbyist"? Doesn't that immediately raise questions that are frankly unnecessary? If there is nothing untoward, nothing going on, why on earth go into that territory?

Mark Ramsdale: The first thing to say is that parliamentary groups are led by Members of Parliament. They simply don't have the time to administer them, nor do their offices. MPs' staff are employed to work on constituency issues and bespoke pieces of research related to issues that the Members of Parliament is interested in—be that debates, questions, motions and so on.

The fact is that a well-administered parliamentary group is run by the Members; the secretariat simply facilitates the action. It may provide counsel, but it acts as a conduit for information to get to Members. In terms of other lobbying practice, a public affairs practitioner—sorry to use that term; I haven't been around as long as Mark, so I stick to the new terms—is able to pull together the sheer volume of information on a particular issue, and that is where Members of Parliament get the best out of parliamentary groups.

Q101 Chair: You don't think you are possibly risking a conflict of interest being both an administrator of a particular all-party group and potentially having interests outside of Parliament, which you may seek to represent formally or informally—not at the bottom of the ruck, but in the bar afterwards, perhaps?

Mark Ramsdale: I would say that there isn't a great deal of lobbying that would go on relating to a game, for example, but I am employed by the sport's governing body, the RFL. The members of the group took the opinion that that would be an appropriate vehicle through which the group might be funded. I drafted a 10-page constitution for the group, which makes quite clear that, if any funding were to be accepted, the members of the group decide where it comes from and, in fact, have turned funding down when it was considered inappropriate. If you look at the secretariat support that is provided to a range of groups, they usually are some sort of charitable interest—a governing body, whatever it might be—and I think they are the most appropriate vehicles.

Q102 Chair: I don't know whether lobbying is the next big scandal, but certainly the use of all-party groups may be the next area of interest for people who are looking for difficulties in the lobbying field. If self-regulation is to work, it may be an area where you and your colleagues want to have another look at how all that works, so that you do not have any semblance of a conflict of interest. I am sure there isn't any, but that may be something you want to have a think about.

Back to the golf course then, Mark. The Public Administration Committee in 2009 said that, "Some of the concerns that exist around improper influence are closely linked to the power of informal networks of friendships and relationships". So, once again, not tapping up the Cabinet Secretary as he is about to make his knee-trembling four-foot putt on the 18th, but nonetheless congratulating him on the 19th hole over a beer on successfully holing that putt, it never entered your mind to have conversations about issues of national importance that were on your mind and perhaps on his, too?

Mark Adams: Chairman, let me begin by saying that I reread—very brave of me—all 80 pages or so of the Public Administration Select Committee's first report on lobbying in the previous Parliament, and it reminded me that they looked very hard, over the course of extensive evidence, to find any wrongdoing. It goes to Mr Hart's question at the start. For example, to quote from it, "In essence, because secret lobbying by its very nature leaves no evidence trail, there could still be a significant problem even with little concrete evidence of one".

In other words, it said, "We have not been able to find any evidence of wrongdoing but we kind of think that it would—" and it is true, isn't it, if there is wrongdoing they are not going to shout it from the rooftops. But, frankly, I don't think that is good enough. I don't think it is good enough to say, "Because people would hardly declare that they are acting wrongly, it still exists even though we couldn't find it". In my view, the other main conclusion from that report is that they said multi-client agencies weren't the problem with the lobbying profession, which of course is precisely the route that the Government is going down with this statutory register.

As it happens, to answer the question directly, I am going to give you an unusually open insight into how lobbying works in practice. I am not offering to do this permanently and regularly, but I think in my relationship with the Cabinet Secretary, when he was Cabinet Secretary—actually, he may have been Permanent Secretary to the Treasury at the time—I only ever had one direct conversation with him on behalf of a client, and that was at the explicit instruction of that client against my advice. They wanted me to convey a message. I rang Sir Gus and I said, "I have been instructed to make this call on behalf of a client. I would ask that you listen while I make this point, and at the end of it I don't expect you to comment in any way at all", and I made—

Q103 Chair: You had that sort of access to the Permanent Secretary at the Treasury, did you?

Mark Adams: I didn't get through him to immediately; I don't have his mobile telephone number on my phone.

Q104 Chair: But you set up a call?

Mark Adams: I am not going to reveal the client—I am happy to write privately to the Committee, if you would find it useful—but it was a client that had very serious relations with government. I was able to place that call, not because of who I was but who they were. I think that is the legitimate point, and we keep saying this. It is about our clients, and they had a perfectly open and perfectly important and natural relationship at senior levels with government. They just happened to want me to be the one who made the call, despite the fact that I advised against it. If that conversation has to take place someone has to make the call, and I have always said, does it really matter if they subcontract the making of the call to someone outside?

You have to ask the client whether they asked me to do it because they thought that, as it was me and I played golf with Gus, he would listen to me more than he would listen to them. My advice, which is why I told them not to instruct me to do that, was that it would make not the blindest bit of difference. Sure enough, at the end of the conversation he said, "Well, thank you, Mark. You did say at the start of this that you didn't expect me to comment. I won't comment, but I hear what you say". I remain convinced to this day that the advice I gave that client—that I should not have been instructed to make that call—remains the correct advice.

To my recollection, that is the only time I ever had a direct conversation with Gus O'Donnell on behalf of a client. Of course we talked about political issues. Of course we talked in the same way that all of us, when we get together in the bars, will gossip about politics. For me, it is a fascinating subject and I love talking about it. I love boring my friends to death about it. But having a direct conversation with him about an issue on behalf of a client, I did once and only once.

Q105 Chair: I am very impressed with your ability to access the Permanent Secretary to the Treasury. We have about 150 years' worth of parliamentary experience around the table; I don't know how many times any parliamentary colleague, any elected Member of Parliament, has ever had that sort of direct access by phone to the Permanent Secretary. No one is taking me up on the offer, so I suspect you have better access than we do.

Mark Adams: Chairman, the point I made in my answer was that the access came not because of who I was but who the client was. That is the important thing, the client—

Chair: We all have some very important clients, Mr Adams. We don't just sit here twiddling our thumbs. We try to represent our constituents—

Mark Adams: Of course.

Chair: —and the national politics on some very important issues, including deficit reduction or going to war, but I certainly have never had that access directly to the Permanent Secretary to the Treasury, so I congratulate you on your portfolio.

Mark Adams: As I say, it is my client at the time you should be congratulating. I am happy to pass that on to them. As I say, I am happy to write to the Committee with further details on a confidential basis about that particular case.

Q106 Chair: Do you think Sir Gus will have fewer golfing partners this coming year than he did when he was Cabinet Secretary?

Mark Adams: I would fully expect him to have more.

Q107 Chair: More? Okay, excellent.

Back to Mark Ramsdale. You were the Executive Secretary of the UK Public Affairs Council, and you met with Cabinet Office officials at least three times. Could you tell us the purpose of those meetings, and did you make any suggestions as to what should or should not be included in the statutory register?

Mark Ramsdale: To deal with the last point first, no. On the initial part of the question, it was essentially an opportunity to share experience. The whole point of meetings with the official was to provide the benefit of that experience, to share the research and the implementation work that we had done, so they could better understand the technical issues and other logistical issues should they wish to take forward a statutory register.

Q108 Chair: Back to Mark Adams. Mark, now Stephen has joined us—Stephen Williams is a Lib Dem. I wonder if we can give him the opportunity of hearing part of the answer you suggested earlier, about why we have this in front of us—because the Lib Dems did not anticipate coming into power and it was in their manifesto and it was a bit of a giveaway for the Tories in the coalition. He may appreciate hearing your line of rationale on that one.
Mark Adams: Chairman, I think you have summarised my answer very succinctly—better than I put it originally.
Chair: Perhaps Stephen might want to follow up on that?
Stephen Williams: All I would say, Chairman, is that my party and myself have a long history of being patronised by people who think we are of no consequence, and perhaps they regret their words now.
Chair: I think you are slightly affronted, Stephen, but is there anything specific that you want to take up with Mr Adams?
Stephen Williams: No.

Q109 Fabian Hamilton: I noticed on your website this morning that you faced 150 15 to 16-year-olds at Grey Coat Hospital, a fabulous school in central London. At the end of your very short piece on the website you say, "Do you think the line of questioning I will get this morning from Members of Parliament will be more sensible than that from the girls?" What is your conclusion?
Mark Adams: I mentioned that exact point to the girls, and promised them that I would feed back the answer to that very question. With the greatest respect to this esteemed Committee and to be fair to the girls—it was a citizenship course, and they were all very engaged—I probably should give that answer first to the girls and then write subsequently to the Committee.

Q110 Fabian Hamilton: We can read it on your website, I assume?
Mark Adams: Or you can read it on my website.
Chair: We look forward to that letter, Mark. Gentlemen, thank you very much indeed. That has been very helpful. Thank you so much for your time. It has illuminated our inquiry. Thank you for coming.

Examination of Witness

Witness: **Elizabeth France CBE**, Chair, UK Public Affairs Council, gave evidence.

Q111 Chair: Hello, Elizabeth. How are you?
Elizabeth France: Hello. I am well, thank you, Chairman.
Chair: Excellent. Welcome to the Committee.
Elizabeth France: Thank you for the opportunity to expand on our written evidence and to answer any questions you might have.

Q112 Chair: You are very welcome indeed. Would you like to give us a couple of minutes' opening remarks?
Elizabeth France: Yes. Just a tiny bit about my background, really, to make clear that I have no past or present involvement in the lobbying industry as such. A major part of my career was as a Home Office civil servant. I resigned from the Home Office in 1994 when I was appointed as Data Protection Registrar. I spent eight years as Data Protection Registrar and Information Commissioner, a further eight years after that as an Ombudsman, dealing first with telecommunications and then, additionally, with energy and surveying.
Since then I have had a number of non-executive directorships, of which chairmanship of the United Kingdom Public Affairs Council is one. I was appointed after a search by Ellwood and Atfield in the spring/summer of 2010, and I took up post on 1 July 2010, along with two other independent directors—I think this is very important—Sir Roger Sands and George Kidd. We were brought in as the last piece of the jigsaw, for the creation of something that was more than simply an industry body or a group of industry bodies getting together. We provided the independent element, the UKPAC.
During the period between the search for independent directors and our appointment, there was a change in direction, in that we had originally been appointed to assist the industry to respond to PASC recommendations. By the time I was appointed on 1 July, we had the coalition Government and a commitment to a statutory register, which slightly changed the emphasis and probably the mood of those of us who were trying to get the new organisation launched.
I am happy to answer questions about how we function as we go through, but if we get to the main issues, which are critical for all of us, about where we are going, what the future for lobbying is and where the Government proposals take us, I want to start by picking up the use of the term "regulation", which I keep hearing. I see no proposals for regulation in this consultation, and I think it is important that we make that clear. A register on its own is not regulation. A register on its own provides transparency, but as a former Information Commissioner who is very keen on transparency, I would say you need to say, "Well, what step does that lead to?" Transparency on its own must take you somewhere.
So I would want to say that we, as UKPAC, would expect to see some link from that transparency to some forms of code of practice. You might be able to create—and I would be content to see created—a self-regulation linked to a broader-based shallow register, with information about everybody who meets the definition and makes clear on that register whether

they subscribe to any self-regulating code. That might be a way forward that doesn't actually involve statutory regulation, but does involve a statutory requirement to be open. That is the first of my points. The second is the definition itself, which has been talked about by Mark Adams and Mark Ramsdale. The UKPAC definition is one that was worked on for many, many months before I took up post and is one that we have found difficult to better. It wasn't drafted by parliamentary counsel and, as it stands, it wouldn't be fit simply to slip into a piece of legislation. But the key thing I would want to emphasise is that it defines lobbying, not lobbyists. It is the activity that we need to be open about and then we can decide whether there are exemptions for certain people who practise it, but first we have to know what it is and what the definition is.

Our definition makes it clear that it has to be done professionally for a fee and be a substantive part of somebody's job; I am paraphrasing. So, definition is key. If it is going to be a statutory register, then the definition also has to be enforceable, so it can't have the soft edges one might like in a self-regulating system because there must be some way of ensuring that everybody who should be on a register is on it.

So definition, scope—I cannot understand the narrowness of the approach. It seems to me that, across the whole spectrum of people commenting, the idea that this should be limited to multi-agency lobby firms makes little sense. It makes little sense for a number of reasons, not only the reasons you heard expressed already—that the larger firms will be the ones with in-house lobbyists and they might be spending more on lobbying. Our view would be, if you have somebody there whose primary job is lobbying, whose job description says that is what they do, they should be included in the register. Although it is also important to think that, if we are going to have transparency, and if we look for what the issue is that we are trying to address, then we can only assume that while it is important to shine a light in dark corners, on the whole most people behave properly most of the time.

So if you are going to take a step it must be a step to address those who are not behaving, who are at the edges of the activity. If you design a system where, when you shine the light in the corner, you find a hole has already been dug and the people have disappeared it is not very much help. My worry is that there would be all sorts of ways of getting round the requirement to register, if it only applied to the third-party agencies and not to in-house lobbyists. For example, what is to stop a large firm, who didn't want it to be known that they were lobbying, from asking one of the agencies to second staff to them for six months? Do they become in-house? All those sorts of difficult issues would arise. It would not be straightforward. If we are going to have a statutory register, it needs to be straightforward, it needs to be simple, it needs to be enforceable, and it needs to cover everybody who meets the definition.

Q113 Fabian Hamilton: In 2010, David Cameron, the Prime Minister, said that lobbying was the next big scandal waiting to happen. Do you think that the proposed statutory register, which you have given us an introduction to, will avert such a scandal and help to rebuild trust in British politics?

Elizabeth France: It can't do it on its own because it is simply a register. As I say, there is no regulation attached to it. There is no requirement to commit to codes of practice or to any guiding principles, such as the UKPAC already has in place. But transparency is a means to an end. As I say, a few years ago we might have argued about the extent to which publication schemes or FOI requests might help our democracy. I believe they have done. So I believe transparency is important, but it does not on its own stop the problem. It gives information to allow people to ask further questions.

Q114 Fabian Hamilton: UKPAC has run a voluntary register for some time now. Is that right?

Elizabeth France: It has sought to run a voluntary register for some time. Only on 15 February this year—that is, a couple of weeks ago—have we launched a register that we think works well and that we would invite you to look at. We would invite you to look at it because we think it provides an example of what you could do. It is limited in scope. It is limited in scope because, as you are aware, we are now including members of CIPR and APPC but not PRCA, and because it is on a voluntary basis we are not currently open to other lobbyists to put their information on the register.

Q115 Fabian Hamilton: Could you just enlighten us as to what those initials stand for?

Elizabeth France: Yes, I am sorry. I shall probably get it wrong now, shan't I? I shall need help. The Chartered Institute of Public Relations is the CIPR. The Association of Professional—I shall have to look up my notes. I am sorry about that. I am hopeless at acronyms.

Q116 Fabian Hamilton: It is all right. They are basically professional bodies?

Elizabeth France: Yes. The three professional bodies; I have the details of the acronyms in here.

Fabian Hamilton: Don't worry if you don't have them.

Elizabeth France: The three professional bodies that came together to form UKPAC. We have two of them now in place, and those two have their members now on there. But the reason I would invite you to look at the register is that I think that it gives you an idea of what a universal register could look like.

Q117 Fabian Hamilton: What were the problems you encountered, though? What lessons could the Government learn from that?

Elizabeth France: When Mark Ramsdale was asked what he was sharing with the Cabinet Office, we were trying to share some of our pain with them in that it wasn't as straightforward as I think we had perhaps thought it would be at first. To start with, we had incredibly limited resources and with those resources we wanted to set up a searchable register online.

What we had not appreciated was that this was not a straightforward exercise. So we under-specified what was needed and the IT response was inadequate. It took us a little while to realise that, to say, "This is not good enough", to go back out to the market to find a new provider and to deliver what we now think—and I know it has only been up for less than a month—does work, and does show you what could be done.

It could be expanded to include people outside the professional bodies that are members; it could be expanded to include individuals, but the point is that the vehicle is now there and you can search it. You can search it by looking at "client", by looking at "employer", by looking at "lobbyist" and it is the beginnings of what we think could be a vehicle that could meet the needs for a statutory register.

Q118 Fabian Hamilton: Finally, did the withdrawal of PRCA damage the credibility of UKPAC?

Elizabeth France: I think that is for others to judge. It was disappointing for us. The industry properly took huge credit for coming together. For the three main trade bodies to come together, to agree to have three independent directors, to agree a common definition and to agree some guiding principles, was a huge step forward. So it is disappointing to me that the PRCA chose to leave, particularly as they chose to leave at the point at which we had just commissioned the new IT provider for the new register and therefore were at the point, we believed, of delivering something that could take us forward.

Q119 Fabian Hamilton: You don't think the register is damaged, though, by PRCA?

Elizabeth France: The register is clearly damaged to the extent that it now covers fewer people, but I believe what we are trying to do at this stage in the process, given that we have launched it during the consultation process, is to demonstrate to you, and to others who are interested, what a statutory register might look like, because if it were statutory everybody would have to be on it. Who runs that in the future is a separate question. I wanted to show proof of concept, and I think that is what we have been able to do.

Q120 Sheila Gilmore: I wanted to pursue a bit further this distinction between registration, with the transparency it can provide, and regulation. Is it possible that the public is going to end up being quite dissatisfied with the outcomes of processes because their expectations have been raised in all this discussion about somehow controlling lobbying, and so on?

Elizabeth France: As I say, I don't think that there is anything in the consultation paper that suggests the legislation is going to control lobbying. If the Committee was minded to think of ways of controlling lobbying—if that is what is thought to be necessary—then again I would say that you are looking at different pieces in a mosaic and there is push and pull. So, it is back to ministerial codes of practice, MPs' registers of interest and FOI requests, and all of those coming together to give you the information you need rather than looking to the register on its own.

If there is anybody out there who is expecting the register to deliver any more than a full list and explanation of who is lobbying, who their clients are, and whether they sign up to any particular professional body's code of conduct, then they will clearly be disappointed. But I am not sure who is looking for that.

Q121 Sheila Gilmore: The point I was making was that the professionals might know that is not the case, perhaps politicians as well, but in the wider context of discussion, where lobbying has been seen as a bad thing or something that has to be dealt with, we may end up with a process that does not really satisfy anybody very much and may be quite an expensive process.

I have an example. It is a different situation, but in Scotland we introduced, about four or five years ago now, a register of landlords. The effort of just even putting the register together has dominated, to the extent that, although there is provision—it does go slightly further than just transparency and there is provision for people having to satisfy a fit and proper person test—somehow there has never been the time or the resource to really achieve that.

Elizabeth France: My experience of 20 months as Chair of UKPAC would echo that. I thought my time was going to be spent doing the things that are the other key roles of the organisation, which involve, for example, an audit of their complaints handling processes and looking at promoting best practice in lobbying, but in fact in our first year we have been entirely taken up with trying to get the register itself sorted out. I would like to think that once we have done that—particularly as we have now designed a register where it is in effect self-registration, so that the accuracy of the data is in the hand of the registrant—that the amount of time we have to spend as a body on that is reduced and time could be given for these other things. But these other things are not included in the Government's proposal.

The other thing I would want to stress is the unintended consequence of the Government's proposal could be that you get less self-regulation. Let's assume there is a fee to pay to join the statutory register, and you are a small lobbying firm and you have to decide whether you can afford both to go on the statutory register, which you must go on, and join a professional body that has a professional set of standards and a code of practice you must adhere to. If we are not careful, the second is going to become a luxury and we are going to end up with fewer people. I hope this doesn't happen. It would be quite the wrong outcome. But an unintended consequence could be that you get fewer people signing up to bodies that have ethical standards and codes of practice, which their members must comply with because they are obliged to sign up to and pay to be on the statutory register.

Q122 Sheila Gilmore: Do you think it would be possible to link in some way, even the form of statutory register that is being suggested here, with an obligation to comply to a code of practice?

Elizabeth France: Yes. I think it would. It would be more costly and it would turn into regulation. There are a number of ways of doing it. As I suggested at the beginning, one way would be to have a hybrid where the register showed whether a particular entrant on the register was signed up to a code of practice, which code of practice and who enforced it. So if you were a member of the APPC or the CIPR, or perhaps if you were a lawyer regulated by the Solicitors Regulation Authority but you were a public affairs consultant, maybe you could put that on the register and then it would be clear to people which body was making sure you behaved ethically and held you to account.

We have a set of guiding principles. An alternative would be to beef up that set of guiding principles and to require anybody, any individual signing up to the register, to comply with those. Additionally, perhaps they would also want to show, because those will never be as detailed, that they comply with a set of standards from a professional body.

So I think it is possible to create a hybrid of that kind, but we need to be clear which we are doing. Is the register just a register? If so, is one of things that should go on the register membership of a body that has a set of standards that is enforceable, or is the register simply for transparency, or is it the beginning of regulation and, therefore, of a bigger construct with more teeth? That is not something I have seen justified, either by the behaviour that is being addressed or by any justification for going against what I think is otherwise the direction of government policy in relation to regulation.

Q123 Mr Chope: On a technical point, surely setting up a statutory register is itself an act of regulation, because it is placing a burden on the people who would be obliged to sign up to the register?

Elizabeth France: Yes. To an extent I accept that. It is just I didn't want people to think that it was doing more than exposing information. It is not actually setting any standards.

Q124 Mr Chope: But in terms of the Government's deregulation agenda, it flies right against that. Can I take you back to the days when you were the Data Protection Registrar and the Information Commissioner? Were you ever lobbied then?

Elizabeth France: That is an interesting thing, isn't it—were we ever lobbied? As a public body, we had consultations and we received responses to consultations and people who came to see us. I don't think I ever asked them whether they had been briefed by lobbying companies, so that is quite interesting. You would have people coming to talk to you.

The key example I have, where I suppose you would call it lobbying but it was very open, was when I was proposing a code of practice in relation to personnel management and the use of personal data by employers. I had a number of meetings with the CBI and with the trade unions, who took different views of the code of practice, which was within my gift because it was within the framework legislation. But it was transparent because it was the CBI and the TUC. So yes, I have been on the receiving end of people who had clear views on policy issues that I was taking forward.

Q125 Mr Chope: But you had initiated the agenda?

Elizabeth France: Yes.

Q126 Mr Chope: Were you ever lobbied on what should be or not be on your agenda?

Elizabeth France: Oh, goodness me. I can't recall any instances at the moment. The big picture is such that there were key areas that we looked at during my time in office. The amendment of the law entirely, of course, but the lobbying there was of government rather than of us when we moved from the 1984 Act to the 1998 Act. There was a lot of industry concern there about the changes that would be brought by an EU directive, but that was lobbying of government. As Information Commissioner, I had to take an independent view on individual cases, and the only times that I was consulting was on codes of practice that were new under the 1998 Act. The key one I recall is that one on employment.

Q127 Mr Chope: It was in fact government lobbying that I was interested in. When you were in that role you were lobbied by the Government?

Elizabeth France: No. I wasn't lobbied by the Government. The Government were looking to change legislation. I was a Crown appointment and I was the servant of the legislation. When we moved from the 1984 Act to the 1998 Act, my powers changed because the statute changed, but I was a creature of that statute so they certainly weren't lobbying me. Of course we did spend a lot of time in Europe, where data protection registrars and information commissioners took a professional view on what was practical, but we were in different committees from ministers who were debating the directives.

Q128 Mr Chope: But you were the independent Information Commissioner. Are you saying that on no occasion did you ever have a conversation with government officials or government ministers saying, "Elizabeth, couldn't you do a little bit more in this direction or not do so much in that direction?"

Elizabeth France: There is a very fine line to be drawn, and I am now chairman of an Ombudsman's service where the same thing applies. When you have a quasi-judicial role, as you have with Information Commissioner and with Ombudsman, it is perfectly proper for government to look at the way you are spending public money and to set key performance indicators. It is not for government to tell you how to use the powers you have to enforce the substance of the law, and I was never lobbied in that regard.

There were occasions when I had issues with ministers about their use of personal data, as indeed you will be aware. It is over 10 years since I was Information Commissioner. You are reminding me of the fact that I had debates over identity cards with the then Home Secretary, where we tried to take a very professional and objective view, but where it was clear that we disagreed with the view of the then Home Secretary.

Q129 Mr Chope: Do you think that, to try to promote transparency, any register of lobbyists should also apply to government, where the Government, either itself or through intermediaries, seeks to lobby independent public bodies such as the Information Commissioner?
Elizabeth France: That is very interesting, isn't it, because the Information Commissioner doesn't make policy; the Information Commissioner interprets policy and takes an independent approach to taking decisions in individual cases. I understand what you are saying, and I can think of some examples where it is important for there to be transparency, but I am not sure that a lobbying register is the way to do it.
FOI publication schemes are there for all government departments; all government departments give lists of key meetings; minutes of meetings are published. These are public bodies caught by the FOI Act. When I talked about different things in the mosaic, we have to run horses for courses. I think pushing further, on some of the other things there to ensure proper transparency in relation to public bodies, is the way to go, not to expect a register to deal with that.

Q130 Mr Chope: Being caught by the FOI Act is very different. That is not transparency, because you need to know the right question to ask before you can get the information.
Elizabeth France: Not if publication schemes are working properly, because publication schemes will give you, as a register does, the baseline data on which to ask your further questions.

Q131 Mr Chope: Just a final question, Chairman. On 16 January this year, two Cabinet ministers and one senior minister had an exercise in lobbying of the Independent Parliamentary Standards Authority. This was private, off the record, designed to influence the Parliamentary Standards Authority to take a particular course of action, which in the end they did—bowed to government pressure.
How do you think that sort of incident can be brought out into the open, the transparency created, leaving aside the propriety of whether it is right that government ministers should lobby an independent body in that way?
Elizabeth France: If we are talking about ministers, then ministers should be indicating what meetings they have had and with whom, which helps you ask the right questions. You can't look for something that will provide the answers to everything. You can try to make sure that the baseline level of information is such that further questions can be asked. In that context, if ministers have gone to see a public body that should be clear from their engagements, which should be published, which should allow further questions to be asked, and then can allow you to frame the question that you want to ask under the FOI Act if you seek to do so.
We can't try to stretch all the bits of machinery we have to cover every issue that arises. We have to look at all the different pieces and try to make them work together. If there is a gap in the middle here, and if that gap in the middle is that we don't know who out there is doing lobbying, and if that is a feeling that is reflected by the public, then we need to have a better register. It needs, though, to be universal because otherwise all the things you are talking about, you have cracks all over the place that people fall through. So you need something as broad based as possible and it is then the trigger for further, more detailed questions or the use of other powers that already exist.
Chair: Talking about stretching the machinery, you have just answered questions from one of the experts in the parliamentary field on that. Working in that last question was ingenious, Chris. Congratulations.

Q132 Stephen Williams: I go back to your answers to Fabian, where you used the phrase "professional bodies and professional institutions", and I think the previous witnesses used that phrase as well. To me, if you are a member of a profession—like the Law Society, the Institute of Chartered Accountants or the Chartered Institute of Taxation, which I am a member of—you have sat exams, you have been admitted to an institute, you have a certificate, there is a code of conduct and you have continuing professional education if you are doing consulting in practice. Is that a description of lobbying?
Elizabeth France: I can't speak for the three bodies that you will be seeing later, but they do set standards for admission, they do have codes of conduct and they do take action against their members if they don't comply with them. They all have slightly different sets of rules, but were all happy to sign up to the guiding principles that we established. But I think you would need to direct your questions to them, when you see them, about how effective that is and what their hurdles for admission are, if any.

Q133 Stephen Williams: Do you have a view on how high those hurdles for admission are?
Elizabeth France: I don't think they should be high if what we are looking for is transparency. If you are doing the job, if you are qualified to do the job, then joining a body that is going to encourage you to be ethical in your behaviour, to continue with professional development, to go to training courses, to talk to your peers and to submit yourself to any code of conduct has to be a good thing.

Q134 Stephen Williams: How do you become qualified to do the job?
Elizabeth France: I am not a lobbyist, but I would imagine that you become qualified to do the job by getting appropriate experience and then proceeding in that way. I don't think it is a profession like the law, where there is an exam that you would sit.

Q135 Stephen Williams: So it is more like being an estate agent, perhaps?
Elizabeth France: I wouldn't want to comment.

Q136 Stephen Williams: From my right it was said, "Or being an MP". MPs are scrutinised—in my case, by 82,000 people in Bristol West. It is an oral examination conducted en masse, I would say. You mentioned that there may be codes of conduct that have to be adhered to. Can you think of any examples where someone has fallen foul of those self-devised

codes of conduct and has been struck off? Indeed, is it possible to be struck off as a lobbyist, or blacklisted perhaps?
Elizabeth France: I think each of the bodies has the right to remove people from membership, but again you will have to ask them what their rules are. Mark Adams referred to the fact that he has made a complaint against Bell Pottinger, and that is currently being looked at by the PRCA. So that is an example that is in the public domain.

Q137 Stephen Williams: In the minutes that have been made available to us of your Council—specifically the ones from 17 November 2010—it refers to you dealing with a query from Imperial Tobacco, which is based in Bristol where I have my parliamentary seat. It was about questions they wished to be raised at your meeting with the Cabinet Office. What sort of worries did Imperial Tobacco have, and have you been approached by any other tobacco companies about their concerns over any regulation or transparency at all in this field?
Elizabeth France: Certainly not. If I recall, the question was a more general question about how we define lobbyists, was it not?

Q138 Stephen Williams: As I asked you, what were the concerns that Imperial specifically had, or indeed any other—
Elizabeth France: They simply wanted to know how broad a definition there was going to be of a lobbyist. I don't actually recall, and I certainly have not spoken to Imperial Tobacco—neither have I taken up any cause for them, nor am I aware of anybody else contacting us. I think it was purely a query that was put through our Executive Secretary about breadth of definition, to which we didn't have an answer.

Q139 Stephen Williams: In terms of the ethics of people who lobby, is it unethical to undermine the reputation of somebody who holds a particular view on behalf of a client?
Elizabeth France: On behalf of?
Stephen Williams: Well, on behalf of a client or on behalf of the interests of a client?
Elizabeth France: As I say, I am not a lobbyist. I have no experience of doing lobbying, but what we have in our guiding principles is a requirement to be accurate and honest, to show integrity and propriety, and those are defined in there. I think any misleading claims or misrepresentation of views would not only fail our guiding principles but would fail the requirements of any of the professional bodies.

Q140 Stephen Williams: Coming back to who is a lobbyist, I suppose is at the heart of all this. If we have a register of lobbyists, who would fall into that definition of a lobbyist? Should it include somebody who is either directly or indirectly engaged by a corporate interest in order to make comments in, say, online forums about a Member of Parliament who holds a particular view?
Elizabeth France: If we look at our definition, a lobbyist would have to be doing that if they were attempting to influence or advise a change policy. If that was their ultimate objective then that might be defined as lobbying. But I can think of other things they might be doing; it might be defamation. I don't know what sort of situation you are thinking of. If it is a professional, and—we say, "Lobbying means, in a professional capacity, attempting to influence, or advising those who wish to influence, the UK Government, Parliament, the devolved legislatures". If they see that as a means of doing that, it might be classed as lobbying, if it is an attempt to modify policy, to get some change in direction. But one would have to look at each case. If there is a complaint to be made about somebody, then it needs to be made and examined.

Q141 Andrew Griffiths: Elizabeth, could you tell us whether there is good lobbying and bad lobbying?
Elizabeth France: Would that the world were that simple. There is lobbying well done and professionally and lobbying that might not be so well done, and I think that is the point. It is not the subject matter; it is not whether I believe in a cause that makes something good or bad lobbying. It is has it been done in a professional way; has it been done with integrity; has it been done in a way that meets at least the guiding principles that we have set out; and has it been done—above all, in this conversation—with transparency and openness?
For example, I don't believe in "good cause" exemptions from the register. Just because you are lobbying for a health charity, for example, that doesn't mean you should be exempt. "Good cause" exemptions are a dangerous route because they require subjectivity. Your good cause might be my bad cause, so you have to be very careful in introducing that sort of subjectivity. Provided that you are not placing an undue burden on those who lobby, that the burden is evenly spread and that what we are asking for is transparency, then I see no reason why there should be any exemptions based on the nature of the lobbying.

Q142 Andrew Griffiths: Very good. That almost answered my second question, which is do you believe that there should be any difference between—I think Stephen used the phrase—a corporate lobbyist and a campaigning organisation, be that a charitable campaigning organisation, a voluntary campaigning organisation or a business engaged in lobbying on a specific subject? Should there be any difference?
Elizabeth France: I don't think there should be any difference at all in terms of the requirement to register. It has to be universal; it has to be as broad as we can possibly make it. That doesn't mean there could not be, if the Government so chose, a difference in view as, for example, to who pays what to be on the register and whether there should be exemptions from a fee.
To go back to my old role, although the Data Protection Register is slightly different now so I might be a little bit out of date: there is a fee for notification, but there are some exemptions. Therefore there is an ability to notify and the fee can be very low, so the two don't necessarily go together. Requiring you to be on the register doesn't necessarily mean everybody has to pay the same fee to be on there. So that is where

you might go into your "good cause" exemptions if the Government chose to do so.

Q143 Andrew Griffiths: Elizabeth, just moving on a little. We read newspaper articles about concern over lobbying and we discuss in Parliament concern over lobbying. Do you think there is a public concern over lobbying?

Elizabeth France: Public concern is always very difficult to judge because, where an issue hits the headlines and people address what they believe to be the problem, then that is when you will see concern expressed.

It is quite clear that, with any of the recent issues that have led to concern about lobbyists, some would not have been caught by a register. If we go back to the earlier trigger, the one that involved Mr Byers, then it is most unlikely that a register would have helped except if you use the push and pull, which I might see as an enforcement possibility, that there would be a penalty for ministers who saw somebody who was not on the register. If you are looking for how do you make a register work, how are you going to make people go on it and how are you going to make ministers use it—just because there is a register it does not mean that you can't see somebody who is not on the register—then that is the only way it would have affected that instance.

But if you ask me are the public generally concerned, I think the public are always concerned that there might be things happening that they are not aware of, so the more open we can be, generally across the way that our administration works, the better. Although that is not an end in itself, as I keep repeating, it then gives you the foundation stone on which to ask further questions if you are concerned. That seems to me a minimal level—if we want to call it "regulation"—of regulation, which is a stepping stone to asking further questions if there is concern.

Q144 Andrew Griffiths: If you went for statutory regulation, where does it stop? For instance, if a solicitor in my constituency asked to see a minister to raise an issue of concern for one of their clients, would they be lobbying? If a community group asked for a meeting with a minister and they represented 1,000 people who had signed a petition in my constituency, would they be lobbying? Where should the definition lie?

Elizabeth France: They would be lobbying, but they wouldn't be somebody who was caught by our definition for inclusion on the register because we say that they have to be acting in a professional capacity, and they have to be providing—

Q145 Andrew Griffiths: But a solicitor would be acting in a professional capacity.

Elizabeth France: Who would be?

Andrew Griffiths: A solicitor acting on behalf of a client, who asks to see a Minister would be—

Elizabeth France: Yes. Provided it is a substantive or sustained part of their responsibilities. These would need to be better defined for statute than they are for a voluntary register, but our view would be: firstly, it has to be in a professional capacity; and secondly, it has to be a substantive and sustained part of their responsibilities. So if you are a partner in a big London firm of lawyers but your title is "public affairs consultant" then I think you are caught. If you are the local solicitor giving some guidance on a one-off issue, we might want to discuss what the threshold is before you are actually a lobbyist.

Q146 Andrew Griffiths: Just finally, Mr Chairman, if I may. What are the consequences of not being on a register with your voluntary code?

Elizabeth France: At the moment the consequences lie entirely with the bodies that I have referred to: the Association of Professional and Political Consultants and the Chartered Institute of Public Relations. They will take any action they think appropriate if their members are not listed. It is difficult while it is voluntary. As I said, what we are trying to do at the moment is a proof of concept. Because this happened during a change of policy direction, then our view is that that is the important thing to do, to show it will work, to show what can be achieved by a register. Then if there is going to be some statutory framework placed around it, that is where you will get the powers of enforcement.

Q147 Andrew Griffiths: Is it not always the case, by definition you could argue, that those who are reputable and would act within a code will register, and those that are not as reputable and would perhaps act in a way that would not be satisfactory are the people who won't register?

Elizabeth France: That will always be the case with any form of voluntary self-regulation. Unless there is a bar to practising in some way, which I don't think you could achieve in lobbying, except, as I say, by trying to show almost by a form of kite mark on the register: who is a member of one of the three professional bodies or a member of something similar like the legal profession, then I don't see any other way of doing that.

Q148 Simon Hart: A couple of quick ones, I hope, to finish off. Can you think of an example of a lobbying scandal—to use the Prime Minister's description—that would have been avoided or could be avoided had there been a register in place, or the register as proposed, I should say?

Elizabeth France: These are always difficult questions, aren't they, hypothetical questions. I think we have already shown that it is difficult to think of an example. The problem with this is that it is not so much the big scandal—although I appreciate that the Prime Minister said that he thought that there might be one coming down the track—as a general desire to improve the confidence of the public in the democratic process, and lobbying is a key part of the democratic process. If there is any question that there is concern that it isn't as open as it should be, then there is justification for improving the transparency, but I am not aware of anything immediately that I can think of.

Q149 Simon Hart: In a sense the whole thing is hypothetical, isn't it, because we are basing this whole discussion on a hypothetical threat. But anyway, we asked a previous witness a couple of weeks ago about evidence. We were trying to push for evidence, not opinion or anecdotal but actual evidence of where the public concern lay. A response that we have had subsequently refers to *The Sunday Times* YouGov poll, conducted in October 2011, which showed that over 50% of people think that lobbyists have too much influence in politics. I wonder what your view is on too much influence. If lobbyists didn't have influence, I would not employ them, and I just wonder whether—

Elizabeth France: That is an example of a result that begs further questions, and the further questions would need to be asked before that could count as evidence. It seems to me that we would need to know what those people responding understood about the process of policymaking. It seems to me that the more information and good information is available, to those of you who legislate, the better the legislation we are likely to get. When you say, "Can there be too much?", I don't think we should say there can be too much. So long as we know—that is the purpose of transparency—who is doing it, then that should help us to make the judgments.

Q150 Simon Hart: Sorry to talk in the hypothetical a bit, but do you have any views or evidence that support the view that, if there was a register, public confidence would improve and people's view on what lobbyists did would be improved as a consequence? Is there any evidence out there that supports that argument?

Elizabeth France: No. We can only look back at other examples of where we will all have our own views of whether transparency has helped. We can go back to the 1970s and Parliament and people—the example was given to me the other day by one of my colleagues—taking fees for making speeches and it was decided that needed to be declared. However the activity carried on until we had the Nolan principles. You have an evolution there of something that I think people would look back and say, "Oh yes, the Nolan principles, they have been an important part of improving our idea of the standards required in public service".

Most of us who are public servants would say, "Yes, that has worked well for us". Whether at the time that seemed to be something that was going to improve our understanding of the process, I don't know. It is the same with freedom of information—some people think it has been helpful, some people are critical of it, but actually on the whole public bodies are much more open now. You can read minutes of organisations on their websites; you have information if you want to ask further questions.

It is difficult to say, "Oh, we don't need to do it because there is no problem". If there is any sense that there are dark corners, it seems to me there is no harm in shining the light. Whether we need to do it by a statutory structure, or whether we could improve self-regulation, is a matter for policy debate, and whether we need to do it in a way that includes further regulation is a matter for policy debate. But what I am quite clear about is, if we do it at all, it must add to what we have on a voluntary basis and it must be as broad as we can possibly make it.

Q151 Simon Hart: To finish, Chairman. The cynic in me thinks that over the last 20 years, each and every time we take a step in that direction, when it comes to openness and transparency and declaration of interests and all these other measures brought in, the graph that measures public confidence in Parliament and parliamentarians appears to be going in the opposite direction. That is an observation.

One last point. In earlier evidence, you suggested that UKPAC might be an organisation that could take responsibility for regulation as part of a statutory requirement that might be imposed by government. Obviously, there is some industry tension; there always is in these things. Do you have any strong views about whether UKPAC would be the only body, one of the bodies? How would you see that happening?

Elizabeth France: I think what we shall be proposing to government in our response—I shall be careful; this is not a view yet shared with all my directors, so perhaps I had better rephrase. My personal view at this stage is that there is no need to set up a separate statutory body to run even a statutory register. If one wants to, one can; there are costs involved.

I see no existing vehicle that would be a ready home. I would suggest a model that I have seen elsewhere of the Government setting up, if they are going to go ahead with this, the requirements for a statutory register, the requirements for a body delivering a statutory register, and that they invite people to come forward and offer to run it. If they did that, UKPAC would consider whether it would offer to do that, and see what changes to its governance structure were needed in order to meet whatever the Government requirements in the legislation were.

Q152 Chair: Elizabeth, you kindly sent us a memo saying you had had no discussion on policy relating to a register of lobbyists with the Cabinet Office. Is that still true?

Elizabeth France: Yes, it is true. Although, having said that, Mark Harper attended an event, a forum that we held last week, but that was an open forum that a wide range of people attended.

Q153 Chair: Isn't it rather odd that UKPAC has not had policy discussions relating to a register of lobbyists?

Elizabeth France: I would say that it was. Going back to my days as a civil servant, I think I would have been recommending that ministers do the sort of consultation that is now going on after the proposals have been issued as a preparation to issuing them, but ministers deliberately chose not do to this; Mark Harper is quite clear that they decided not to do it.

When I went to see him in July 2010 with Sir Philip Mawer, which is the only meeting I had with him—which was when Sir Philip handed over the embryonic UKPAC to me and introduced me to the Minister—I had the impression that we would have a dialogue in the run-up to the delivery of the recommendations, but that was very early days. It was early July and when they reflected, the Cabinet Office took the view that they wanted to produce their consultation based on research that they were able to do themselves without engaging any of the stakeholders, and they are now doing that at this stage.

Provided the Minister and his officials listen to all the comments that are coming in, as the Minister says he is doing, then we may yet have proposals that add value. As things stand, I think that opportunities to benefit from what others have done, and what others have found difficult to do, were not taken up earlier.

Q154 Chair: So far, UKPAC have not spoken to the Cabinet Office about any of this stuff, and the Cabinet Office have not spoken to UKPAC about any of this stuff?

Elizabeth France: No. We had the meetings that Mark Ramsdale referred to between Mark Ramsdale and an official, which were to share some of our early learning. That was very early on. We have prepared, but not yet submitted, our full response to the consultation. I would hope once those responses are in, and the Government starts to consider those, that officials will want to talk to a number of us who will have put in substantive responses.

Q155 Chair: Looking at your website, I see there are minutes that record three meetings between the UKPAC Executive Secretary and Cabinet Office officials in September and October 2010 and in June 2011. Also, the minutes of UKPAC's meeting on 17 November 2010 state, "The Executive Secretary should stress to the Cabinet Office our view that emphasis should be on regulation/transparency of the activity, not the entity carrying it out".

Elizabeth France: Yes.

Q156 Chair: Also, the minutes of the UKPAC meeting on 27 July 2011 state, "Executive Secretary to circulate a note to all board members on conversations with the Cabinet Office, immediately".

Elizabeth France: That was the June 2011 meeting that has already been referred to.

Q157 Chair: That strikes me as some very serious interaction with the Cabinet Office.

Elizabeth France: No, it was—

Q158 Chair: At that point, you managed to undertake those meetings without mentioning your policy in relation to a register of lobbyists.

Elizabeth France: This shows how transparent we are. The meeting between the Executive Secretary and the official—

Chair: We will see.

Elizabeth France:—in June 2011, and you have already spoken to Mark Ramsdale, was referred to by him orally at that meeting, and one of our directors was quite determined that if such a meeting had been held he wanted to know exactly what had been said. It was actually in order to make sure policy had not been discussed, because the view was that only directors ought to be discussing policy with the Cabinet Office.

Q159 Chair: So, on these five separate occasions of interaction with the Cabinet Office, there was no discussion of a register of lobbyists by UKPAC, which is meant to represent the lobbying industry?

Elizabeth France: No. When you say, "There was no discussion", we were discussing the practicalities. We did not try to suggest a policy way forward. We were never invited to. Although there is reference to where we thought there would be interaction, we were not then invited. We were prepared.

When I went in July 2010, I thought we were going to gear up to some serious debate about policy issues. We prepared for that. Indeed, we have a letter from Mark Harper agreeing that regular meetings between our Executive Secretary and his officials might be helpful. That was in July 2010. He then took a different view. So, although we were prepared for those discussions, we were never invited to share views on policy. What we did share views on were the practical difficulties that we were experiencing in getting a register up, in getting a definition that worked, in getting something that actually made sense.

Q160 Chair: So you distinguish between practical difficulties and policy related to the register?

Elizabeth France: Yes. We were simply trying to share our experience on what we were doing and what it was clear in the public space we were trying to do.

Q161 Chair: But using your words, you have nonetheless interacted with the Cabinet Office on possible difficulties, practical difficulties, related to a register?

Elizabeth France: At an executive level. No directors have had any discussion with ministers or officials.

Q162 Chair: From memory, I don't recall the distinction between executive officers and directors in your memo.

Elizabeth France: In my memo? Yes. Well, it is quite clear. The Executive Secretary had meetings in September, October and June and I had a meeting in July 2010. Those are the meetings.

Chair: Do any colleagues have anything further to add on these issues? No. Elizabeth, thank you very much for your time this morning. We appreciate it. You have helped us considerably in our thoughts about the report we will write. Thank you so much.

Thursday 15 March 2012

Members present:

Mr Graham Allen (Chair)

Mr Christopher Chope	Simon Hart
Paul Flynn	Tristram Hunt
Sheila Gilmore	Mrs Eleanor Laing
Andrew Griffiths	Stephen Williams

Examination of Witnesses

Witnesses: **Francis Ingham**, Chief Executive, Public Relations Consultants Association, **Jane Wilson**, Chief Executive Officer, Chartered Institute of Public Relations, and **Helen Johnson**, Chair, Association of Professional Political Consultants, gave evidence.

Q163 Chair: Welcome to the Committee, and thank you for coming along to help us with our inquiry on lobbying. I hope you will find this a helpful conversation. Neither you or we are on trial, so feel free to relax and tell us your views. I think it might be useful if we had a couple of minutes' opening statement. Jane, would you like to go first?

Jane Wilson: Yes, certainly. Good morning, everyone. I am Jane Wilson, CEO of the Chartered Institute of Public Relations, one of the bodies that represent the professional interests of lobbyists in the UK. Thank you for the opportunity to give our views in response to your questions today, and I am very pleased to be here alongside my colleagues, Francis and Helen, from the PRCA and the APPC. The CIPR represents the public relations and public affairs professional through individual membership. We have a membership of over 9,500 professionals and an active group of around 700 members who work in the broad discipline of public affairs. We offer training, professional development to support careers in public affairs, including the CIPR Public Affairs Diploma, which I believe is the only qualification of its kind awarded by a professional body. Above all we provide a code that regulates the professional conduct of our members, which, along with the PRCA and the APPC codes, is the cornerstone of industry self-regulation.

Our view of lobbying goes beyond the Government's description of it as a legitimate activity. We see it as an essential part of the democratic process with an important part to play in the relationship to freedom of speech. However, we also accept that influencing public policy is an issue of public interest, and that lobbying should be open and transparent to be better understood and ultimately accepted. We therefore welcome the consultation insofar as the Government states that it wants to introduce a register that will improve knowledge about lobbying, accountability of lobbyists and more information on who and what influences public policy decisions.

However, the Government has expressed a preference for a register that includes only third party lobbyists, exempting by some estimates up to 80% of the active lobbying profession. If the aim is knowledge and accountability in the lobbying process, a register that omits in-house lobbyists would simply not achieve it. Along with the APPC, and initially the PRCA, we founded the UK Public Affairs Council, UKPAC, following the original Public Administration Select Committee report.

UKPAC was founded to provide a model for how a register could be developed and maintained independently of government. It achieved this not without a learning curve, not without some difficulties, but it is a learning curve that the Government could heed and it is the only current attempt to provide a publicly searchable register of both individual lobbyists and their employers. It was set up as a register to cover the membership of the founding bodies, so it would need to be adapted to meet statutory requirements, but we believe it could be one option for consideration as a delivery vehicle for a statutory register but only once the definition that would determine the scope of the register has been set. There are a number of questions arising from the consultation, which I am sure we will cover here today. However, should the opportunity not arise in the rest of the session, I would like to stress that government attempts to register lobbyists should be complementary to industry structures of self-regulation, industry codes linked to professional conduct that are backed up by rigorous disciplinary structures that provide a process of accountability that clients, employees and members of the public can have confidence in. A register that covers all lobbyists and provides reasonable levels of accurate information could assist in making the process of lobbying better understood. Unfortunately the proposal in the consultation document is fundamentally flawed, and I urge the Government to reconsider its proposals as part of the consultation process. Thank you so much for bearing with me.

Q164 Chair: Thank you, Jane. Can you tell me why there are so many bodies in the field? Did they all fall out at one point?

Jane Wilson: Why there are so many what, sorry?

Chair: So many professional bodies.

Jane Wilson: I think the history is that—well, the Chartered Institute of Public Relations, as I said, covers the broad church of public relations as a whole, and public affairs is part of that and lobbying is a subset within public affairs. So it is set up for individual professionals and their professional development. I believe the PRCA was set up separately as a body initially that looked after the interests of organisations, although that has emerged and evolved over time, and the APPC is specifically for public affairs only. So I hope we are complementary. We have a lot of cross-pollination between our members. Members who join us individually, professionally, may themselves now be members of the PRCA and their companies of the APPC.

Q165 Chair: Francis or Helen, do you want to make a little statement?

Francis Ingham: Yes, thank you. My name is Francis Ingham, I am the Chief Executive of the PRCA and prior to assuming that role I was Assistant Director General of the CIPR and I was a lobbyist to the CBI, in the charitable sector.

Q166 Paul Flynn: You had a sort of religious conversion, did you?

Francis Ingham: I do not think there was any sacrament involved, no. I was also a Conservative Party councillor.

Paul Flynn: You are—

Q167 Chair: Paul, I have just invited the witnesses to make an opening statement. Let them finish, if you would be so kind.

Francis Ingham: But I will not be going into holy orders.

Chair: And you too, Francis, stay on message.

Francis Ingham: The PRCA is a membership body founded in 1969, and together the three of us represent and regulate the public affairs industry. We represent agencies, so from the very large ones down to very small ones, in-house teams from multinationals to charities to the public sector, and individuals as well. We hold, as a requirement of membership, a register, which all of our members must complete four times a year, and we have held that for over 10 years. It identifies the clients and the individuals who offer public affairs services. There are about 1,000 people on it and slightly more than 1,000 clients. We also require our members to sign up to two codes of conduct, a generalist one and a public affairs-specific one. Those codes are often written into their work contracts by their employers.

Regarding the consultation paper, we welcomed it and we would have wished to have seen it earlier. We welcome the Government's proposal for a statutory register and we believe that is essential to improving transparency and public confidence in the industry. Our problem with the Government's proposal is that it has a very narrow definition. It will cover only, as Jane said, a quite small part of the industry. It will exclude anybody who works in an in-house team, whether that is a corporate, a charity or the public sector itself. It will exclude lawyers who lobby. It will exclude management consultants who lobby, accountants who lobby. It will not cover very many people. So we think that that is not only unfair to the people who will be covered, but that it will also fail to meet the Government's objectives, which we share.

Two further final comments. As Jane said, we did help to found UKPAC in 2009. We left it in December of last year. We left it with regret because of its inability to put together a comprehensive and accurate register of public affairs individuals and because of, in our view, the lack of confidence the industry has in it. We believe it would be a very grave mistake if the Government were to give UKPAC the responsibility for holding any register that it creates.

Our final comment would be that, in our view, the Government ought to listen to the criticisms made of its plans, I hope constructive in many regards. It ought to amend its plans to take those on board, broaden the scope of the register, and then get on with implementing it rather than wasting any more time. Thank you.

Helen Johnson: I am Helen Johnson. My day job is managing director of a small public affairs and policy consultancy, but I am here today in my capacity as Chair of the APPC, which I stress is both part-time and unpaid, but I am here as a volunteer and not as a pressed woman.

The APPC is the self-regulatory and representative body for political consultancies only. So that is firms or agencies with third party clients and, therefore—you will have seen the proposals—we have a particular interest in the proposals on the table.

We currently have 68 member firms across the whole of the UK.[1] We employ a total of 1,152 political consultants and we are providing consultancy services to currently 1,877 clients. We were formed in 1994, specifically to encourage openness and transparency and to promote high standards of ethical behaviour in dealings with institutions of government. We have been operating our own register of consultants, staff and our clients now for nearly 17 years. Our register, like the PRCA's, is updated quarterly, published on the APPC website, and we also require all of our members to adhere to a code of conduct, which is enforced through various compliance mechanisms, including being written into consultants' contracts of employment. We have an independently run complaints and disciplinary process too.

We were very pleased and proud to be founder members of the UK Public Affairs Council and, along with the CIPR, we continue to be supporters of the Council going forward.

I should emphasise from the outset that there is a wide spectrum of views and opinions on a whole range of issues among APPC members. That is probably inevitable with 68 firms in membership. We are still consulting on our detailed response to the Government's proposals. I will do my best to share with you the APPC view but I am aware that some of our members will have written to the Committee separately, or will be responding to the proposals separately, and may be expressing different views from the ones that I do today.

We are absolutely not opposed to statutory registration. We have been running our own client register for nearly 17 years. We do that because we believe it is the right thing to do and we believe it should be the norm for anyone lobbying in a professional capacity. We welcome the consultation as a starting point but we are disappointed in what is being proposed. The primary reason for that, as you have already heard from Jane and Francis, is the

[1] Note from witness: correct as at the date of our last quarterly register, 29 February 2012

starting premise that the register need only extend to lobbyists who are acting on behalf of a third party. Not only do we think that is flawed, we think ultimately it is pretty pointless for a number of reasons.

By and large, we are the sector, as you have heard, that are already self-registering. We are the sector that are already registered. Secondly, again the vast majority of lobbyists are not working for multi-client firms, as you have heard. They are working in-house or for charities or think-tanks, unions, law firms, and so on. Thirdly, in the case of the APPC, with the exception of the proposal to list previous public office, we already declare voluntarily on our register more information than the Government is proposing we should do through a statutory vehicle, which seems at best to be a duplication of what we already do and at worst an unnecessary regulatory burden. By and large, also I would say, it is not firms like ours that are doing the lobbying. For the most part we are advising our clients, they are doing their own lobbying, so that does call into question who is the lobbyist here in many of these situations.

The net result with the proposals on the table at the moment is that you end up with a statutory register not of lobbyists but of a particular subset of lobbyists and a minority of lobbyists at that. At best, as I said, that would duplicate information already available. At worst you could end up with less information in the public domain than currently, which of course then decreases transparency rather than increases it. If a register is to be introduced, it has to apply universally to all those who lobby on a professional basis. We feel that anything falling short of that will fail to deliver the increased transparency that the Government is looking for.

Getting the definition of lobbying right is absolutely key in this respect, and I would just finish on this point—as bizarre as it may sound, as the proposals stand currently it is not clear that the current Chair of the APPC will be required to add herself to this statutory register. Thank you.

Q168 Paul Flynn: How many of your members have you expelled in the 17 years you have been going, Ms Johnson?

Helen Johnson: Let me just turn to the relevant piece of information there. We have a number of procedures in place.

Paul Flynn: The question is how many have you expelled?

Helen Johnson: I am looking for the information. We have suspended—

Paul Flynn: Perhaps Mr Ingham can tell us. How many have you expelled?

Helen Johnson: We have suspended, Mr Flynn, two members that have been brought to my attention and one member was persuaded, for want of a better word, to resign for failure to comply with the requirement to complete registers. We have a range of sanctions attached to our code of conduct, including reprimand, public reprimand, public apology, remedial action and so on and so forth. Our disciplinary process has a range of sanctions attached to it, but in terms of suspension, the information I have been given, and this obviously pre-dates my chairmanship is that we have suspended two.

Q169 Paul Flynn: One expulsion and one suspension?

Helen Johnson: Two suspensions.

Q170 Paul Flynn: What was your total membership in that period?

Helen Johnson: Total membership?

Q171 Paul Flynn: Yes. How many organisations, groups, individuals, do you have in your organisation? That is about 0.1%, I would think.

Helen Johnson: We currently have 68 firms in membership who between them employ 1,152 political consultants. I could not, off the top of my head, tell you how many members we had at the time of those suspensions.

Q172 Paul Flynn: Yes, okay. The behaviour of the other 99.9% has been immaculate in that time, not requiring any interference from you?

Helen Johnson: We have a complaints and a disciplinary procedure that by definition requires that someone brings a complaint to us. I do not have the full complaints history in front of me.

Q173 Paul Flynn: I just want to probe how effective you are as bodies that discipline your own members.

Helen Johnson: No, that is fine.

Q174 Paul Flynn: Mr Ingham, how many have you expelled?

Francis Ingham: Since I have been the Chief Executive over the last five years we have handled five complaints, I would say. None of those have led to expulsion.

Q175 Paul Flynn: So, it is none. Okay, thanks very much. Ms Wilson?

Jane Wilson: One in the last 12 years.

Q176 Paul Flynn: Out of how many members?

Jane Wilson: 9,500 members.

Q177 Paul Flynn: Do you think the fact the three organisations are fighting like cats in a sack is any recommendation that you should have self-regulation when you clearly can't regulate yourselves or even come to an agreed form of single association? Is it not right that you need someone to bang your heads together from outside?

Jane Wilson: No. I think it is a leap to go from saying a small number of members have been expelled to saying that we can't self-regulate. We do have a process that goes, like Helen's, through conciliation. We have reprimands, we have suspensions. We had eight cases between 2000 and 2008. Since then we have seen a massive increase in the amount of cases coming forward and we have a fully independent—I do not see the evidence that—

Paul Flynn: It seems clear—that is okay, I will not reach any conclusions.

Chair: Paul, you must let the witness finish otherwise I will not let you finish. Jane, carry on.

Jane Wilson: So I think there is a leap. Certainly between 2009 and 2010 there were 120 hours spent on our disciplinary procedure; 2010 and 2011 there were over 400 hours. We have cases ongoing at the moment. We do take this incredibly seriously and to say that we have found people to go through the process and it has not resulted in expulsion does not mean it is not working. It perhaps means that some of the complaints are unfounded. It perhaps means that those who are within our codes are behaving well.

Q178 Paul Flynn: I am trying my best to understand your answer to the question. In your period of existence how many members, how many have been expelled?

Jane Wilson: In the past 12 years, one expulsion.

Q179 Paul Flynn: That is the answer, okay. What percentage would that be of your membership?

Jane Wilson: It is about 9,500, so it is 0.001%, I guess.

Q180 Paul Flynn: 0.001%. That is a remarkable organisation of saintly people, isn't it?

Jane Wilson: But remember those are—

Paul Flynn: That is the extent of your discipline, that you have expelled 0.001%.

Jane Wilson: No, that is not the extent of our discipline. That is one part of the disciplinary procedure.

Q181 Paul Flynn: Okay, what are the other parts?

Jane Wilson: The other parts would be yearly reprimand or suspend and there is a hearing process that takes place. But remember those who are within our code of conduct, and Francis' and Helen's code of conduct, have chosen to do so. When they join up they sign up to behave in an ethical and transparent way. They sign up to a code of conduct. I do believe in all of our organisations people are taking it more seriously. The register as it is proposed is not one that is about code of conduct; it is about registration.

Q182 Paul Flynn: 99.9% of your members that abide are worthy of a hagiography, I would have thought, on this. It is remarkable to hear of such virtue. Ms Johnson, I believe our paths have crossed in the past involving an all-party parliamentary group here.

Helen Johnson: Indeed.

Q183 Paul Flynn: There was an all-party parliamentary group on rheumatoid arthritis that became an all-party group on inflammatory arthritis. Were you involved in that change?

Helen Johnson: No, I was not involved in that change. My firm was involved in providing secretariat support to that all-party group with effect from the beginning of January 2006.

Q184 Paul Flynn: What happened when it changed to the other group? Were you involved then? You were not involved at all when it changed?

Helen Johnson: I was not involved in the group prior to that change at all, no.

Q185 Paul Flynn: When you were involved in the group were they supported by pharmaceutical companies?

Helen Johnson: I was not supported by pharmaceutical companies. What happened with the funding and support for that group was the secretariat to that group was provided by a charity called the National Rheumatoid Arthritis Society and they received funding and support from a range of sources. It was the charity NRAS who paid for me to help support that secretariat, as declared in the all-party group register.

Q186 Paul Flynn: It was NRAS that was supported by Abbott, by Wyeth, by Roche, and by a whole range of bodies. The point I want to put to you is whether the role of lobbyists and people in that group is a benign one, because in my view the role of that group, which I do not think exists any more, was undermined because it became a mouthpiece, not for patients but for the drug companies. I am just curious whether your involvement changed it from that.

Helen Johnson: My involvement, my firm was retained to support the National Rheumatoid Arthritis Society and not anybody else. I can't speak for the funding arrangements that that charity had with its supporters. I am not party to those; I am not familiar with those. My firm was appointed to help support the group on behalf of the National Rheumatoid Arthritis Society.

Q187 Paul Flynn: Who have now formed a different mechanism. They now have sort of friends of the NRAS. I think they have come out of the all-party group. You have no involvement in that?

Helen Johnson: The all-party group was disbanded at the time of the general election in 2010. My understanding is it was not reformed. I do not know necessarily the reasons for that and, no, we are not involved in supporting that work at all at the moment.

Q188 Paul Flynn: Can I ask the others about how lobbyists are involved in all-party parliamentary groups here? This is an instance where a group was set up by well-meaning patients and was reasonably successful but then was infested by money and—corrupted is possibly too strong a word because there were still good people involved. But certainly their aims were undermined by the influence of the drug companies who came in to advance the cause of their drugs rather than what was necessarily beneficial for the patients, and the organisation has now collapsed and does not exist. Is it your view, Mr Ingham and Ms Wilson, that this is what happens with other all-party groups here, which is a subject being investigated by a Committee?

Francis Ingham: I believe we have submitted evidence around all-party groups. Let me say this about our members and how they declare their interests. They all declare their clients four times a year, so if they are working with an all-party group they will declare that four times a year. It is in the public domain, anybody can see it. They declare the names of all of their staff who work in public affairs. Anybody can see that as well. As Helen said, our register, like the APPC's register, has been there for years. If you believe that the involvement of private companies or of consultancies is corrupting all-party groups, then the parliamentary authorities ought to take action here. The responsibility for appropriate behaviour of party groups does not rest with me and my members, it rests far more so with the parliamentary authorities. If you wish to regulate all-party groups more so, then feel free.

Q189 Paul Flynn: In the general approach you all take, it seems to me the whole of the lobbying industry wants to widen the scope of regulations that have come out. Should all my 60,000 constituents be registered, because most of them lobby me?
Francis Ingham: I do not think they lobby you professionally.

Q190 Paul Flynn: A lot of them do. Over the years I have had as many as 10,000 lobby me on one single issue and there is 62,000 of them.
Francis Ingham: Within any sensible definition of lobbying you would not include everybody's constituents, because it would be so wide as to be utterly meaningless.

Q191 Paul Flynn: Is that not what you are trying to do? You are trying to take a proposition, which is manageable, about corporate lobbyists and spread it so that it becomes not more effective. It actually becomes weaker if you have to apply it to tens of thousands of charities and trade unions and other bodies that we do not see as a problem. The problem appears to be corporate lobbyists.
Francis Ingham: Let me say this, having worked for the CBI and for charities. If you go to the CBI, you will find a floor of over 100 lobbyists; none of them would be included in this register that is proposed. Having worked in the charitable sector, you will find thousands of lobbyists. None of them would be included either. If you want transparency about the lobbying industry you would make it wide to include everybody who lobbies professionally, not somebody who drops you a line saying, "Please don't close my hospital; I live there and I like it", but somebody who does stuff for money or in a board role within an organisation. That seems to me very well defined, not at all broad to dilute it in any way whatsoever.
The problem with this is that the register that has been proposed by the Government will have less detail than the current voluntary registers and include fewer people. I do not see how you can make a call for greater transparency by reducing the amount of information that is required and reducing the number of people who are required to give it.

Q192 Paul Flynn: The public's concern about lobbying is largely involving corporate lobbyists and large sums of money or important decisions taken at a very high level, and there is not any evidence I know of public disquiet about people collecting to repair the village roof.
Francis Ingham: If you have any primary research to back that up I would be delighted to see it, but that is not my understanding of the situation.

Q193 Paul Flynn: Why do you think there is public concern about lobbying?
Francis Ingham: I think there is unwarranted public concern that there are relationships between the lobbying community and parliamentarians or former parliamentarians or former ministers that is inappropriate, but if you go back to the Byers and Huhne and so on material there was not a single lobbyist involved in that. Every one of these scandals around lobbyists are of people being stung, frequently parliamentarians and former ministers, with not a lobbying company in sight. This idea that my people who already register, put all their clients in the public domain, sign up to a code of conduct, sign that into their contracts, are the problem is completely disingenuous.
Chair: Last one, Paul.

Q194 Paul Flynn: I will make it the last one. There is a conclusion there. I ask you briefly, would you regard the experience of Canada, with Karen Shepherd in Canada running the reforms there, as a model to emulate?
Francis Ingham: Not necessarily. I think that our Parliament is quite able to come to its own decision about what kind of model. Why do you feel the need to imitate somebody else's?
Paul Flynn: Because it is better, possibly.

Q195 Chair: Thank you, Francis. Helen, do you have a comment on that?
Helen Johnson: I would endorse all the comments that Francis has just made, but the only additional point I would make at this point is coming back to the Government's proposals. It seems to us that the Government has started by asking itself the wrong question. It started from trying to define who is a lobbyist and therefore who should be in and who should be out, who should be on the register, who should not be on the register. The starting point should be what is the activity that we are concerned about? Where is the public concern? Where is the parliamentary and the government concern?
If lobbying is a problem, we need to know what that problem is and what activity it is that is causing concern, and we need to define lobbying. Once we have defined what lobbying is, it is very easy to define who a lobbyist is and who should or should not be on the register. It should be anyone who lobbies in a professional capacity.
Jane Wilson: I wholeheartedly agree with both those points. We need more clarity, particularly on the act of lobbying. In the same breath you mentioned charitable organisations and charities and somebody who wants to fix a village roof or the roof of the village church. Those are two very different things and we must not get confused, just because something is a charity, is set up as a charitable organisation, an NGO or a not for profit, that it is in itself, one, without controversy and, two, incapable of huge influence in its lobbying activities. Some of the best lobbyists in the business

do work for charities, because it is an important but tough job.

Q196 Paul Flynn: As professional persuaders do you not think you are likely to put yourself in a position of being implausibly sanctimonious?
Jane Wilson: Am I putting myself in the position? No.
Paul Flynn: All of you. Particularly you—
Jane Wilson: I am not trying to be sanctimonious, plausibly or implausibly so.
Paul Flynn: This is better than the lives of the saints.
Jane Wilson: I do believe that humans are flawed creatures, whether you are a professional working in lobbying or whether you are a parliamentarian or whether you—
Chair: We will leave the philosophy for another day. Thanks very much.

Q197 Mr Chope: Can I ask Helen Johnson, first of all. You said there needs to be a definition of lobbying. What is your definition of lobbying that you would like to be endorsed by Parliament?
Helen Johnson: This is not something we have a definitive APPC view on at the moment. I should make that clear. There is a distinction between lobbying and public affairs. What APPC members declare on the register at the moment is all of the clients on whose behalf they provide public affairs consultancy services. That might include advising clients on the political system, how it works, who the members of a particular committee are and what their interests might be. It might include preparing briefing materials, organising events, parliamentary monitoring, report writing, policy analysis and so on. It might also include lobbying, which you can define either narrowly or more broadly. A narrow definition of lobbying, we believe, would be triggered in some way by direct contact or interaction with institutions of government or legislators. We would assume that if we were meeting with a Member of Parliament, meeting with a minister, writing a letter to a Member of Parliament in a professional capacity, that would be lobbying. There is an argument that the broad definition of lobbying should include advising clients on how to make that direct contact themselves, which is what we would be doing. As I say, by and large the services we are providing are advising the clients and supporting the clients. When it comes to meeting with Members of Parliament and ministers, in the majority of cases the clients are doing that themselves. I am not doing that on their behalf.
A lot of work has gone into trying to define lobbying over a period of many years. All of our three organisations have sat down to try to agree that. It was a primary job of setting up the UK Public Affairs Council: could we agree a common and workable and practical definition of lobbying? You will have seen in the proposals that the Government has rejected the UK Public Affairs Council's definition of lobbying but has not proposed an alternative. So we have to get that definition right. I think we are all agreed on that. At the moment it is an open question as to what that definition should be, because the Government has certainly rejected so far previous attempts to put a definition on it.

Q198 Mr Chope: What you have said is your attempt at a definition. That is very helpful, what you said about direct and indirect lobbying. Is that a definition with which Jane Wilson would agree?
Jane Wilson: Yes, I would agree. It is seeking to influence public policy and doing so in a professional capacity, regardless of who you work for and what kind of organisation they are.

Q199 Mr Chope: That is not an identical definition to the one that was given by Helen Johnson. That is your alternative?
Jane Wilson: I support what Helen said. I would add to it that I think you can probably start from that position. But I do think a proper working definition is important and the lack of one in this document is the fundamental flaw, because the definition itself and the work that is done on the definition will influence every other decision that is made of who is included, the scope of the register and ultimately who runs it. It will influence the size, it will influence the funding. I do think it is a shame that that work on the scope, the size of the problem, what the problem is we are trying to solve, was not done because that would have led us to a definition. So we are going to propose a more robust definition that is more appropriate to statute, and perhaps the Government wants to look at a working group just to work on the definition to tighten it up beyond just this bigger consultation process on the register itself. It is that important.

Q200 Mr Chope: Mr Ingham, do you agree with the definition that has been given so far?
Francis Ingham: Yes, I do. We have consultancies in membership, we have in-house teams in membership, and we have individuals. So either they provide advice on how others ought to interact with the Government or they interact with government directly themselves. Having been one of the founder members of UKPAC and having agreed with that definition that is on the UKPAC site, clearly we do not resile from that either. I think there is broad agreement within the public affairs industry it is those two elements, and there is a broad despair within the industry that the consultation paper does not provide a definition of its own.

Q201 Mr Chope: Jane Wilson, you said in your evidence at the beginning that a statutory register was essential. Why do you believe a statutory register is essential?
Jane Wilson: If we are to go for a statutory register, a statutory register that is universal is essential. I think it is important that if we want more transparency in the decision-making process, if we want more transparency and to make it clear who influences and what the influences are on government decision-making in public policy, then a statutory register would go some way towards doing that.

Q202 Mr Chope: You are not saying a statutory register is essential. What you are saying is if there is

a statutory register these essential elements should be in it?
Jane Wilson: Yes, and it would have to be universal.

Q203 Mr Chope: In a scenario where you have focus groups and the focus groups are being asked about issues relating to public policy, would that come within your ambit of lobbying when the purpose of those focus groups is to help a body or organisation that is wanting to influence public policy?
Jane Wilson: It depends what you do with the information. The act of having a focus group is an information-gathering exercise. It is what you then do with that information, how you seek to influence using that information. Yes, I think that does fall under the act of lobbying when you then do something with it and use it to influence.

Q204 Mr Chope: You think the people who are on those focus groups should be informed about who is funding the focus group, effectively?
Jane Wilson: I think usually that is the case. I have certainly never been involved in a focus group where it has not been clear who is running the focus group.

Q205 Mr Chope: As Members of Parliament, we quite often get surveys, some from public relations organisations, which we are asked to fill in, and sometimes those surveys are funded by the Government. The Government is basically using intermediaries in order to find out the views of Members of Parliament. This may seem bizarre. It certainly seems to me to be bizarre, but that is what happens. There is a total lack of transparency. Members of Parliament do not know when they fill in these survey forms that the questions are being asked not by their own Whips directly to them but indirectly through the taxpayer-funded Government. Do you think that is satisfactory?
Francis Ingham: I think it is bizarre.
Jane Wilson: Kafkaesque.

Q206 Mr Chope: Do you think there should be transparency there? Do you think this is something that should be caught by a register?
Helen Johnson: I am not sure I can comment on what the Government is or is not doing in its activities. Coming back to ourselves again, it is certainly a requirement of our code that any of our members interacting with legislators, with people in public office, with government departments, with officials in those departments, are very clear on whose behalf they are calling up or writing, and that they are transparent about that, so that there should not be any question as to who you are meeting with and indeed why.

Q207 Mr Chope: Would the world be a worse place if there was no legislation on this at all?
Chair: We are heading back to philosophy again, I suspect.
Mr Chope: Do you think our country is going to suffer if we do not have this legislation carried through?
Francis Ingham: I think in order to provide greater public confidence in the lobbying industry it will be a good thing to have legislation that is universal and transparent. When we left the UK Public Affairs Council in December, we said that we believe the Government ought to introduce as a matter of urgency a statutory register because the existing voluntary registers are never going to be universal. There will be plenty of charities and think-tanks and lawyers who do not register as lobbyists but who are lobbyists or lobbying organisations, and if lobbying transparency matters to the Government, then it ought to go the whole hog and introduce a statutory register.
Helen Johnson: I know previous witnesses have discussed this with the Committee, but we have to be clear about what a list of names of staff and clients can deliver in terms of transparency. I am not entirely sure that that case is fully made as to why a register, as currently proposed, is the right solution to whatever the exact problem is perceived to be. If there is no registration, if there is no statutory register, we will continue, as APPC members, to do what we have always done, which is to complete our register on a quarterly basis, to list which of our clients are fee-paying, to list which ones are pro bono, to list our monitoring only clients, to list our clients across the whole of the UK, not just those who are lobbying at Westminster and Whitehall. We will continue to do that and to publish that information.
Francis Ingham: The same would be true of us and our consultants, members, in-house teams and individuals as well. We will keep on doing that.

Q208 Tristram Hunt: I think we are agreed the Government's plan is pretty hopeless in terms of, for example, your example of the CBI not being included. Do you see any difference between the CBI or trade unions or charities, or do you think if you are going to include big corporates you also have to include organised labour?
Francis Ingham: I think you need to include everybody who lobbies. Let me say I spent a couple of very happy years in the CBI. I was a lobbyist there. Not in a confessional sense but I was a lobbyist there. We lobbied in the interests of our members, which we would categorise as UK business. It was not an indifferent activity but what we believed we were doing we believed to be beneficial to the country. The TUC would lobby in a slightly different way at the same time. We would lobby from different perspectives. We were both doing something we thought was beneficial to the UK but with very different objectives in mind. I think we both ought to have been covered, or going forward ought to be covered. I make no distinction between a commercial company lobbying for something that is in its interests and a charity lobbying for something that it believes in either. They are to me the same thing. They are undertaking the same activity and they ought to be covered by the same rules of transparency and ethics.

Q209 Tristram Hunt: But I think trade unions regard themselves as very different organisations to that. They have, yes, on the one hand a concern about a piece of legislation about health and safety or whatever, but also they have a much broader civil society role and political role. Without disparaging, I think they would feel uncomfortable being placed in the same sort of bracket as whatever Tim Bell's latest company is called. They would regard themselves as a very different type of organisation to a sort of textbook, classic lobbyist, and their members certainly would.

Francis Ingham: Yes, but once you go down the route of saying that there will be a special case here, if you believe you are lobbying in a good cause and you are not caught by this, then very quickly it becomes highly subjective and very narrow and probably you end up just with public affairs consultancies being on a register, which already, by and large, exists. So it becomes a rather fruitless, pointless exercise.

Helen Johnson: I would endorse what Francis said, and clearly I am not in a position to speak for the trade unions. If it is minded to do so, perhaps the Committee might want to speak to the unions. From comments and discussions I have had informally, there is some acceptance within unions, and certainly within the charitable sector and indeed other firms, that they do lobby as part of their work or a proportion of their work and they should be subject to a statutory register too. It may be worth speaking to some of those other groups.

I am also happy to share my career history because it is relevant to the point around lobbying activity. I started my professional career as a lawyer. I then went and worked for the pharmaceutical industry and then I became a lobbyist in my own firm, so I have spent the last 20 years being a social and professional pariah from that perspective. When I was working in a law firm, one of my functions was to lobby government. When I moved in-house into the pharmaceutical industry, I became an in-house lobbyist subsequently and would lobby government. Now I head up my own small firm and I actually do less lobbying and have less interaction with Members and government than I had in either of my two previous professional capacities.

It seems to me and my members to be a nonsense that we are trying to decide who should be on a register based on who their employer is or based on the type of organisation that they work for. I think we come back to the point it should be about what is the problem around lobbying, what is the activity we are concerned about. Once we have defined the activity we are concerned about, anybody who engages in that activity in a professional capacity on a professional remunerated basis should be on the register if it is to be introduced.

Q210 Tristram Hunt: Do you think think-tanks will be caught by this? Think-tanks are not influencing policy for clients but they are seeking to influence policy for broader, often political objectives. They might have a broad base of funders who will not be asking for direct action but there is a climate of opinion that think-tanks seek to shape, which are often implicitly potentially in the interests of those who provide core funding.

Francis Ingham: Absolutely, they should be.

Q211 Tristram Hunt: Forgive my ignorance, on the Government's current plans are they—no, they are not at all?

Francis Ingham: No, they are not.

Q212 Tristram Hunt: But you think they should be?

Francis Ingham: Yes.

Q213 Tristram Hunt: So something like the Institute for Public Policy Research should be?

Francis Ingham: Yes.

Q214 Tristram Hunt: Why?

Francis Ingham: Because they lobby professionally. Their remit is to influence public policy and to influence government decisions. It seems to me absolutely obvious that they are professional lobbyists and they ought to be on such a register.

Q215 Tristram Hunt: But they would not be going for a meeting to worry about a piece of health and safety legislation. They would be publishing or holding conferences or writing articles to shape a broader political discussion rather than a concern with a particular—any decent think-tank is involved in a conversation of ideas rather than narrow public policies.

Francis Ingham: I suppose it is quite sad to admit this, but I do read think-tank publications quite frequently. They do relate both to the broader public sphere, I accept, but they also make detailed recommendations for how public policy ought to be changed, clearly linked to specific changes and, in my view, do come under the definition of lobbying.

Q216 Tristram Hunt: How on earth is this going to work? Who is going to run it, because the Cabinet Office is not going to run the statutory register, is it? So who is going to run the statutory register, do we think?

Francis Ingham: We would say an independent body funded via the industry. We do not think it is appropriate—

Q217 Tristram Hunt: So no existing body at the moment?

Francis Ingham: Absolutely. It should not be us, it should not be either of my colleagues' organisations, it should not be the UK Public Affairs Council. It ought to be an independent body, independent of the industry but funded by the industry.

Q218 Tristram Hunt: Is that your view too?

Jane Wilson: I agree it should be an independent body. I believe the funding mechanism, it should be funded by industry, and that is where you can have good cause exemptions because if this is—we want it to be a low burden. We do not want this to be red tape for the sake of it and lots of bureaucracy, but you could have good cause exemptions for organisations that are not for profit, organisations that are registered charities. It is quite easy to work those out because they will either be a registered charity or they will not. We could have revenue thresholds for payment. One of my colleagues, Lionel Zetter, who is on the board, believes it should be wide and shallow, which will spread the burden and spread the cost.

On who runs it, I believe it should be a non-government organisation. I do believe UKPAC could be considered, depending on what the final recommendations from government are on scope, definition of what it is there to achieve. I do believe it could be considered because it has run a register, albeit a limited register, albeit one that has limited finances, and one that had limited support of our organisations initially.

Q219 Tristram Hunt: Within that you would not be averse to a differentiation of lobbyists; on one hand we have charities, on one hand we have in-house lobbyists within corporations, on one hand you would have think-tanks—you would have trade unions?

Jane Wilson: I think I would. I am not sure hierarchy would work or how it would work. I would be interested to hear views on how that could happen, but I think you could state the type of organisation you are, "I am a publicly listed company. I am a charity. I am not for profit. I am a think-tank". So you probably could have categories but I would not necessarily call it a hierarchy. That does suggest—

Tristram Hunt: No, hierarchy is not—colour-coded or something, something non-judgmental.

Q220 Simon Hart: During the course of our investigation into this particular topic we have had a number of witnesses and we have asked largely the same questions every week. One question we keep asking, for which we have not had an answer so far—and perhaps we should have Paul Flynn as a witness because I suspect he might have one—is precisely what is the extent of the problem, whatever the problem is, and is there any evidence to support the claim that there is a public appetite for this register? If there is evidence, rather than opinion, that there is an appetite for a register, what are the concerns that are uppermost in the public's mind that leads to the demand? David Cameron described it as the next big scandal; nobody quite knows what he meant by that. I am interested to know if you know what he meant by the next big scandal and what this public evidence is.

Jane Wilson: I have not seen any evidence of the demand from the public. I think if there had been evidence it would have been in this document and it is not. It is not in the impact assessment, which I would have expected it to be in. If one does an impact assessment on a problem, it is always good to have the problem there and some evidence of why you are doing it. This does feel like a compromise to deliver an election pledge, a coalition pledge. It feels like the lowest possible compromise to do so. Whether it is or not is not for me to say.

I have not seen that evidence, but I do think there probably is, in this country at the moment, a general feeling in the public that it wants more transparency in government, media, establishment processes in general, so that is the conduct of our parliamentarians, of our Government, of those who seek to influence, of those who do or do not pay taxes at a corporate level and what those levels are, those who are in the media and how they relate to the police and how they relate to government. I think this is one part of that bigger sense that there is an issue, or not an issue but a demand, a direction of travel for more transparency. The proposals as they currently stand do not take us forcefully in that direction of travel. They sort of say, "Well, if we have to do something let's just do this". That is not a good thing.

Helen Johnson: Yes. I would absolutely endorse what Jane said. Clearly I can't speak for what was in the Government's mind when it developed these proposals, but it seems to us that the public concern, if there is one, is much broader around how people in public office behave and how they interact with other interests, external interests, and how those interactions are perceived, whether they are open, whether they are transparent, whether they are subject to inappropriate influence. I think the point has already been well made that for a number of reasons the proposals on the table are not going to take us forward in terms of addressing public concerns there.

Q221 Simon Hart: If I could just interrupt, on that particular point do you agree with a claim, which has been made by earlier witnesses, that if one of your members is faced with the choice of having to sign up to a statutory register, which carries no particular codes of practice, the consequence of that might be that they then surrender the membership of your organisations for which there is a code of practice, and the consequence of that is the opposite to that which the Government is attempting to achieve? You have less accountability and transparency rather than more. You have the warm feeling of having imposed a statutory register and tick the coalition Christmas list, but have you achieved the objective?

Helen Johnson: I think that is a possible unintended consequence, but it depends on the definition and scope of the register that we end up with. It depends on things like funding and the regulatory burden. Let me just make two points on that. Firstly, we still have firms looking to join the APPC. We have four applications for membership pending at the moment, so even with the suggestion of a statutory register on the table we still have a group of firms who want to be part of our framework, sign up to our code, and to demonstrate that they are being open and transparent before government forces them to do so. So I would make the point that there is still an appetite to demonstrate openness and transparency voluntarily.

Secondly, if I just take the example of my own firm on the unintended consequence. My firm has four client-facing members of staff. Our subscription to the APPC is an annual subscription of £428, £107 per member of staff. If the statutory register imposed a fee on me of, for example, £1,000 as an annual fee, I might look at, "Well, if I have to pay £1,000 to the Government, do I also want to pay my £428 to the APPC?" Clearly I have to comply with the statutory requirement, so I will save my £428, pay my £1,000 to the Government, and the risk then is exactly as you suggest, Mr Hart. I have taken myself out of the code of conduct piece, which is absolutely critical to supporting what a register may or may not be able to deliver. I think what we are probably all very clear on is that a list of names of clients and staff does not do anything at all to address how people behave, whether they are ethical, whether their interactions are appropriate or follow some degree of appropriate practice. That is where our codes of conduct are so critical, and it is vital that we do not have people taking themselves out of that framework because they are trying to comply with a statutory requirement instead.

Francis Ingham: I would endorse that broadly. My consultancy members frequently make reference to the fact they have signed up to a code of conduct when they are pitching for new business or to retain existing business because it reassures clients that they are engaging an ethical company. My in-house members like to sign up to a code of conduct, not for those commercial reasons, obviously, but because they like to reassure the broader market or the people with whom they interact.

There is that unintended consequence problem that might be there. But I would hope that on a statutory register we could in some manner identify those people who also had signed up to a code of conduct and those who had not. That is certainly feasible. But what I would not want to see, obviously, is a reduction in ethical standards within the industry as a result of this.

Regarding the document itself, it is a kind of grubby little document really. It has "compromise" stamped all over it, and the fact it has taken so many years to get to this point I think probably indicates the level of compromise involved in it.

Q222 Simon Hart: One last question, if I may. An earlier line of question was, I think, suggesting that because as organisations you had a relatively low expulsion rate per member, that somehow was an indication of weakness. I wondered whether you saw that as an indication of weakness or an indication of strength when taken against perhaps other institutions, whether it is the General Medical Council or the Market Research Society or these other self-regulatory bodies as opposed to statutory regulatory bodies, who have a similar low rate of expulsion but argue that that is a sign of effective regulation rather than ineffective regulation. I wondered what you thought.

Francis Ingham: No, I understand the question. I view it as a sign of strength. You only sign up to being a member of the PRCA or one of the other bodies if you believe you can adhere to its code of conduct, because otherwise your membership of it will be short-lived and your expulsion will be public. So there is a kind of self-selecting element here. I do not think that is a terrible thing either. Companies, when they sign up, if they have had loose ethics in the past realise they have to amend those ethics and behave in a different manner. It improves standards within the industry. Clients and other people with whom our members interact know that if these people behave in a bad manner they have a form of redress. I think that is important, and I do think it has been effective. The fact we have a low expulsion rate is not something I am at all ashamed of. I am quite proud of it actually.

Q223 Simon Hart: Do the three of you support the proposal for a statutory register simply because it is a little bit embarrassing not to? We all say, of course, we support the Government's general principles when it comes to it, knowing full well that we do not really but we feel we have to say so. Yes or no?

Francis Ingham: I think public debate has moved on a little bit too much for this to be anything other than inevitable. I want to make it the right register that is created rather than the wrong register. I think the right register could be very helpful. The wrong one could be very damaging.

Jane Wilson: I endorse that view.

Helen Johnson: I would agree with that. It would be bizarre for us to not be happy with the idea of registration, given that we have already been doing it for the last 17 years and are very happy to continue to do so.

Jane Wilson: As long as it is registration because we think it will lead the process of democracy and transparency and not because we think we as a profession are doing something wrong or illegitimate. That is a very important point.

Q224 Mrs Laing: Can we explore what lobbyists actually do and how you and your members interact with Members of Parliament and Members of the House of Lords and ministers? I am particularly interested in the cost to the public purse of lobbying activities. First, are you aware of how often your members send out an email or a circular letter to all Members of Parliament? Nowadays, presumably, instead of having to address 650 envelopes, they simply make up a database once and then by pressing a button send emails to every Member of Parliament on whatever issue they wish to influence a few Members of Parliament. Are you aware of the fact that all of those emails have to be answered and that whenever an invitation is sent to all 650 Members of Parliament for events that are usually attended by perhaps 10 Members of Parliament, the other 600-odd Members of Parliament have to reply to those invitations? In my office I say to my secretary, "That pile there that has come in, don't reply to those invitations because it is going to take you two hours to do that and I have this other work that requires to be done". She says, "I can't not do it, because if I don't reply, they will phone".

I suspect that there are literally hundreds of people in this building and that building over there who are spending several hours a week replying to invitations and emails from your members. Are you aware that this is a cost to the public purse? But I am giving you the opportunity to justify it.

Jane Wilson: I am not aware of the extent to which that takes place but one thing I would say is, because we have public relations and public affairs and other disciplines within the CIPR, I would think that is a really bad practice. I would urge through our professional development, through our Public Affairs Diploma, through our workshops and training, and also the workshops and training and courses that PRCA would do, there is plenty of evidence there that shows that those kind of scattergun approaches are not good. They are not productive. It is not best practice. So if that is happening on a regular basis—and I take your word, Mrs Laing, that it is—then I would urge my members not to do so, but I have no evidence to suggest that it is our members that are doing it.

Francis Ingham: I have no idea if that happens on a regular basis or not. I would not advise my members to do it because I do not think it is terribly productive. We have never invited parliamentarians to an event, but if we ever do you are very welcome to ignore the invitation. We will not ring up and chase about it.

Q225 Mrs Laing: This is very interesting, because you reacted immediately and very positively—or negatively as the case may be—to what I have just told you, but I assure you it is the case. If this message could be got over to your members it would be enormously helpful and I promise it would save the public purse a lot of money. Sorry, Helen.

Helen Johnson: No, I completely agree with everything Jane and Francis have said. I am not aware of the extent to which our members might be implicated in the practice that you are sadly on the receiving end of but completely agree that it is poor practice and not an effective use either of their resources and certainly not of yours.

Mrs Laing: I am extremely pleased to hear that, and if only some lobbyists would learn that lesson, because I seriously object to the amount of money that it is costing for people to have to deal with these things, never mind my own time. That is not the important point; the point is that matters have to be dealt with.

Chair: While we have been sitting here I have had two messages from the Labour Whips, no doubt other colleagues in other parties have had messages. Perhaps we can include them in the list of lobbyists and stop them sending us these things

Mrs Laing: I know the answer to that. It is leave your pager at home and let the battery run down. Did I say that? There might be somebody listening.

Chair: The transcript will be in the public domain. You are in trouble now.

Mrs Laing: It is all right, I think I have already told them that.

Chair: Sorry to interrupt.

Mrs Laing: It is absolutely right. But it is not appreciated that when MPs say we get hundreds of email every day it is not an exaggeration. It makes it more difficult to do the work you want to do because before you can get to the email that matters you have to open the other ones. If an email is from Jane Wilson, you don't know whether it is your friend Jane Wilson or your constituent Jane Wilson or Jane Wilson representing a particular interest. Before knowing whether that is something that requires immediate attention, you have to open it and read the email. People might say, "Well, yes, okay it only takes 30 seconds to do that". Yes, it only takes 30 seconds to do one but if you are dealing with 100 of those every morning before you can get to the work you have to do, it does matter.

Chair: Is there a question there?

Q226 Mrs Laing: Sorry, that was me responding with thanks to the response that I had. Can we go on to other ways in which lobbyists generally engage with parliamentarians and, in particular, with all-party groups. Once again, looking at the costs to the public purse, for example of holding meetings of all-party groups here in the Palace of Westminster, let me put the question this way to allow you to consider it. If all-party groups were restricted so that lobbying companies could no longer operate all-party groups, or let us say provide the support and secretariat for all-party groups, how significantly would it affect the activities of your members?

Francis Ingham: Very marginally I would have thought. It would not be something that as an organisation we would have any degree of fight against really. All-party groups are highly variable in their quality and in the return on investment, if you want to put it that way, made in them by outside organisations. I think their behaviour, their performance could be improved considerably. I do not think as an industry we would fight tooth and nail against having consultancy involvement in them. But I think some of what they do can be valuable; I just think that most of what they do is not valuable.

Q227 Mrs Laing: That is very helpful. How could the performance be improved? Forgive me if that is too wide a question, but you said so yourself.

Francis Ingham: Yes, sure. It is quite a wide question. I have rarely read a report that had any particular insight included in it. In my experience they have fairly low levels of attendance and engagement but are presumed to speak with more authority than they really have. That is partly a problem here rather than the public affairs community.

Mrs Laing: That is very helpful. Thank you.

Chair: Did Helen or Jane want to come in on that?

Helen Johnson: I will happily add a word about all-party groups. I think they can serve a very useful function and purpose. I think it is important that there are those forums for members to come together and discuss single issues or particular issues that they are particularly interested in. I think the external organisations have an important role to play in bringing insight and intelligence about those issues to the table, to the all-party group meetings. I would endorse what Francis said, that I think some groups are perhaps more effective than others. Some are certainly more active than others in terms of the number of meetings, events, inquiries and so on that they hold. That is clearly a matter for the officers of those particular groups as to how they want to run and organise them.

So far as the role of consultancies and lobbying firms in that process is concerned, I am perhaps interested to know what the concern is and whether it is a concern that they have some kind of undue influence over the direction of the group or that they are somehow inappropriately steering the direction of the all-party groups. Again, I would hope and trust that the officers of the group are able to set their own sort of programme of work and be able to determine that for themselves rather than have it directed by a third party. The point that I made right at the start of the session is, of course, that all financial and administrative support from whatever quarter has to be declared in accordance with the parliamentary rules on the register, so there is a level of transparency there. But if the concern is over something inappropriate going on or some kind of conflict of interest affecting those groups then I think that is something that perhaps needs to be looked at probably separate from—it would not be addressed by what the Government is proposing at the moment.

Jane Wilson: Yes, I agree too that the effectiveness of any group is dependent on its composition and the level of engagement of the Members themselves. If there is an undue influence from any external force then I do think that is an issue that has to be dealt with. *[Interruption.]*

Mrs Laing: It is the Whips again.

Jane Wilson: Is that an ad? Have we just heard a sponsor? Do we have to declare a sponsorship?

Chair: You will have to think about it and I will tell you at the very end.

Jane Wilson: I know what it is, I know the brand.

If there is an undue influence externally then I think that is something that has to be dealt with here. If the existence of those groups is wholly dependent on external support, either funding or administrative assistance, and if those groups are deemed to be important then that is an issue, but that is an issue for this institution.

Q228 Mrs Laing: That is very helpful, thank you. If I may go on to the register that we have just been discussing: can you foresee an instance, or has there ever been an instance of which you are aware, where your members would be reluctant to disclose or would not wish to disclose they are acting on behalf of a particular client or where they would not wish to disclose where they had had a meeting, for example with a minister or with Members of Parliament?

Francis Ingham: Yes. We have in the past had the very, very occasional exemption where a member can provide advice from a credible source, for example police or the Ministry of Defence or something of that nature, that to reveal a client would be a dangerous thing to do. For example, if you were working for the RUC in some manner, putting that on a public register would put potentially the lives of your staff in danger, or something like that. In that case we have very occasionally given people an exemption, but we would never give somebody an exemption from revealing a client purely because they were embarrassing, purely because they were working on behalf of an organisation that might embarrass them. They would never, ever get an exemption for that, and I do not believe they should, under any statutory register.

Jane Wilson: I agree. Those would be the cases where there were personal safety issues or high-level security issues.

Helen Johnson: We have exactly the same exemption. I can think of one case where on the advice of the police force we did not declare—it was not a client but the name of one of the political consultants working in one of our member firms was kept from the register because of concerns about that person's safety. But that would be the only situation. As I have already said, our members are already declaring a much broader range of services and clients than just what you might call pure lobbying, if we can call it that.

Q229 Mrs Laing: In that case, would the register have to have an exemption in it or a point where information could be registered but not publicly disclosed?

Helen Johnson: What we have at the moment is management committee discretion on that point. It is not formally written into our codes or our procedures. I think from a Government perspective, from a legislation perspective, there is probably an example around some of the life sciences industries and so on. There are Companies House exemptions whereby certain directors do not have to be disclosed on Companies House registers and it might be that there is a parallel there that government could look at for this register of lobbyists.

Q230 Stephen Williams: Can I come back to this question of transparency that we have all mentioned, and what the register is designed to expose to that transparency. I suppose this might be a question that is appropriate to start off with Helen because of your association of political consultants. We will all know and can think of examples of Members of Parliament who left the House in 2010 who have become lobbyists. We have probably also met since 2010 people who used to be lobbyists who are now Members of Parliament. What is your estimate of the flow of traffic over the last few years?

Helen Johnson: I am afraid I can't answer that, Mr Williams. I have no idea as to what the flow of traffic would be. If it is helpful I can go back and dig through records and find out for you, but I can't answer that today.

Q231 Stephen Williams: So if you speak for four-fifths, by turnover anyway, of the trade of political lobbying and you have no idea how many ex-elected politicians are now lobbyists or how many current elected politicians who have had a very recent and financial connection with lobbying are in that trade, then that does demonstrate the need for a register and transparency, doesn't it?

Helen Johnson: We would have that information in the sense that we would be able to go back through our registers. I just can't give you a figure today off the top of my head, I am afraid. But we would have that information and I am sure we can send that into the Committee if that would be helpful.

Q232 Stephen Williams: Can we come on to who would actually be on a register, because obviously it is a register of people, I suppose, who are engaged in lobbying. How could you test what boundary you have to cross to be engaged in lobbying or whether your influence over, say, an elected politician is of the nature that you can influence their opinion but you are not actually a lobbyist? To give an example of, let's say, a trade union general secretary who phones up a Labour MP—probably the most typical example—and says, "We don't terribly like what your stance is on public sector pay; we want you to change your

behaviour", is that lobbying or is that influencing or is it blackmail? What is it?
Helen Johnson: I am afraid I keep not answering your questions very straight, but it comes back to what the definition of lobbying is, so far as this register is concerned what the definition of lobbying is that we end up with. Once we have got that, whoever engages in that activity would be a lobbyist. But I think what you are alluding to, perhaps, is whether there could or should be some kind of threshold or some kind of de minimis rule applying whereby perhaps certain people would be taken off the register if they lobbied as only a small proportion of their time, 20% or 10% or whatever it would be, or if they only lobbied once or twice a year. I know I have heard people talking about you could have two wildcards a year and only if you lobbied on a third occasion would you have to go on to the register. My concern is that to try to set any kind of threshold based on percentage of time, numbers of occasion of lobbying or whatever it happens to be is fraught with difficulty. I think any kind of threshold or level on whatever basis has a risk that you then start having people trying to take themselves under that threshold and therefore outside of the registration regime that we are talking about. I come back to the point that we have to define the activity correctly and then that will determine who should and should not be on the register.

Q233 Stephen Williams: I don't know whether the other witnesses want to answer my first question, though it was really for Ms Johnson.
Francis Ingham: Well, there is no point talking for its own sake. I endorse pretty much what Helen has said. The definition is critical. In my view, if you are a general secretary of a trade union you should register as a lobbyist just as if you are the chief executive of a trade association or something you ought to register. That seems pretty clear to me, but it is a grey area.

Q234 Stephen Williams: That is a clear answer. Jane?
Jane Wilson: Yes, I wholeheartedly agree with that. The issue of transparency is about what an organisation is doing. Whether it is a big supermarket in planning or whether it is an energy company or whether it is an organisation like Greenpeace who is trying to influence energy policy, then what you begin to find out is the sheer volume of the number of people who are engaged in the lobbying process, which will tell you quite something about the level of interest they have in lobbying and the numbers and the cost of the lobbying activity then. You will begin to build up a picture by the numbers of people engaged in lobbying in any one organisation.

Q235 Stephen Williams: Tristram raised earlier the subject of trade unions in general, whether they could be included. If I can give an example of lobbying by a trade union that may not, on the face of it, seem to be to do with health and safety or the welfare of its members. I am just disclosing that I am the chair of the all-party group on smoking and health. UNITE are busily lobbying Labour MPs against plain packaging of tobacco products at the moment. Is that an activity that should be disclosed by them?
Francis Ingham: Yes.
Jane Wilson: Yes.
Helen Johnson: Yes.

Q236 Stephen Williams: Is a register enough in order to ensure transparency? A register will say who is engaged in lobbying, maybe it will say what sort of lobbying activities they are undertaking, but if we receive these invitations, for instance as Mrs Laing referred to, or these round robin emails and newsletters, which may be very interesting and have nice pictures on them, maybe there is a nice reception to go to, you do not know who is paying that lobbying firm in order to circulate that email or the letter. Has the fact that they are on the register as a lobbyist, and they are engaged in this particular activity, joined up all the dots so there is full transparency, both for us so that we know who is trying to influence us and for our constituents who need to know that as well?
Francis Ingham: It would be a register of individuals but also of organisations, I should have thought. Our own register you can search by individuals or by organisations, ditto the APPC's. If an agency were to be handling this mailout, which I would say is quite rare and not very well advised, on behalf of British American Tobacco, for example, British American Tobacco would be listed as one of their clients on either this—I would hope—statutory register or certainly listed at the moment on our current existing voluntary registers. So there is that element of transparency there.

Q237 Stephen Williams: But if Mrs Laing's poor secretary receives a newsletter from a trade association of corner shops, for instance, which says that tobacco control is desperately damaging to their turnover and they are all going to go out of business and Mrs Laing then gets very worried about it, should Mrs Laing know that that public affairs agency that is doing that work has been funded by BAT, to give your example?
Francis Ingham: It is not going to have an agent's imprint on the bottom, I suppose, saying, "Printed and published by X", but if you wanted to look up does BAT retain an agency, you would be able to do so just by going to a document and typing in BAT, search. There is that degree of transparency.

Q238 Stephen Williams: Mrs Laing has already told us her secretary is very busy with this huge pile of invites, which in my office tend to go in the bin. Should any of our PAs, secretaries, whatever, have to think, "I wonder who is paying for this. Shall I check the register of lobbyists to see whether this firm is engaged in a particular activity or who their clients are?" Of course, they may have lots of clients. Or would it just be better if on the invite it said that, "We are undertaking this promotional activity on behalf of our client BAT, Japanese Tobacco, Imperial Tobacco", whoever it is?
Helen Johnson: The short answer from an APPC perspective is going back to our code that in making representations to the institutions of government,

political consultants must be open in disclosing the identity of their clients and must not misrepresent their interests. So if there is a concern that on material coming through it is not clear or transparent on the face of that material who the ultimate client is who is funding and paying for that activity, then I completely agree that, firstly, Mrs Laing should be able to find that information out readily and easily and, secondly, if she were to put the question to the agency they should be able to tell her immediately who has funded that activity. If you have examples of where that is not happening, I hope you will make a complaint to the APPC and bring it to my attention, please.
Francis Ingham: We have exactly the same wording, word for word, in our code of conduct, yes.

Q239 Stephen Williams: Helen used the phrase the ultimate payer of the bill, the top client I suppose, but there may be several chains in between that client and the Member of Parliament who the client is seeking to influence. What is the assessment of the three of you of the use of intermediate groups, not just the lobbyists themselves but other groups that may, on the face of it, have an innocuous air to them but in fact are acting for a corporate interest in the background? Oil companies may have done this, tobacco companies certainly do, and many other corporate interests will as well.
Helen Johnson: Our advice to our members is that they should be listing everybody in that chain all the way back to the ultimate client.

Q240 Stephen Williams: That is your current advice to your members?
Helen Johnson: That is our advice to our members. A number of our members are very small firms or sole traders who might be contracted on certain projects by some of the larger firms. In that case the larger firm is required to list the smaller firm as a client or as a supplier, whichever way round it happens to be. Similarly, we have a number of our members who perhaps are working on behalf of coalitions or alliances, a whole range of interest groups in different sectors. What happens there is that the member concerned will name the alliance or the coalition and then look to list the funders or supporters or individual members of that alliance.
Jane Wilson: Exactly the same as our code and the principles of the code are those of integrity, transparency, honesty, ethical behaviour, but I do think those sorts of front organisations—I may be wrong and your experience may be different—are diminishing because we do generally live in a more transparent world. I think social media has done a lot, citizen journalism has done a lot to open this world up, and this is part of that bigger picture of a movement towards transparency, the things that we are talking about today. I do think that is diminishing anyway, but I do think absolutely best practice because why would you want a Member of Parliament to come along to an event or show initial support for something that then turns out to be not what it seems? That is not good business; that is not best practice. So just from a purely effective professional approach position, we would advise against it, not just on the ethical transparent point.

Q241 Andrew Griffiths: Apologies for my late arrival. We have talked about trade unions and we have talked about the trade bodies. Can we talk about the charitable sector and the voluntary sector a little bit more? NCVO say that nobody in their organisation is involved primarily in lobbying and so therefore those organisations, those charities, should not be included on any sort of statutory register and should not be required to be registered. Could you tell us whether you agree with that? What are your views on charitable organisations and also campaign groups? Do you think they should be registered and do you think they should be required to identify where their funding comes from?
Jane Wilson: My understanding of the NCVO position was that—and I have to declare an interest, my husband works for the NCVO—it would not have a problem with considering charities perhaps having to be on a register but Sir Stuart Etherington recently said that this proposal as it stands is not one that he would recommend NCVO members would sign up to. As we have all said previously today, we do not think it is about the type of organisation you work for, it is the act of lobbying, and charities are not without conflicts and they are not without issues of public interest. I do want to know if there is a climate group that may be a charity seeking to influence policy on energy, for instance. I might want to know if there is a church group seeking to influence policy on gay marriage, for instance. So there are a lot of instances where just because someone is working for something that they perceive to be a good cause does not mean they do not have undue influence, and I think there are many NCVO members who would fall into that category.
Francis Ingham: I consider the NCVO claim to be literally incredible. I doubt even Stuart Etherington believes it either. Charities lobby on a regular basis, they employ fulltime lobbyists. I was one of them. The idea that charities do not lobby is absurd. The idea that if they do lobby it is only at the margins is laughable. We have charities who are members of the PRCA who do declare their lobbying activity on our voluntary register. They would not be caught by the Government's proposal. There ought to be no good cause exemption, because that is incredibly subjective and would narrow down the register to the point of pointlessness. I have to say that I saw Stuart Etherington's comments. I thought it was more with happiness than with regret that he was reversing the NCVO's position and I think it will be a very poor register that does not include the hundreds and thousands of charities that register.
Helen Johnson: I completely agree with both Jane and Francis. I don't think there is anything I can add other than to completely endorse what they have just said.
Andrew Griffiths: Could we move on to meeting with ministers?
Chair: Just before you go on, Andrew. Eleanor, did you want to jump in on that particular point?

Q242 Mrs Laing: May I, please? Just on charities, having asked you a question about the general activities of many lobbying companies and others who send emails to everybody and it is irritating, to put it simply, let me ask you about the activities of particular charities. Can I give you the example that yesterday I happened to have the adjournment debate in the House of Commons and it was on the subject of controlling dangerous dogs, because of an incident that happened near my constituency to one of my constituents. As soon as the order paper was published with that subject and my name on it, I got lots and lots of information from the RSPCA, the Dogs Trust, the Kennel Club and other charities. I think this is the question, Mr Chair. Would you consider that that is good lobbying activity and ought to be encouraged?
Francis Ingham: I do not think it is very effective from the way you are phrasing this, so clearly not.

Q243 Mrs Laing: Sorry, I should explain myself. I was trying to put it as a question. I really wanted to say it was good lobbying activity and that it was extremely helpful in preparing for a debate yesterday to have flooding into my office information from those organisations, charitable organisations, who have been involved in this subject with good intentions.
Francis Ingham: Well, it informed you, it was well intended, but it was absolutely definitely lobbying, and that is why those organisations ought to be on a register.
Mrs Laing: Thank you.

Q244 Andrew Griffiths: Do you think that ministers and civil servants should refuse to meet with organisations that are not on a statutory register?
Francis Ingham: Yes.

Q245 Andrew Griffiths: If they have those meetings, do you think it should also be incumbent on ministers to declare why the meetings are taking place?
Francis Ingham: I would have no reason to think that was a bad idea. Ministerial diaries could be improved considerably; they are frequently late or inaccurate. I think transparency cuts both ways and it would be a good thing for ministerial private offices to be a bit more open about who they meet, as well as the demand for lobbyists to be more open about what they do as well.
Jane Wilson: Yes, I entirely agree that transparency goes both ways. I think it is a very good way to put it. I do think if you use these different pieces of information together you could build up a picture, so with freedom of information, with ministerial diaries, with a register, and actually a statutory register could be a licence to operate. If somebody calls up your office and says, "Can I have a meeting with you?" or speaks to your secretary, they should be able to check the register. If that person or their organisations or their client are not on that register then they should not get a meeting.
Helen Johnson: Again, I completely agree with the point that everybody involved in this process needs to be transparent and we need not just to be looking at the lobbyists but potentially the lobbied and, yes, there is certainly a strong argument there for that information to be disclosed.
Francis Ingham: But I would add that if you are going to restrict people who are not on a register from meeting people who make policy decisions, you need to make being on a register not financially prohibitive because otherwise you make it those three horrible words "cash for access" really, don't you? You would restrict the ability of people to lobby depending upon the financial strength of their organisation, and that is not necessarily something any of us would want to encourage.

Q246 Andrew Griffiths: Do you have an idea about how much that level should be set at, Francis?
Francis Ingham: No. I think we will put some formal proposals in our response, but I know that some of the examples bandied around seem to me to be extremely high. For a simple register listing people and clients, and maybe if they have been former MPs, I don't see why that is an expensive operation in any way. It can be done quickly and efficiently without incurring great cost.
Jane Wilson: I agree, and the broader it is the less that the burden is on a few people. We mentioned that is where the good cause exemptions could come in on funding and it could be a mixture of the status of your company or your organisation, so it could be, are you a registered charity, are you a chartered body or are you not-for-profit or are you a trade association. So there could be status but there could also be profitability limits set as well and that would be fairly straightforward to do.
Helen Johnson: I completely agree that the fees have to be proportionate for what it is that people are being asked to pay for, assessed to a level that is not punitive or prohibitive for individuals to register. I notice that the Government has said that it would be committed to keep the regulatory burden and cost to micro businesses as small as possible, and I think that is to be welcomed. We do not have a set view on the amount that would be appropriate. Again, we do not really know what the definition and scope is at the moment, so that is difficult, but I think our inclination is we would be talking tens of pounds per individual to register rather than hundreds of pounds or anything even higher than that.

Q247 Simon Hart: Ministerial meetings are FOI-able anyway. As you said earlier, part of your job is to advise your clients about how to go about their lobbying. You might advise your clients, as I used to do my own members, that perhaps the ministerial meeting was quite a difficult thing to arrange. What was not difficult to arrange was a constituency visit from a constituent who had a particular interest in our affairs to go and see their MP who might also be the Minister, thereby getting round that problem. If we put too many obstacles in the way, will people find a way, as we did, of simply getting into the constituency surgery on a Friday afternoon, having greater impact that way and thereby bypassing the whole purpose of the register?

Helen Johnson: As a very general comment, yes, the more hurdles that are put in place, the more regulations that are introduced, the greater the potential risk is that people will find ways to work round those regulations and identify loopholes. That would clearly be a very concerning consequence if that were to be the case.
Francis Ingham: That is true, but if a member of mine were to organise that sort of meeting, they would probably be breaking my code of conduct on several counts.

Q248 Simon Hart: The fact is that a member of yours—and this is where the whole thing is vague—might be a charity that might have members who want to speak to their MP or a minister on a certain topic and might say, "How do I go about doing that?" A member that is a campaigning charity would say, "Well, look, the thing you need to do is you need to make an appointment at the constituency surgery and go and speak to him or her and these are the points you need to make". That cannot possibly be an unethical approach. That is an entirely legitimate piece of advice you can give to a member of your organisation in order to enable them to undertake democratic activity. I cannot believe that that would fall foul of anybody's code of conduct.
Francis Ingham: No, I think it depends on which way round it is. If you are a supporter of the Countryside Alliance and you say, "I'm concerned about this, I would like to make clear my views to my Member of Parliament", and the Countryside Alliance say, "Well, there's your Member of Parliament's details and this is how best you might approach them", I think that is entirely valid and legitimate. If it is the other way round, if it is the Countryside Alliance going out to friendly supporters and saying, "Look, do you mind dropping a line to your MP saying I am concerned about this and here is a briefing paper for you, and not saying that we have made this recommendation to you", that seems to me slightly different.
Simon Hart: How very interesting. Thank you.

Q249 Sheila Gilmore: Apologies if this area has been covered already, but where on the spectrum would you place some of the organisations that present as research organisations or think-tanks and again send us reports saying that—well, I suppose climate change has been a big one of these on both sides of the argument to some extent, but it seems to be perhaps an increasing practice. If Friends of the Earth sends me a report, I know it is Friends on the Earth and it is very clearly that. There do seem to be a growing number that use that kind of think-tank approach and there are queries that arise out of who funds them and other things. Do you see that as a lobbying activity and should they be required to register?
Francis Ingham: I think we covered this a little bit earlier on. We were all in agreement that they ought to be registered if they lobby on a professional basis.

Q250 Sheila Gilmore: What does it add for the single issue groups? Obviously what voluntary organisations do is lobbying and they do it very effectively in lots of different ways, but if they have a particular focus what does having them registered add to that?
Jane Wilson: Well, you would see to what extent they are lobbying, to what extent their activities are purely lobbying or if they are fundraising or if there is mobilisation of communities. So if they are a small organisation, single issue, but they have four people on the register, that will tell you something about that organisation's lobbying activities and how they are seeking to influence. I think it is important to be able to say, "Is this an organisation that is just about mobilising communities to do good things or are they seeking terms to influence public policy?" If they are seeking to influence policy, they should be on the register. The fact that they have somebody there doing the act of lobbying, they should be on the register. It gives them clarity in the nature of their activities.

Q251 Sheila Gilmore: Yes. It is quite a fine line, though, especially for perhaps more localised organisations, who will not generally perhaps be lobbying but might on two or three occasions because they are fired up about it.
Jane Wilson: The one thing we have consistently discussed is the big flaw in this consultation document is a lack of definition, a lack of work that has been done on the scope of the problem and a problem does exist, a proper impact assessment, and then saying, "Okay, so what do we define as lobbying, first of all, and then how does that affect the scope of a register?" That work has not been done and I think that is the most important thing we have to do to figure out the detail of this issue.

Q252 Sheila Gilmore: That would help those organisations as well because they might genuinely not see themselves as—
Jane Wilson: Entirely. Make it clear. Make the principle of universality but make the detail very clear.

Q253 Chair: Any other colleagues? So, Jane, you have had half an hour. What do you think the ringtone was?
Jane Wilson: Lloyds TSB.
Chair: No, Grand Designs.
Jane Wilson: Oh, Grand Designs; I thought it was a brand.
Chair: So I would like to thank all three of you for being part of our grand design, which is to make something workable from the Government's proposals on lobbying. I do not know if you have made our task harder or easier, having heard your comments today, but certainly we are much better educated. Thank you very much, Jane, Francis and Helen, for your time this morning. I think it was a very good and productive session. Thank you so much.

Thursday 22 March 2012

Members present:

Mr Graham Allen (Chair)

Mr Christopher Chope
Paul Flynn
Andrew Griffiths
Fabian Hamilton
Simon Hart
Tristram Hunt
Mrs Eleanor Laing

Examination of Witnesses

Witnesses: **Ben Kernighan**, Deputy Chief Executive, National Council for Voluntary Organisations, and **Nigel Stanley**, Head of Campaigns and Communications, Trade Union Congress, gave evidence.

Q254 Chair: Welcome to our Committee, Ben and Nigel. As you know, we are doing an inquiry into lobbying. As you also know, we are the Political and Constitutional Reform Committee, the baby of the Committees, but we hope we are kicking and screaming as loud as possible on some of these key issues and we intend to produce a report on lobbying in the not too distant future. I think you are among some of the last witnesses that we are going to hear from but don't read anything into that. We are very, very pleased to see you and you are very welcome. Would you like to make an opening statement, Ben?

Ben Kernighan: Thank you, and thanks for the opportunity for coming and talking to you today. As you will all know, charities have a great deal of experience of working with people on the ground, including some people who do not always get a loud voice in terms of influencing public policy. That gives them, often, a unique insight into how public policy shapes our society, and it is not surprising that many of them want to use that experience to influence public policy. So we see lobbying as an essential part of democracy and it is right that outside interests inform public policy process. Often, lobbyists can help parliamentarians and others and be a beneficial source of information, improve debate and strengthen the law-making process. However, we also recognise that there is a need to regulate lobbying activity in order to prevent further ambiguity and mistrust of the political system.

It is important to remember that charities lobbying government are different in a number of ways from other types of lobbyists. For example, they are accountable to a board of trustees, usually unpaid, they are legally required to act for public benefit, and all but the tiniest of them are regulated in their lobbying activity by the Charity Commission. NCVO has previously argued that lobbyists should be subject to the same rules and regulations, regardless of whom they lobby for. Indeed, we think it important that there is a high level of public trust. But when we look at the proposals that government has come up with we don't think there is an argument in favour of charities being part of that register. The reason for that is that we think it is pretty self-evident who it is that charities are lobbying for. The nature of what they do is pretty clear to organisations and they do that quite specifically and are only allowed to do it, by law, for their charitable purpose. We think that the Government has missed an opportunity in its proposals in taking a wider look at lobbying, which may have led to a greater increase in public trust and confidence, and there are two key things that we think are missing. One is setting out clear standards of professional conduct for lobbyists, and the other is making it clear who is lobbying whom. If all those things were in place, we could see a value in terms of charities being involved in that process. But in the very narrow register that is being proposed, we don't think that that would add value, and the added cost and regulation burden would not warrant their involvement in the proposals as presented by the Government.

Q255 Chair: Thank you, Ben. Nigel.

Nigel Stanley: Thanks very much for inviting me this morning. I have to say that, having looked at some of the previous sessions and some of the evidence submitted, I am finding this a rather confused and confusing debate. The problem is that the register seems to be being advanced to solve a number of completely different problems and there are, therefore, a number of different agendas getting confused together.

At the broadest, there is a broad concern that people with wealth and power have superior access to decision makers over others. Whether the register can deal with what is a fundamental, society-wide issue, I don't know. But there are also rather precise and narrowly focused concerns about the role of third-party lobbyists, and we share some of those. On the other hand the professional third-party lobbyists say, "Not just us, guv. We should be treated the same as everybody else, so everyone should be registered", so you then immediately get into a broad agenda again. Then there are other concerns that have been put into the Government's consultation paper. Unions have been singled out, along with charities and think-tanks—a concept that has no legal meaning at all, I think—as giving rise to some special concern in this process. But it is an odd list. Even the 19th-century Combination Acts at least maintained the pretence that employers and unions would be regulated in the same way, but there is no mention of employer groups in this, despite the fact we are both registered by the Certification Officer process and by the same Act of Parliament. There is a missing category of groups as well: the rise of what you might call campaign groups that are not charities, not unions, not professional lobbyists, and that clearly get a lot of money from somewhere—one doesn't really quite know where—but are very influential in the way that they brief MPs, talk to ministers and dominate the media agenda. There is no mention of these coming into the scope of a register at all.

So, if I could just sum up our approach. We do think there is a particular problem with lack of transparency around professional lobbyists—knowing that a minister has met one of them, doesn't quite know what the issues are and what the clients are there. We would support much more disclosure about that, their clients, the issues they are lobbying on and their finances. The TUC is already fantastically open, transparent and highly regulated and we don't understand why we have been singled out. You may disagree with us, of course, but there is nothing mysterious or secret about the TUC. There is also the problem of who needs to be registered. I can't go round the TUC staff and say, "They're a lobbyist and they're not a lobbyist". Anyone who works on policy in the TUC may well meet an MP, meet a minister, meet a special advisor, because on the whole we like to send the people who know what they are talking about to see ministers. Do we register all the staff or not, even if they don't lobby anyone for a year because their issue is not in the limelight? So, we have an issue there.

We have no problem in being added to another register to reveal all the same things that are on there and all the other registers that we are already on, but we would be a bit resentful if we were singled out as some special category of people that needed registering. We think there is a basic problem here—that the real onus for transparency should be on those being lobbied. Whatever rules you have around lobbying, people will try to get round them, but they are all aimed at the same decision makers, so really the onus should be on the decision makers to declare their contacts and attempts to lobby them. That seems to us to get round a lot of the rather tricky administrative issues that we can see in the approach set out in the consultation document.

Sorry, I have probably spoken for too long but—

Chair: No, that is fine; very helpful.

Q256 Tristram Hunt: I agree with your analysis and I think in the Government's proposals at the moment there is no appreciation of the broader civil society role of trade unions, and to reduce them to the same as Lowe Bell Communications or whatever seems a rather reductive approach. Can you spell out more in terms of the complexities of how trade unions, as you understand it, will have to apply themselves to the register? Obviously, you have the TUC but then you will have all sorts of individual unions; you might even then have regional branches. In terms of the consultation document at the moment, how will it affect union declarations?

Nigel Stanley: These are difficult questions. I don't think the answer is clear in the consultation document, because one gets the impression that unions and charities and think-tanks were rather a last-minute addition to it. One can read the consultation document as being originally a proposal about third-party lobbyists with a few bits bolted on to it. But I think that is a very good question. It comes back to whom exactly do we register as lobbyists. Is a voluntary union activist in your town who comes to see you—not necessarily a constituent, but someone acting on behalf of the general interests of trade union members in Stoke—a lobbyist? I don't know. It depends what your definition is. They are certainly trying to influence you, so in one broad definition they are; but are they a paid lobbyist for hire like Lowe Bell, who are doing it because they make money from it? I think that is so distant a part on the spectrum of lobbying that you can't force them into the same compartment.

Q257 Tristram Hunt: That seems exactly right, because I will have branch members of a union of the CWU or the FBU come to see me, probably both as constituents and as members of trade unions. Whether I will then have to, on your idea, register them as being lobbyists, or they themselves will have to register, seems to me perverse.

Can you spell out your hesitations about those organisations whom you don't think are covered by this? Do you mean campaigning groups and organisations such as the TaxPayers' Alliance?

Nigel Stanley: I think the TaxPayers' Alliance are a very good example because they are particularly opaque about their finances. They claim to represent taxpayers but they certainly do not ever ask me my views as a taxpayer. All we generally know about their financing, I understand, is that one of their main financiers is a tax exile from France who is not even a taxpayer. So, the idea that they are in some way representative—*[Interruption.]* I don't wish to enter into controversy in my evidence this morning, but the idea that they are not covered in any way—do they come under this rather nebulous term "think-tank", which is an interesting catch-all? Some think-tanks are registered charities and very proper and precise, and other people call themselves a think-tank and are not registered charities, and may well be proper and precise in different ways but have very clear political alignments. I do worry that because companies and individuals have to declare political donations to political parties now—I think rightly so—there is a kind of new breed of quasi-American organisations set up to get round this, so people can give money for political campaigning without having to declare it. Fine, they should be allowed to do that, but we should know where people get their money from and how much they get and what issues they are pursuing. That is the real transparency gap, and that has not even begun to be mentioned in the Government's consultation document.

Q258 Tristram Hunt: But it also seems to mean, does it not, that this slightly poisons the well of debate? Once you make think-tanks—whether it is the Centre for Policy Studies, the Adam Smith Institute, Demos or whatever—and trade unions lobbyists, the nature of political debate sometimes becomes a very mechanical exchange. Actually, however, what is involved—both on left and right—is a discussion and a search for ideas, rather than a utilitarian exchange of access for money, for influence, for policy.

Nigel Stanley: There is an interesting debate about what professional lobbyists can actually achieve. I often think that effective lobbying is not about the big political ideas and the big political issues. I recognise Members sitting around this table have a number of very different ideological views, and the idea that by somehow spending money on top-rate lobbyists you are going to shift those views seems to me absurd. It is in the narrow little bits of policy, the precise implementation, the detail, where I think professional lobbyists can help their clients. In some ways that can also be helpful to government. All of the meetings I have had with officials in the last year have been at their request, not my request, because they value TUC views and insights into the world of workplace pensions, which is my particular policy interest. Of course they talk to a whole range of stakeholders as well, and I have no complaints there is inappropriate access at all. But in terms of the narrow implementation—who gets this contract; what precise form does that regulation take, because that might benefit me or my competitors in some way?—that seems to me where more of the problem with lobbying is. There is a separate and important issue—but it is separate—about people with more money having more influence over political debate because they can fund more. But I don't think you solve that particularly with a register, because it is rather obvious that the TaxPayers' Alliance have as much money as they possibly want, and putting that on the register isn't going to tell me anything—although I would quite like to know who gives them their money.

Q259 Tristram Hunt: Finally, without wishing to lead you in any particular direction, if you looked at the politics of this, would it be fair to suggest that on the one hand we have a Liberal Democrat manifesto commitment to have a register of lobbyists, and in the coalition carve-up there might have been views on the Conservative side of life that this would be a good vehicle to bring in the trade unions? Secondly, are there those within the professional lobbyist community who wish to undermine what might be a register for professional lobbyists by broadening it out to the Charity of Landscape Architects and whatever?
Nigel Stanley: That is a good interpretation of what is happening. There is a narrow and precise point about the role of professional lobbyists. There is not enough transparency about their clients, the issues they are taking on and how much they are receiving for that. I think there should be more transparency about that.
Trying to deal with all the other issues, some of which are real issues, using the same tool is not right. I was always brought up to think that you should use one tool for one purpose: the purpose it was designed for. Attempts to use a register for dealing with a whole number of different problems—you can't put a screw in with a hammer.

Q260 Mrs Laing: If I may say so, Mr Stanley, that is something we should all remember—you can't put a screw in with a hammer.
In trying to work out what we should do, may I go to Mr Kernighan first? You represent an enormous variety of charities and voluntary organisations. Do some of those organisations receive grants from government departments—from taxpayers' money?
Ben Kernighan: Yes.

Q261 Mrs Laing: Do they have to apply for those grants?
Ben Kernighan: More often than not, yes, certainly.

Q262 Mrs Laing: In doing so, do your organisations then disclose what that money is used for?
Ben Kernighan: They would certainly disclose that, in that they will have some agreement with the statutory organisation that is providing them with a grant, in terms of what that is used for. They will provide summary financial information to the Charity Commission, as well.

Q263 Mrs Laing: Thank you. Do some of those charities seek to influence government?
Ben Kernighan: Yes, certainly they do. The Government often wants to be influenced by them and will frequently seek their views, because it will recognise the expertise that they have in terms of working with a particular group of individuals. For example, in working with people with disabilities and providing support—sometimes paid for by the Government—when at a local or national level they are looking to develop their policies, they will recognise that that charity will have real expertise, grounded on an understanding developed through the process of delivering those services.

Q264 Mrs Laing: Indeed. Can I just clarify that point? Would you agree that it is often the case that a particular government department will recognise beyond doubt that the organisation that can best implement its policy is a voluntary organisation that has the expertise?
Ben Kernighan: Yes, and furthermore they will sometimes also recognise that that charity can help the Government to influence their policy positively, not just to implement their policy.

Q265 Mrs Laing: Indeed, that is a very good point and I am glad we have put that on the record. Thank you very much.
Can I turn to Mr Stanley. Can you just remind us, Mr Stanley, what is your title within the TUC?
Nigel Stanley: I am the Head of Campaigns and Communications.

Q266 Mrs Laing: So, do you campaign?
Nigel Stanley: I do campaign, yes, but I would define the TUC as a campaigning organisation. We have a number of roles, but one of them is speaking up for people at work and trying to influence the public policy agenda and employer activities—to treat people better at work. That is why I find quite tricky this idea that some of the people who work at the TUC are lobbyists and some are not, because for anyone who works on policy, part of their job is influencing across the piece—whether it be Ministers, MPs or the media—the way public policy is agreed and decided in this country.

Q267 Mrs Laing: Thank you. You have anticipated my next few questions. That is very helpful.
Nigel Stanley: We are very keen on improving productivity.

Q268 Mrs Laing: That was very good, yes. Mine isn't usually improved so dramatically; I should come to you more often. So, the TUC seeks to influence government?
Nigel Stanley: Yes.

Q269 Mrs Laing: Given that that is an open role and that everyone assumes that that is what you do, and you have just said that is what you do, what is the problem if you were to register your interest in influencing government?
Nigel Stanley: I don't think there would be a problem in us joining another register that revealed the TUC was entirely open and transparent about what it did. Whether it would add anything to the sum of human knowledge having it in more than one place, I don't know, but I think it would also be quite hard for us to do it if it was a list of named individuals. I don't quite know how you capture the definition of a lobbyist in organisations like the TUC, or in many charities and voluntary groups—even think-tanks—as well.
If it was a list of organisations then, yes, we would be happy to join it. We would be a little resentful, though, if we were singled out as a special category of organisation that needed to be registered when, say, employer organisations—which have a perfectly legitimate role in influencing public policy in the same way that we do, and in many ways are rather analogous—don't have to join that register. I think we would feel a bit cheesed off if that happened.

Q270 Mrs Laing: Thank you. Does the TUC gather money from its members in order to fund its activities?
Nigel Stanley: We are an umbrella body for Britain's unions, whereby unions join as organisations and pay an affiliation fee, depending on how many members they have. That is our major source of income.

Q271 Mrs Laing: You have, over the years, been successful in many of the campaigns that you have run.
Nigel Stanley: I am not sure that all our member unions often appreciate that sufficiently, but yes.

Q272 Mrs Laing: I think you probably have and you are still there. What I am getting at here is that you stated earlier that you were concerned about those who have wealth and power. I put it to you that the TUC has wealth and power.
Nigel Stanley: Yes, but not as much as Mr Murdoch.

Q273 Mrs Laing: It is a matter of opinion whether anyone has as much as Mr Murdoch, but I do not think he is the touchstone. Would you agree that the TUC has wealth and power?
Nigel Stanley: Yes, I think that's right. Let's answer that question more seriously. I think the reason why organisations like the TUC and other civil society organisations arise is that we are speaking up for people who, just left to themselves, would not have much of a voice—ordinary people without much wealth or money. By aggregating their interests together in a democratic umbrella body and seeking to represent their views collectively, yes, I think we bring some weight and influence to public discourse. I think it has more to do with the fact that we have, between our unions, over 6 million members—which makes us the biggest voluntary movement in Britain—that gives us or should give us some entry into civil society and the policymaking process. Actually, in terms of our central resources in the TUC they are not that huge. I don't have big budgets generally for my campaigns. I have to think of smart arguments, rather than things to spend money on.

Q274 Mrs Laing: Let me just clarify your argument. You were saying that the exercise of power is not always done through the spending of money. It can be done through the actions of a great many people.
Nigel Stanley: Indeed.

Q275 Mrs Laing: You have just made the case for the power of the TUC.
Nigel Stanley: Yes.

Q276 Mrs Laing: So, even if it does not have wealth, it has power?
Nigel Stanley: Well, it has some influence; I am not sure power is the right word. We live in a pluralist society, and that is a good thing, and I think that public policy discourse should recognise that and should recognise there are legitimate interest groups. Trade unions are a legitimate interest group, employer bodies are a legitimate interest group. I think some of the concern about this is that some people, because they have wealth, power, connections, can barge a bit more into that discourse than perhaps they deserve, given whom they represent or the interest groups they represent. I think that is the wider concern that I meant to refer to in my opening remarks.

Q277 Mrs Laing: Are you saying then that there is a difference between power and influence?
Nigel Stanley: Yes. I think governments have power; people can seek to influence them. If they are successful at that, then you could argue that they are shaping the way government exercises its power. I am not sure that unions have power. We almost were formed because ordinary people at work have very little power. The relationship between an employer and an employee is fundamentally unequal, but by joining together and giving workers a collective voice you restore some of that balance—both legitimate voices, but you restore that balance. To say that we have power is not quite right, but to say we have influence, yes, and to say that governments of all stripes should listen to us and recognise that we are a serious organisation with a serious role in civil society and a pluralist democracy is right.

Q278 Mrs Laing: I would entirely agree with you on everything you have just said, for what it is worth. But what I am getting at is that in your opening remarks you showed some concern about those who exercise wealth and power. I am seeking to find the difference between the TUC and those whom you put in that category who have wealth and power. That is why I was putting it to you that the TUC has wealth and power, but I accept that perhaps it is not power, but influence. So are there other bodies or organisations that you see as having not just influence but power? Why should the TUC be treated differently from those other organisations? Who are those other organisations that you are worried about?

Nigel Stanley: I think I may have used the precise term "power" in a rather loose way and in different ways in different arguments; I think you are right to pick me up on that. In the way that people talk about trade union power, people on our side of the argument will talk about other organisations having power. In a formal sense that may not be true, because governments, we hope, act without being influenced in an inappropriate way for a power relationship. But there is a sense that, because governments respond to public opinion and what is in the media, it is not unfair to use the word "power" if you are talking about the power of the media to set an argument and set a debate. That may not be a very precise transmission belt—that the media can therefore get minister X to do thing Y on day Z—but it does mean that the media, by setting the terms of public debate, by influencing people, have a pretty powerful influence, but it is a powerful influence rather than direct power. So, perhaps that is what I meant in my earlier remarks about power.

Q279 Mrs Laing: Thank you for clarifying that, but I don't think it adds much light to differentiate the media. What I am trying to get at is, am I right in thinking that you are putting the case that there are organisations that should be regulated by the Government because they are lobbyists, but that the TUC is not one of those organisations because they are not lobbyists? What I am getting at is, what differentiates the TUC from those people about whom you are concerned in the exercise of their influence, power, wealth or whatever it might be, in order to affect the actions of government?

Nigel Stanley: My argument is that we can see a strong role for a register for the precise group of paid-for third-party lobbyists. We think there is a problem when you go wider than that to include a random list of organisations, as in the Government's consultation paper—unions but not employers, think-tanks but not campaign groups. We would not object to being part of a register if absolutely everybody was on it, but I can see problems with defining who everybody is and what organisations are covered by this, which makes us sceptical that this is the right route to go down. That is why we think that the onus is on ministers and special advisors to declare who is lobbying and seeking to influence them, rather than trying to get everyone who seeks to do that—whether successfully or completely unsuccessfully and ineffectively—to declare their interest. Does that clarify what I am saying?

Q280 Mrs Laing: It does, thank you very much. Can I ask Mr Kernighan if he has anything to add to that?

Ben Kernighan: Yes. The perspective we are coming from is that there is a very high level of public trust in charities, so we don't think charities are what is leading to a decrease in trust in lobbying activity, but we think that lobbying activity should be properly regulated. We do not think what is proposed by the Government would do that, because it does not address two issues. It does not put in place a code of conduct and it does not address people reporting the issues on which they are lobbying. Because what charities lobby on is so narrow and self-evident, we don't think it would be of value to have charities on this particular register.

There are some practical issues for charities that it is important to consider. We anticipate that about £3 billion of charitable income is going to be reduced between now and the end of the next Parliament because of reductions in public spending, and a large majority of charities are very small organisations. We are concerned about a regulatory burden, both in terms of what that might mean for the time people have to spend, and in terms of costs. So, it would need to be proportionate if charities were to be involved. There is another issue, which is that quite a lot of small organisations, small charities, are nervous about taking on any kind of activity in influencing policy, and we would not want them to be deterred from doing that, in the sense that this is seen as another obstacle for their engagement, particularly small local charities.

Mrs Laing: Thank you very much.

Q281 Simon Hart: At last, I think, we have got suddenly to where I hoped we would get, which is to talk about "what" rather than "who". It seems to me that we have spent quite a lot of the evidence session talking about who might qualify rather than what might qualify. Surely—and I would be interested in your view on this—you can have good corporate lobbyists and bad charitable lobbyists. Do you agree?

Nigel Stanley: It depends whether you mean good as in effective, or good as in moral. Which do you mean?

Simon Hart: Well, to be good I think you need to be moral. I should have clarified that.

Nigel Stanley: I think that is right. In any democracy it is entirely legitimate for anyone to put forward their views. It is legitimate for them to seek advice on how best to put forward those views, and I don't think you can object to that. One can be a bit worried that one side of the argument may have more access to that kind of good advice, which may make it harder for politicians to hear both sides of an argument properly; but there is certainly nothing fundamentally immoral about anyone attempting to influence decision making in a pluralist democracy.

Ben Kernighan: I think my answer to that would be that to be a charity in law you have to be working for the public benefit. In order to be a charity, most of your activity also has to be around providing services. You can, from time to time and to varying degrees, lobby on the basis of the knowledge that you get from the provision of those services. Most of the time you will be accountable to an unpaid group of trustees and that group of trustees, by law, has to ensure that the activities of that organisation are for the public benefit and consistent with their charitable objectives. So, I think there are a range of reasons there, which means that more often than not lobbying activity within charities will be for the good. I agree with you, of course, that in theory at least there will be good and bad lobbyists in a variety of different sectors. That is also why we are not making the general case that charities should not be subject to good practice in terms of lobbying—something this consultation misses out—or indeed in terms of transparency more generally. I am making the case that for the proposed register, there wouldn't be value because so little information is required and because the public generally are aware of what it is that charities are lobbying on, because they are only allowed to lobby on their charitable objectives.

Q282 Simon Hart: I'm not sure I am any clearer, because surely the whole purpose of us having this inquiry and of the introduction of the register in the first place is to deal with a problem, either existing or potential, in a proportionate manner. But so far—and you must be the sixth or seventh group of witnesses we have had here—nobody has been able to put their finger on precisely what the problem is, existing or potential. Given what you have just told us, unless we can identify the problem, should we be doing this at all? We can make the argument—which I happen to support—that this is a complete waste of time and we shouldn't be doing it, or that it has to be much more of an all-encompassing proposal that deals with a problem that we can all clearly identify, and which there is evidence to suggest exists in the first place. There is a lot of strong feeling about it, there is a lot of anecdote, but nobody has actually sat where you are and said, "This is the problem". When I have asked the question of previous witnesses, "What was David Cameron meaning when he said lobbying is the next big scandal?" nobody, but nobody, has been able to answer the question. So I am optimistically hoping that perhaps that drought of answers is about to come to an end. Perhaps you can help us.

Ben Kernighan: It would seem sensible to ask David Cameron what he—

Simon Hart: Unfortunately, he has not come before the Committee but I would very much like him to. We have to settle for the Deputy Prime Minister here.

Ben Kernighan: He is obviously subject to a great deal more lobbying than I am, so he will have an insight that I do not have. What we know is that the level of public trust in the political system has taken a dive over recent years, for a number of different reasons. There is a public perception that part of that is to do with the extent to which there isn't a sense of fairness regarding who influences that political process. To be clearer about who is influencing that process and on what issues, and to have enshrined some good practice around what good lobbying activity is, could go some way to increasing both public trust in and public understanding of the political process. I agree with you that what is proposed—which doesn't make many requirements and doesn't, for example, put in a code of good practice or require people to say on which issues they are lobbying—would not achieve a great deal. So I have some sympathy with your view that either more needs to be done, or that to do this amount, on a cost-benefit analysis of cost/regulatory burden versus benefits, may not achieve that end.

Nigel Stanley: What is the precise problem? I think there is a narrow but real problem about the transparency around professional third-party, paid-for lobbyists, whether they are public affairs companies, lawyers or whatever. I think there is insufficient disclosure about who their clients are and what issues they are seeking to raise. Having that in the public domain—

Q283 Simon Hart: Disclosure to whom?

Nigel Stanley: To the public, the electors, and sometimes perhaps even those being lobbied, who may not be quite aware of the full agenda. So, there is a strong argument for a degree of openness. Going beyond that gets you into fantastically difficult areas where there are genuine issues of debate but they are rather different, which goes back to my point about the hammer and the screw. I think there is an argument for what I rather suspect was the first draft of the consultation paper, which concerned paid-for lobbyists. One can go through the detail and argue it in various ways, but there is an issue there. Trying to bring these other things into this exercise is a mistake. That is another series of debates and we might have proposals on that, but I am not sure that this is the best place to capture those.

Q284 Simon Hart: I have one further question, which deals slightly more precisely with charities, and particularly arm's-length lobbying as opposed to third-party lobbying, if there is a difference. We touched in earlier evidence sessions on the manner in which some lobbyists and some charities work, which is to provide the information and the ammunition to facilitate its members to undertake the lobbying. One rather good example, which I am keen on, is, oddly enough, the Women's Institute who undertook a very effective lobbying campaign on food labelling, which was organised at a constituency level. As I have indicated, I am very happy and keen to be lobbied by as many different people as possible and I have never been conned by a paid-for lobbyist into not understanding where he came from or what he was trying to do. But I think it would be a mistake to think that charities can't be extremely aggressive, and often very effective and penetrative, lobbyists. I personally have met many, and full marks to them for being so effective. But in those circumstances, do they fit into the lobbying model we are looking at, as I suspect they don't, given what you have told us so far? If they do, who is the lobbyist? Is it the member who comes to a Friday afternoon surgery in one of our constituencies; is it the person behind them who is providing them the information and the technique to be as effective as they possibly can; or who? Again, if you cannot answer that, would these people appear on a register anyway? Should they?

Ben Kernighan: Clearly, you could not register the members of even the major charities because you would have a register of most of the population of the United Kingdom. There are major charities that have millions of members who at certain points may get engaged in some kind of activity in terms of trying to influence. If there was to be a register, you would have to have some way of defining a lobbyist as somebody who perhaps spent most of their time on lobbying activity. It would be impractical for each member of the Women's Institute to be on such a register.

Simon Hart: Of course—which is my point, really. They are effective lobbyists, they are attempting to influence government through MPs—either members of government or backbenchers—and very good at it they are, too. They are, by my definition, lobbyists, but they should not be anywhere near a register; but that is just an opinion. Thank you.

Q285 Mr Chope: Do you both think that it would be better not to have any legislation than what is proposed in this consultation paper?

Nigel Stanley: I am not sure there is a well-thought-through proposal in the consultation paper that could be legislated. I think at its kernel is an idea about a register for third-party lobbyists, and one can discuss the detail but there is an argument for knowing that. Whether people fall for third-party lobbyists is a different question. I think people need to know what is going on. That is a transparency argument. Having a proposal that included trade unions but not employer associations, think-tanks but not campaign groups—I don't see how you could have that kind of legislation. In using the kind of rather loose language there at the moment, it is not legislatable. It is a very hypothetical question, because I don't think you could even draft legislation with that in.

Ben Kernighan: A better solution than the one proposed would be to have a register that makes it clear who was lobbying whom on what and put in place a code of good practice. I think I am neutral on whether or not the proposal as it is is better than nothing, but I am very clear that with the proposal as it is there would not be an added benefit to either charities or the public if charities were engaged with it.

Q286 Mr Chope: Underlying all this is alleged to be public disillusionment. There was quite a lot of public disillusionment in my constituency during the lifetime of the previous Government when, in the same way as I have to explain now that the Government is constrained by the coalition agreement, I then had to explain that the Government was constrained by what was called the Warwick Agreement. Mr Stanley, I wondered if you could tell us how the Warwick Agreement came about, whether there was transparent lobbying in advance of it and so on?

Nigel Stanley: I am not sure I can provide the insight that you want, because this was a process within the Labour Party and the TUC is not affiliated to the Labour Party and most of our unions are not. I know many people in the trade union movement who would have a diametrically opposite view of the last Government—who would have said they were terrified of doing quite common-sense, practical things because they were so terrified of being tagged as being in the pocket of the trade unions. There is more than one way to look at that particular relationship.

Q287 Mr Chope: Do you think that there was a problem about the Warwick Agreement yourself?

Nigel Stanley: I think political parties should be free to have whatever policymaking mechanisms they wish.

Q288 Mr Chope: But this was not a question of a political party. This was a group outside politics, of trade unionists who were funders of the Labour Party, basically making their continued funding and support conditional upon the Government of the day, the elected Government, pursuing particular political policies.

Nigel Stanley: I wouldn't agree with your characterisation that it was some way outside the Labour Party. As I understand it, although I wasn't there and am not an expert, what happened at Warwick was a meeting of Labour's national policy forum within the party's democratic structures. I think that it would be a dangerous road to go down to start legislating for the internal democratic structures of political parties.

Q289 Mr Chope: So you do not think that what happened at Warwick would be a cause for public disillusionment, or sufficient cause to want to have legislation and more regulation?

Nigel Stanley: I think it is probably one of the reasons why you are a member of the party you are, and why people vote for you rather than for some of the other people around this. It is in the public domain, people have that information, and they know about it before they go to the ballot box. I am very happy that those issues are decided by the people when they go to cast their votes.

Q290 Mr Chope: I think we are probably in agreement on this: less regulation, more transparency and leave people to judge on the basis of what they see as to where they wish to put their support in political elections?

Nigel Stanley: I think sometimes you need regulation to secure transparency, but I think the objective of all of this is to secure transparency.

Q291 Mr Chope: You do not think the way this draft is going is the right direction?

Nigel Stanley: I think I have already explained why.

Q292 Chair: Are political parties lobbying organisations?

Nigel Stanley: It depends how you define lobbying, is the only answer to that, but I think it does go to some of the problems. Am I lobbying you this morning? That is an interesting question; I will leave you to decide that one.

Q293 Chair: So it is possible that political parties may have to be registered under the current proposals if the definition was broadened?

Nigel Stanley: It is possible, although of course you could argue, just as unions are registered by the

Certification Officer and charities are regulated by the Charity Commission, so political parties are highly regulated and have to declare all their sources of income. I think that is right. That is an example of where you did need regulatory or legal changes to secure transparency, and I think that is a good thing. But adding political parties to provide exactly that information again in a different register strikes me as a bit bizarre, given they will all be available in your internet browser.

Q294 Paul Flynn: Your presence here this morning is proof that the lobbying industry has been very successful in lobbying to ensure that this issue has not become one concentrated on corporate lobbying but is spread as wide as possible to make the future register as shallow as possible. You were not invited to the previous inquiry, either of you, because the previous inquiry never thought for one moment you were the problem. Do you think that when the Prime Minister talked about the future scandal, he had your union or your charities in mind as causing that scandal? If he didn't, what did he have in mind?
Nigel Stanley: Like Ben, I would not claim to have any special insight into the Prime Minister's mind. I think that he may—and this is a guess—have been using the word "lobbying" to talk about corporate relationships. You could say that News International was a fantastically successful organisation in lobbying ministers of all parties. They didn't do it through corporate lobbyists; they didn't need to. They seemed to have their own office in Downing Street for at least some of the time. So there is an issue around that—that excessively close relationship between politicians and one narrow commercial interest. That is rather different from the wider concern. But to answer your first question, you are right, and of course the lobbying industry does employ an enormous number of smart people, and one should only admire their ability to have broadened this debate into these fields.
Ben Kernighan: I am pretty confident that most politicians and most of the public would not see charitable lobbying as being a major cause of the problem. The evidence for that is the very high levels of public trust and confidence that exists in charities, and indeed the public nature of a lot of their lobbying. So the public know that we do it and generally the public are happy that we do it. I don't leap from that to saying therefore that there shouldn't be any more transparency in what we do under any circumstances, but I do say you have to think about which circumstances. It has to be proportionate and must not affect small charities in an unhelpful way. It has to add to what the public already know and understand about charities.

Q295 Paul Flynn: Would you accept that the lobbying industry was shocked by the previous report by the Public Administration Committee that called for a much stronger register than they were expecting? They now look at the present Government and decide how they can weaken any future lobbyists, so they pick on cuddly charities to be involved—nobody wants to be beastly to them—and appeal to the erogenous zones of the Conservative Party on trade unions, because the Government and Conservative MPs find it almost irresistible to take an opportunity to give the trade union movement a kicking. But by dragging this into the wider group, do you think that this is the strategy of the lobbying industry, as presented by them in a unified form: "Let's not concentrate on the corporate lobbyists who were involved in previous scandals, but let's apply it to everybody so we can't have stricter regulation"? Isn't that what is behind all this and why you are here?
Nigel Stanley: I think the waters have become rather muddied. You have at this table different yet in some ways similar organisations, in as much as I think people know what we do. They may agree or disagree with us based on what we do, but there is nothing secret about us. Making us be more transparent about what we are already highly transparent about achieves very little. However, the more secretive world of professional lobbying—in which there are many perfectly good ethical performers, but there is a degree of secrecy—seems to me a much more valuable subject for investigation and transparency.

Q296 Paul Flynn: Mr Kernighan, I think we all accept the benign nature of the mass of charitable organisations, but do you accept that there are lobbying wolves in charitable sheep's clothing that are active in trying to corrupt the nature of charities?
Ben Kernighan: There are more than 100,000 charities.

Q297 Paul Flynn: Would it be helpful if I gave an example of one? The Depression Alliance was set up in 1990 in order to publicise depression as an illness. It may be very successful, but 300% more people take time off for depression than ever before. It was set up ostensibly as a charity, as a patients' association, but was in fact 100% funded by pharmaceutical organisations selling antidepressants. There are many other examples of lobbyists cleverly using the sheep's clothing of charities in order to disguise what is a crude commercial aim to sell their products.
Ben Kernighan: The way charitable law is set up means that charities can only act, by law, if it is for the public benefit and they can only lobby on issues related to that. If there are abuses of that process, there is a regulator in place. I would be open to considering other ways in which any abuses should be dealt with, but I am not clear that the current proposals would help solve the problem that you are suggesting, which, I would also say, in the scale of the more than 100,000 charities, is a small problem.

Q298 Paul Flynn: If you take the activities of charities in this building, where there is an investigation going on into all-party groups—virtually every illness has its own all-party group, and many of these have services provided by the pharmaceutical organisations, which provide remedies for the illness in question—is this a matter of concern to you? Is this a way of lobbying that, although ostensibly charitable, is really deeply commercial and should be considered as an area the register should cover?
Ben Kernighan: I think most charities think very carefully about where they accept money from, the

strings attached to those resources and the expectations that funders have. Charities are usually careful in terms of the strings that can come from rich individuals, from government or from companies. But it is their job, and I think they mostly do a good job in ensuring that their activities are for their charitable purpose and that they act independently.

Q299 Paul Flynn: As two people who have studied the evidence of the witnesses coming before this Committee, do you think it is the duty of the Committee to look beyond the evidence as presented by professional persuaders? The people who come before us actually train people on how to give evidence. Should we look beyond that, as the previous Committee did, and ensure that their conclusions are based not so much on the evidence provided by those who have a vested interest in selling their own case but, in the words of the past Prime Minister, recognise that there is a paramount need to restore the reputation of Parliament and to avoid the potential great scandal that David Cameron envisaged in opposition?
Ben Kernighan: Absolutely, yes. Lobbyists are one stakeholder in relation to this consultation but the public is an important other stakeholder.
Nigel Stanley: I think there is an important point about the reputation of politics and democracy, although I think the responsibility lies primarily with politicians to restore faith in politics. I come back to my point that trying to regulate or register everyone who seeks to influence politicians, ministers or special advisors is really quite hard to do, although one should have more transparency around all the people trying to do it in various ways, using different routes perhaps. But the prime responsibility is with the politicians to behave properly, to ensure that they seek views on all sides of an argument when they are taking decisions, and to be open about the contacts they receive, rather than having random slots for official meetings that are subject to freedom of information requests and declarations, and for private or personal meetings where the same things can be discussed, but which are not subject to that. That leads to a lack of trust and people seeing conspiracies even when there aren't any.

Q300 Paul Flynn: Just a final question, Mr Stanley. You said, quite fairly, that if you are going to be regulated, so should the employers associations, and that then, the register becomes fantastically difficult. Don't you think that introducing complexity is the aim of the lobbyists, making it as complex and impossible to regulate as possible, so that they can't come up with a strong register that is targeted on the real problem: the corporate lobbyist? Isn't that precisely what the lobbying industry has done in this instrument to defend their bad practices?
Nigel Stanley: I think I have already answered that question by saying, essentially, yes. There is a particular issue around third-party, paid-for lobbyists that a register would help illuminate. I think there are a whole set of other agenda items but they are not best caught with that register.
Paul Flynn: Thank you.

Q301 Chair: Nigel and Ben, we had Tamasin Cave here from the Alliance for Lobbying Transparency and she told us that there was a massive disparity in the financial resources that various lobbyists can bring to bear. What is your view on the importance and centrality of financial disclosure in any register of lobbyists?
Nigel Stanley: I think it is important, because seeing how much money is being spent—without necessarily getting down into the precise details, but in broad bands—does provide some sense of what resources are going into the influencing process.
Ben Kernighan: I agree with that. As I understand it, the United States has a model—clearly, there is some complexity involved—in which people are asked roughly to assess the level of resources.
Chair: Ben, Nigel, thank you very much for your time this morning; it was a very enlightening session. Thank you so much.

Examination of Witness

Witness: **John Wotton,** President of the Law Society, gave evidence.

Q302 Chair: We now have Mr John Wotton, President of the Law Society. Welcome, John. Thank you for joining us this morning. You know we are inquiring into lobbying. We are coming, hopefully, towards the end of our inquiry and you are one of the last witnesses that we are going to see. Would you like to make an opening statement?
John Wotton: If I may, just briefly. First of all, thank you very much for inviting me to give evidence to the Committee this morning. The Law Society, as you will be aware, is the professional body for the solicitors in England and Wales, who number about 150,000 at present. It is, in a sense, a representative body rather than a regulatory body, as the regulatory function is delegated under the Legal Services Act to a separate board: the Solicitors Regulation Authority. The Law Society is very supportive of the principle of transparency in lobbying. We recognise that, as a professional body representing our members, we are from time to time a lobbying organisation ourselves, a responsibility we take quite seriously as law reform is really at the heart of the Law Society's mission.
We have considerable experience of the development of lobbying registers from the European Transparency Initiative, in which we have engaged very actively from an early stage. The Law Society is registered as an interest representative under that register in its role as the professional body. We have also engaged in quite detailed discussions with the European institutions on the definition of lobbying specifically in the context of legal advisors. The scope of the European Transparency Initiative, and indeed the potential scope of the Government's proposals on lobbying, would extend to lobbying government

departments as well as Parliament, and potentially even a wider class of people. In many cases, therefore, it could extend to interactions between individuals—whether people or corporations—and government departments in their capacity as people engaged in the administrative process, whether themselves applying for a decision or on the receiving end of an investigation or other inquiry. I don't think the role of legal advisors in that process is normally regarded as lobbying. For that reason we have had discussions with the European institutions, which have led, I think, to a fairly well-crafted exclusion for legal advice and representation, designed to particular processes and structures in Europe. One of our core points in relation to the Government's proposals is that some similar exclusion would be appropriate in any register that was contemplated for this jurisdiction.

Another distinction we regard as quite important is whether the register is voluntary or statutory. A voluntary register presents a number of difficulties. One is the more general point that if it is voluntary, it would be possible for people to engage lobbyists who are not on the register and so bypass the transparency process. The other is that, quite rightly, legal professional privilege and the duty of client confidentiality binds a lawyer and the only basis on which that confidentiality can be breached is with the express consent of the client. That makes it quite difficult to deal with the European Transparency Initiative voluntary provisions. If the register were statutory, then, with proper notification to the client, the duty to disclose would, in certain circumstances, override the duty of confidentiality and make it possible for the purposes of the register to be achieved if any activity in which lawyers were engaged strayed into the area of lobbying.

Lobbying has not become a very big activity as such for lawyers in this country. Very few law firms have identified a specific public affairs or lobbying activity. Most of their activity—if it could be described as lobbying—would at most be incidental to their role as legal advisors and representatives in proceedings.

That is all I want to say by way of introduction, if I may, but thank you.

Q303 Fabian Hamilton: Mr Wotton, welcome. The Government's consultation paper claims that their aim is to increase the information available about lobbyists without unduly restricting lobbyists' freedom. Do you think that the current proposals for a statutory register of lobbyists will achieve the Government's aim?

John Wotton: I think they can do so because they are designed to make transparent the capacity in which a lobbyist is lobbying, whether on their own behalf or on behalf of an identified client, and I think that is a very important distinction. If an organisation is lobbying on its own behalf then it is transparent to all—the institution and the public—who they are and what they are about. It is only where there is a client involved that there is an additional need for transparency.

Q304 Fabian Hamilton: Notwithstanding what you said in your opening remarks, the Law Society has historically been against the idea of a voluntary register of lobbyists. In your written evidence you state that a statutory register would appear to level the playing field. Can you add to the comments you made earlier as to why you think a statutory register would be preferable? You made some very important points and I wonder if you could add to that.

John Wotton: Yes. The key public interest point is that unless the register is statutory, it is difficult to see how it can become observed universally unless there are other non-statutory and non-transparent sanctions for not registering. One of the unsatisfactory aspects, for example, of the voluntary register in Europe is the spoken or unspoken threat that parliamentarians or officials will not speak to you unless you are on the register, even in matters where properly, in the interests of the client, they should do so. That is not the sort of process—it is not transparent and it is not fair, whereas a statutory register should avoid that. I don't think it is special pleading in relation to lawyers, though, to say that the statutory register provides a more practical solution to balancing the duty of confidentiality with the public interest in disclosure than any voluntary arrangement could do.

Q305 Fabian Hamilton: Do you think that charities, therefore, trade unions—we have just heard from them—and law firms, obviously, should be on that statutory register of lobbyists?

John Wotton: You mention three quite different categories. A trade union is an example of a representative body where it is clear for whom they are engaging in lobbying activity—for their members. It seems to me there is no great difference in principle between a trade union and a professional body like the Law Society or the Institute of Chartered Accountants in England and Wales, or indeed a trade association representing an identified group of companies. I am not sure that I would understand a logic that said that trade unions should be exempt whereas professional associations should not. So that would be one question.

I don't claim any great expertise on charities, to be honest. I would have thought that if a law firm is retained by a charity, whether on a pro bono or a paid-for basis, the interest of transparency is broadly the same. If it were thought that there should be, in terms of greater accessibility, an exemption for pro bono arrangements on behalf of charities, I doubt whether that would seriously undermine the public interest. But, as I say, I claim no special expertise in that area.

Q306 Fabian Hamilton: I suppose the difference here, and it may be a false difference, is between lobbyists who carry out lobbying for private gain—for the profit of the lobbying organisation—and those trying to do it for the public good: Greenpeace, Friends of the Earth, Amnesty, for example, charities that just want to promote a better environment or fairness and justice in parts of the world. They are not doing it to make a profit. They are not doing it for shareholders. They are doing it because they believe they want the world to be a better place, through their lobbying of parliamentarians. Is that a false difference, or is it all the same thing?

John Wotton: I don't see it as a difference. As you put it, it seems to me part of the principle, which I think is rightly identified in the Government's Green Paper, that where organisations are lobbying on their own behalf, they should not have to register. It is fairly clear who charities like Greenpeace or Save the Children are, and I don't think any public purpose would be served in placing them on the register. On the other hand, if they retain a lobbying organisation, presumably it is just as important that Parliament, government and the public should know that that organisation is representing Greenpeace or Save the Children as it is that it is representing Unilever or ICI or whatever.

Q307 Fabian Hamilton: Surely the important thing is that parliamentarians know that that third-party organisation is representing those other organisations, rather than whether they are doing it pro bono or not. Is that relevant, the pro bono aspect? For example, if a law firm had a passion about the environment, justice abroad or prisoners and it was happy to represent Amnesty for the public good and for the good of people who were being perhaps tortured in jails abroad, but it didn't want to charge a penny because it felt it was a public benefit, is that different from that same firm taking on a client for profit? Should there be a distinction there?

John Wotton: I am not convinced there should. In professional terms, the client is still a client whether the engagement is pro bono or for reward, and the professional duties to the client are the same. The interest on the part of government or Parliament, or indeed the public, in knowing on whose behalf this law firm is acting is probably just the same whether it is pro bono or paid for. I think it most unlikely that such activity would be concealed, though. Generally, a law firm engaged in socially responsible pro bono work, as long as the client permits it, would wish it to be known.

Fabian Hamilton: Yes, absolutely. Thank you. That is very helpful.

Q308 Mr Chope: Can I extend your argument about the need for confidentiality? What about newspapers? A lot of newspapers have undisclosed agendas on particular campaigns. How do you think they could be brought into this net, or do you think they should be?

John Wotton: It is a very interesting question and not one that I have ever considered, and again I claim no particular expertise on the press and media as such. For a news medium, it is at the heart of the agenda—and a requirement, of course, for broadcasting media—that they be impartial, so they shouldn't be carrying a torch. Equally, broadcasters and newspaper proprietors are commercial organisations that may engage in lobbying in pursuit of commercial interests, just in the same way as any other commercial, industrial or financial company might do. I am not sure that I see a need for any very different treatment. If a media organisation is on a campaign, it is generally fairly clear that it is on a campaign and its editorial content will make that clear. That does seem to me rather different from lobbying, though. It seems to me to be part of the fundamental role of the press.

Q309 Mr Chope: But it may be that the campaign is encouraged by the fact that one of the people on behalf of whom they are campaigning is giving them a lot of advertising revenue, editorial content or help in some way. How does that differ from the situation you are describing with your clients? You are saying you have to have a statutory register, because otherwise you wouldn't be able to disclose on behalf of your clients that you are lobbying on behalf of those specific clients.

John Wotton: This is trespassing rather close to Leveson territory that it's probably not appropriate to go into. But if a law firm is advising a newspaper, then I can't see that there is any difference in terms of the duty of confidentiality, the right to legal professional privilege or the public interest, as compared with any other client, whatever their interests. If a firm is advising on a lobbying campaign, the same level of transparency should be required whoever the client is lobbying for.

Q310 Mr Chope: So the Law Society thinks it would be a worthwhile exercise having such a register, provided it was a statutory register?

John Wotton: I think so, provided it is a statutory register, provided that the area of legal advice and representation in proceedings, decision making and so forth is carved out and provided the level of representation is appropriate. Perhaps a pragmatic approach to not just law firms but to all organisations where lobbying is only incidental to their other activities should also be looked at. One might envisage a situation in which a client who wishes to produce a paper to lobby Parliament or government asks for legal advice on all or part of the content, which might be provided as legal advice. The legal advisor would have no hands-on involvement in the lobbying process. If they entered or took part in any meetings, they would be doing so quite transparently as a representative of the client in just the same way as if the client used their in-house lawyers for that advice. Under the current proposals, that would be regarded as lobbying in your own interests and not requiring specific registration. As we said in our initial evidence—I must emphasise that we have not yet responded to the Government Green Paper; we are still formulating our thoughts—there may be some scope for a de minimis or incidental lobbying type of exemption.

Q311 Mr Chope: Say we are about to discuss the Finance Bill in Committee. You are a firm of solicitors; you have a big client with global interests; you want to lobby on particular parts of the Finance Bill, perhaps dealing with exploration and the tax regime or something else. How do you see this working? Do you think that when you write your letter to the Treasury saying how you would like to see these provisions tweaked in a particular way, you should say, "By the way, I am writing on behalf of"—whatever large oil company is the client? How do you see that working?

John Wotton: I do see it working normally, rather in the way you have described. I don't think a law firm would normally write a paper to Government where it was putting a case on behalf of a particular client without disclosing that to the recipient. Normally speaking, one is engaged in a transparent capacity as legal advisor and representative. Occasionally a law firm may put in their own representation but then they would make it clear that those are their own views and not those of their clients. The professional ethical standards and code under which solicitors and barristers operate contain general principles that would certainly mean that any misleading of government or Parliament as to the capacity in which representations were being made would not be regarded as good professional conduct.

Q312 Mr Chope: I am not suggesting you would be misleading. Have you, in preparing your response, worked out what definition of lobbying you think is best?
John Wotton: No. We are still in the process of that exercise, but we do think that aspects of the UKPAC definition are perhaps unduly broad and that an exemption for legal advice would be helpful, just in the interests of clarity.

Q313 Mrs Laing: I don't think I really have to declare an interest but, erring on the side of being careful, I should declare that once upon a time I was a member of the Law Society of Scotland but have not been for many years. I have not paid a subscription for many years, either; nor, as I keep on telling my constituents, do I carry professional indemnity insurance and I can't give them advice. Mr Wotton will understand that if nobody else does.
John Wotton: Particularly in the case of your world, if I may say so.
Mrs Laing: I was interested in what you said in your opening remarks—that lobbying is incidental to the work of your members. I was trying to think if there are any obvious examples of the way in which your members might become involved in what might be deemed as lobbying, and where the fine line can be drawn between acting on behalf of or giving advice to clients, and lobbying on their behalf. If a firm has been advising a client, or indeed putting the client's case in law, at what point does it become lobbying if the firm is then making the client's case to government, let us say? If that is not an easy question to answer, then that itself is an answer.
John Wotton: Yes. I think there are principles that would guide one towards an answer. Where one is assisting the client in the client's interactions with the decision maker, which may be an investigating body or a licence-granting body or whatever, then I think that is clearly not within lobbying activity. That is the legal advice and representation area. When one moves into the area of seeking to influence other parties or the legislative process, then that is probably within the area of lobbying. So in the case of a law firm that has a significant activity, let us say, in advising clients on lobbying Parliament on legislation, I think that is lobbying in principle. It might be regarded as outside the definition if it were all done in the back room—providing legal advice to the organisation that then represented itself in all dealings with Parliament.

Q314 Mrs Laing: Thank you. I can think of an example that concerns an accountancy firm, but I think it is the same principle as a law firm, where a large company is advising a professional body on a matter of tax and VAT. There was a point where the company was representing the professional body in writing on an appeal against VAT and so on. But now the professional body has decided to put the case to government that the law in this area should be changed, and therefore the accountancy firm is now seeking, on behalf of its client, to change the law. Would you say that that goes over the line, the grey area?
John Wotton: I think the case you describe has the potential to fall within a sensible definition of lobbying, yes. If there were a statutory lobbying register, I anticipate that the Law Society would register and if its tax law committee, let us say, had proposals on law reform to make they would be put forward within the scope of that registration.
That reminds me of a point I did wish to make, and that is the practicality of identifying the individuals within an organisation who would be identified in the registration. If the registration extended to professional bodies, I think that would be pretty cumbersome, because a professional body like the Law Society has views on law reform across an extraordinary range—from legal aid at the one end to company and tax law and international law at the other. In order to be effectively representative of the wider profession, of course we endeavour to engage as many of our members as possible in that activity. I think it would be unfortunate to be constrained to certain named individuals in any lobbying activity that we were to take part in. I don't think that would be in the interests of the legislative process.

Q315 Mrs Laing: Likewise, when the matter is examined from that angle, at what point would there be a conflict between preserving client confidentiality and privilege, and an obligation for disclosure in a statutory register?
John Wotton: If the professional body is making representations in what its members believe to be the public interest then there is no client, as it were, and no duty of confidentiality arises. The professional body would not normally be acting as a legal advisor to any individual member or firm, so again that issue would not arise. But if a law firm is putting forward a paper or a submission, I think it should be clear in what capacity it is doing so. If it is in fact acting on behalf of a client, I would have thought that the principle of transparency requires the identity of the client to be disclosed.

Q316 Mrs Laing: That is encouraging. Taking that further, you would not then have a problem with a statutory register?
John Wotton: No. I think the statutory register is potentially practical for lawyers, because a statutory duty of disclosure in the circumstances—probably quite limited—in which it applies to a law firm's activity would override the duty of confidentiality. There might well be a duty imposed on the law firm to make the client aware before instructions were

taken that there were circumstances in which the statute would require disclosure if lobbying, as defined, were undertaken, but I think that is how it would work. At the moment, we have had to produce a very cumbersome practice note to deal with the European Transparency Initiative, which involves obtaining the consent of every client for whom one has done or may do lobbying work to the disclosure of their identity and the turnover that one has had on lobbying work with that client over the past year before the registration can be made.

Q317 Mrs Laing: You have already had this?
John Wotton: Yes.

Q318 Mrs Laing: Winding back for one minute, to whom is this disclosure made? I am sorry, this is just my not having—
John Wotton: That then goes on the public register maintained by the European Commission and Parliament.

Q319 Mrs Laing: Right. So, to a great extent your members are already dealing with the sort of registration that would be required?
John Wotton: I would say to quite a limited extent, because the number of law firms that have registered under the European Transparency Initiative is very low, reflecting the fact that most lawyers take the view that the work they are doing in Brussels is legal advice and representation rather than lobbying. But of course, one has to reach that conclusion based on the terms of the joint agreement between Parliament and the Commission in which the definition of lobbying is set out and the quite detailed exemption for legal advice in proceedings is contained.

Q320 Mrs Laing: Could the experience of the operation of that system at present shed any light on what ought to happen in the UK in future?
John Wotton: Yes, I think so, particularly on the specific aspect of defining the boundary between lobbying and legal advice.

Q321 Mrs Laing: I was concerned that the boundary between lobbying and legal advice would be too much of a grey area and would be very difficult to define, but you are putting my mind at rest to a very great extent. You consider that it can be defined?
John Wotton: I think a proper area can be carved out that is legal advice and representation as properly understood, and not lobbying, yes.
Mrs Laing: Thank you very much.

Q322 Andrew Griffiths: Can we go back to that discussion you were having about the European register and the fact that lots of law firms are not registering because they feel that the work they are doing is legal advice and not lobbying? Do you think that is a deliberate interpretation? Do you think that those firms are choosing not to register as lobbyists because it is cumbersome, onerous and expensive, or because they just don't feel that they are undertaking any sort of lobbying activity?
John Wotton: I think they are taking the issue very seriously. Indeed, as chair of the Law Society's EU Law Committee before I became president, I was involved in very detailed and serious discussions with a number of law firms, particularly those who have a substantial presence in Brussels, over a number of years on how this matter should be dealt with. I know that they have all taken that issue very seriously indeed. The pattern is largely repeated around Europe that very few law firms from any of the member states have registered under the European Transparency Initiative, but by contrast almost all the bar associations and law societies around Europe have done so as interest representatives of their members.

Q323 Andrew Griffiths: Do you think there is anything we should learn from that process in relation to implementing a register in the UK?
John Wotton: Yes. I think that going beyond the identification of the client is probably not worth the effort. I know that for those organisations that have mixed businesses—in my experience, principally law firms who may do some lobbying work—identifying the lobbying turnover for particular clients is an awful waste of time and effort. Of course, if the business that is being carried on is not purely a lobbying activity, then there is no equation between the lobbying income from a particular client and the client's influence on the organisation or its contribution to its finance.

Q324 Andrew Griffiths: Can you tell us a little bit about the driver, the motivation, in Brussels for the implementation of the transparency register?
John Wotton: I think it was very similar to the motivation here—that it was important that the legislative footprint on European measures should be clear, and that officials, legislators, commissioners and the public should be aware of who was influencing the legislative process and in what capacity.

Q325 Andrew Griffiths: Could I just turn, if I may, to the statutory code as set out. We heard from Elizabeth France, the Chairman of the UK Public Affairs Council, and she suggested that a register without a code of conduct could lead to less regulation of lobbying activity. Could you tell us whether you think a requirement for all those who sign up to a statutory register to adhere to a code of conduct would be a workable suggestion?
John Wotton: I am not an expert on the lobbying industry at large. In relation to lawyers, and the same would go for barristers, I think that the detailed and principle-based professional code of ethics under which we operate should be a sufficient safeguard. I can see that it could well be useful if other lobbyists also had an appropriate code of conduct. I would not favour, though, a lobbying regulator. I think we are seeing some of the difficulties of having a number of regulators in the legal sector already. I think it works better to have an operation under the jurisdiction of one well-resourced and experienced regulator. In our case it would be the Solicitors Regulation Authority, which is a uniquely well-resourced regulator in the

legal field. I don't think that requiring lawyers who undertake lobbying activity also to subject themselves to regulation under a new code would serve any particular purpose.

Q326 Andrew Griffiths: Finally, do you have any information, any view, on the relative size of the companies engaged in that lobbying activity? Do they tend to be the larger firms or the smaller firms? The reason I ask is in case you have a view about the level at which fees should be set for registration, and whether that would impact on smaller or larger firms.
John Wotton: My impression is that they are quite a mix. I am not sure that any of them are large in terms of lobbying business themselves, but some are associated with larger groups involved in related activities. I am not sure that the level of fees should be set by reference to the size of the organisation that is the lobbyist. It seems to me desirable that, with proper transparency, decision makers and legislators should be as accessible as possible to those whose vital interests are affected by what they do. It would be unfortunate if fees were set at an unreasonably high level, either for those who are doing lobbying as a commercial activity or for those, such as you mentioned earlier, Mr Hamilton, who are doing it on a purely pro bono basis.

Q327 Fabian Hamilton: Mr Wotton, the USA's Lobbying Disclosure Act 1995 and the Canadian Lobbying Act 2008 require only those who spend more than 20% of their time engaged in lobbying activities to register. Do you think that a threshold of time spent on lobbying would be a workable way of defining those who need to register, or would it simply create a loophole to be exploited and drive up the costs of running a register?
John Wotton: I am not sure that is necessarily the right test. I can see that it would be cumbersome to administer from the point of view of the lobbying community, and cumbersome to administer from the point of view of the register. I think, though, having put forward the idea that there should be some de minimis or incidental exemption, it is incumbent on us to develop those thoughts in our response to the Green Paper, and we will. I am not at this point sure whether we will incline towards a quantitative or qualitative test of what is incidental. I am sorry I can't—

Q328 Fabian Hamilton: Presumably you do not know much about the workings of the Canadian and USA Acts?
John Wotton: No, I don't. We did make some reference to them in the course of the discussions on the ETI, but we didn't go into their operation in detail.
Chair: John, thank you so much for your time this morning. It has been very helpful.
John Wotton: Thank you very much, Chairman.
Chair: You have given us lots of food for thought. Members are getting ever more interested in this topic and I have a feeling we are going to produce quite an interesting report at the end of all of this. Thank you, John. It was good to see you today.

Thursday 26 April 2012

Members present:

Mr Graham Allen (Chair)

Mr Christopher Chope
Paul Flynn
Sheila Gilmore
Andrew Griffiths
Fabian Hamilton
Simon Hart
Tristram Hunt
Mrs Eleanor Laing
Mr Andrew Turner
Stephen Williams

Examination of Witnesses

Witnesses: **Dr Raj Chari**, Lecturer in Political Science, Trinity College Dublin, and Author, *Regulate Lobbying: A Global Comparison*, and **Rob McKinnon**, Who's Lobbying, gave evidence.

Q329 Chair: Rob and Raj, welcome to our Committee. As you know, we are in the middle of a long-running evidence-taking session on lobbying and we are looking forward to your contribution today. Would you like to begin by making an opening statement?

Rob McKinnon: Certainly.

Chair: Fire away, Rob.

Rob McKinnon: Thank you to the Committee for the opportunity for me to provide evidence. My name is Rob McKinnon. I run the Who's Lobbying project, which is a spare time experiment to collate publicly available data on lobbying and public affairs in the UK. Since September 2010, Who's Lobbying has run the website whoslobbying.com. Whoslobbying.com is a publicly searchable collection of information on organisations that have engaged in public affairs activity. Currently it has entries on the activity of over 9,000 organisations. Each organisation has a page on the website listing its government ministerial meetings, oral evidence given to Parliament, lobbying firms hired as disclosed on industry registers, Lords parliamentary passes, and a description of the organisation from their Wikipedia entry in the cases where there is one.

The public are able to filter this information by organisation categories derived from data at Wikipedia. For example, if you are interested in pharmaceutical companies or defence companies, there is a filter that lets you see the information in that sense. Over 3,000 organisations have been matched to a Wikipedia entry, which is where we derive this category information from.

Currently, it is the only attempt to provide a publicly searchable collection of this collated lobbying information. It collates data from government department reports, the Parliament website, industry registers and other public sources. Potentially, it could be one option for consideration as a delivery vehicle for a statutory register.

Motivations for the Who's Lobbying project include: to provide the public with easy access on the web to information about who is trying to influence government and public affairs, and on what issues. Another motivation is to inform the Government as to what information is and is not available, at a time when they are proposing to create a statutory register of lobbying activity, or at least of lobbyists. The third thing is to demonstrate to government how to put this type of information on the web in an easy-to-browse, consistent format for the public.

Just to note, Who's Lobbying is extremely disappointed that departments have not released the last seven months' worth of ministerial meeting reports. Departments last published meeting reports for the period July to September 2011. All ministers are in breach of the ministerial code May 2010 requirement that "Departments will publish, at least quarterly, details of ministers' external meetings".

Themes I hope we cover today are that transparency delayed is transparency denied. The case of the public having to wait up to nine months for departments to publish reports is a denial of transparency in a way. Another theme I hope we explore today is that incomplete transparency is also transparency denied, and I am sure we will explore those themes in more detail.

Q330 Chair: Thank you. Raj, would you like to say something to begin?

Dr Chari: Yes, thank you. Thank you very much for inviting me to the Committee today. I suppose I will tell you a little bit about myself. I am an Associate Professor at Trinity College in Dublin, although I was born and raised in Canada myself and spent a number of years living in Madrid, Spain working out of the Juan March Institute. The research that we have been doing—together with John Hogan and Gary Murphy, both out of Dublin as well—has been looking at the regulation of lobbying legislation throughout the world and trying to analyse it from a global comparative perspective. My research has been funded by the Irish Research Council.

I suppose it is important to say that, other than publishing our book, which we have done, we have given policy advice to different organisations, either at the domestic or intergovernmental level—including: the Czech Government, the Council of Europe, Venice Commission, as well as the Irish Government—in terms of bringing our experience of understanding legislation from other jurisdictions to policymakers, that experience of when they are drafting lobbying legislation. I am hoping that being here we will be able to give you some insights as to what the global trends in lobbying regulation are about.

I suppose it is important to note, right from the beginning, which jurisdictions in the world have lobbying rules in place. It basically started in the United States in the mid-1940s. Germany then pursued legislation in the early 1950s. The next iteration came with Canada in 1989. It is also important to note here that different countries, even though they introduce legislation at a certain time, also make amendments to the legislation after that. For example, in Canada legislation was first introduced in 1989, but there was a different amendment to it in 1995 as well as 2003 and 2008. Generally what happens is the countries make amendments, so that the legislation becomes more robust in terms of fostering transparency and accountability. After Canada, the European Parliament pursued legislation in 1996. Those were the forming ones in the century of 1900. Then after 2000 we see the number of countries that have pursued lobbying legislation actually double. That starts with Lithuania in 2000, Poland 2005 and Hungary in 2006. That was actually taken off the books when Fidesz came to power in 2011, so Hungary no longer has lobbying legislation. We also see other countries that have recently done it including Slovenia, Israel and France. I would be happy to talk about the experiences of those countries in general.

I note that our book is a co-authored book, and so I would be more up-to-date, up-to-speed and more knowledgeable of regulations that exist in Canada and the European Union, whereas my co-author, Gary Murphy, would be on the United States and John Hogan on Australia. I would be happy to talk about both of those jurisdictions, Canada and the European Union. However, by any definition, I am not an expert on British politics or developments in British politics, so I come with no particular agenda.

Chair: Thank you, Rob. Thank you, Raj. I ask Members to question now.

Q331 Paul Flynn: Good morning, gentlemen. I am sure the Committee will be very grateful for the work you have done, which will certainly enrich the report we produce. First of all, David Cameron memorably said, on 8 February 2010, that lobbying was the next great scandal. Do you think that the Government's proposals are ones that will avoid the scandal that has been predicted? Unless it has already happened of course, is this the answer to the worries that the Prime Minister has?

Dr Chari: Is lobbying regulation an answer to—

Paul Flynn: The Government's proposals before us, do you think they are going to make sure that we will not have major lobbying scandals in the future? Is that the answer? If not, what is?

Dr Chari: The proposals as they stand right now, again I am not an expert in British politics—

Chair: Could I ask colleagues to speak up just a little bit. The acoustics are not very good in here, I am sorry.

Dr Chari: I can answer that question, not from an expert in British politics perspective but from understanding it from a global comparative perspective of different regulations that exist elsewhere in the world. From that perspective, I suppose the proposals are quite narrow on different fronts. The lobbyists that are covered would be professional consultancies solely. For example, it does not include in-house lobbyists, in-house corporate lobbyists, trade associations, NGOs and other organisations as well, which most other legislations in the world would consider to be lobbyists. From that perspective it is slightly narrow, so you can have potential for scandal existing from lobbying from other than professional consultancies.

From what I understand of the proposal, the details that are required when you register are a lot less than required by other jurisdictions in the world, particularly the United States and Canada where you would have to give full details as to who you were lobbying, who the members of your organisation are, which ministries you want to lobby and how much money is being spent on your lobbying activity. That is related to a third point, I suppose, of a very narrow focus, by not focusing on spending disclosures within the proposals. It is unclear from the proposals how the independent regulation of this will actually take place. There doesn't seem to be a real independent regulatory authority, which is free from partisan interest, which will be able to hold the register. It is also wanting in terms of having specific rules for cooling off periods. So we know that politicians oftentimes go into the world of lobbying, after they are done with their political career, and with that they sometimes take inside information, which is beneficial to whichever lobbyist or organisation that they work for. As a result, in the medium- and high- regulated systems, most legislation would have a cooling off period of at least two and sometimes five years before politicians can go into the world of lobbying. So to answer the question succinctly, it is pretty narrow from a comparative perspective.

Rob McKinnon: If you consider what makes something a scandal—and I just tried to think of things that are common across the different events that have been publicised in the last several years—one thing that makes it a scandal is if it is non-disclosed, non-public information that is released after some form of activity has occurred. Often it is involving some allegation of privileged access or undue influence, and then also it is sometimes the nature of the activity or what is being lobbied on. As it stands, the Government's proposals do not include covering what issues are being lobbied on. I think that in itself will prevent the proposal from being able to help us perhaps prevent scandals of the nature we have seen. Lobbying is a very complicated area. As we have seen, a lot of the scandals involve relationships that you need to explain with a narrative rather than with data. I appreciate it is difficult to actually define what data needs to be collected in order to prevent these issues, but I am sure that my fellow panellist will be able to provide examples in other jurisdictions where they have been able to define more comprehensive data collection that would help prevent scandals.

Q332 Paul Flynn: "Transparency delayed is transparency denied", was the striking phrase you used. Have we seen a denial of transparency in the past two years? How has the situation changed?

Rob McKinnon: After the 2009 Public Administration Committee report into lobbying, the previous

Government promised that they would publish ministerial meetings. This was before the election. Several months later I went to look for these—they said they would publish them quarterly—they weren't there. I had to send an FOI request to every department. After the election it was a joy to see the ministerial code actually specify a requirement for departments to publish ministerial meetings quarterly, along with some other information.

In May 2010 they promised this requirement and several months later, in October, I was looking for these reports. They were not there and I had to send an FOI request again to every department. So it seems this theme is one of promising but not necessarily delivering. Just to give you an example—because sometimes it is a bit hard to visualise what we are talking about—Liam Fox resigned last year from a ministerial position. The department in which he was a Minister has still not released all of his meetings. We are still waiting for the last seven months of government meetings. This is an example of the denial of transparency, even when there has been a scandal, so I think the Government could be improving in that respect.

Q333 Paul Flynn: Are you happy with the workings of the ministerial code, since the independent adjudicator resigned at the time of the Liam Fox debate? He expressed unhappiness because he was not called in to adjudicate on it. A civil servant was brought in.

Rob McKinnon: I am not an expert in these matters, so I don't have an opinion on it.

Q334 Paul Flynn: Dr Chari, appreciating the differences in all groups of countries, could you point to one that you regard as a model in which we could frame an alternative proposal to the Government? Would it be Canada? We were going to take evidence from Canada. It is not going to happen now. We know they changed recently, but there is still unhappiness about the way it is working. Are things so much better in Europe? In the last Committee's report we went across to Brussels. We were very unimpressed by the embryonic system they had for the control of lobbyists there, which seemed to be just a free-for-all.

Dr Chari: I suppose the first point to note about the European Commission Register is that it is voluntary, which basically means that it is not mandatory. So if you want to register, you can—if you don't, you don't have to—and there is really no effective penalty for not registering. From that perspective, in terms of models to follow, if you are seeking a statutory register, where you have lobbyists having to register, that obviously would not be a model to follow. To contextualise my answer as to which model is the best, I can't answer that. What I can answer is that, in our research, we have tried to conceptualise three different types of regulatory environments that exist from a global comparative perspective. The first would be very low-regulatory environments, where basically not much information is required by the lobbyists when they register. There are really no spending disclosures that are ever made. There isn't a real independent regulatory authority that verifies or falsifies the information that is given, and generally speaking there is very limited public access to what details the lobbyist has given when they register. So you would find that, particularly in the European Commission, in the Parliament. You would also find that in Poland as well as Germany.

In the second step you have what we call "medium-regulated systems". In medium-regulated systems you would have a lot more information given by the lobbyists, with regard to the name, not only just the senior chief executive officer, if it is in-house corporate or the people in charge of the consultancy or the NGO, but the staff members that would be involved in lobbying activity as well, the issues that they are going to lobby in, which are the potential ministries they are going to lobby in and which are the specific bills they may be lobbying in.

In the case of Canada as well, you would have monthly updates being given if lobbyists meet, which are referred to as "designated public officeholders" who are senior members, including ministers and senior civil servants. Sometimes you would have audits and reviews of the information. But in these medium-regulated systems you wouldn't really have penalties that are given precisely because the rules are followed, as I am sure they are in Canada. I know there have been a couple of cases where they found that there could have been potential breaches, but mostly penalties aren't given. You will find those jurisdictions, particularly in the Canadian provinces and at the Canadian federal level. You would also find it in terms of the legislation in Lithuania, the old Hungarian legislation and the Australian legislation as well.

Then on the other extreme you have the high-regulated systems, where full information is given, penalties are enforced if there is a law broken, complete public access. What distinguishes the high-regulated systems from the medium or the low is that there are full spending disclosures given by the lobbyists.

Q335 Paul Flynn: Is there any objective evidence on which of these systems produce benefits that could be objectively measured?

Dr Chari: Yes. Look, from an objective point of view, as social scientists we have to think of things in terms of pros and cons of every system. In high-regulated systems the obvious pro that you would have is increased transparency as to who is lobbying whom, for which reasons and how much money is being spent on doing it.

The disadvantage is that you might have regulatory offices that are highly staffed, which could cost a lot of money to the state. Medium regulation, again, it provides much more information in terms of transparency for the public to see who is lobbying whom. But oftentimes you don't see very severe penalties that are being laid down by regulatory authorities. In low regulatory systems, it is there, it is window dressing. It looks good but its effectiveness, in terms of regulating lobbyists, can be considered wanting. So that doesn't particularly answer your question, but I guess when any political system is deciding which model to follow each comes with pros and cons.

Q336 Paul Flynn: I don't know if you gentlemen accept the Government's definition of lobbying as, "Those who undertake lobbying activities on behalf of a third party client or whose employees conduct lobbying activities on behalf of a third party client". Is this an appropriate definition?
Dr Chari: It is a narrow definition. With that definition, what you are basically focusing on is the activity of professional consultancies, public relations and public affairs firms. It does not include in-house corporates. It does not include trade associations, non-governmental organisations, different types of charities, religious organisations, and think-tanks. There are plenty of other lobbyists.
To put that into context, it is interesting that in looking at the registry data in the European Commission we tried to see which percentage of the registered lobbyists belong to the different categories. If you actually look at the percentage of the in-house lobbyists and trade associations that are registered, that would represent about 50% of all of those that are registered in the Commission's transparency registry. NGOs and think-tanks would represent about 30%, other religious organisations and academic organisations about 10%. Effectively now we know that the uptake of registering professional consultancies in the European Commission has been very low, for different reasons of confidentiality. I suppose the question would be: of all lobbyists that are in the UK, what percentage do professional consultancies represent? I don't know the specific data, but in other jurisdictions it would be around 10% to 15%, and that is a very small percentage of all lobbyists. So that is why it is a very narrow definition.

Q337 Paul Flynn: I should imagine you would agree with that, Mr McKinnon?
Rob McKinnon: Yes. I agree with people who have previously given evidence to this Committee that it is the activity that needs to be defined, and then anyone engaged in an activity should be included in the legislation as being required to register. I would go a step further and say it is actually the activity that should be registered and, as a consequence, you will eventually find other people performing that activity.
Just to provide some numbers that I have. In the Who's Lobbying database I have almost 8,000 meetings that were declared by departments. Of those, at present only 18 of those meeting included a lobbying firm. That is less than a quarter of a percent of all of the government meetings. In comparison, law firms have twice as many at 34 meetings, which is about 0.4% of government meetings. Organisations that are in Wikipedia's political and economic think-tank's category have had 163 declared meetings with government, which is about 2% of the meetings I have in my database. We can see that in comparison think-tanks have almost 10 times as many meetings with ministers. As we probably all know that is obviously a very small part of the activity that is performed by people who are lobbying. So these are really just indicative levels of activity.

Q338 Tristram Hunt: Does a meeting with a think-tank mean a speech at a think-tank event, because that is a rather different thing?
Rob McKinnon: That is a good point. Unfortunately, the level of information provided by department reports is fairly limited, so I could delve into those numbers and give you a breakdown, but in some cases it would require me making a judgement call. Another point perhaps I should make is the current Government meeting reports do not provide a date. They only provide the month of the meeting, so it makes it very hard to do further analysis.
Chair: Eleanor, did you want to follow up?

Q339 Mrs Laing: Basically, I didn't catch what you said. You said "10 times" but you did not say what. Ten times what? Could you just go over that again, sorry?
Rob McKinnon: Sure. Of the meetings I have in my database, which are derived from the government department reports, lobbying firms have been in 18 of those meetings and political and economic think-tanks have been mentioned in 163. So there are almost 10 times as many meetings that think-tanks have been referenced as being in the meeting as meetings where lobbying firms have been mentioned in the meeting.

Q340 Paul Flynn: A current theme that runs through our investigations is whether there is a need for a statutory code of conduct for lobbyists, based on the concern that self-regulation is often no regulation. What views do you have on that; is this necessary in a reform of the system?
Dr Chari: A code of conduct in terms of professional behaviour?
Paul Flynn: Yes, indeed.
Dr Chari: Yes. There are certain principles I think that are established in most legislation, which say that you can't give dishonest information to a public officeholder and that you have to be honest in what you do. However, it is very difficult to fine someone based on breaking a code, per se, because it could be somebody's interpretation based on another. I think where you do see prosecutions taking place within the legislation, particularly in Canada, is when there is misinformation that is given at the registration stage; for example, saying that you are going to lobby ministry X when effectively what you are doing is lobbying ministry Y. So, based on giving false information or incorrect or inaccurate information when you register, you can prosecute somebody on that. It is very difficult in terms of monitoring codes of conduct, though, to prosecute someone, I would have thought.

Q341 Paul Flynn: We are not seeking perfection on this. We are seeking improvement if we can. Mr McKinnon, do you go along with the view that a statutory code is going to be helpful to strengthen the regard that the public have for the political system?
Rob McKinnon: I am not an expert in these matters and I actually don't have an opinion on this issue.
Dr Chari: I would estimate that it would increase the faith in the political system in many ways. It would increase transparency, people would see what

lobbyists were doing, politicians can openly say they are speaking with lobbyists, and you can decrease an amount of cynicism within the general public, yes.

Q342 Paul Flynn: There was a defence given recently by someone who is a lobbyist for another country. His claim was that he was lobbying government and not Parliament and, as such, lobbying government should not be restricted in any way. Do you agree with this concept?
Rob McKinnon: What we are talking about is transparency of lobbying activities. I would imagine what would be important, in terms of legislation in this area, is whether that activity would be required to be registered. As I understand it, it would not be. So I think it is really for the public to decide whether that is a legitimate activity or not on behalf of this Member of the House of Lords. What would be important, in terms of the legislation, would be whether that activity is actually recorded in a publicly accessible place.

Q343 Paul Flynn: Some evidence we have had has drawn attention to activities by other countries who sponsor visits—sometimes they do—to their countries, and are very active in presenting an acceptable PR case for their countries. Often these are countries with dreadful records on human rights and various others. Is this a matter of concern to you and something that you believe needs additional regulation?
Rob McKinnon: I come from more of a technical perspective on these things, so a little bit of background: I am actually a software developer rather than a professional in the actual industry itself. But as a member of the public I would expect there should be a record of this that is easily available for me to make my own decision and, as someone who is producing software that tries to collate this information, I would like there to be requirements that this type of information be published in a very consistent, machine readable format, which would make it easy to automate analysis and reporting of this type of activity. To a certain extent, some of this information is published in the financial disclosure of Members, which is published on the parliamentary website, but it is not always published in a manner that is easy for someone to extract out the name of the organisation providing the sponsorship, or in this case maybe the country providing the hospitality. So in a way I think there needs to be an evaluation of how rigorously and consistently this information is reported, in a way that can be consumed by third-party services.

Q344 Paul Flynn: Any view, Dr Chari?
Dr Chari: On the foreign diplomats, I think some different legislation has clearly stated in some cases, particularly Canada, that if you are a foreign diplomat, you don't have to register with the state when a lobbying activity takes place, because it is assumed that this is an interaction between states and this is not a lobbying act, per se, in terms of experienced institutional actors lobbying the political system. I think what is at play here, in terms of conceptualising what Rob is saying and what I am saying, is the big question that has to be asked—that the Committee has to ask itself, and maybe the Government has to ask itself—is: who is responsible for getting the information out? You can go through ministerial releases as to whom, where and which venue or whatever. But in the case of Canada, for example, or systems with regulation that is robust, it is not the state's responsibility to say with whom elected representatives or civil servants have met. It is the lobbyists' responsibility to give that information and update that information on a regular basis. Theoretically, the question is: should it be the lobby that have to give the information, or should those that lobby be the ones that have to give the information? Finding information on the internet is very important but if you have a centralised system, where lobbyists themselves give all that information and they update that information, you will have that housed in one central registry.
Paul Flynn: I am very grateful to you, gentlemen.

Q345 Mrs Laing: I think that is the most interesting thing is that the balance of responsibility is the other way around. If lobbyists are required to provide that information, what is the sanction if they don't do so?
Dr Chari: It depends on the jurisdiction. Generally, it would either be a monetary fine and/or a jail fine. For example, in the Canadian legislation if you were found to have broken the rules, you can get a maximum of up to a $200,000 fine and up to two years' imprisonment. There are different jurisdictions that have different penalties; some it is less. I think even in some Canadian provinces it might be X thousand dollars, which would be a lot less. But there would be a monetary fine or a jail sentence—
Mrs Laing: It is a pretty substantial sanction.
Dr Chari:—and they would be struck from acting as a lobbyist for the next whichever number of years according to the register.

Q346 Tristram Hunt: Is it your view that, in terms of where the balance of responsibility lies, that is the most effective system?
Dr Chari: I think that is the way that most systems have worked until now, in the sense that it is not the onus of the state to collect the information but it is the onus of the lobbyist to give that information to a regulatory agency that independently monitors it from any partisan influence.

Q347 Tristram Hunt: But has a big stick?
Dr Chari: Has a big stick, yes.

Q348 Tristram Hunt: Just on the Government's current proposals, as I understand it—obviously, we are in the middle of this rather interesting debate with the Leveson inquiry and the role of various lobbyists within News Corporation trying to allegedly influence the DCMS—the in-house lobbying of the former News Corporation lobbyist, Frédéric Michel, would not be listed because it is not a third-agency lobbyist; it is an in-house corporate lobbyist. Would that be right?
Dr Chari: If it were based on your proposals, from what I understand it would not be required. No, it

would not be. To answer the very first question, that is why the proposals are quite narrow. You would not have been able to pick that up if you had this registry based on that proposal.

Q349 Tristram Hunt: Rob, in terms of the kind of transparency you are interested in seeing, what is your reflection on what we have seen over the last 48 hours of this rather interesting data-trail case study of lobbying?

Rob McKinnon: I would like to say I have had time to follow it in detail. I have not. Because I have spent the last several nights after work trying to get more department meeting reports into my database. In general I think it highlights that this is a complicated area, but I was trying to ascertain from my datasets whether any of these communications were actually described as ministerial meetings. It becomes very difficult to do that because they might have been phone calls; the communication might have been happening at levels below that which is currently reported. In general, it highlights the need for maybe a broader definition to be included in an activity that should be registered. I am more familiar with the US situation, where the registration that is made by the lobbyists, whether they are in-house or consultant, includes information on who within the Government they are lobbying.

Dr Chari: Yes, it would be the same in Canada as well. You can go do a search on any company and you can find out the different types of meetings that they have had in the last month, and you would see the names of the people that have been involved.

Rob McKinnon: What is interesting there is you said "in the last month".

Dr Chari: Yes, it is updated. If you meet with a designated public officeholder you have to do a monthly return at the federal level. Yes, that is correct.

Q350 Tristram Hunt: Dr Chari, from your comparative analysis, and then looking at the Government's proposals, do you get the sense that there has not been a great deal of research done in terms of what is out there?

Dr Chari: Without making any criticism I wouldn't want to answer that question, but there is certainly a whole wealth of information out there from the international perspective. International experience, there have been good things that have gone in highly-regulated systems, there have been bad things. So it is important to learn from both.

Q351 Tristram Hunt: In terms of that comparative analysis, the Canadian model for a UK perspective—I know you wouldn't want to answer that, but if pushed, would you say that was the most applicable?

Dr Chari: You are dealing with parliamentary systems that have a lot of similarities and there is certainly a very big historical link. I would have thought that, given the experience, a model from where to start from would be the Canadian federal model. But, again, keep in mind that there is different legislation at the provincial level. Different provinces have different legislation, but the federal legislation is probably considered the more robust of them. But it has had its glitches as well.

For example, one of the issues is that basically the rules say that in-house corporate lobbyists have to register if 20% of their time is spent on lobbying. I think the Office of the Commissioner have themselves been very critical of this and would like to see it changed, precisely because how do you quantify if an in-house corporate is spending 20% of their time on lobbying? It is very, very difficult, and this is where you come to misinterpretations and, "Well, I actually didn't spend 20%. I spent 18%", and the lobbyist might say, "I think he spent 25%", and it gets into something that is very difficult to make a judgement on.

If you were to follow the Canadian model then avoid things like trying to quantify it in terms of percentage of time. This is also seen in the United States as well: that if you work 20% over six months, then you are required to register. So this threshold of 20% is very contentious. It is necessary to broaden the scope of lobbyists who you are dealing with in terms of your proposals, but it is also necessary to be very clear as to what is considered a lobbying act.

Q352 Tristram Hunt: On that point, one of the issues that we are wrestling with is this world of charities, think-tanks, trade unions, some of us regard those organisations as having a slightly different place within the political ecosystem in contrast to professional consultant lobbyists. How do other countries deal with that issue, or do they approach trade unions and charities in the same field as a professional lobbyist company?

Dr Chari: No. Roughly speaking, they would treat them similarly. A lobbyist is any individual or group of people, each with varied and specified interests, who attempt to influence political decisions. Public consultants or professional consultancies, yes, try to influence political decisions; so do NGOs, and so do trade unions. This is a normal legitimate part of any democratic society that outside interests will try to influence it. So you have to create a level playing field, in the sense that you can't call some lobbyists and others—well—charities that don't lobby. Everyone is trying to influence political decisions, and they should be treated on an equal footing. I think this is the view of most legislation in the world. Does that answer the question?

Tristram Hunt: It does. Not necessarily the way I want it to, but it does.

Rob McKinnon: What is also interesting, in terms of what is currently transparent, is there is no distinction between the types of organisation. For example, when you report this Committee meeting you are not going to distinguish the organisation I represent, or whether I am representing myself, when you report that I was here meeting you. In that sense, it has been quite interesting to use the oral evidence witness lists as a data source for the Who's Lobbying website, because along the way I get the name of the person, their role within their organisation and also the organisation name. From that I have probably got most of your register—well, I don't know—and I am definitely able then to produce a list of people who have titles in their name, which make it sound like they are in-house lobbyists. So, when you report who gives you evidence, you are not distinguishing what type of organisation they are from. So I don't see why we need to make that distinction now that we are regulating other information disclosures.

Q353 Tristram Hunt: The level of transparency and complexity you are interested in, Rob, does that have financial implications? Does that cost a lot to produce?
Rob McKinnon: Currently I am self-funding the project. I am not receiving any external funding. The cost is mostly my volunteer time. The actual IT costs are probably in the order of £30 a month for web-hosting, and I am using open-source software to develop the website, which comes at no cost. I know UKPAC had some issues developing their online website, and I think what this highlights is part of what we are talking about is a process and information technology issue. If executed correctly, the actual cost of this, in terms of financial cost and the cost of the time of the people who are required to enter this information, should be fairly low.
Also, by treating this as an IT problem you can then produce a single source of information that is updateable in a timely fashion, that can produce information that is reusable by third party services, or itself provides fairly comprehensive public transparency services, like search, browsing by category, being able to be indexed by Google so that people in a search engine are able to find the content.
Dr Chari: Could I ask a question? Why is there no single source of all the information together right now? If all this information is collected at the ministerial level—this is not knowing anything about the developments in UK politics—what is the issue in making the next step and just putting it together in one centralised databank? That someone outside of the state has to do this, it seems slightly surprising—
Tristram Hunt: We have the Minister next week or in two weeks' time, so we shall ask him.
Dr Chari: Okay. It just occurs to me that it is a simple step to do, and that someone from the outside is actually doing it—I guess, from an international perspective, I think it is great you are doing it—it is slightly surprising it needs to be done.
Rob McKinnon: I just wanted to show it was possible, and you can have a fairly interesting website on the back of it. Yes, it is an example to government that they can do this. It is possible to do it.
Just to answer your question, I think right now what has happened is they have made it a department responsibility to publish this information. Some of the problems that go along with that are there are over 24 department websites you need to visit to find this information. Currently, it has been published in over 150 different files. If you had a researcher trying to collate this information, it might take them days just to collate the activity of a single organisation right now if the Who's Lobbying website was not there.
The other issue is each department is publishing in a slightly different format. Some publish only in PDF format, which is notoriously difficult to extract information from. Some publish in Comma Separated Value file format. A memo the Prime Minister sent to departments was that all data should be in a machine readable format. They have made some attempts there but once again it is not standardised, so any efficiency gain on my part, by writing software that can automatically extract this information, is dramatically diminished every time there is a different format. That is really where all the work has gone right now on my part in just finding ways to extract this information.
In comparison, because Parliament published the witness lists of Committee meetings in a fairly regular format, I can automate that. Every day I have software that actually takes the lists of witnesses and automatically updates the website and I don't have to do anything, so Parliament can perhaps pat itself on the back there that it is doing a more consistent job of reporting some of this information than government.

Q354 Chair: We should all be careful of extrapolating from media events that are occurring as we speak. But with that health warning could I ask, from what you have both said, it would appear that the questions that have come to light in recent times, around the interaction of News Corp with the Department for Culture, Media and Sport, where an in-house lobbyist is alleged to be in contact with either the Secretary of State, or people close to the Secretary of State, Mr McKinnon, none of that would appear on your website because none of it would have been available in publicly available sources?
Rob McKinnon: It would only be available to the extent the department reported a meeting.

Q355 Chair: If a physical meeting had taken place?
Rob McKinnon: I don't think they have actually defined what a meeting is.

Q356 Chair: From your knowledge of the Government's proposals, nor would anything have been required to have been registered around the issue that has been in the newspapers in the last 48 hours?
Dr Chari: Not to my knowledge. If it was an in-house corporate lobbyist from the corporation that was directly talking to a public officer or a public official, minister's assistant, according to your proposals, no, that would not have been captured by that.

Q357 Chair: When the Prime Minister talks about the next big scandal and lobbying, I think he believes it is this sort of issue that should be in the public mind and yet, both from existing sources and from proposed sources, an issue of that kind would escape disclosure?
Dr Chari: That is correct.
Rob McKinnon: That is correct in my understanding.

Q358 Mrs Laing: I am a bit concerned about the contrast you have made between the information that is available about witness lists, Select Committee and parliamentary activity, and information that is available from departments about meetings, simply because this is an open public meeting. This meeting right now is being broadcast. I don't know if anybody is watching.
Chair: Millions of viewers.

26 April 2012 Dr Raj Chari and Rob McKinnon

Mrs Laing: It is being broadcast. This is as open as you can get. We are taking evidence and we are having an open discussion, and anything that happens in Parliament is open, is minuted in Hansard or in Committee reports, is in the Order Paper beforehand. That is the nature of Parliament. Are you comparing that with departmental meetings and meetings of ministers, because I would ask you, is it appreciated in your analysis that these are two completely different parts of the democratic process?

Dr Chari: I think within the democratic process you have different stages when policy is made. Quite clearly, when you have a committee that meets, which gets different views from experts or witnesses, or when you have a debate in Parliament between the two different political parties, that is one stage of the policymaking process; particularly in Parliament, after either the blueprint or the details of the actual policy has been made, either at the executive level, or if it is a single Member bill when the single Member has decided to present the bill.

But we know most legislation from most Western democracies is spearheaded by core executives, which includes your most important ministers, working alongside their own cabinets and different secretaries within the different ministries. It is within that black box of policymaking that you don't have the cameras that you have here, or that you have in Parliament. In these meetings the actual details of the policy, or the important aspects of the policy is made, which may favour certain interests over others. So the regulation of lobbyists is simply to say, "Okay, we know that is the important part of the policymaking and policy shaping process, what's going on? Who's talking to whom?" What the regulation of lobbyists would allow you to see is who are those extra institutional actors working, effectively in that black box behind the scenes, trying to shape policy.

Q359 Mrs Laing: Can I just take you further on that. This is a rhetorical question. This is not expressing my opinion because that is not what I am here for. Why is that important?

Dr Chari: Because this is when you basically see what are the objectives of the policy, and who wins and who loses and who does it benefit. For example, you can take liberalisation, and telecommunications before liberalisation took place. You may have had outside interests from different operators that would say no to liberalisation, "We don't want it to happen". If they are able to block liberalisation of telecommunications—which is not the case in the UK, but if they were able to do it for years, then that would give them a privileged market position, right? So that is why it is important because it can benefit—

Q360 Mrs Laing: No, I am not suggesting it is not important. I just want to get it on the record what is important about it.

Rob McKinnon: Just to provide an example, the Prime Minister commissioned a report into copyright law. In that report Professor Ian Hargreaves stated on copyright issues, "Lobbying on behalf of rights owners has been more persuasive to ministers than economic impact assessments". In summary, this report says that copyright law should be based on evidence, not lobbying.

In terms of why transparency is important, the Government consultation asked the question, "How can public participation in the development of Government policy best be safeguarded?" In response I said, "Making paid lobbying activity fully transparent in a timely manner is the best way to safeguard public participation in the development of Government policy. Timely transparency gives the public an opportunity to provide an alternate view to Government before Government has made decisions. Closed door lobbying jeopardises public participation, as it denies the public an opportunity to present timely alternative viewpoints to Government". In my view, part of this lobbying transparency is merely just to level the playing field. Right now I imagine you can access some information by paying for it that is not publicly available, and in a way that was harmful to the—

Q361 Mrs Laing: Which information?

Rob McKinnon: I presume these lobbying firms have been paid to provide information, in addition to other activities. So—

Q362 Mrs Laing: Sorry, you said you can access some information that is not available by paying for it. Who can access it and what information?

Rob McKinnon: I don't have any evidence of this, so maybe I should stop there.

Q363 Mrs Laing: All right. It would be very interesting if you were saying that there is information that the Government ought to make available, which some people get because they pay for it.

Rob McKinnon: When I say "pay", they pay for the services of people who know things, either the workings of government—and I presume this is what—

Q364 Mrs Laing: People who know—you mean, in the same way as if there is a legal case somebody pays a lawyer to advise on the law and to represent them in a legal argument, someone can pay a government affairs company to give them advice on government affairs and possibly to represent them?

Rob McKinnon: I take your point. I have no evidence for that.

Mrs Laing: No, I am not making a point; I am asking a question.

Rob McKinnon: I don't have any evidence, so I take back that comment.

Q365 Mrs Laing: All right. Can I take you to a completely different matter that you mentioned earlier? You said something about—and I am not sure exactly what you said, so I am asking you to go back to that—people who have been involved in politics having a time restriction on being able to go into any kind of public affairs business once they have left politics. You said something about that in your opening remarks.

Dr Chari: So that would be referred to in the legislation as a cooling off period or revolving door provisions. Basically what that would stipulate is that, once a politician leaves his or her post—and there may be some conditions—whether it is specifically related to their post or not, they can't get into the world of lobbying, particularly if it involves going back to talk to officials with whom they have worked before.

Q366 Mrs Laing: When you say "a politician", do you mean a minister, or do you mean—
Dr Chari: Yes, sorry, it could be a minister. It could also be a high—
Mrs Laing: Can I just make the distinction that there is a huge difference between a minister, who has been party to information and the workings of government within a department, which is not known to anybody outside that department, by the very nature of the fact that people never know exactly what other people do in their workplace. There is a big difference, is there not, between that and a Member of Parliament? So when you say "politician" what do you mean by "politician"?
Dr Chari: In the Canadian legislation it would be what is referred to as DPOH or designated public officeholder, which can include ministers to senior members of their staff to parliamentarians, as well as high level civil servants. See, the concern here is that if you have contacts already established in your previous life, either as a politician broadly speaking or as a civil servant, you will use that information on the inside as a lobbyist to help either the firm or the consultancy you are working for gain contracts, gain money and so on, or have undue influence when it comes to public policymaking. So you have inside information.

Q367 Mrs Laing: In the UK we have rules to that effect, as far as ministers are concerned. They are not allowed to leave their ministerial office and then immediately go and earn money from a similar sort of job with the same people. But are you suggesting that that should be what—
Dr Chari: Sorry, what did you mean by "the same people"?
Mrs Laing: Sorry, I am just trying to summarise the law for the sake of brevity. We have rules that prevent someone who has held ministerial office from going immediately from ministerial office to a position where they would earn money from the immediate contacts that they have.
Dr Chari: For example, if someone worked in the Exchequer, they couldn't go and work for a bank after?
Mrs Laing: There is a time period.
Dr Chari: There is a cooling-off period?
Mrs Laing: Yes.
Dr Chari: Okay.
Mrs Laing: I would not call it "a cooling-off period". There is a time period. I can't remember the exact restrictions, but what I am asking you is are you saying that that should go further to Members of Parliament?
Dr Chari: From a normative perspective, my own personal point of view, yes. What I talk about is what exists in the pre-existing legislation around the world—and particularly Canada—and, yes, that is the rule.

Q368 Mrs Laing: Thank you. I wanted to take Mr McKinnon to the issue of TheyWorkForYou. I understand that you have been involved in the New Zealand TheyWorkForYou?
Rob McKinnon: That is correct, yes.

Q369 Mrs Laing: Are you in or do you have knowledge of the TheyWorkForYou website working here in the UK?
Rob McKinnon: Yes, I do. I do not have any direct involvement in the UK theyworkforyou.com, but I am acquainted with many of the people who have contributed to making it. I often see them at events and, in fact, they did encourage me to create the New Zealand version.

Q370 Mrs Laing: What I wanted to ask you about was the collation of statistics, presentation of statistics and analysis of statistics. I will just give you an example. I was very surprised when someone drew my attention to my own entry on TheyWorkForYou, on what people have been saying about me, because each of us knows our own activity better than anyone else's, I guess. The publication of the statistics, how many times you voted, which bills you voted "Yes" or "No" on and which motions you voted "Yes" or "No" on, of course is absolutely fine and it is very good to put that in one place. It is publicly available information and most of us would encourage that. But what I would like to take you to is analysis of that information. Because I have read that I personally am on a particular point on the left-right spectrum of politics, because of an analysis done by TheyWorkForYou, and frankly it is wrong and very crude.
Rob McKinnon: As I said, I have no involvement in the UK theyworkforyou.com. On the New Zealand site, such analysis is prohibited because we changed to a proportional representation electoral system, some 17 years ago, and since then most divisions in the New Zealand unicameral Parliament are party votes, which means the whole party votes together. In my mind, this makes it much easier as a voter to be able to vote for a party and that party votes in the Parliament. There is no possibility to record rebellion.
Chair: That is all very, very interesting, perhaps we need to do some lobbying and we can give Eleanor some private advice.

Q371 Mrs Laing: All I was seeking to explore was the analysis of statistics, and you have given me a good answer; thank you. Looking at the analysis of statistics, I was concerned that the last issue that Dr Hunt was looking at was the way in which publication of information solves the problem. The way the discussion was going alarm bells rang in my head, that if the Government were to be encouraged to collate information—as Mr McKinnon said, it would be possible to do because the information is there, and I think you said, Mr McKinnon, in 26 different places—but if you can collate it, then why can't the Government collate it? My concern is that if that were done it would look as if the job was done and that the information is all there, whereas what you have said in your evidence suggests that the information in fact is not all there. So what I was getting at was presentation of information and that in fact, in a complicated subject like this, can it be summed up on a website with numbers of meetings? What is a meeting?

Dr Chari: It is a good question. The experience of lobbying regulation in North America, for example, is that that information is given by the lobbyist to the regulatory authority. That information is then updated if necessary and there you can see the different information. If you look at this act of registration of a corporation in Canada, you can see the information of the company, a description of its activities, all of its subsidiaries, the lobbying activity information, in terms of the federal departments that it is actually seeking to lobby, the senior officers of the organisation, communication techniques that have been used or that are going to be used by the organisation, information about the subject matter, and specific descriptions on policies and programmes. Then if there is a meeting with a public officeholder that is recorded and summarised every month, in which you have, "This is the organisation, this is the responsible officer, and this is the designated public officeholder that they have talked to and this is their position within the ministry". If you click on that, you get a more detailed analysis, not necessarily of the content but of actually what was the subject matter of the communication.

So, all of that; if you do a search of corporation X or consultancy Y or NGO Z, you can do a search on the database, you get the information, you click on it, and you can see all of that information neatly aligned.

Rob McKinnon: We know in the United States that, because the information is fairly detailed and comprehensive, you have a whole ecosystem of websites that process, analyse, collate and consolidate that information. My concern with the current proposal from the Government is that they haven't specified that the clients of lobbying firms provide their company number or charity number if they are not a company. What I have found, in trying to collate existing information, is that almost 30% of the organisations that are declared in government meetings have been put into reports with a variant of their name, which makes it very difficult to collate their activity by organisation. I would strongly recommend any proposal by the Government require that any time a legal entity is mentioned, if it is a company, that the company number be provided, if it is a charity, that the charity number be provided, And if it is registered in a different jurisdiction, that the jurisdiction and the registration number in that jurisdiction be provided. Otherwise I agree that there are concerns with the ability to analyse and report on this information.

Q372 Mrs Laing: Bringing all of that together, given that you have both made a very good point that the point of this is to know how policy is arrived at and constructed. If the political cycle was at the stage where it was, let's say, 18 months to a year before a general election and, given that a change of government would therefore be possible, while information about activities of government ministers would be required, do you consider that such information about shadow ministers and their meetings with lobbyists should also be disclosed, because surely a government in waiting is also constructing policy?

Dr Chari: I agree with you, and—

Mrs Laing: No, I am not making a point; I am asking a question.

Dr Chari: Okay, let me clarify that answer then. Full information is a good thing because it helps with transparency, it helps the public understand who is trying to influence whom, including from the Government side or the Opposition side. I guess my suggestion would be that we are looking at this from the wrong way, in terms of what is the information that either the Government or Opposition has to give with regard to meetings. All I am simply saying here is that if you had a proper register of lobbyists, which made the lobbyists detail all the information of every public official he or she was meeting with, all of this information would be clearly on the public record.

Q373 Mrs Laing: By "public official", and I have to get a definition here, you see, because "public official" to us doesn't mean a Member of Parliament. It means somebody paid by the Government, on the Government payroll, and the Leader of the Opposition and his team don't count as public officials. Forgive me we are trying to put it into UK language. What do you mean?

Dr Chari: I will repeat what I said earlier with regard to what is referred to as a designated public officeholder in the Canadian legislation, and that would refer to anyone who is either in government at the ministerial level or a Member of Parliament. It could refer to any Member of Parliament. It could refer to any high-level civil servant in any ministry, and it also can include a member of the armed forces as well.

Mrs Laing: Thank you.

Q374 Sheila Gilmore: Sorry, I missed the beginning of the meeting due to another commitment. This is primarily to Mr McKinnon. The website Who's Lobbying: could you tell us a bit more about the relationship between your website and data.gov.uk? Why does the Government website, listing ministers' meetings, actually send users to your website for further information?

Rob McKinnon: Last year I was asked by data.gov.uk if I could provide a report to them of all the meetings that I had collated, which I did so, and they chose to present it in the manner you described.

Q375 Sheila Gilmore: So they are linking to you?

Rob McKinnon: Yes, but you would need to ask them as to their reasoning for why they do that.

Q376 Sheila Gilmore: I think you also said in your written evidence that there are a number of government departments that haven't published up-to-date details of ministerial meetings. In fact I think the

date you gave was June 2011. Some departments seem to have no difficulty publishing photographs of meetings much more regularly. Do you know of departments that can publish photos but don't appear to be able to give any further details?
Rob McKinnon: Yes, many government departments now have a photo publishing account on a website called flickr.com, and they are regularly publishing information in quite a timely fashion there. Here is an example from the No. 10 stream. I am holding here a photograph of a meeting David Cameron had in May 2010. In the same month that photo was published on flickr.com, and then we had to wait until October 2010 before the report of that meeting was published as part of the regular ministerial meeting reports from the departments.

Q377 Sheila Gilmore: Do you have a view about how often details of meetings should be published, and are there any departments that we could look to for the practice?
Rob McKinnon: The more often, the more frequently and the more closely to the event the information is published the better, for transparency and the ability for the public to participate in government and Government policy formation. Given that pretty much all departments now have a social media account on twitter.com, where they are regularly updating and many have photo accounts at flickr.com, there seems to be no reason why they could not be equally forthcoming with who the minister is meeting in the same sort of fashion. I would imagine if the technology was in place they should be able to update that on more like a daily or weekly basis. The evidence is they are paying for staff right now to provide regular updates to the public, so I don't think there is any additional cost burden to departments to do this.

Q378 Simon Hart: Sorry, I had to disappear, and also I apologise if I raise topics that have been raised already while I have been elsewhere.
Can I go back to a reference to the cooling-off period—which I think, Dr Chari, you mentioned earlier on, and I know Eleanor Lang did also in the last few moments—as I want to explore it a bit more. It seems to me that an MP or a minister when they leave here will carry with them information that may benefit some future career. That career may be in industry; it may be in journalism; it may be in a range of things, as well as possibly within lobbying. In many ways that they will have, though no fault of their own, privileged information which they can use to their advantage in a future career, apparently any future career other than lobbying, according to what you have told us. If the Government was to impose the register as currently proposed, and that was to become law and there was a proper register, and let's say there was also some voluntary code of practice, what is the problem? Why should an MP not go into a highly regulated, highly transparent industry where his or her skills can be effectively deployed? Why should they be barred from so doing?
Dr Chari: Precisely because they would be able to take some inside information of how things go on in the ministry, or wherever they worked before, that could be used.

Q379 Simon Hart: They could do that in any industry.
Dr Chari: Yes, they could.

Q380 Simon Hart: So why not bar them from that too?
Dr Chari: Let's look at this by way of an example. Let's say I am working as a minister in industry and I go to work for a big oil corporation. Quite clearly, if there is any new legislation, which may be relevant to the oil corporation and that the oil corporation might want to influence so that it is better off by changing something in the legislation, or by adding something to the legislation, that minister is in a privileged position as a member of the that corporation, as a lobbyist, to influence policy. He or she is able to influence policy based on inside information in a way that other corporations or other lobbyists can't.

Q381 Simon Hart: But if he was a lobbyist for a third-party company that is representing a multi-client company—
Dr Chari: A consultancy.
Simon Hart:—or equivalent of, you have made your point and we can accept it or not. However, he or she may go into one of the organisations that regularly lobbies us, either as ministers or MPs, but won't fall within the Government proposals because it might be a charity or an NGO. They will still take with them powerful insider information, which they can deploy but will not be caught as a consequence of the proposals, either as they are or as they might be.
Dr Chari: There are varying views on that in the legislation. Some legislation internationally might say you cannot be a lobbyist in the area that you specifically worked in before because you would be able to take insider information. There are others that would say that, "Okay, if you can clearly demonstrate that the information you take as a politician will not be used in a way that is disadvantageous to other lobbyists or in a way that will mean that you will use your contacts from your previous work, well, then that is fine".

Q382 Simon Hart: Two more questions. How would you do that because a lot of this information is contained in people's heads? When people leave any industry they take with them industry knowledge, which they could go to a competitor with. However much you might tie it up in a contract you cannot remove the knowledge that they have acquired and the use to which they may put it.
Dr Chari: That is right, and that is why it is probably just best to have a cooling-off period altogether.

Q383 Simon Hart: In two years that knowledge has ceased to be of relevance; is that what you are saying?
Dr Chari: I don't know the psychology—if someone remembers the information or not that is up to them—but I think the idea is that in two years or for those two years at least, or five years as in the case for the

federal level in Canada, you will not be exercising influence in the way that is not fair.

Q384 Simon Hart: Last question for Mr McKinnon; leaving that where it is, a slightly different point. As I left you mentioned lobbying scandals, and one of the things we have struggled with, with previous witnesses, is to actually clearly define what a lobbying scandal is. We haven't got very far with having examples of lobbying scandals that would have been prevented had the Government's proposals been in place. Unfortunately I couldn't wait to hear you expand your argument, but I know you touched on Liam Fox. Of course, we all take the view that Adam Werritty would not have qualified as a lobbyist so he would not have been caught by the proposals, therefore that particular scandal would not have been avoided as a result of the proposals. So I wonder if I can ask you for some more examples of scandals that might or might not have been prevented by the proposals; recent ones?

Rob McKinnon: We did cover this earlier.

Simon Hart: Apologies.

Rob McKinnon: Earlier I tried to identify what makes something a scandal, and I think it is a combination of there is closed, non-public information that involves some degree of privileged access that at a later time becomes public, and that the public, or the media, or the two together come to the conclusion that there was undue influence or privileged access that would not be considered publicly acceptable. As we know, the current Government's proposal does not require lobbying activity to be registered. As currently proposed, I don't think the register would aid or mitigate these types of scandals. Whether that is the sole purpose of the register, I don't think it is. It might be exciting for the media to think that that is why we are going to have a register, but just from a general public interest point of view it is quite interesting to know that, yes, there are lots of different organisations that are involved in lobbying government and to what extent they do so.

Q385 Simon Hart: I did say specific examples that illustrate your point: anything from the last couple of years that you think really illustrates the need for a register and which would have been avoided if that register had been in place. Is there anything specific you can point us to?

Rob McKinnon: As I said, I don't think that is the sole purpose of a register, so I would be hesitant to—

Q386 Simon Hart: Except you mentioned lobbying scandals. I am only trying to find out which ones you were referring to when you made that comment.

Rob McKinnon: There have been so many.

Q387 Simon Hart: Give me two.

Rob McKinnon: Okay; so this current situation, where you've got an in-house public affairs professional having direct communication with people at a fairly senior level within a government department. As my co-panellist has suggested, if that activity were required to be registered we would then have that on the record, so it would cease to be a scandal if in a fairly timely fashion that type of communication was on a public record.

Q388 Fabian Hamilton: Apologies to our witnesses for being late. I was detained by a Bill Committee. Dr Chari, in your research, which I believe is entitled *Regulating Lobbying: a Global Comparison*, you suggest that many lobbyists who are working within regulated systems are in favour of detailed registers because it allows them to gain information about their competitors. Did the lobbyists that you interviewed—and indeed politicians—state that there were any other benefits in working within a regulated system?

Dr Chari: That is an excellent question. We talk about four positive kick-backs with any register, and it has to do with benefits not just for the lobbyists but also for politicians as well and citizens alike. The first one would be that lobbyists would be able to get information on what their competitors were doing. Particularly when we were interviewing in Ontario, what we found was that religiously lobbyists, whether they are in-house corporates or whether they would be consultants or NGOs—and the NGOs would do this quite a bit—would see basically there are other organisations that would work in their area, "Let's check the registry to see if they have updated their register or what they are working on now; if there is anything different". So this isn't a new finding, in the sense that in the late 1990s other academics in the literature were saying that one of the biggest consumers of an actual lobby register would be the lobbyists themselves. There is a perception that innately lobbyists are against a register. There is that preconception. Our experience shows that, over time, it is the lobbyists that become the most passionate users and defenders of the register in a lot of ways because it gives them that sort of competitive advantage.

It also gives them a second advantage—and this would be the second positive kick-back—and that would be being able to demonstrate to either members of their organisation or their clients what they are doing. We see this particularly with the non-governmental organisations. For example, the Cancer Society every year can tell its members, "If you want to see how we have been trying to influence health policy, these were the bills that we lobbied on; these were the Members of Parliament or the ministers that we talked to. So you can see that we are active in trying to better your interests as members of our organisation". In-house corporates could also use it the same, to show the members of the corporation what they are trying to do and how they are trying to do it.

The third kick-back in all of that is that citizens, in having access to this information on the web, can see that lobbyists are a legitimate, open and transparent part of the democratic process and are not hiding what they are doing. All of the information is there. Any citizen who wants to hold either a politician accountable for talking to corporation X because they don't like that they are talking so much with their Member of Parliament, well, they can be accountable because they might not necessarily get the votes they want. On the other hand, they can be very transparent in terms of saying, "Well, this is the different organisations that are lobbying" simply in terms of interest. I suppose the assumption here then is that consumers of the registry would be a citizenry that do want to understand about politics; that do want transparency.

The fourth benefit would actually then be from the politician's side because the politicians do not then have to hide that they are talking to lobbyists. They can openly say, "Yes, I talked to this lobbyist on this day about this event", and that is perfectly legit and it is on the public record.

Q389 Fabian Hamilton: That is helpful. Thank you very much. Can I move to you, Mr McKinnon, and just ask you this. In your written evidence I think you identified 167 organisations with lobbying activity in the UK and the USA. You stated that there was a combined disclosed spend in the United States of about $3 billion. In your view, is an element of financial disclosure necessary to ensure transparency about the differing resource capabilities of those who do the lobbying?

Rob McKinnon: Yes. But what was more interesting when I did this research was to also find out what issues these organisations were lobbying on. In the United States they are also required to say what issues are being lobbied on, and that includes bills that are going through. Right now the monetary financial figures provide an indication of the extent to which resources are being put into lobbying. But I think for the public it is much more interesting to know what issues are being lobbied on. The two combined then can also provide fuel for public debate and participation.

Fabian Hamilton: Thank you for that. Can I just ask one final question, which is one that I know that my colleague Paul Flynn wanted to ask: do you think it would be a progressive move if the Government nationalised your enterprise, Who's Lobbying, which obviously operates at a fraction of the cost of a government department? Forgive me if it sounds frivolous, but there is a serious intent here.

Rob McKinnon: That is definitely something that could be possible. The current website is a combination of two things: it is bespoke software code that was written, and then the time it takes to nurture some of the data and clean it on the way in to the system. So there is definitely a cost for anyone engaged in this enterprise of doing the two things.

The other thing to consider is the Government has now set up a Government Digital Service, the GDS, and they are in the process of developing a single government domain, which was a Martha Lane Fox recommendation for the Government. Once again, this was a cost reduction measure that each department need not be spending money on maintaining the infrastructure necessary for a website when that could be centralised. I would imagine that that Government Digital Service would be a good candidate for a part of government that would be able to rapidly develop the software required to maintain such a register.

Q390 Fabian Hamilton: You will forgive me here; I was not trying to be frivolous. There was a serious intent here. The point is that organisations like yours, entrepreneurs like you, can do these things at a fraction of the cost, and we all know the extraordinary inflation in costs of any government computer, IT or digital programme. So would it not be better to get entrepreneurs like you to develop the Government's Digital Service or people in your situation?

Rob McKinnon: I am definitely available to have a conversation.

Fabian Hamilton: I can't let the contract, obviously.

Rob McKinnon: I think we are all in agreement that this is a useful resource. It was an experiment. It is done in my spare time. It is not necessarily going to continue. I do this at some personal cost right now. But definitely if someone in government wanted to talk about either taking the software, or even just having a conversation about how I do things, because I have probably discovered some workarounds for merging information from different sources.

Q391 Fabian Hamilton: I think you will agree there is no point in re-inventing the wheel, is there? Why spend huge amounts of money doing what you have already done? We might as well just pay you for it.

Rob McKinnon: As UKPAC have said—it really depends on what the requirements are. So I think we have not really got to the bottom of what the requirements are for such a service.

Fabian Hamilton: Thank you. Thank you, Chairman.

Chair: Thank you, Mr Flynn/Hamilton. There was some heavy lobbying there, which I hope will be declared if Mr McKinnon makes a million out of it. But I would have to say, having had some recent experience with the speed with which civil service can let tenders, I want to ask Mr McKinnon to carry on doing the work in a private capacity for the foreseeable future.

Q392 Andrew Griffiths: Gentlemen, we have heard a lot about how you feel there needs to be more transparency in government, about how they are lobbied. Doesn't that also apply to the Opposition, who you could say have a huge influence over policy, and that the public have a right to that information also?

Dr Chari: That is right; Yes, I would agree with that. But I think that the important point to underline there—and I am talking particularly of the Canadian experience or the more robust regulatory systems in general, which would be found in North America—the general rule would be that is if any attempt is made to influence political decisions that should be recorded. As a lobbyist you would have to give your details and specific registration details, and other things we have mentioned before, when you register as a lobbyist. If you have robust or even half-robust rules, you are clearly shedding light in terms of policymaking processes, and generally speaking adding some transparency of what goes on with either the Government or Opposition. That is the important point to underline here: that lobbying when it takes place—and you are totally right—can take place not just with the Government officials but also those who are not. But if there is an attempt to influence, broadly speaking, that is what is recorded.

Q393 Andrew Griffiths: Mr McKinnon, do you agree with that? Do you think we should know what is going on with the Leader of the Opposition and who he is meeting just as much as the Prime Minister?
Rob McKinnon: Many of us have come before this Committee and said it is an activity that needs to be defined, and then anyone engaged in the activity would need to register that. So if it is considered any approach to a Member of Parliament is of public interest, then it is just a matter of definition that that activity would then be recorded.

Q394 Andrew Griffiths: We heard that legislation has been introduced in various countries and then amended later. Are there any examples where legislation has been amended because the burdens have been particularly onerous or costly? Are there any examples where it has been watered down?
Dr Chari: Not really. Generally it has been amended because the regulations either didn't ask for enough information, or it was deemed by the Government of the day that more information on the lobbyist was deemed necessary, so they made it more robust and asked different questions, or there could have been loopholes in the legislation. For example, you may have rules saying that if you meet with a lobbyist and you are a minister, that lobbyist has to be registered, but if the minister invites the lobbyist, then they don't need to be registered. That was a loophole that existed in Canadian legislation in the beginning, but then they realised that this was a loophole so they made it so that that could not be done any more.
I don't know if you were here when we talked about how we tried to make different sorts of regulatory systems. In our research we talk about low-, medium- and high-regulatory systems. What we have basically seen in the quantitative point scale of 1:30 for low, 31:59 for medium, and 60:87—which is our maximum for Washington State—for high, that when there have been amendments that have been made the legislation has become more robust. In fact the federal legislation in the United States was at one time medium-regulated, but with the last change in 2007 it became highly regulated. I don't know if that answers your question, but generally speaking there is a lot of policy learning going on here. That is the other thing to keep in mind as well, as you are considering developing legislation, is that it doesn't necessarily have to be the last word. You can develop some proposals, you can get them into law and maybe you will see some other things are needed and you might make amendments within five to 10 years. That is how it has been in other countries.

Q395 Andrew Griffiths: It is always a ratcheting-up of the legislation rather than down?
Dr Chari: The only case we have seen where there have been lobbying laws that were then abandoned altogether was the Hungarian Government with Fidesz.

Q396 Andrew Griffiths: Am I right in thinking that in Canada the onus is on the lobbyist to register their meeting?
Dr Chari: Correct. That is right. That is an important point I tried to underline before. One thing we have is in the case of ministerial meetings where the State gives the information to the public as to who they have met with. In the case of lobbying legislation throughout the world, not just Canada, the onus is on the lobbyist to provide the information with an independent regulatory authority. That information goes on a centralised database that is open for the public to scrutinise.

Q397 Andrew Griffiths: What is the maximum fine anywhere in the world for failure to declare?
Dr Chari: To my knowledge the maximum fine would be in Canada with, as we mentioned before, a maximum fine of $200,000 with a potential for up to a two-year jail sentence for giving misinformation.

Q398 Andrew Griffiths: Can I just go back in relation to Who's Lobbying. It says in our sheet here that there were 1,560 entries in different public documents. What percentage of all the entries was that, just to get a perspective on the scale?
Rob McKinnon: You are talking about the issue of different name variants being used for organisations?
Andrew Griffiths Yes.
Rob McKinnon: Yes, so I have some updated figures on that. Just to explain the situation: currently when the name of an organisation is provided in either a government Department report or one of the industry registers provided by APPC or PRCA, the name of the company is just a piece of text that can be typed in by someone. I have found, as you have identified now, over 1,700 of these, in the case of government reports, have been provided with a variance of the name. That is about 26% of the entities that have been disclosed as meeting government, so about a quarter there.

Q399 Andrew Griffiths: Do you think that is deliberate variance or do you think that is accidental?
Rob McKinnon: There is a combination of things. Acronyms are very popular in the United Kingdom so often acronyms will be provided. Also, just misspellings or just saying "Authority" instead of "Association" in the name, or just common mistakes humans make. There is also the fact that a number of bodies are going through rebranding exercises so a lot of charities are changing their name. Obviously companies can do the same as well. Companies can operate under a trading name and have a different registered name, so different combinations of that can be provided. That is why I have said that it would be best to require the publication of a company number, in the case of the entity being a registered legal company, or a charity number if it is also a charity. This is similar to the way the UK Electoral Commission political donations register works. It requires that the company number be provided. It makes it a lot easier for someone coming along to analyse and collate this information by legal entity, which I think is an important thing—an outcome we should consider to be important—that that be possible.
I just had a look at this Canadian disclosure from

Dr Chari and all subsidiary companies also had to be disclosed. So this is very crucial as well: that we have the combination of the parent company and all of the subsidiary companies related to an issue.

Q400 Andrew Griffiths: Just one final question for Dr Chari. Where this legislation has been introduced, have there been any surveys or quantitative work done to show that public confidence in government and politicians has improved as a result?
Dr Chari: That is an excellent question. Our own research did surveys to politicians, lobbyists and administrators, so we didn't do a public opinion survey per se. I am not aware of any data that has been collected with regard to public opinion on registries. The general assumption is that if you add some sunshine into the policymaking black box that there is a benefit for mass publics. I am not entirely sure that surveys would capture that. At least the theoretical perspective is that you are empowering citizens with knowledge, and you are giving them the opportunity to see exactly who is trying to influence who when policy is made. That can only be good for your policy. By empowering them with knowledge, they understand how government works, and you decrease cynicism.

Q401 Andrew Griffiths: You could argue that we could get the Prime Minister to wear a head-cam 24 hours a day and we would know exactly what he was doing at any moment in time. What I am saying is, can we demonstrate that these measures actually have any impact on the public's perception of politicians, or is it a small group of people who have a particular interest who say it would?
Dr Chari: No. Again, if you are asking for public opinion surveys on a large end scale that have been performed on this, I am not aware of any, so I can't give you that data. What you might want to do is go back to your constituency and ask. I think it is generally assumed within countries that have high to medium regulation that interested parties—and not just lobbyists themselves or politicians or administrators—do have that ability. It gives citizens the ability to find all of this information if they need it and if they want it, and they can see that maybe a corporation is lobbying a ministry on a law and having a position that they are not in agreement with and they might not buy that company's product. They might see that a politician is talking to 500 corporations and not once to an NGO and they might not vote for the politician. It is an interesting idea for a study to see where the hits come from—we can ask the regulators to give us their data on that—but we know from talking to the regulators themselves that they get thousands of hits every day, and invariably that is not just going to be people working in the profession; it is going to be citizens.

Q402 Andrew Griffiths: So there is evidence that these registers are well-thumbed?
Dr Chari: They are widely consumed, yes. In fact registrars will get third-party complaints all the time about citizens knowing—or I suppose competitors as well—that people are lobbying without having registered, and they will file that third party complaint to a registrar and the registrar will spearhead an investigation into that. Yes, it has happened several times.
Chair: Thank you very much indeed, Raj and Rob. You have been very informative—very interesting. Certainly we will pick up, between now and when we do our report, the question about the way in which government is responding currently to its mandate under the ministerial code to have some of this information in the public domain. Whatever we come up with in our report, it is not satisfactory if the deadlines are not being met for putting this stuff into the public arena, and I will take that up directly with the Cabinet Secretary.
Thank you so much for your evidence today. You have been extremely informative and helpful. Thank you for coming along. Thank you, colleagues—a very good session. Thank you very much indeed.

Thursday 17 May 2012

Members present:

Mr Graham Allen (Chair)

Mr Christopher Chope
Paul Flynn
Sheila Gilmore
Simon Hart
Tristram Hunt
Stephen Williams

Examination of Witness

Witness: **Mr Mark Harper MP**, Minister for Political and Constitutional Reform, Cabinet Office, gave evidence.

Q403 Chair: Good morning. We are going to discuss lobbying today. Is there anything you want to tell us, Mark, just to kick us off?

Mr Harper: We will obviously go into detail, but given that there has been press comment calling into question the Government's commitment to getting this job done, I thought it might be worth saying at the beginning that we are committed to getting it done during this Parliament. I have said in other places—I cannot remember whether I have done so in Parliament—that we have done the consultation, which is now closed. You are obviously undertaking your inquiry. The consultation responses are being analysed, and we will look closely at them and your report. We will then publish a White Paper and a draft Bill during this Session of Parliament for pre-legislative scrutiny. We will also publish the summary of responses to the consultation, with details of our next steps, before the summer recess.

We may not be going as fast as some people would like, but I think you have probably discovered from your evidence sessions—we certainly did from the consultation responses and the six public events that I did—that the devil of the subject is in the detail. I would rather get it right, with a long-lasting solution that we do not have to return to, than rush off and do something in haste and have it unravel. We are taking a sensible approach, but we are determined to get it done during this Parliament. Some of the press coverage was a little misleading.

Other than that, I am happy to dive straight into dealing with questions from the Committee.

Q404 Chair: This is a nice lob to get you warmed up. Obviously, people keep referring back to the Prime Minister's comment that this was "the next big scandal waiting to happen." Do you think the work in front of us will stop that next big scandal happening?

Mr Harper: I very much hope so. One of the interesting points that came out during some of the events that I did is that it is worth being clear about what problem we are trying to solve, because that will help to inform why our proposals in the consultation document are as they are.

The problem that we identified is not lobbying per se. We said in the consultation document that lobbying is a perfectly reputable activity. When governments do not listen to people who are affected by their legislation, they normally make very poor decisions. It is about making sure that the lobbying is transparent and that people know who is lobbying the Government, so that when they look at the decisions that are made they can draw their own conclusions. We said that when ministers meet external organisations, we would publish the details of those meetings, so that it is transparent. We said that there was a gap in the level of transparency. If we publish the fact that there were meetings in which ministers met companies that lobby for third parties, it is not clear who they were actually being lobbied by. The Minister may know—in fact, will know—but the outside world will not, and that is the gap we were trying to close in our proposals. Clearly, the evidence that we have had, that I have listened to publicly and that you have had is that people want us to have a much broader scope for that. The problem we were trying to solve was that gap in transparency, which explains why our proposals look as they do.

Transparency in this area is dealing with people, ensuring that they feel that government are listening to those who have a legitimate point of view, weighing that up, and then taking decisions in the public interest, rather than for some other reason.

Chair: I will bring in Paul, but first I am going to Chris, because he has a particular question around definition that picks up the Minister's opening remarks. Do you want to drop that one in now, as it seems appropriate?

Q405 Mr Chope: We know that people are suggesting that there should be more discussion about the specifics of what we mean by lobbying. You cannot have clear legislation, unless the people who are affected by it know whether or not it is going to apply to them. Are you minded to have further consultation with organisations such as the Chartered Institute of Public Relations, which thinks that it has now got a more workable definition of lobbying? Surely that is the fundamental basis of the whole process of setting up the legislation.

Mr Harper: Sure. We absolutely agree that getting the details right is important, which is why we have not rushed off to do something and then found that it has all unravelled. I have seen what the CIPR has said. I was a little worried that it said that it had asked a law firm to come up with a workable five-page definition of lobbying. It did not seem to me that that necessarily met the spirit of what we were intending. It comes back to what we intend the legislation to do, and we will reflect on that when we look at the consultation responses. If we are trying to create a register that captures everyone who does lobbying, whether or not you call them a lobbyist, and tries to influence government and Parliament, that clearly is one definition. The alternative definition that we set out in our consultation is where we are trying to capture those who lobby for third parties, because we felt that that was a gap in the transparency.

One of the issues is just deciding what problem it is that we are trying to solve. We have set out in the consultation document the problem as we see it and how we think that we should solve it. One of the things that has come through from the consultation and the meetings is that other people, including many people in the industry, think that it is a different problem that we are trying to solve. What we propose to do when we set out our White Paper and draft legislation is be clear about the problem and how we intend to solve it. Part of the reason why we want to publish a draft bill for pre-legislative scrutiny is to make sure that we get those definitions right, that they are workable, and that everyone who will be captured by them—whether that is industry in the narrower definition or whether we go for the register with a wider scope—is clear about whether they would have to register on such a statutory register. That is why we want to do this in a deliberative way, rather than rushing off and getting it wrong.

Q406 Mr Chope: Will the draft bill have two alternative definitions of lobbying, depending on whether or not you go for third-party lobbying?

Mr Harper: No. The Government's intention is that we will look carefully at the consultation responses. The consultation has only recently closed. We have not finished that work yet. We will do that and we will look carefully at the report that this Committee publishes—both the evidence that you took and any conclusions and recommendations that you reach. We will reach a policy decision, which we will set out in the White Paper, and then we will publish a draft bill for pre-legislative scrutiny. That is a sensible way of doing things. People will still have the opportunity to comment on our White Paper, our policy intention, and the way we have defined it in draft legislation.

Q407 Chair: Thank you, Mark. When we have operated as a select committee should, as a partner for government—an often critical but friendly partner—on, for example, electoral registration and administration issues, what has been produced as a result of that process is far better than what we started with. That is not a criticism of the earlier part of the process. It is just that the full process can work to everyone's benefit.

You have pointed out that the devil is in the detail. I hope that you will take the same view—the view that we have had so far—on this potential legislation. There are a lot of strong-minded people with their own views on this Committee, but I hope that we will produce something that is helpful in making it even more workable.

Mr Harper: Sure. One thing that would be very helpful, Chairman, is specifically to come back to the point about defining the problem. We have set out clearly what we think the problem is. Some people from the industry think that it is a different problem. One of the things that they have enjoyed pointing out, I think, is that a number of the so-called scandals involving lobbying have involved politicians in some part of the process. They have often pointed out that that has often been the case. It would be helpful, therefore, to hear from a committee of parliamentarians on what you think the problem is, and therefore what you think the appropriate solution is. The Government will listen very carefully to what you have to say and weigh that up against what the public and other interested parties have said in the consultation.

We have heard mixed views. Even when listening to audiences from the industry, I have heard different views about the problem and the solution. It is a case of trying to get something that generally people feel correctly identifies the problem and sets out a sensible, workable solution that does not burden everyone and make genuine discussion with government difficult. That would be helpful.

Chair: We will try to be as helpful as possible and respect the spirit of openness in which you have addressed the issue. Thank you.

Q408 Paul Flynn: Not the press but serious commentators have pointed out the gulf between the Prime Minister's splendid rhetoric in February 2010 and the reality of what you have presented. Mark Adams, a lobbyist, has described the paper as "possibly one of the most shoddy documents I have ever seen government produce." Sir Stuart Etherington, Chair of the National Council for Voluntary Organisations, said of the register: "Basically it's so weak now there's no point in us joining it." Do you accept that the Government's proposals are weak and in no way represent the spirit of what the Prime Minister said in February 2010?

Mr Harper: No, I do not. Part of this comes down to what problem you are trying to solve. The problem that we are trying to solve is a lack of transparency about those who meet ministers.

Q409 Paul Flynn: You have said that a number of times. There are a number of things that I would like to ask you, if I can go on to that. You think it is okay. Fine; we have got that point. Let's take not what the Government say, but what they actually do. The ministerial code was set up five years ago. There are three instances that possibly should have been investigated by the independent adviser—Sir Philip Mawer, as it then was, or the new adviser. One of them is the current case involving the Culture Secretary. There is also the case involving the Communities Secretary and one involving Mr Adam Werritty and the former Defence Secretary. All those are potential breaches of the ministerial code. None of them has been investigated. Why is that?

Mr Harper: I will let the Chairman decide how far he wants me to go. On the point about the Culture Secretary, the Prime Minister has made the position very clear. He is responsible for enforcing the ministerial code. He does not—

Paul Flynn: Shall we—

Chair: Paul, the minister has to answer the question.

Mr Harper: I shall try to keep the answers fairly brief, but you have asked me the questions, so I will try to answer them. As far as the Culture Secretary is concerned, the Prime Minister has made it clear that he is responsible as the arbiter of the code. The Secretary of State is going to set out all his evidence at the Leveson inquiry. The Prime Minister's view is that the Secretary of State has not breached the ministerial code. The Prime Minister has made it clear that if, after having looked at all the evidence that is laid out, he takes a different view, he will act. That seems to me a perfectly sensible process. You have a judge in a public inquiry at which witnesses will give evidence under oath; that seems to be a much more robust process, in this case, than asking Sir Alex Allan to carry out a parallel process.

Q410 Paul Flynn: Do you know the details about the Communities Secretary? The Communities Secretary had a dinner—a five-star dinner at the Savoy—with Bell Pottinger and one of its clients who had a case that they were bringing before his department. His reason for not registering it was that on that day he was eating privately and not ministerially, so we are not sure on what day he eats with his ministerial stomach and on what day he eats with his private stomach. Apparently, the Government accepted that defence, and that he did not have to register it. Is that an advance in transparency?

Mr Harper: This Government are far more transparent than any previous Government have been in terms of publishing the details of ministerial meetings, who ministers are meeting, when those meetings are with external organisations, and the purpose of those meetings. It is clearly for ministers to make a judgment about the extent of that publication, and then for the Prime Minister to judge whether that is in accordance with the code. I know you have raised this case before, and I think the Communities Secretary responded to those allegations publicly—I cannot remember, off the top of my head, what he said—but I think people were broadly content with his response. Clearly that is an issue for the code. It is interesting to come back to this case, though, because it raises one important issue that the Committee might want to take a view on. We said in the consultation document that this was about not just lobbyists meeting ministers, but how they engage with Parliament. Clearly, if you take the view that there is only an issue about meetings with ministers, one potential solution that has been put forward by some in the industry is that you solve the problem completely by beefing up the extent of the disclosure that ministers make about their meetings. I would argue that it is about not just ministers, but meetings that lobbyists might have with parliamentarians because, after all, individual parliamentarians can change the law—they can change what is in legislation—so it is not just about ministers. If you limit it only to ministers, you are missing out a whole load of interactions that lobbying organisations have with Members of Parliament and Members of the House of Lords. That is why we have set up the register solution, as opposed to just dealing with it through transparency about ministerial meetings.

Q411 Paul Flynn: Other Members will take up that point.

The investigation into the case of Adam Werritty and a former Defence Minister was conducted by a person who had no authority to conduct it. The sole enforcer of the ministerial code is the independent adviser. It was then Sir Philip Mawer, who said that he should have conducted the investigation, and who then resigned. The result of that investigation was certainly illegitimate, and many suggested it was inadequate as well. There was a resignation, which halted a full inquiry. How does it advance transparency when we still do not know the role of Mr Adam Werritty, who was in the pay of a number of think-tanks, most of them outside this country, and who, it is alleged, had an agenda to encourage a war between ourselves and Iran. This is the allegation: that a private defence policy was being pursued by a Defence Minister and his adviser—the most serious allegation one could make. It has not been investigated by the sole enforcer of the ministerial code. Why?

Mr Harper: I do not think you describe the adviser on ministerial interests correctly. The enforcer of the ministerial code is the Prime Minister, and the Prime Minister is able to call on the independent adviser to investigate if, after consulting with the Cabinet Secretary, the Prime Minister thinks that investigation is necessary. In this case it was not, because after the Cabinet Secretary had carried out some investigations and information came to light, the former Secretary of State for Defence decided that it was appropriate for him to tender his resignation and he ceased to be a member of the Government. It seems to me that, in that case, he accepted that he had behaved unwisely and he is no longer a member of the Government. It seems to me that the code, in that case, worked perfectly as it is supposed to.

Q412 Paul Flynn: If the allegations are true, the worst possible outcome—just to repeat this—is that having been drawn into a war to get rid of non-existent weapons of mass destruction, and having stayed in Afghanistan to defend ourselves against a non-existent Taliban terrorist threat to Britain, we could have been drawn into a war on the basis of non-existent Iranian long-range weapons, carrying non-existent Iranian nuclear bombs. That is the agenda of some of the people who were paying Adam Werritty, and he was possibly influencing a Minister of the Crown. We do not know; it has not been tested or investigated. In fact, you have not used the ministerial code at all in the two years in which you have been in government, although there have been three cases. Doesn't this mean that instead of building up trust in politicians, we are further undermining it?

Mr Harper: Mr Flynn, I am perfectly happy to sit here and expand on the Government's foreign and defence policy on a range of issues for some time, but I do not think that is what the Committee asked me to come here for. Your characterisation of the British Government's foreign and defence policy is not one that I or, I suspect, most people share. You are entitled to your view, but it is not one that we share. I do not think that the allegations you have put forward are supported by even a shred of evidence.

Q413 Paul Flynn: I would be happy to provide you with that. Each of the self-regulatory bodies that has appeared before us has made its comments and submissions on this. The previous PASC suggested that we needed a statutory code that people had to abide by. You have pulled back from that. You have retreated from what happened in the previous Government—from recommendations that, disgracefully, were not taken up by the then Labour Government, though they should have been. Why didn't you propose a statutory code of conduct alongside the register this time? What is your response to the argument that a register without a code of conduct will lead to less regulation of the lobbying industry, and that self-regulation usually means no regulation?

Mr Harper: On the point about a code of conduct, we made it clear in the consultation document that we published that we do not intend to set up a regulator for the whole industry or everyone who carries out some kind of lobbying. We are trying to set up a register to increase the transparency about those who meet with ministers and parliamentarians, so that people are aware of who is meeting who and the purpose of those meetings. Transparency is how you deal with the concerns that people have. It is a different point of view. We do not want to set up an industry-wide regulator—another quango to regulate the industry. We think that if we have transparency, that is how we will deal with it.

On your specific point about regulation and a code of conduct, one of the things that came through in a number of the meetings that I attended was an idea that we will consider that was put forward by some in the industry. They pointed out that a number of the professional bodies have a code of conduct. They suggested that it should be made very clear in the register if anyone registered was a member of an organisation that had a code of conduct and a mechanism for ensuring high standards.

The other thing that the Government will consider is whether ministers would meet with people who did not belong to an organisation that had a code of conduct and therefore tried to drive up standards. That may be a way of driving up standards and enforcing them. Government will consider that when we bring forward our final proposals.

Q414 Paul Flynn: A final question: Unlock Democracy has fairly made the point that what you are suggesting might include details of meetings with ministers, but not necessarily the subject of those meetings. Clearly, there is no worthwhile transparency unless subjects are published. Have you any intention of doing that? Do you think that it is essential to publish the subject of the meeting and not just the meeting itself?

Mr Harper: The details that are already published on meetings that ministers have with external organisations include the meeting's purpose. Certainly, when I have meetings with external organisations, we say what the purpose of the meeting is. I know that there have been some concerns that if meetings cover a wide range of subjects, there is not enough detail, but there is a balance between publishing a minute of the meeting and publishing something that is meaningful, and people will have different views. We already publish not just the fact of meetings and who ministers are meeting, but the purpose of the meeting, which therefore gives an indication of the topics that are being discussed.

Paul Flynn: I am grateful to you.

Q415 Chair: Just following that up briefly, Mark, I wrote to the Cabinet Secretary—I hope you received a copy—about the publication of information. It is fine to publish it, but it has got to be published on a timely basis. The Cabinet Secretary has said that he has asked departments to continue to work to speed up the process. I would just make a comment, and you may wish to respond or not. Clearly if we are serious about this, just fulfilling the technical nature of the commitment is not good enough, and it would be very helpful if, perhaps even through your good offices, you could support the Cabinet Secretary on getting this information made available in a timely way. That will avoid any suspicion that there is some other agenda, which I am sure there is not.

Mr Harper: That is a very fair point, Chairman. In an earlier debate—it may even have been the one in Westminster Hall that Mr Flynn inspired—I made exactly this point. A colleague who had their iPad available looked up the details and pointed out exactly that: that the timeliness of publishing the meetings was not all it could have been, shall we say. I have spoken to my colleague, the Minister for the Cabinet Office, and work is under way to speed up the publication of that information while making sure it is still accurate. There is a real push to make sure that that is published on a more timely basis, so that the transparency agenda is dealt with better and the information is available more speedily. That is not just a commitment from the Cabinet Secretary; it is a commitment from ministers. Your Committee will no doubt hold us to account if we fail to do that.

Chair: That is really helpful, minister. We will follow that up with a few questions as the report progresses, so that we can hopefully help you keep them to the task on that.

Q416 Mr Chope: May I ask you about what is happening in Canada and the United States, where the lobbying register includes provisions for financial disclosure? We have heard evidence saying that it is not going to work unless there is a provision for financial disclosure. What do you think about that?

Mr Harper: We said in the consultation document that we thought there was a case for a certain amount of financial disclosure, and we floated the idea of something similar. We said we did not think that detailed financial disclosure was appropriate, and we could see that there would be issues around commercial confidentiality there, but we posited the idea of something akin to what Members of Parliament, for example, publish when they have outside remuneration. That information is published in bands to give an indication of the size of financial commitment that lobbying companies might have with their clients. Obviously we will look very carefully at what responses come back on that issue.

Q417 Mr Chope: So have you rejected having a look at the Canadian or US-style model of the lobbying register, which includes proper financial disclosure?
Mr Harper: We have not rejected that. That was not what we set out in our consultation document as our first port of call. We thought a better balance was some financial information. Part of the reason is that we want to have a proportionate register. What we want is something that is workable, sensible, and reasonably easy to comply with, and something that delivers transparency. We are not trying to create a wall of useless information, which would have an issue surrounding commercial confidence.
We set out our proposals in the consultation document. I have not seen the details of the responses that have come back. We will look at what people have said. It is an issue that becomes more complex if the scope of the register is wider. So, for example, in the register as set out in the consultation document, where you are talking about those who lobby on behalf of third parties, it is reasonably easy to see what we would mean by financial information; it would be the nature of the contractual obligation between the two. If you start bringing into the register, as some argue you should, in-house lobbying, charities and trade unions, it is not then clear what financial information you would be asking for and how easy it would be to disclose. Indeed, if you had very detailed regulations, it is not clear how easy it would be for people to get round then. We will look carefully at what people have said in the consultation and we will listen very carefully to what the Committee has said.

Q418 Mr Chope: On the issue of proportionality, the proposal at the moment is that, effectively, a register, if it were brought in, would be self-financing and the people who are on the register or who applied to go on the register would have to pay fees. That would include sole practitioners, small organisations and not-for-profit organisations. Do you think that there is a case for exempting those small organisations from the burden of effectively having to pay?
Mr Harper: We do think there is an argument there. It is one of the things we set out in the consultation document—people's views about whether there should be some kind of exemption from cost for small organisations. It is worth saying that we did think about whether we should exempt small organisations—the micro-businesses—from having to be registered in the first place. We decided against that, because it seemed to us that many of the organisations that operate in this industry are small organisations, and if you were to exclude them completely, you would be missing a lot of transparency. If you are going to include them, we think there is a case for asking how much of the financial burden they should pick up. That was one of the questions we asked in the consultation document, and we will look carefully at the responses.
There seemed to be a reasonable amount of agreement that this should be self-funding, but it was not unanimous, so we will look carefully at the consultation responses. There is clearly an argument. It could be like some registers that are self-funded and delivered by the industry at no cost to the taxpayer. There is another argument—that what we are doing is delivering a public service by making information transparent, and the taxpayer should pay for it. The Government's starting position was that it should come at no cost to the taxpayer and should be funded from fees. People will have different views about that.

Q419 Mr Chope: The Government also have a policy of not increasing burdens on business through regulation. My understanding is that you specifically exempted these lobbying proposals from the burdens-on-business analysis of "one regulation in, but only if another regulation is removed", so why are you making an exemption from your own policy in relation to lobbying?
Mr Harper: Because we think that there is a real problem to solve here, which we want to deal with, but it is exactly for that reason, Mr Chope, that we want a proportionate response. We do not want to create something that will be a disproportionate burden on industry, or a sledgehammer to crack a nut; we want something that deals with the issue of transparency in a way that is proportionate to the problem and easy to comply with, but does the job. We do not want to do any more than is necessary to deal with the problem at hand.

Q420 Mr Chope: This is my final question. This paper is very much about government being on the receiving end of lobbying. Do you think there is a case for increased transparency the other way, where government are doing the briefing, but doing it anonymously?
Mr Harper: There are two issues here. I will deal with the one that I think you are asking about secondly. The first point is about taxpayers' money being used for lobbying. We have already set out very clearly, in codes of practice, that local government should not be using taxpayers' money to lobby government. We have also made it clear that non-departmental public bodies should not be engaging in lobbying other parts of government to bid for more money for themselves. Those are two very important measures. On what you are saying, are you talking about the Government briefing the media about stories?

Q421 Mr Chope: Yes—not just the media, but government briefings.
Mr Harper: I do not think there is anything wrong with the Government seeking to communicate their message. The Government do that all the time—that is what the Government communication offices and government press departments are for. I think that the Government communicating their message and why they are doing what they are doing is a perfectly legitimate thing. I am not really sure that that would fall under the definition of lobbying. It is by its very nature transparent, because it appears in the media and you have either the Government spokesman or ministers being quoted. I am not quite sure of the point you are trying to get at.

Q422 Mr Chope: Is it not arguable that, when the Government brief the media through their spin doctors and all the rest of it, in a sense the Government are lobbying the general public, but doing so, quite often, under the cloak of anonymity? They can deny that any of the briefing actually came from any named individual, so there is a total lack of transparency in that respect.

Mr Harper: That may be a very interesting question in another debate that we could have, but I am not sure that it is particularly something that we could deal with under the purview of the lobbying register. I have to say that, if we are talking about the general public being lobbied by the Government, I think the general public are more than capable of weighing up what they are told by the Government and all sorts of other people, and coming to a sensible conclusion when they cast their votes.

Chair: Sheila, did you have a quick interjection?

Q423 Sheila Gilmore: This is about voluntary organisations and so on. Umbrella voluntary organisations, such as the National Federation of Housing Associations, will lobby on behalf of their members who will, on the whole, be a variety of housing associations. Are they required to register, or is it self-evident from what they are that they do not need to? At what point does that line get drawn? I suppose it is very clear what the NFHA is. The NCVO represents a rather wider and disparate group. That is where for some of the groups there are questions such as cost. How would they be affected by this?

Mr Harper: Your question raises two different aspects of this problem. The first is the scope of the register. Clearly, if you argue that we should capture everybody who lobbies government, organisations of that kind would be captured by a register of that sort. One thing is not clear, and this is part of the reason why we consulted. Take an organisation that represents housing associations. It may be a membership organisation, with housing associations paying fees to that trade association. Should they be covered?

There is one argument that says it is obvious on whose behalf those organisations lobby. I had that conversation when I spoke to the Trade Association Forum. Someone from the Airport Operators Association—I am not picking on them for a bad reason—made the point that in that case, it does what it says on the tin. It is fairly clear what his organisation does, but there are trade associations where it is not entirely obvious for whom they are lobbying. That is one of things on which we have asked for responses in the consultation.

There is an argument that if you are bringing in organisations, some of which are not well funded, what sort of burden should they bear, in terms of funding the register? What we are not trying to do is discourage organisations and individuals from lobbying their Members of Parliament and the Government. We want to hear their views; we are not trying to put people off. That is another reason why we want a proportionate register. We do not want to discourage the giving of legitimate information to government when they and parliamentarians are making decisions. That is not the purpose of the exercise. If we did that, we would all be worse off: the Government would make poorer decisions and the public would get worse-drafted laws. That would be a reduction in the quality of decision making.

Q424 Tristram Hunt: Minister, can I take you back to the celebrated speech of David Cameron in 2010, when he talked about the "next big political scandal"? He said: "I'm talking about lobbying—and we all know how it works", not least because David Cameron had actually been a lobbyist for Carlton Communications, so he probably did know. He added: "The lunches, the hospitality, the quiet word in your ear, the ex-ministers and ex-advisers for hire, helping big business find the right way to get its way. In this party"—I think he meant the Conservative party—"we believe in competition, not cronyism. We believe in market economics, not crony capitalism. So we must be the party that sorts all this out."

As a general question, would you regard the contact between the Culture Secretary's special adviser, the curiously named—in this context—Adam Smith, and News Corporation's Frédéric Michel as an example of market economics or crony capitalism?

Mr Harper: Let me go back to the speech that the Prime Minister gave when he was Leader of the Opposition. I will come to your specific question about BSkyB. Several of the things he addressed in that speech we have dealt with in government. Part of the reason why we published the details of meetings that ministers have is exactly to deal with transparency. We have dealt with the issue of former ministers who lobby the Government in the code, in which we have prohibited ministers when they leave office from being able to lobby government for two years. That provision, which was not there before, is now a mandatory part of the code. We have taken some specific steps, which we did immediately upon taking office, to deal with a number of the issues that the Prime Minister set out.

On your specific question, I know only what I have read in the papers about the contact between Adam Smith and Frédéric Michel. I would prefer to wait. We have seen one side of that argument with some of the information that has been published. I want to see the information that is published by the Culture Secretary and the explanation that he gives, before reaching a conclusion. I think that that is the right thing to do. I am not, I am afraid, going to be drawn on that question.

Q425 Tristram Hunt: On the extraordinary level of contact between one company and a department? If you believe in market economics, where everyone has—

Mr Harper: There are two issues there. First, we know some of the information, because some of it has been published. What we have not seen, and we will not see until it is published at Leveson, is the information that the Culture Secretary is going to publish, which he is adamant demonstrates that he has behaved at all times with complete integrity. I think that it is right to see that evidence, and the Prime Minister has made that clear, and then people can reach a judgment.

On what we already know, Adam Smith said himself that he felt that he had gone beyond what he had been instructed and authorised to do by the Secretary of State. He accepted that some of his contact had been inappropriate and that was why he tendered his resignation as a special adviser, and I think that that is appropriate.

Q426 Tristram Hunt: On the broader question of lobbying and the code of lobbyists, many of the criticisms we have had suggest that exactly that kind of contact would not be covered by what the Government are proposing. Whether it is News International, BP or BT, the army of in-house lobbyists who attempt, quite understandably, to influence government would not be covered, whereas a one-man-band lobbyist would be. Is that a rational way to approach your end point, which is about transparency and the electorate understanding where influence is?

Mr Harper: I think that the argument, and the reason why we reached the conclusion that we did in our consultation document with our initial proposals, is that if a minister meets an external organisation, and it is from an in-house lobbyist, we say, "The minister is meeting a man from Tesco"—just to pick someone at random—and it is clear that you are meeting someone from Tesco. If you say that you are meeting someone from a lobbying company, it is not entirely clear. That lobbying company could be acting for any organisation. Just saying that you are meeting them does not make it clear who the end client is. That was the gap in transparency that we were dealing with. It has been put to us in some of the consultation responses, and indeed when I did a number of the meetings, that that is not really the problem that we are trying to solve.

The problem that we are trying to solve is to deal with, not just meetings with ministers, but also those organisations' meetings with people involved in the political process, so with parliamentarians and that slightly wider look at the issue. It comes down to the definition of the problem. If you accept that the problem is about transparency, ministerial meetings with organisations being disclosed deals with it being clear if you are meeting in-house lobbyists, because you know on whose behalf they are arguing.

It comes back to the point that Mrs Gilmore made: if you are meeting the national association of housing associations, it is very clear what that is about, but if you are meeting a lobbying company representing them and you do not know that it is representing them, you are not aware of what the discussion might be about. It kind of depends what problem you think that you are trying to solve.

Q427 Tristram Hunt: But it also goes back to Mr Chope's point about financial transparency. Given the resources inherent in a Tesco, a BP or a BT, relative to the group against the development of whatever site, which wants to lobby you at the same time, even if you can have an equality of meetings, the kind of influence that might be brought to bear on a minister will be relatively different in terms of lobbying capacity, won't it?

Mr Harper: First, if you had a number of meetings with organisations, you would be publishing the number of meetings that you had, so that would be clear. I am not sure that having more people doing lobbying, having thicker documents or producing more information necessarily changes the result that ministers have. Ministers are going to weigh up information from lobbying organisations legitimately saying what their view is and how their industry might be affected. They are going to weigh up views from community groups. They are going to listen to parliamentarians and take advice from civil servants. Ultimately, ministers have to weigh up all that information, and then they have to take a decision in the public interest and make a judgment about how they think that is best served. I am not sure whether how much money companies spend on their lobbyists necessarily changes the result of that.

Q428 Tristram Hunt: Is it the Government's view also that, essentially, trade unions are no different from lobbying organisations?

Mr Harper: The reason why we put the question in the document is because trade unions clearly lobby government and political parties on behalf of their members. On the definition that we had set out—lobbying on behalf of third parties—you probably would not include trade unions in that. If you go for the more expansive definition of everyone who does lobbying, you probably would, because trade unions absolutely do try to change the law. They try to campaign for changes in decisions, and they do that with the Government and political parties. Again, it is about being transparent. We asked in the consultation whether it should apply to think-tanks, charities and campaigning organisations. We wanted to hear what people had to say. We want something that is transparent, but equally we do not want to stop the legitimate lobbying activity of people setting out their concerns and their views to government. That is not what we are trying to do. It is about the scope of the register.

Q429 Tristram Hunt: Does that then necessarily lead, as it were, to a system with a register of subsections in which you have a clear delineation—what Bell Pottinger does compared with what the Centre for Policy Studies or IPPR does? They are parts of the political process, but they are not, I would suggest, conceptually the same thing.

Mr Harper: If you were going to go for the argument that a number of people have used—for a more expansive, wider scope for the register—clearly there would be an argument about whether you said everybody should have to disclose the same information. Would you have a different level of disclosure depending on the size of the organisation? Again, as you said, would you have categories of types of organisations? Those are the kinds of things that you would need to deal with if you were going to go for that more expansive type of register, and you might want to have differential fees and all sorts of things. If you go for that, you may need to answer some of those questions.

In our initial proposals, we were not going for that more expansive register, but it is clear from an initial analysis of the consultation responses that quite a lot of people think it should be a much broader register. That was certainly the view that I had from a number of the meetings that I held. Interestingly, that view was not just from the lobbying industry, but from a number of the campaigning organisations. Mr Flynn mentioned Unlock Democracy. They take the view that they should be included. They lobby and try to change our minds. Their view is that they should be included on a register, and that it should be a much more expansive arrangement. We will have to look at all the responses and listen very carefully to what you say before we come to a decision.

Q430 Tristram Hunt: Finally, do you not regard it as slightly curious that the way people find out about ministerial meetings—on the question of government transparency—is that you go to the website data.gov.uk and then you link through to Who's Lobbying, which is a privately run website, run by the gentleman who came to give evidence to us and who does it in his spare time after work?
Mr Harper: The information is actually published on individual departmental websites. That is the source of the information. That organisation takes the information and presents it in what they would argue is a more user-friendly way. It comes back to one of the things that I think the Minister for the Cabinet Office set out about how the Government wanted to deal with transparency. We would put the information out there—we would publish it—and we were confident that people would then take that information and present it in different ways and analyse it. It could be done by media organisations or third-sector organisations. Some people may even be able to create a business out of presenting that information, and that is a very good example.
The information is published on departmental websites. It is all there. What that organisation does, I understand, is take the information that the Government publish and cut the data in all sorts of different ways and publish them in a way that they think is very helpful and meaningful for the end user. The data are published on departmental websites, albeit, as the Chairman said earlier, not on as timely a basis as perhaps they could be, which is what the Government want to work on. The Government publish that information on departmental websites, so it is available to the public. If you go to a departmental website, you can access all of that information at first hand.

Q431 Tristram Hunt: You are happy with that model of the departmental website and it being up to the other individuals, and you do not think that it should be the role of the Cabinet Office to help citizens understand what is going on more actively?
Mr Harper: There are two views. We publish the raw information. If I think of how it is published on the Cabinet Office website, it is not in an unhelpful format; it is fairly straightforwardly published in a spreadsheet format and, I think, a PDF format. Last time I looked at it, Who's Lobbying publishes it in a way whereby it cuts the data in different ways and presents them in terms of the most common meetings that have been held and, for each department, who are the people that they talk to most frequently. They cut the information in all sorts of different ways, which they think is helpful.
I think that one of the interesting things is that it shows that most of the lobbying that goes on is exactly what you would expect. If you look at the Department for Education, surprise, surprise, it spends a lot of time meeting the teachers' unions and people representing parents. On the children side of things, it meets people who represent social workers and who deal with child protection. I looked at a number of departments, and the sorts of people that ministers talk to are the sorts of people that you expect them to talk to and, actually, if they were not talking to them, they would not be doing their jobs properly. That is quite interesting. That website has an innovative way of presenting the information, but it is also presented by departments. The raw materials are there. I think that other organisations present it more creatively, in a way that it is very user-friendly, and that is a good thing and to be encouraged.

Q432 Chair: I am very impressed with Rob McKinnon. He does a day's work and then he goes home and puts a shift in every night. We floated, half-humorously, the idea that he should be nationalised and he did not seem to find that an unacceptable suggestion. Perhaps I should just leave that with you.
Mr Harper: If I may say so, I suspect that he does it much more efficiently, much more cost-effectively and much more quickly than if he were nationalised and it was done by a nationalised industry or a quango. I think that I am content to leave him working in the private sector.

Q433 Paul Flynn: There is a precedent. In the 1980s, I ran an operation publishing the questions from next-step agencies, which were not published in *Hansard*, and the Tory Government at that time nationalised my private enterprise, so it has happened before. The question I wanted to ask—a one-word answer would suffice—is: if a former minister, during the two-year period from retiring, does in fact lobby, what can the Government do about it?
Mr Harper: I have been asked this question before and it is very clear in the code that they are prohibited from doing so.

Q434 Paul Flynn: Yes, but what can you do about it?
Mr Harper: I am confident that ministers will comply with the terms of the code.

Q435 Paul Flynn: I think that the word that you are looking for is "nothing".
Mr Harper: We have not had a case yet where a former Minister has behaved in a way not in accordance with the code. Let us see what happens.

Q436 Paul Flynn: If it happens, what do you do?
Mr Harper: Rather than always looking on the black side—

Q437 Paul Flynn: You have claimed that this is a reform.

Mr Harper: I think that it is worth saying that this is a new provision in the code. It was not the case before that ministers were prohibited from doing this. Without mentioning any particular names, there have been cases in the past where, five minutes after ministers stopped being ministers, they went off and were paid for going back and lobbying their former colleagues for the private sector, so I think that there has been a step forward. It is very clear that, when ministers take office, they have to abide by the code. All those who are now former ministers, so far as I am aware, have abided by it. Let us wait and see how effective it is and not just assume that it will not work.

Q438 Paul Flynn: And what will you do? It is a simple question. What can you do?

Mr Harper: I tend to take the view that people who are made Ministers of the Crown will abide by the code and follow its strictures. Let us just see and let us not be so pessimistic and look on the black side of human nature.

Paul Flynn: I do not understand how you can take this utopian view.

Chair: It is open to the Committee to adopt a view on whether sanctions should exist and, if so, what they might be. We will cross that bridge if and when we come to it.

Q439 Simon Hart: I would start off by following that point, because I am quite interested in the argument. In my area, once you have finished your 25 years of being a planning officer for your local authority, you leave on a Friday and walk in again on Monday morning as a planning consultant, using all the knowledge and assets that you have acquired over 25 years at the public's expense in order to run a lucrative consultancy. So if you are going to apply that rule to ministers, which, I happen to think, would be a bit peculiar, should you apply it to civil servants at all levels? If you can take your knowledge into all sorts of other industries apparently without a second question, why should a former Member of Parliament or minister, who is able to take it into industry and pretty much everything else, not be able to do it for lobbying? It seems very inconsistent just to pick out ministers and say, "You can't use your knowledge and therefore compromise your ability to earn money for two years," when apparently everyone else on the public payroll can.

Mr Harper: If we take government, both senior civil servants and ministers, there is already a body, the Advisory Committee on Business Appointments, which looks at ministers and senior civil servants who want to take up appointments after leaving office. It has to look at those and judge whether an appointment is appropriate given the role they had. It is trying to deal with the issue of the revolving door, where people may be influenced in office by what they thought they were going to do afterwards.

I think the Select Committee on Public Administration either has done or is doing a review into that Committee and how effective it is. Forgive me for not knowing whether it has completed that report. The Government will clearly look closely at its recommendations.

This is effectively a tightening up of the detail in the code, specifically to stop ministers, for two years, being able to come back and lobby government. I think that is appropriate. It deals with the point in a speech, from which Mr Hunt quoted, made by the Prime Minister before the election about that concern. I think it is appropriate. I think ministers who take office need to ensure that people are confident that they make decisions in the public interest.

Q440 Simon Hart: You expressed complete confidence in ministers' integrity in your reply to Mr Flynn, about how they would behave afterwards. Yet you seem to be concerned about how they might behave in the final years of their office on the basis of what they might do afterwards. On the one hand, you are saying that these are people of integrity, with which I agree, and therefore let's not be too pessimistic; on the other hand, you are saying that we do not trust them quite enough not to impose these rules, because it might influence their thinking in the run-up to an election or when they might be retiring from Parliament. I wasn't going to raise this; it is just an aside.

Mr Harper: Briefly, it is about two things. It is partly about dealing with what is and is not acceptable, just making it clear what is acceptable. But it is also about public perception and making it clear that, "Here are the rules. Here is what is expected", and raising the bar on them. I think there was a general view that having ministers leave office and immediately come back and lobby both former departments and their former colleagues was not appropriate. But equally, your point about people having a legitimate ability to earn a living is why there is a time limited bar. I do not think it is reasonable to say that ministers can never engage in lobbying. It is about getting the balance right.

Q441 Simon Hart: They could go into Tesco and advise lobbyists on how to lobby, but they cannot actually be a lobbyist themselves. That seems odd to me.

You lead nicely on to the point that I intended to ask you about first. Turning the clock back to the beginning of the conversation, how have you or the Government assessed the extent of the transparency problem? Did you go out? Whom did you go to speak to? What sort of public opinion test did you apply, if any? What was the evidence on which you based your decision to proceed with the proposal as it is?

Mr Harper: The most obvious reason why we decided to proceed with our proposal is because there is a commitment in the coalition agreement. The two coalition parties said that we felt that having a statutory register was a necessary step to increase the transparency that you could not deal with purely through what ministers have decided to publish. We had a commitment to do it, and this is about delivering the commitment. The question that we had to deal with when we were thinking about the initial proposals that we put into the consultation document was: how are we going to deliver that in a way that is proportionate—picking up on Mr Chope's point—and effective? The problem that we identified is this gap in transparency. If you publish the details of ministerial meetings with people who represent third parties, there is a transparency gap, and that is the problem that we are trying to solve, and our case, as argued in the consultation document, follows. That is why we have set out our proposals. Clearly, some of the evidence that you have had and some of the responses to the consultation document effectively say that there is a different problem, and people posit evidence for that and therefore propose a different solution.

Q442 Simon Hart: I take your point, but it also seems that the commitment was made before the problem was identified. I was wondering what led to the commitment being made in the manifestos and the coalition agreement in the first instance. What compelling public pressure and evidence were you put under that necessitated its inclusion in the manifestos and the coalition agreement?

Mr Harper: Mr Hunt, when he quoted from the Prime Minister's speech from before the election, showed that we had identified that there was a problem, and there were a number of issues before the election that meant that people had been concerned about undue influence on the Government and some of the things that had happened. We and the Liberal Democrats had, and Labour did have, some proposals before the election for dealing with this. When we were negotiating the coalition agreement, the blending of the two Government parties then led to a commitment to deliver this statutory register. That is how we got to that point.

Q443 Simon Hart: A feature of the evidence sessions that we have had on this topic in the last few weeks has been that, every week, we have asked witnesses—either from the industry or those who monitor the industry—if they could put forward one tangible, real example of a lobbying scandal in the last three or four years that would have been averted had the Government's proposals, as they are, been in place. Not to be flippant, but, to date, nobody has actually come up with any such example. Can you?

Mr Harper: We were very clear about the problem that we are trying to solve with the register. There are other issues, but it depends on how you define the problem. If I just pick up—without going through them in detail—the points that Mr Flynn raised, you could argue that some of those are not actually about lobbying per se; they are about the conduct of ministers and whether they have breached the ministerial code. The solution to those problems is either about what is in the code or how the code is enforced. It is not necessarily about making lobbying more transparent.

What we wanted to deal with was perception, and I was asked at one of the meetings whether I thought that lobbyists had undue or improper influence. I said that I did not, but I also said the public do not necessarily think that that is the case. Part of this, therefore, is about being transparent, so that people are confident that ministers meeting people who are lobbying is above board and transparent, and people cannot make accusations of secret meetings, because it is all out there in the open. If ministers make decisions and the Government bring forward policies, people are aware of whom they have met and they are aware of those discussions, and the public can make a judgment on whether they think ministers have reached the right decisions in the public interest, having listened to all the views, or whether they have done something else. That is the problem that we are trying to solve. We are not pretending that this register solves every problem that there has ever been that people might say involves lobbying. Some of those problems may be more about the ministerial code and the conduct of ministers or about something else. They may have lobbyists involved in the process, but we are not trying to solve every problem; this is about solving the problem of transparency, much of which is about public perception, rather than reality.

When I think about how I have made decisions, you listen to different views, you weigh them up, and you take a decision in the public interest, but if I am not transparent about whom I have met, the public might not believe that to be the case. This is about giving the public confidence that those decisions are properly reached.

Q444 Simon Hart: On many topics that we have discussed with you on this Committee, there has always been a question about the extent to which the public are lying in bed worrying about this at the moment, and we could have that discussion perhaps on another occasion.

I do, however, want to pick up on one point you made. Obviously, you will not try to solve all the problems in this one measure. I think we all agree that lobbying techniques have changed quite a bit over the last few years. Do you think there is a risk that by imposing conditions or regulations, or however you might like to describe them, on traditional organisations such as Bell Pottinger, you end up driving lobbying into a different area? As you know, I am a former lobbyist of sorts. I would probably not have come under the register—although, strangely enough, I think I probably should have done—because most of my lobbying was done through third parties. We seldom sat down in a Minister's office and engaged them. We facilitated people meeting their MPs in their constituencies, armed with the necessary evidence and information—and very effective that was.

Paul Flynn: Or invaded the Commons Chamber.

Simon Hart: Absolutely. There were several ways in which we could make our point. There is some quite aggressive charity campaigning, which is often very effective and very controversial. It may be online or it may come in a million different forms, all of which stand a chance of influencing the direction that a government may take, but it will not appear here, although it may have quite a powerful impact. Are we at risk of them thinking that they will get something that is completely transparent and will eradicate whatever the problems are, when it will make no difference at all?

Mr Harper: You highlight a risk, and we must make sure that being more transparent about some things does not cause inadvertent problems. That is partly the point of doing this thoughtfully and carefully, and not rushing off to a short-term solution that has inadvertent consequences. Picking up your specific point about some of the campaigning that organisations do to persuade members of the public of a view, and then encouraging them to raise that with their Member of Parliament, it seems to me that that is legitimate.

Q445 Simon Hart: I think it is a good thing.
Mr Harper: We are absolutely not trying to stop or to get in the way of constituents raising issues with their MPs.

Q446 Simon Hart: Yes. This is really important. The 38 Degrees online campaigning site had a mass-campaign on forestry, and the Government changed their mind about their policy—some would say rightly—yet if the 38 Degrees agenda and the people who make up that lobby organisation had been known to the wider public, the argument might have been slightly different. I am sorry to interrupt, but that is a classic example of when transparency was not available to everyone, yet the effect on government policy was huge.
Mr Harper: You make a good point about organisations. In that case, the organisation did not directly lobby the Government. It effectively gave information to the general public, who decided whether they wanted to raise it with their MPs. The source of some of the e-mails that Members of Parliament receive has become fairly obvious, and MPs can make a judgement about the extent to which they want to rely on them. In the forestry case that you raise, I do not think it was just the volume of e-mails. MPs received representations from their constituents. As a Member for a forest, I received correspondence from and had conversations with constituents and, as a minister but with my constituency hat on, I made my views known privately to my ministerial colleagues. There has been quite a lot of that going on as well. The credit for the Government's rethink of their policy lies a little more widely than just a lot of e-mails, but I take the point.
It depends on the scope. If we go to everyone who lobbies the Government more widely, these organisations may be in scope. They were not in our initial proposals, but some of the views we have received are that all campaigning organisations should be captured, but that would make the register a much wider beast than we initially set out. We will look at the responses that we have received. We have had responses from several campaigning organisations that have encouraged members of the public to respond on this issue as well, but they will respond only if they find the arguments that they are given compelling. In some senses, the public have a check—a role in controlling that sort of lobbying.

Q447 Simon Hart: You mentioned that a meeting between a minister and a representative of Tesco was what it appeared to be, whereas a meeting between a minister and Bell Pottinger might not be, in terms of transparency. The question I would put to you is that it is a simplistic way of looking at it, because there are 1,000 different issues that Tesco might want to raise with the minister, varying from planning to pricing. In terms of organisations, particularly larger organisations—the Countryside Alliance, which I worked for, lobbied government on 20 or 30 different issues—it is simplistic to suggest that it is obvious because of what their name is. Likewise, if you are determined enough, and some of our witnesses clearly have been, there are already ways, through FOI and other existing legislation, to discover what it was that Bell Pottinger was in your office talking about, and to demand much more than the register is going to provide by way of copies of exchanges, letters and e-mails.
Mr Harper: Let me pick up that point. The register is not designed to be the solution to every problem. One important thing about transparency, and about increasing transparency, is that it enables people to use other tools at their disposal to do some of that work to get more information. For example, even if you do not publish the information in the register, if it is information that is within the scope of the FOI legislation, you can use that, but often you cannot use it unless you know that a meeting has happened. If you know that a meeting has happened with an organisation, you can then ask a question about what was discussed and those sorts of things, and then obviously the Government will apply the appropriate rules in the Freedom of Information Act.
You need the raw material, unless you are just going to encourage people to send in FOI requests, asking for any meetings you have had with anybody ever. You want focused questions. Some of the transparency that we are talking about here will help people—it could be individuals, other organisations or the press—ask those focused questions and use some of the other tools at their disposal to then do that work. We are not pretending that the register is the complete solution. It is an essential tool in that level of transparency, but then there is the further work that people can do using other tools to put things into the public domain.

Q448 Simon Hart: Will you put a sunset clause in there so that we can review its effectiveness after a year or two?
Mr Harper: As a standard rule, government look at things post-legislatively, and select committees can do that as well. Certainly, it is always sensible to review things to see if they have had the desired effect and have delivered what you wanted. That is a sensible way of governing. As well as government looking at it, we will also look to the select committees to see whether what we have delivered does what we wanted it to do.

Q449 Stephen Williams: There is not a great deal left to ask. That is the danger of going last. Simon was asking Mark about what problem this was trying to solve. I come in from a different perspective. Where is the demand for the problem to be solved coming from? Is Mrs Jones in Lydney or Mr Smith in Coleford saying, "Mark, I want to know what you are up to"?

Mr Harper: It is one of those things where there are peaks and troughs. When there are scandals, for want of a better word, or a particular focus in the media on these stories, people may decide that they want to know. It is probably unlikely that most of my constituents spend any significant part of their day trawling the Cabinet Office website to see who I am spending my days meeting. When various stories happen, people want to know that ministers are being transparent about who they are meeting, and that if they wanted to know, they could. It is also about making sure that we have good government. If you have an appropriate level of transparency and ministers make it clear who they are meeting—even if people do not check the information, they are happy that it is out there and that things are above board—things function better. It is probably not the sort of thing that keeps people awake at night, but I suspect that when there are issues about it, those are the sorts of things that you either do not want to happen or, if they do, the Government want to be able to turn around and say, "No, actually there isn't anything to this. We had some meetings with this organisation; we published the details of them; we know what they were about. It is fairly straightforward. You don't need to be concerned about this because we have been very transparent about what we've been doing." It is part of the general move we have made towards being more transparent. A lot of the information we have published about procurement, meetings and things like that improves the way that government is conducted overall.

Q450 Stephen Williams: How easy do you think it would be for the residents of Lydney and Coleford to find out what their Member, who happens to be a minister—or any minister—is getting up to? Mr McKinnon has been mentioned several times by colleagues; he tells us that, at the moment, in terms of the information that the Government publish, you would have to view at least 24 departmental websites. There are other bits of the Government that are not in a department, including you. There are 150 different files, so it is pretty difficult to get just a snapshot at a moment in time of who is meeting who and talking about what. Once we get this register in place, how easy is it going to be for our constituents to find out what their government ministers are doing and who they are meeting?

Mr Harper: That comes back to the point that I think Mr Hunt was alluding to, which is that the Government have published the raw material in a reasonably accessible format. It is pretty straightforwardly published in the two different file types. The question then is the extent to which other people cut and interpret the data and present them in a way that people find meaningful. It seems that, yes, the Government could try to do that, but I suspect, knowing a little bit about the IT industry, which I used to work in, and looking at a lot of the innovative ways people use IT now to display information, that other people are likely to do that much better than the Government—whether it is people like Mr McKinnon, who gave evidence to you, or media organisations. Often when media organisations are covering particular stories, they will take the raw material and publish it either in their printed copies or make it available on their website. They will cut it in different ways. It kind of depends what you are looking for. The raw material is out there, but often people are not just doing it in a random way to say, "I want to see who every minister is meeting with." They will have a particular reason or subject they are interested in, or they may have a particular range of organisations they are concerned with, and they will want to cut the data in different ways.

The important thing for the Government is that we put the data out there; then people can cut the data and display and look at them in different ways, depending on what their need is. There will be private individuals, organisations or media organisations who will take care of presenting the information in a different way. If the Government tried to present it in a way that was interesting to everybody for every possible use, I suspect they would fail.

Q451 Stephen Williams: Is that not an admission—perhaps you are preparing the ground for this fact—that the way you propose to publish the information will make it very difficult for an armchair auditor, which is how the Prime Minister described citizens, to do this for themselves? They will have to rely on third-party organisations that have their own agendas putting this information together. If we suppose that Mr Jones in Lydney wants to see how many ministers a particular lobbyist has met, it sounds as though he will not be able to find that out from what the Government are proposing, other than by going through every single departmental website.

Mr Harper: This is one of the questions about the register, the information we publish in it and the way it is published. In terms of what is published in the register, clearly this will be, again, partly about making sure that it is proportionate. Having enormous quantities of information that is not very useful is probably a good way of making sure it is difficult to find stuff out. That is partly why we are trying to understand what information needs to be on the register and what should be published. Something we did not really talk about in the consultation document—it sounds as though, in light of the evidence you have taken, you may be giving us some advice on this—is how to publish it and make the information easily available. In the consultation document, we did not really go into any great detail about the register, how it would be available, how you would pool the information and some of that level of detail. It sounds as though you may well be thinking about giving us some advice in that area, and that would be welcome, to make it as easily accessible as possible.

Q452 Stephen Williams: Otherwise, it is sort of bathroom-window transparency, isn't it? You know something is going on, but the view is obscured, which may be a good thing. Some transparency would be in order for you to see clearly through the information that the Government are providing. In terms of what information the Government already

provide—this may not exactly be best practice to base the future on—with ministerial meetings, only the month in which the meeting took place is published, rather than the exact date. If you are having a three-star lunch—as opposed to Mr Pickles's five-star lunch—in April, that is interesting to know, but it would be more interesting to know that you have had a three-star lunch five days before a White Paper comes out. Why are the Government not publishing information more precisely at the moment?
Mr Harper: That is a point of view. The fact is that the Government are publishing the information that they publish, which was not previously published, so I think we have taken a step forward. Clearly, people will argue that we should publish it in ever-tougher degrees of detail. There is a balance in terms of what you publish. I do not know the extent to which the Committee has looked at what ministers already publish, and whether you will have any views about whether there should be any changes in that. Clearly, if you make recommendations, we will look at those seriously. We have published stuff that we think is useful. If you have recommendations about that, please make them, and we will look at them seriously. It is important that when we publish the information, it is accurate.

Q453 Stephen Williams: You can be accurate about dates, surely?
Mr Harper: One of the things that slows it down is checking what is published, so the more you publish, the more it has to be checked. Again, there is a balance there, but that is why we are working on speeding it up and publishing it on a timely basis. If you make recommendations, we will absolutely look at those and take them seriously.

Q454 Stephen Williams: An analysis has been presented to us, which I think comes from Mr McKinnon as well—he is clearly very busy. It says that of 8,000 meetings currently disclosed on a monthly basis by the Government, only 0.2% have been with third-party lobbyists. Does that not rather undermine the whole basis of the Government's proposal that only third-party lobbyists should be on the register, when quite clearly, an awful lot of meetings are taking place with other people who seek to influence government and will not be required to register?
Mr Harper: You can look at that the other way round, of course: of those 8,000 meetings, in 99.8% of cases, it is very clear who the minister is meeting and the purpose of the meeting. Actually, you could argue that the Government are being incredibly transparent, and we are trying to close the gap that is left, because there is, perhaps, a disproportionate perception issue. To be quite frank, some of this is about perception. Ministers clearly know when a lobbying company comes to see them, and they will ask who they are coming on behalf of. It would be extraordinary if that were not known to the minister, and I was challenged on that at some of these meetings that I held. I said, "No, of course ministers know, but it is about making sure that the public know and are confident that it is all transparent and above board." The way I would prefer to look at the information you have just given me is to say that we are being 99.8% transparent, and what we are dealing with here is ensuring that we go the last mile.

Q455 Stephen Williams: Trade unions, charities and other people have already been mentioned, but what about think-tanks? I read yesterday—in *The Times,* I think—that the Government are to contract out some more policy-making analysis to think-tanks outside the civil service. If Ministers are having more meetings with think-tanks, should they not be registered as lobbyists, too, particularly as their role potentially seems to be becoming more important, in terms of policy formulation?
Mr Harper: If ministers are having meetings with external organisations, think-tanks would fall within that definition already. If a minister either has a meeting with, or people come to see him from, a think-tank, my understanding is that that would be covered by the existing disclosure regime, so people would know that that was happening. We have put down think-tanks as a particular case in the consultation document, along with trade unions and charities, in terms of whether they should have to be in the register. Some people think they do and some do not, so, again, we have asked for views on that. I think I am right in saying that we have heard mixed views about some of those other organisations and whether they should be included. I do not know yet where the balance of that falls.

Q456 Sheila Gilmore: The 2009 Public Administration Select Committee report on this issue noted the following: "Some of the concerns that exist around improper influence are…linked to the power of informal networks of friendships and relationships." Obviously, that issue has come up a lot again recently. There is the archetypal round of golf, but there are also the Sunday walks and the meeting at a dinner party or whatever. Will these proposals allay in any way people's concerns about those more informal networks? Is there anything we can do about that?
Mr Harper: To some extent, this brings us back into the debate some of the issues that I raised about the ministerial code in answer to Mr Flynn's questions. Clearly, you could take an extreme position and say that once somebody became a Minister of the Crown, they were to cease ever having contact with any other human being on any basis, but I think that would be ridiculous. Ministers have to conduct themselves in a way that is appropriate.
For example, if ministers meet people socially because they happen to know them, they should discuss things in a way that would be appropriate publicly, so they should be perfectly happy to disclose what the Government's policy is on something that has already been announced, but if the minister wants to have a discussion with the person about the detail of something, they should do it in the proper way. That person should come to see them and they should have a meeting, with a civil servant to take notes, in a proper way. That is how the minister would protect themselves from any allegations. That was part of the

concern and part of the reason why the former Defence Secretary said that he resigned—because he accepted that some of the ways in which he had behaved had caused concern. He accepted that.

Some of this is about how ministers conduct themselves, and it does say in the ministerial code that it is not just about what we do, but about conducting ourselves in a way that does not lead to the perception of wrongdoing. As I said, some of this is about how ministers conduct themselves. I do not think you could say that every single time you talk to anybody for five seconds at a reception, that somehow has to be registered. I think that would be ridiculous. It would have the opposite effect. The effect would be that ministers never talked to anybody, never listened to anybody and were terrified to engage with anybody. We would get worse decision making. What we want to do is to encourage ministers to listen and to engage, but to do so in a transparent way.

My view is therefore that ministers should be perfectly happy to explain to people what the Government's policy is in a way that has been disclosed publicly, but they should not go beyond that. If they want to have a discussion with somebody about a policy area, if they want to listen to some evidence from or hear the thoughts of people who are involved in that area, they should have them in to the department and have a meeting, with notes taken by officials so that everybody knows that it has been done in a proper way. Clearly, it is perfectly appropriate for Ministers to listen to the views of their constituents, but equally if I had a constituent who had a professional interest in one of my policy areas, I would want them to come to see me in my ministerial capacity and I would deal with that in the proper way.

This is partly about how ministers conduct themselves. That is dealt with through the code, rather than by making the register a diary of ministers' social engagements. I think that is the way you have to handle it.

Q457 Sheila Gilmore: Do you think that there is almost a danger of people getting so anxious that they become less likely to disclose things? There is the idea of the media running around with cameras and sitting outside your door to see who you meet on the way to the local post office or whatever. People may be disposed to be less than candid about some of their social engagements, but then again, in the end, that makes people even more suspicious.

Mr Harper: Some of this is about judgment, balance and being sensible. It is about ministers always having to ask themselves about how they are conducting themselves. Are they comfortable with how they are conducting things, and would they be comfortable if people knew about what they were doing? That is one of the tests. When I was in business, one of the tests we had when we were thinking through how we conducted ourselves was very appropriate for politicians: the, "Would I be happy if this was on the front page of the newspaper?" test or, alternatively, the, "Would I be happy explaining it to my mother?" test. Those are actually quite good, common-sense ways of deciding how you are conducting yourself and whether you are comfortable with it, but they are more about the code than about the register; that is my view.

Q458 Paul Flynn: We have just emerged from the worst parliamentary scandal for 200 years. The urgent priority of any incoming government was to try to rebuild confidence and trust in the political system. In the past two years, thanks to the Bureau of Investigative Journalism, we have seen on our televisions Bell Pottinger boasting that it can sell access to the Prime Minister, and we have seen an official of your party, Mr Cruddas, saying that it costs £250,000 to buy access, for a meal, with the Prime Minister. These are not speculations; we have actually witnessed these things.

We have seen a new doctrine of absolution by resignation in the Fox case and in the SpAd case in the Culture Department—that once you resign, there is no investigation. That is, I think, a new method of sleaze. We have seen allegations of the influence of McKinseys on the Health and Social Care Bill. You have given two examples of how the Government have improved things. One, I think, was entirely spurious—there were no sanctions involved in the ACoBA one.

We should all feel passionately. I have just finished a book, which goes off to the printer today, about one of our colleagues who I think died prematurely—an entirely innocent, honourable gentleman—because he was part of the collateral damage from the expenses scandal. If we are passionate, we have a task which will take a decade before we restore the confidence that people previously had in politicians.

Don't you really think that the tardiness with which your Government have behaved in trying to get a proper register for lobbyists—all the allegations, the disregard of the ministerial code—means that the judgment, after two years, is that the public have less trust in us now than they did when you were first elected?

Mr Harper: I do not accept the premise. Yes, the expenses scandal was very serious, and that is why Parliament took the decisions about setting up IPSA. We touched on this when the Deputy Prime Minister and I gave evidence, but I think that now—it took a while—the normal mechanism has demonstrated that people were actually held accountable. People who had committed the worst abuses—those who had actually breached the law—went through a trial, were found guilty and went to prison. Before the election, there was a lot of scepticism about whether that was ever going to happen. We have cleaned up our act: we have an independent body to do expenses—it has not been trouble free, and it has not been entirely popular with all colleagues, as I know—which is now working reasonably well. In that area, if you look at polling, people are confident about that.

On your various accusations, I do not accept your argument in the Culture Secretary's case. That is not done and dusted. My understanding is that Frédéric Michel, Mr Smith and the Culture Secretary will all give evidence under oath to a judicial inquiry. On the idea that nothing is ongoing—that is a pretty high bar for them to have to deal with—I just do not accept that premise.

In terms of tardiness, I absolutely reject that. The previous Government did nothing on this issue for 13 years. We came into office with a commitment. We have published our proposals and we are going through a proper process. There is an argument that we could have rushed off and brought in legislation, not having paid attention to the consultation or waited for this Committee's report. Looking at the consultation response, we would have ended up with legislation that was immediately controversial, that did not deal with the problem that people agreed existed, that was badly drafted, and—picking up Mr Chope's point—that was probably not delivering what we wanted.

We are going through a proper process. It takes time, but I think it is better for Parliament if we are all clear about the problem, clear about the solution, bring forward well-drafted draft legislation, which your Committee can then scrutinise, pass a bill this Parliament, and then not have to come back to it again, because people will be confident that we have the right solution. The last thing we want to do is rush off in haste, cobble something together and then come back in six months and do it all over again. I would rather get this job done properly—get it done. Then, to pick up Mr Hart's point—he is not in his place at the moment—we can get on with discussing the issues that the public do worry about at night: jobs and growth, and ensure that they are confident that we have a robust political system. We need to do the job properly rather than in haste and make a bodge up of it.

Paul Flynn: Haven't you forgotten—

Chair: No, Paul, you have come back three times and some colleagues have only been once.

This has been a helpful session, Minister. You have also pointed us towards one or two areas that it would be particularly helpful for us to look at in depth. We will obviously look at the whole thing in depth. I leave you with the thought that where we have been successful has been where we have interacted effectively with government. I think we managed to move the show forward when you have listened to us and we have presented a rational case.

Mr Chope: Chairman, I thought we were going to ask the Minister one or two questions outside lobbying.

Chair: There is time and, if the Minister is willing, I am happy to allow other questions outside the lobbying sphere.

Mr Harper: The Minister is content.

Q459 Mr Chope: Since the Minister was last here, we have had the Queen's Speech and the announcement about a bill being introduced in relation to the composition of the House of Lords. Could you tell us any more about the specific timetable for that bill? What is meant by the expression the Prime Minister used of "seeking consensus"? Does that mean that the threat that was hanging over this legislation of it being "Parliament-Acted" has now been lifted?

Mr Harper: As colleagues will know, the Joint Committee that was scrutinising our draft bill did that very thoroughly and published its report not very long ago. We are, obviously, considering its recommendations. It made a number of recommendations. It is worth saying that it broadly endorsed the approach we adopted. It accepted by a significant majority that there should be an elected House—that was not actually one of its narrower decisions. It broadly endorsed our approach on 80/20 and on a number of other things. It also accepted that the primacy of the House of Commons could be maintained, and made some recommendations in other areas that we are seriously considering. On timing, the Leader of the House said last week at business questions that he expected the legislation to be brought forward before the summer recess. I would not demur from or add anything to what he has said.

In terms of its parliamentary passage, it will be a Government Bill, taken through in the usual way. I think that the point the Prime Minister was making about consensus is that of course there are different views in all parties on this, but it was in all three parties' manifestos and all three Front Benches agree that it is something we should do. It is absolutely true that the public do not have it at the top of their list of things that they grab us to talk about when we knock on their doors or pass them in the street, but they broadly agree that we should elect at least most of the people who sit in the upper House of our legislature. It is a fairly uncontroversial proposition for the public. They think it is pretty straightforward. We should deal with the detail, but we should get on and do it, and that is what the Government intend to do.

Q460 Mr Chope: What about the Parliament Act—is that now removed as being a threat? Obviously, it is rather inconsistent with the approach of trying to get consensus to have a threat hanging over heads that, if their Lordships try to amend the bill in any way that the Government do not like, they will force it through under the Parliament Act.

Mr Harper: On the context and the Parliament Act, we want the bill to pass in the usual way. We would expect that, when the Commons passes a bill, particularly on this subject, and sends it to their Lordships' House, it would be debated and almost certainly amended. There is a question about whether you are talking about a bill that will be amended or one that their Lordships will try to block. I think it is perfectly in order for their Lordships to debate and amend the bill to improve it, but I do not think it would be appropriate on this subject, if the House of Commons has taken a clear decision, for their Lordships to try to block it. That was the context in which the Prime Minister was asked the question about the Parliament Act. I very much hope that we will not have to use the Parliament Act. I hope we will be able to pass the bill in the Commons, with a significant cross-party majority, send it to the House of Lords, have the bill improved, and then have a more democratically legitimate legislature in our country, which is something that the public support.

Chair: With colleagues' consent, I will close the meeting. We expect to produce our report towards the end of June, Minister, and look forward to taking some of its proposals forward with you, when we finally see some legislation towards the end of the year, we hope.

17 May 2012 Mr Mark Harper MP

Mr Harper: I look forward to it. Thank you very much indeed.

Chair: Thank you so much for your time this morning.

Written evidence submitted by Tamasin Cave, SpinWatch

INTRODUCTION

1. SpinWatch has been engaged in a programme of research into the public relations and lobbying industry in the UK and Europe since 1996. In September 2007, we established the Alliance for Lobbying Transparency (ALT), a coalition of NGOs and unions—many of whom are lobby groups, including Unlock Democracy, Friends of the Earth and ActionAid—who are concerned about the growing influence of lobbying on policy-making in the UK. We were greatly encouraged by the Public Administration Select Committee's recommendation in 2009 for a statutory register of lobbyists.

2. We therefore welcomed the commitment in the Coalition Agreement to introduce a statutory register. However, we have since been concerned by the lengthy delays in bringing forward plans, and the lack of senior ministerial ownership of the proposals. We are also increasingly concerned that the Government's proposals have been unduly influenced by the lobbying industry, and that the Cabinet Office has sought to keep its discussions with lobbyists secret. This could lead to the conclusion it has not approached the policy with an open mind.

THE GOVERNMENT'S PROPOSALS FOR A STATUTORY REGISTER

3. *The Committee asks: Does the Government's consultation paper represent a balanced approach to the idea of a statutory register? Does it contain the right questions? And which lobbying contacts are of greatest legitimate public interest?*

4. We are extremely disappointed by the Government's proposals as set out in its consultation paper *Introducing a Statutory Register of Lobbyists*. We do not think that it represents a balanced approach, and have serious concerns about the very narrow framing of the issues. Partly as a consequence, there are a number of key questions that have not been raised in the consultation. We also believe that the paper contains serious errors, including in its evidence base, and is in parts misleading. Our key concerns are outlined below.

5. Two are fundamental: first, the minimal information that lobbyists would be required to declare and second, that it would only apply to a minority of lobbyists, those working for agencies.

6. First, the Government is proposing that the register should only reveal minimal details, namely who is lobbying for whom. Lobbying agencies would only be required to list the names of an agency's individual lobbyists and the names of their clients.[1]

7. The reason for this approach of very minimal disclosure by a small section of the industry is justified by minister Mark Harper as follows:

> Ministers already have to say who we meet. If we've met with outside organisations, we say we've met with them. So that's very transparent... The gap is that if you meet with a lobbying company you know you've met with them, but if people don't know who their clients are, they don't know who they're representing, then there's a gap there, and that's what we've sought to address in our proposals.[(i)]

8. In essence, the problem that the Government is seeking to address is one of lack of transparency in who agencies represent. The key benefit for both the lobbying industry and the Government in taking this narrow approach is that the solution mirrors the current voluntary system of registration operated by the industry, while forcing lobbying agencies that have so far stood outside the system, to join.

9. It is the register model that has long been pushed by the lobbying industry. In July 2010 it was reported that Mark Harper had given the "thumbs up" to a blueprint for a lobbying register drawn up by the industry. "It would essentially look very similar to the current APPC and PRCA registers," one senior industry source told *PR Week*.[(ii)]

10. In January 2011, Elizabeth France, Chair of the UK Public Affairs Council, which was created by the three lobbyists' trade bodies, described the industry's approach as: "persuading government that what they need to do is embrace [UKPAC's register] with a statutory hug rather than invent something else".[(iii)]

11. The Government appears to have been persuaded. However, in defining the problem as simply one of a lack of transparency over agency clients in respect of ministerial meetings, the Government is both showing a gross misunderstanding of public concerns over lobbying, and misrepresenting the facts.

12. The consultation paper states in setting out the "Purpose of a Statutory Register":

> "The government already publishes quarterly information about Ministers' meetings... But under the current system, when ministers meet lobbying firms it is not transparent on whose behalf they are lobbying."

[1] We agree with the Government's proposal that information should be supplied on previously held public office, but think it should be widened to include any public office, not just senior. Financial information should also be provided (based on a good faith estimate of lobbying spend). However, for the purposes of this paper, these are not central concerns.

13. According to the website whoslobbying.com, which collates government logs of ministerial meetings, of the 5,144 meetings logged since May 2010 only about 10 were with lobbying agencies. The Government is therefore suggesting setting up a register that would address a lack of transparency relating to just a handful of ministerial meetings. The records of five of these meetings also name the agencies' clients, along with the agency.

14. The data underlines something that lobbyists giving evidence to the PASC inquiry in 2008–09 were at pains to point out: that they do not advocate a view to a minister on a client's behalf: "a client is their own best advocate". In other words, it is seldom the case that ministers will meet with lobbyists without the client being present, and therefore declared.

15. **The problem, narrowly defined by the Government, appears then not to exist**, or could be solved much more easily: ministers should be required to log the names of specific clients represented on the occasions that they meet lobbying agencies.

16. In setting the parameters thus, the Government could be accused of willfully **misrepresenting the problem in order to justify a system of absolute minimal** disclosure, and one that is broadly in line with the industry's wishes.

17. In so doing, the Government has completely misrepresented the actual purpose of a statutory register, which is ultimately to increase government accountability by allowing a degree of public scrutiny of its interactions with lobbyists. The consultation's Impact Assessment describes the benefits to government from a register as: "greater transparency in their interactions with lobbyists, leading to greater public confidence in decision-making process".

18. Essential to this, therefore, is information on *government's interaction* with lobbyists: whom is being lobbied in government, and which policies, legislation, regulation and government contracts are being lobbied on. Without these key pieces of information the register would be a relatively meaningless list of names.

19. Under the Government's proposals the register would include no information on lobbyists' interaction with decision-makers. However, there is an explicit acknowledgment of this need to see what lobbyists are lobbying for in the consultation's Impact Assessment:

> The purpose of the UK register is to increase transparency by making available to the public, to decision-makers and to other interested parties authoritative and easily-accessible information about who is lobbying ***and on what issues***. This will help ensure that those seeking to influence decisions do so in a way that is open to scrutiny, improving knowledge about the process and the accountability of those involved in it.

20. However, this critical piece of information has been deliberately taken out of the consultation paper's description of the register's purpose:

> The purpose of the UK register is to increase transparency by making available to the public, to decision-makers and to other interested parties authoritative and easily-accessible information about who is lobbying ***and for whom***. This will help ensure that those seeking to influence decisions do so in a way that is open to scrutiny, improving knowledge about the process and the accountability of those involved in it.

21. The consultation paper itself makes no reference to the possibility of lobbyists being required to disclose whom they are lobbying, or what they are trying to influence (other than in passing in the Annex describing disclosure systems in other countries).

22. The Alliance agrees with the Government that registration should not create an undue burden on lobbyists. However, it would be no more trouble for lobbyists (who will be in full possession of the details) to add information on issues lobbied on, than it would be to list lobbyists names, clients and whether they've previously held senior public office.

23. Imagine the case of outsourcing company X: It hires lobbying agency Y. This much would be recorded on a public register under the Government's plans. How is the public to know if a firm that operates across local and central government, education, transport, health, pensions, insurance, and other sectors such as financial services, is meeting government officials to discuss government contracts (future or existing), employment, planning or tax issues, or a specific problem it is having with a regulator, such as the FSA?

24. It is not true to say, as Mark Harper did on the World at One: "If [a minister's] meeting someone from a company, you pretty much know what that's about." **The register must reveal who is lobbying whom in government and on what issues.**

25. This leads to the second key concern we have with the Government's proposals: its decision to exclude in-house lobbyists from the register.

26. "Should in-house lobbyists be covered?" the consultation asks before concluding: "Given that it is clear whose interests they represent, it is not evident that an extension of the register to in-house lobbyists would provide any additional transparency".

27. In the context of a register whose purpose is limited to "providing information about who is lobbying and for whom", this makes a degree of sense. However, in the context of a system designed to "make sure that lobbying is out in the open, it's transparent, so that everyone knows what's going on", as Mark Harper described it in interview, it is a glaring omission.

28. Here, **the Government appears to have distorted the figures on the number of in-house lobbyists in the UK in order to support its case for excluding them.**

29. In the consultation's Impact Assessment "Evidence Base", the Government puts the total number of lobbyists at 1,500. It states: "Based on their definition of lobbying, UKPAC have estimated the possible coverage of a statutory register. That data suggests the register would cover... around 1,500 people engaged in lobbying."

30. It provides a summary of UKPAC's calculations to reach this figure:

Type of organisation	*Number of organisations*	*Employees engaged in lobbying (total)*
Public affairs specialists	100	1,000
Companies with in-house staff	60	100
Charities/voluntary sector	40	120
Unions	30	50
Trade associations	25	50
Law practices	20	50
Others		130
Total	275	1,500

According to these figures, the number of in-house lobbyists, which includes company, charity/voluntary sector, union, trade association (and possibly "others"), is between 320 and 450, fewer than half the number of agency lobbyists ("Public affairs specialists").

31. However, these figures are significantly different from earlier calculations done by the three lobbyists' trade bodies, which went on to form UKPAC. In May 2009 they published a paper, *Towards a Public Affairs Council*, which puts the total number of registered agency lobbyists on the main voluntary register at 825, broadly similar to the table above. However, it goes on to note:

> A far larger contingent of lobbyists work "in-house"... That is they work directly for representative bodies, corporates, charities, NGOs and other campaigning groups.

32. Citing academic research, the industry estimates a ratio of 4:1 in-house to agency lobbyists. The figures in the consultation give a ratio of fewer than one in-house lobbyist to every two agency lobbyists.

33. The industry's 2009 figures also put the total number of dedicated lobbyists working in the UK at between 3,500 and 4,000. This is 2,000–2,500 more than the figure in the Cabinet Office's Evidence Base.

34. It is difficult to work out how the Government has arrived at these figures. For example, it calculates that there are 100 in-house company lobbyists working in the UK. Given that a quick search reveals that Tesco alone employs at least six in-house lobbyists (including a former member of the Downing Street Policy Unit, former private secretary to Blair, another of Blair's closest aides, and an ex-press officer at CCHQ), this seems a gross underestimation.

35. In conclusion, according to the industry's original figures, **the Government has chosen to exclude roughly three quarters of the lobbying industry from its proposals.**

36. The obvious, illogical consequence of this would be that the lobbying activity of, for example, Tesco's well-connected in-house team would not be open to public scrutiny. But if the supermarket took on an agency to give it additional capacity, perhaps on a particular issue, the agency's limited activity would be registered.

37. The consultation appears to justify the exclusion of in-house lobbyists by claiming that information on their lobbying is already in the public domain, through the disclosure of ministerial meetings. The consultation states:

> The Government already publishes quarterly information about Ministers' meetings. Information about which stakeholders are meeting Ministers to put forward their views on policies is therefore already in the public domain. But under the current system, when Ministers meet lobbying firms it is not transparent on whose behalf they are lobbying.

38. Disclosure of ministerial meetings provides very little transparency and cannot be used as justification for limiting the scope of the register.

39. First, it is far from clear from the descriptions given in the ministerial meeting logs what issues are being discussed: of the 5,144 ministerial meetings recorded, Over 1,100 of these meetings are reported simply as "introductory meeting/introduction", general "catch-up" or "discussion".

40. Second, while the consultation underlines the requirement in the ministerial code to publish, at least quarterly, details of external meetings, disclosure is often delayed. For example, the last ministerial meetings logged by the Treasury, BIS, and Mark Harper's own department, Cabinet Office, are April-June 2011.

41. Third, it is not the case that all meetings between ministers and agencies are recorded. For example, it was recently revealed that Communities Secretary, Eric Pickles had accepted a dinner with lobbying group Bell Pottinger. Pickles said he was not required to register the dinner because he had attended in a "private" and not a "ministerial" capacity.[(iv)]

42. Finally, the focus on face-to-face meetings with ministers shows a misunderstanding of the nature of lobbying. It excludes approaches made to countless other public officials, such as regulators, special advisors and civil servants. Disclosure of ministerial meetings does nothing to address the lack of transparency in lobbying of other public officials.

43. The Committee asks: *How should the Government deal in policy and practice with how it might be lobbied on the issue of a statutory register of lobbyists? Are you confident that the issues covered are ones on which the Government has an open mind?*

44. Lobbying by the lobbying industry on the issue of a statutory register, and the way the Cabinet Office has conducted itself in regard to its discussions with lobbyists, provide compelling evidence of why a robust system of disclosure in lobbying is urgently needed, and why the Government's proposals are inadequate. It also shows the Cabinet Office's opposition to transparency in lobbying up to this point.

45. It's understood that Mark Harper made the decision not to meet with outside interests to discuss the Government's plans until the Cabinet Office had published its consultation. The Alliance for Lobbying Transparency received a letter to this effect from the minister in October 2010 in response to a request for a meeting.

> I do not think at this stage in the process a meeting would be appropriate, but I look forward to receiving your contribution to our consultation, which we hope to launch in the coming months... I think it is helpful to be clear that the government intends to consult fully on proposals for a statutory register of lobbyists. We will take note of the voluntary register run by UKPAC, and no doubt UKPAC will wish to respond to the consultation paper and provide the benefit of their experience in this area.

46. However, according to minutes of an UKPAC board meeting in September 2010, Mark Harper had already given the go-ahead for regular discussions to be held between his officials in the Cabinet Office and the industry. Minutes from the meeting state:

> A letter from Mark Harper to the Chairman had been received acknowledging receipt of the UKPAC's progress and plans to date. He agreed his officials meet monthly with the [UKPAC] Secretary.[(v)]

47. As reported in last week's *Sunday Times*,[(vi)] UKPAC had four meetings with Eirian Walsh Atkins, who until last week, was responsible for drafting the Government's proposals for a statutory register. UKPAC describes its discussions with her as "productive and positive". According to minutes from one UKPAC meeting:

> Ms Walsh Atkins outlined the timetable for the introduction of legislation for a statutory register... She made clear that the Cabinet Office would be working closely with the Department for Business, Innovation and Skills to draft the consultation and legislative framework, including discussions on the possible sanctions for non-compliance. Ms Walsh Atkins and the Secretary will have close contact to discuss progress, meeting at least once a month.

48. It is clear from this that the Cabinet Office, and the minister specifically, have granted industry lobbyists privileged access to influence the drafting of the register, while denying access to others, including those pushing for greater transparency, until the consultation had been published.

49. However, as the *Sunday Times* also reported, the Cabinet Office has sought to keep its discussions with the lobbying industry secret. Walsh Atkins herself led the Cabinet Office's rejection of a Freedom of Information request to disclose details of its contact with the industry.

50. SpinWatch has submitted a series of Freedom of Information requests to the Cabinet Office for this information. The way in which the Cabinet Office has handled the requests does not point to a department in favour of lobbying transparency.

51. It was not without irony that the Cabinet Office initially refused to disclose information on its dealings with lobbyists. In December 2011, the Information Commissioner ruled in favour of disclosure, some 17 months after the request was first submitted. In the year and a half that the Cabinet Office fought to block the release of information, it broke ICO guidance on the time it took to process the request (its internal review process took five months instead of 20 working days), it was threatened with contempt of court proceedings by the ICO (for not providing the commissioner with the information necessary to make a judgement), and was found in breach of the Act (for withdrawing its original exemptions and applying a second set of late exemptions without informing the requestor).

52. Despite the ICO's ruling, the Cabinet Office is blocking disclosure of a further three requests concerning its discussions with lobbyists.

53. Further evidence of the Cabinet Office's opposition to the idea of transparency in lobbying was also published last weekend. Walsh Atkins, in charge of drafting the Government's plans, tweeted on 22 December 2011: "I wish Unlock Democracy would die. I am prepared to help it along."

54. Unlock Democracy is a member of the Alliance for Lobbying Transparency, which had encouraged its members to write to the Cabinet Office with their concerns about the lengthy delays in publishing its plans for a register.

55. Walsh Atkins has since apologised, but faces an internal investigation for possible breaches of the civil service code of conduct. She resigned as Head of Constitutional Policy at the Cabinet Office last Friday.

Conclusion

56. The Government's proposals for a statutory register of lobbyists are fundamentally flawed, and will deliver little more than the system of voluntary self-regulation that currently exists. While we believe that the plans have been unduly influenced by an industry long opposed to statutory regulation, it is clear that the Cabinet Office has not approached the register with an open mind.

57. More concerning, however, is the fact that the Cabinet Office has failed to behave transparently over its interaction with the industry, which is both suggestive of a culture of secrecy and a complete failure to understand the nature of the problem that the register is designed to address.

58. We believe the consultation paper must be amended, without delay, to properly reflect public concerns over lobbying, with accurate information on the industry, and a fuller and more balanced account of the options for, and potential benefits of, a register of lobbyists. Submissions must be sought from as wide a range of people as possible, and their views must be given proper weight. Otherwise, the danger is that a policy designed to restore public trust in politics will have the direct opposite effect.

January 2012

Notes

(i) Interview with Mark Harper on BBC's World at One, 20 Jan 2012.

(ii) Public Affairs: Register blueprint developed, PR Week, 16 July 2010.

(iii) Interview with Elizabeth France, CIPR TV, 16 Jan 2011.

(iv) Gaping hole in rules lets Eric Pickles keep five-star business dinner "private", TBIJ, 22 October 2011.

(v) UKPAC board meeting 2, minutes, 16 Sep 2010.

(vi) "Abusive" lobbying reform chief quits over tweets, *Sunday Times*, 29 January 2012.

Further written evidence submitted by Tamasin Cave, SpinWatch

SUPPLEMENTARY EVIDENCE: INTRODUCING A STATUTORY REGISTER OF LOBBYISTS

1. During the first session of the Committee's inquiry into the Government's proposals for introducing a statutory register of lobbyists (2 February 2012), Members asked for evidence that there is growing public concern with lobbying.

2. To date, very few public surveys have focused specifically on attitudes towards lobbying in the UK. However, a number of opinion polls and reports do exist, which reflect public concern over issues of access and influence in politics.

3. Most notably, a Sunday Times/YouGov poll conducted in October 2011 showed that over 50% of people think that lobbyists have too much influence in politics. The poll also showed that three quarters of people now support a register of lobbyists.[2]

4. This supports the conclusions of the Public Administration Select Committee's lengthy inquiry into lobbying. The Committee's 2009 report *Lobbying: Access and Influence in Whitehall* states:

> There is a genuine issue of concern, widely shared and reflected in measures of public trust, that there is an inside track, largely drawn from the corporate world, who wield privileged access and disproportionate influence.[3]

2 YouGov/Sunday Times poll, 23 October 2011.

3 Public Administration Select Committee (2009) *Lobbying: Access and Influence in Whitehall*, p 3.

5. The Committee's central conclusion was that "reform is necessary", and it highlighted the dangers of ignoring public concerns:

> The result of doing nothing would be to increase public mistrust of Government, and to solidify the impression that government listens to favoured groups—big business and party donors in particular—with far more attention than it gives to others.[4]

6. A 2008 report by the Conservative Party Democracy Task Force, Trust in Politics made a similar observation:

> In recent years, a crisis of trust has enveloped governments of both parties. The Conservative government of 1992–97 was constantly accused of "sleaze" and the loss of the party's reputation for probity was a significant factor in the massive defeat of 1997. The New Labour government that followed promised, famously, to be "whiter than white". The subsequent disillusionment has been, if anything, still greater. A steady troop of forced ministerial resignations has been accompanied by serious questions over the access to power and patronage that money can buy.[5]

7. This acknowledgement of the link between money, access and influence, and a decline in public trust was strongly reaffirmed in a speech on lobbying by David Cameron in February 2010, called Rebuilding Trust in Politics:

> I believe that secret corporate lobbying, like the expenses scandal, goes to the heart of why people are so fed up with politics. It arouses people's worst fears and suspicions about how our political system works, with money buying power, power fishing for money and a cosy club at the top making decisions in their own interest.[6]

8. There is insufficient data to show that the public concern expressed by the Prime Minister, PASC and others is greater now than in the past. However, we do know that the size of the lobbying industry in the UK has grown dramatically in recent years, and that it is likely that public concern will have increased as a result. One estimate suggests that the industry has doubled in size since the early 1990s.[7]The industry estimates that there are now 3,500–4,000 full-time lobbyists (consultants and in-house) in the UK.[8]

9. However, data from the 2006 Power inquiry, which sought to discover why disengagement from formal democratic politics in Britain has grown in recent years, does provide further evidence of public concern with lobbying.

10. A key finding of the inquiry was that "business is widely cited by the public as having greater influence over government than citizens", a point, it noted, that was raised many times in the evidence it took. It cited a number of indicative quotes from the submissions it received, such as: *"It is not just perception that corporate lobbying influences government policy—it is actuality. Until the actuality changes, the perception will not.";* and: *"The influence of big companies is endemic; they have the time and the money whereas most individuals do not."*[9]

11. This finding reflects an ICM "State of the Nation" poll in 2004, which showed that 79% of people said they felt large corporations had influence over government policies, while only 34% felt they ought to enjoy such influence.[10]

12. The Power inquiry took evidence from people both inside Westminster and the general public. It is worth noting that the inquiry recorded a "palpable difference" between the public response and the "insider" response: "The politicos have no idea of the extent of the alienation that is out there," it said.

February 2012

Written evidence submitted by Mark Adams OBE

INTRODUCTION

1. My name is Mark Adams and I am a lobbyist. I have worked as a professional lobbyist since 1998, having been a senior civil servant before that, including six years in the Prime Minister's Office, 10 Downing Street, under both Sir John Major and Tony Blair.

2. I am the Director of standup4lobbying, a campaign to promote the reputation of professional lobbying, which I established in January 2012. I write a daily blog on lobbying, which attracts a regular audience of around 200 daily readers. As I suspect it is not read by many machine tool operators in Glasgow, it is fair to assume that the majority of those reading it are involved in the debate about lobbying, plus of course my mother, Mrs Anne Bebbington.

---

4 Public Administration Select Committee press release, 5 January 2009
5 Conservative Party Democracy Task Force (2008) *Trust in Politics*, p 1.
6 David Cameron, 8 February 2010, "Rebuilding Trust in Politics" speech.
7 Thompson, S and John, S (2002) *Public Affairs in practice: a practical guide to lobbying*, pp 4–5.
8 APPC, PRCA, CIPR Working Party (2009) *Towards a Public Affairs Council Issues Paper*, p 8.
9 Power Inquiry final report (2006), *Power to the People*.
10 ICM poll of 2,000 people, June 2004.

3. I am the Chairman of an independent lobbying company, The Professional Lobbying Company. I previously worked as a lobbyist at four other companies. I am a former Deputy Chair of the Association of Professional Political Consultants. I was heavily involved in the work to establish the UK Public Affairs Council. I chaired a working party to devise a strategy for the establishment of UKPAC; then was Deputy Chairman, under Sir Philip Mawer, of the UKPAC Implementation Group. I have not been involved in UKPAC since its launch and have gone on record to criticise the way that the profession has handled the evolution of UKPAC.

Regulation of Lobbying

4. The lobbying profession has a key role in the democratic process. Lobbyists advise their organisations (if employed directly) or their clients (if employed by a consultancy) on how to influence government most persuasively. Concern has been expressed—in my view wrongly—that lobbyists can achieve undue influence over policy decisions. In the light of this, and because it is the right approach, I believe that it is important for the lobbying profession to be regulated effectively.

5. In my view, it is purely an empirical question whether regulation is more effective if it is carried out on a voluntary basis or on a statutory basis. As a general rule, I believe a system of regulation that participants choose to join is likely to be more effective than a system where participants have to be forced to take part. Therefore a clear and strong case must be made before a voluntary system is replaced with a statutory one.

6. Some have argued that lobbying "scandals" prove that self-regulation has failed. In practice, there have been very few cases of lobbyists being shown to have contravened the profession's Code of Conduct (as laid down by the Association of Professional Political Consultants and the Public Relations Consultants Association). Occasional revelations in the media have been more often about the actions of politicians rather than lobbyists (although it is perhaps understandable that politicians are in denial about this). Where lobbyists are exposed in the media, it illustrates how difficult it is for them to avoid detection. It would be as ridiculous to suggest that because lobbyists occasionally behave inappropriately that self-regulation has failed, as it would be to suggest that because crime still happens the police have failed.

7. No system of regulation will be perfect and I remain to be convinced that statutory regulation will be any more effective than self-regulation. What I am convinced about, is that the Government's proposals for a statutory register as set out in the consultation paper are considerably less effective than the current system of self-regulation.

Response to the Select Committee's Questions

1. *Does the Government's consultation paper represent a balanced approach to the idea of a statutory register?*

— *Does the paper present the evidence in a balanced way?*

— *Are you confident that the issues covered are ones on which the Government has an open mind?*

— *Is the Government clear wherever it has a preference for a particular option, and is this preference in each case a reasonable one?*

8. The proposal is a nonsense. The consultation paper argues that it is necessary to have a statutory register of multi-client lobbying companies (but not of anyone else) because it is not clear when such companies meet ministers whom they are lobbying on behalf of. However, as the evidence of Tamasin Cave revealed, a very small number of meetings are with multi-client lobbying companies. Additionally the publication of a client list does not mean that the identity of the client represented in any specific meeting is revealed. A far more sensible mechanism to achieve the Government's objective would be to require multi-client lobbying companies to reveal their client at the start of any meeting.

9. In meetings attended by the Minister, Mark Harper MP, he explained that the Government is concerned with meetings with MPs as well, not just ministers and that the register is needed for that. Again it would make more sense for the House authorities to agree that a register of MPs' meetings, with appropriate exemptions to exclude meetings with constituents, should be introduced as a simpler solution to this problem.

10. Given how poorly argued the consultation paper is, there is a real suspicion that it is written simply to deliver a coalition agreement commitment, in turn building on an ill-considered Liberal Democrat manifesto commitment, even if it makes little sense. It is difficult to see the Government agreeing not to proceed, whatever the consultation reveals, when not to do so would break the coalition agreement.

11. It is in places difficult to understand the Government's preference for the outcome. It does seem to be clear that the Government currently intends the proposals to apply principally to multi-client lobbying companies. This is a fundamental error. It will capture only a small proportion of the overall number of professional lobbyists and covers the very sector that is, by and large, already covered by the voluntary system in place.

2. *Does the consultation paper contain the right questions?*

— *Is each of the questions asked in a balanced way?*

— *Are there any important questions that are not asked?*

12. Any public policy development should involve a coherent and incisive analysis of the problem and the advance of a convincing public policy solution. Unfortunately the Government's consultation on a statutory register does neither. It should ask what evidence there is of harm to the political system with the current system, as there is precious little evidence; and ask what will be achieved by the changes proposed. The Government claims that a number of individuals and Members of Parliament have written to express concern about the activities of lobbyists. However, they give no information on the scale of the representations, of the nature of these concerns and whether the concerns are in the slightest bit justified. I have made a Freedom of Information request to uncover elements of the evidence, but it is an area that I hope the Committee chooses to explore, should they invite the Minister to appear before them.

13. I feel I may be being a little naive, but an important question that does not seem to have been asked is what exactly is the problem that the Government is trying to solve? The Government cannot possibly justify a public policy intervention without answering this question and demonstrating that the scale of the problem justifies the response. The consultation paper spectacularly fails to do this.

3. *Which lobbying contacts are of greatest legitimate public interest?*

— Does the consultation paper envisage the capture of appropriate information about these contacts, as opposed to other kinds of contact?

14. Contacts that public servants, including Members of Parliament, ministers and civil servants have with outside interests are of legitimate concern to the public to ensure that such decision makers are receiving a rounded set of representations. It would seem to be obvious that the way to achieve this is through a register of meetings by such people, already in place for ministers, rather than through a completely different (and largely irrelevant) mechanism. A register of lobbyists and their clients will obviously reveal precisely nothing about their contacts with public servants on behalf of their clients.

4. *How should the Government deal in policy and practice with how it might be lobbied on the issue of a statutory register of lobbyists?*

— *How open should the Government be about such lobbying contacts?*

15. It seems reasonable for the Government to be carrying out the consultation, so long as they have some intention of paying any attention to the responses. Consistent with sensible government policy, the Government should be open about the representations they receive.

16. The critics of the so-called "lobbying industry" have suggested that, while their requests for meetings with the Government have been declined, the Government has met "representatives" of the industry. As I understand it, the Government declined to meet any of the representative bodies for the profession, namely the Association of Professional Political Consultants, the Chartered Institute of Public Relations and the Public Relations Consultants Association. Instead meetings were held with the independent element of the UK Public Affairs Council. It strikes me as entirely sensible for the Government to want to investigate whether UKPAC would be a suitable body to police a statutory register, subject to any changes in the governance structure that might be required. Therefore I think any meetings that the Government may have had with UKPAC—rather than with the representative bodies of the profession—are unlikely to have been meetings to consider representations from "the industry".

5. *How should the Government analyse the consultation responses, and seek to balance the weight of opposing argument?*

17. I am always mystified by how governments weigh up responses to consultations. On the one hand, it appears to be some kind of plebiscite, where they compare the numbers in favour of a proposal with the numbers against. That rather encourages campaign groups to organise their members to submit essentially the same arguments many times over. Companies are increasingly adopting this tactic as well.

18. Instead, my rather naive view is that government should consider the strengths and weaknesses of the views and arguments that have been put forward and adjust their decisions accordingly. They should listen to views on what the problems are and what the potential solutions might be. Then the final outcome should be based on what most effectively achieves the public policy objective that emerges from the consultation.

6. *Do you have any comments on how any proposals emerging from the consultation should be implemented?*

19. I support what I understand to be the process that the Government intends to follow. Once the Government has considered the responses to the consultation, they intend to publish a White Paper and a draft

Bill to implement any proposals that require primary legislation. I look forward to giving evidence to the Committee that will consider any draft legislation.

February 2012

Written evidence submitted by Mark Ramsdale

INTRODUCTION

1. Below is a summary response to questions asked by the Political and Constitutional Reform Committee's call for evidence[11] in relation to the Cabinet Office's consultation Introducing a statutory register of lobbyists.[12]

2. It is my intention to submit a response to the Cabinet Office consultation.

ABOUT

3. My name is Mark Ramsdale. I act as an independent public affairs consultant, often referred to as a lobbyist. I have worked for a Member of Parliament and as a public affairs and policy specialist for over 10 years, including for several organisations responsible—directly or indirectly—with the regulation of those who lobby, including the Chartered Institute of PR (CIPR) and the Public Relations Consultants Association (PRCA). I held the position of Executive Secretary to the UK Public Affairs Council from July 2010 to December 2011 and prior to that provided support to the working group tasked with its creation.

4. I have worked as an independent consultant since 2008, operating via a limited company since April 2010. I am a member of the Professional Contractors Group (www.pcg.org.uk).

5. I currently provide advice and services to a range of clients, details of which on my website: www.markramsdale.com.

6. All responses are provided on a personal basis, independent of my current or previous employers or clients and may not reflect their views.

REGISTRATION AND REGULATION OF LOBBYISTS

7. I agree with the Government when it states in its consultation that "lobbying serves an important function in politics—by putting forward the views of stakeholders to policy makers, it helps in the development of better legislation. But it needs to be open and transparent."

8. However, I disagree that a register containing solely "third party lobbyists" would be open and transparent. To be truly transparent, all lobbyists, regardless of whether they practice independently (as in my case), in-house or as part of an agency should appear on a register. Furthermore, they should do so irrespective of whether they are employed by or represent commercial or charitable bodies, trade unions, religious groups or any other professional organisation that lobbies as part of its activities.

9. Constituents, including ad hoc groups that come together on constituency issues should not be required to register as they are dealing with the Member of Parliament they elected and whose duty it is to represent their wishes.

10. The key element—one which is difficult to prescribe—lies in the definition of lobbying. This affects who should register. An unclear definition that is open to interpretation could cause some to question whether they should register and offers the potential for others to challenge whether they lobby. A definition of lobbying must make clear to whom it applies and it should stand up to legal scrutiny.

11. By appearing on a register, a lobbyist or their employer or clients is demonstrating their commitment to transparency. This is to be welcomed. However, whilst a register (containing details of all those who lobby, not just "third party lobbyists") addresses issues around transparency, it is of little use without a regulatory framework, adherence to codes of practice, and appropriate sanction regime.

12. Explicit codes relating to public affairs practice exist within the three PR and public affairs industry bodies (APPC, CIPR and PRCA). Therefore, a register without any adherence to these or other suitable codes offers a retrograde step for the industry. I believe it would be preferable to ensure people agree to at least a common standard of practice, a requirement of which is to appear on a register. Failure to adhere to that requirement, including registration would result in penalties. Whilst sanctions are discussed in the Cabinet Office paper, the focus is on failure to register rather than on failure to behave ethically.

13. In terms of the approach to the consultation and the next steps the Government will take, the Minister for Political and Constitutional Reform has stated publically his approach to contacts regarding lobbying on a statutory register of lobbyists. In response to a questions posed by a Member Political and Constitutional

---

[11] http://www.parliament.uk/business/committees/committees-a-z/commons-select/political-and-constitutional-reform-committee/news/call-for-evidence—lobbying/

[12] http://www.cabinetoffice.gov.uk/sites/default/files/resources/Introducing%20a%20Statutory%20Register%20of%20Lobbyists.pdf

Reform Committee during a Westminster Hall debate on Parliamentary Lobbying on 2 November 2011,[13] the Minister stated he had "one meeting with the independent Chairman of the UK Public Affairs Council on the subject. I have had no meetings to discuss the issue with lobbying companies and no meetings with anti-lobbying companies either."

14. The Minister sanctioned meetings between the lead Cabinet Office official and the Executive Secretary of UKPAC. As Executive Secretary of UKPAC I took meetings with said official in September 2010, October 2010 and June 2011. Meetings are referred to in minutes of UKPAC Board meetings which are published on the UKPAC website and were used as a means to share the experience of UKPAC and its working group in order to understand better the technical and other logistical issues faced in creating a register of lobbyists. The meetings were not used as a means to lobby or put forward UKPAC position.

15. The Minister has reiterated publically that the Cabinet Office consultation is the first step in creating a register and I am aware that he has taken meetings to discuss the paper. As such, I feel the consultation document provides a focus for debate both within the industry and without. A White Paper, further consultation and impact assessment would be appropriate.

February 2012

Written evidence submitted by the UK Public Affairs Council (UKPAC)

Introduction

1. UKPAC will be responding in full to the Government's consultation paper on introducing a statutory register of lobbyists (Cm 8233). This paper, which we hope will be of assistance to the select committee, summarises the Council's views on the main elements of the Government's proposals.

2. The circumstances of UKPAC's founding by the three main representative bodies in the public affairs industry—the Association of Professional Political Consultants (APPC), the Chartered Institute of Public Relations (CIPR), and the Public Relations Consultants Association (PRCA)—are referred to in section 4 and Annex A of the Consultation Paper and do not need to be repeated here. In December 2011 the PRCA withdrew its support from UKPAC, it said because of UKPAC's failure at that point to deliver an updated, searchable, online register of public affairs consultancies and individuals engaged in lobbying. Following a change to a new IT contractor in November 2011, UKPAC launched, on 15 February, an updated register covering consultancies in membership of the APPC and relevant practitioners in membership of the CIPR. The register can be found on the UKPAC website: .

3. In view of recent public comment it should be understood that UKPAC has no special relationship with the Cabinet Office and has so far been involved in no discussion on policy relating to a register of lobbyists. In July 2010 the Chairman was introduced to the Minister for Political and Constitutional Reform by the outgoing Chairman of the Implementation Working Party, Sir Philip Mawer. It was agreed then that dialogue between the relevant Cabinet Office official and the UKPAC Executive Secretary, to share the learning of the working party and to track the lessons UKPAC might learn in seeking to establish a voluntary register, would be valuable. There was one introductory meeting and two follow up meetings between the Executive Secretary and the Cabinet Office official; these were in September and October 2010 and June 2011. The first two of these meetings are referred to in the minutes of UKPAC meetings to be found on the UKPAC website.

4. The views expressed in this response are the collective views of the independent and industry directors of UKPAC. They do not necessarily correspond with the views of the APPC or the CIPR, each of which will be responding separately to the Government's consultation.

Summary Response to the Government's Proposals

5. UKPAC agrees with the Government that lobbying is a legitimate activity in an open and democratic society, and indeed performs a vital role in ensuring that legislative and executive decision making takes proper account of the views of those businesses, communities, individuals and organisations likely to be affected. We also agree that current anxieties about lobbying are in danger of undermining public confidence in the decision making processes of Government and Parliament and need to be addressed.

6. The Government's consultation paper appears to attribute these anxieties solely to an alleged lack of transparency surrounding the activities of "third party lobbyists", and its proposed solution is accordingly limited in scope to that issue. We disagree with that analysis. In our view there is also clear and legitimate interest in the ways in which large corporations, trade associations, organised pressure groups and others seek to influence and inform policy. A statutory register which is limited to professional public affairs consultancies and consultants will therefore fail to achieve the stated purpose of restoring public confidence in the decision making process.

---

[13] http://www.publications.parliament.uk/pa/cm201011/cmhansrd/cm111102/halltet/111102h0001.htm

7. One obvious anomaly which would result from implementation of the Government's proposals would be that a statutory regime would apply to the lobbying activities of medium-sized companies and organisations, which tend to find it most economical to use the services of a consultancy for public affairs purposes, but would not apply to large companies and organisations which have the resources to employ a permanent, in-house, public affairs team. It is also not clear whether the proposed regime is intended to apply to the large number of representative bodies such as the CBI, the National Farmers' Union or the British Bankers' Association. A statutory register which did not include such bodies would give a very unbalanced impression of lobbying activity in the UK.

8. UKPAC particularly regrets that the Government, in no more than a brief paragraph, has set its face against linking its proposed system for the registration of lobbyists to a code of conduct or set of guiding principles. We think it would be a significant lost opportunity if the debate which is conducted around the Government's consultation and the Select Committee's inquiry did not extend to address the arguments for and against setting out the standards of behaviour expected of those who lobby and, potentially, the implications if these are not met.

9. The APPC, CIPR and PRCA all operate their own codes of conduct, observance of which is a condition of membership and inclusion in their respective registers. The paradoxical consequence of implementation of the Government's proposals would therefore be that it would be less onerous for third party lobbying agencies or individuals to observe the requirements of the statutory regime than it is now to observe the requirements of the representative bodies to which nearly all of them variously belong. In page 15 of its consultation paper the Government expresses its support for the industry's efforts to improve standards. But ministers should take account of the risk that the industry may scale down or even discontinue these efforts if it is burdened with the additional expense of maintaining a statutory register and feels that it is being treated in a discriminatory fashion by comparison with other professional lobbyists.

10. The Government's stated justification for limiting its proposed regime to third party lobbyists is that ministers' meetings with direct lobbyists are transparently published in the "Who's Lobbying" section of the website, whereas meetings with third party lobbyists are not transparent when so recorded because the client—the third party—is not known. We believe that this argument is fundamentally misconceived because it is based on a misapprehension of how public affairs consultancies normally conduct their business. The services that such consultancies provide to clients include monitoring parliamentary and government activity and policy development, alerting clients to relevant proposals and draft legislation, drafting briefing and position papers and advising clients on how representations may best be made to government or evidence given to parliamentary committees. Rarely, if ever, do the services include making such representations directly on behalf of the client. Public affairs consultants may accompany a client to a meeting with a minister, civil servant or politician, but will not normally attend in their own right. If they do, their code of conduct will require them to declare the identity of their client and the nature of his business.

11. It is therefore not surprising that a selective trawl through the www.data.gov.uk website has revealed no record of a meeting with a public affairs consultancy. If there are indeed a number of such meetings, they can easily be made transparent by imposing a requirement on Government Departments to record them by reference to the ultimate client rather than the consultancy. The establishment of a statutory register of third party lobbyists, under independent supervision, would be a wholly disproportionate solution to what is, on the most generous interpretation, a limited and arguably different problem.

12. In the paper which it intends to submit to the Cabinet Office before the close of the consultation period, UKPAC will give its responses to the more specific questions and issues raised in the consultation paper. But those responses will need to be read in the light of our fundamental doubts over the Government's approach to implementing the Coalition agreement on a statutory register of lobbyists and with the arguments in favour of that approach which are advanced in the consultation paper.

February 2012

Further written evidence submitted by the UK Public Affairs Council (UKPAC)

1. UKPAC is pleased to have submitted its response to the Government's consultation on the Introduction of a Statutory Register of Lobbyists, a copy of which can be found on our website at www.publicaffairscouncil.org.uk.

2. I wanted to add to that response by writing separately to let you know of the progress UKPAC has made with its register. As you will be aware we re-launched the website and register on 15 February 2012. We have since had two quarterly updates. The quarter to 30 November 2011 has been archived and can now be viewed as a PDF document, while the period to 29 February 2012 is the current searchable data. Registrants are now updating or registering for the quarter to 31 May 2012 which we will publish in mid-June.

3. The most recent searchable data, for the period to 29 February, has 2041 entities listed as clients by lobbyists (this figure includes clients listed by more than one organisation or individual who lobby on its behalf). There are 1,387 individuals listed; these are employees of lobbying companies and individuals in CIPR membership. Under organisations, there are 67 APPC member companies registered along with the companies

and other bodies who were named as the employers of individual CIPR registrants. It is interesting to see that the register already includes some voluntary and public bodies and law firms where these organisations employ members of the CIPR.

4. We are proud of the step change that this represents from the single membership organisation, flat registers which had existed before (a comparison with the current PRCA register demonstrates the added value the new approach gives). We wanted to provide proof of concept and I consider we have, after a challenging start, now demonstrated what can be done. We have: simple self-registration, the possibility of adding other groups or individuals; the ability to add to or reduce data fields; and a data base readily searchable on a range of criteria.

5. I do hope that you will take the opportunity to have a look at the UKPAC register.

April 2012

Written evidence submitted by the Association of Professional Political Consultants (APPC)

1. The Association of Professional Political Consultants (APPC) welcomes the opportunity to offer its views on the Government's proposals for introducing a statutory register for lobbyists.

Key Principles

2. The APPC is continuing to consult its members on its detailed response to the Government's consultation. However, the following key principles that we believe should underpin any statutory registration scheme have already become apparent:

- The APPC supports the principle of a statutory register, providing that it treats all those who engage in lobbying equally.
- This means, as well registering lobbyists who work for multi-client agencies, the far larger number of lobbyists who work for law firms, management consultancies, planning consultancies, think tanks, trade associations, trade unions, charities, NGOs and in-house for businesses, should also be covered by the register. To exclude such lobbyists would mean the register would fail to achieve its objective of improving transparency and building public confidence.
- We support the proposed level of information to be included in the register.

3. In addition, consistent with the Government's concern that its proposals should not place undue burdens on business and others in their day to day dealings with government, we are keen that the system should be as cost-effective and as simple to administer as possible. To achieve this:

- We think the administration of the Register should be added to the functions of an existing organisation rather than creating a new additional and costly body.
- The APPC already runs such a register, and should be used as a benchmark for the level of costs that it can be run for in the public sector.

4. We agree with the Government that lobbying serves an important function in politics, but that it needs to be transparent.

5. We support the principle of a statutory register, providing that it treats equally all those who engage in lobbying on a professional basis. That means not only public affairs consultancies, like our members, but also law firms, management consultancies, planning consultancies, trade unions, think tanks, charities, NGOs and those who work in-house for business or other organisations who lobby on their employer's behalf.

6. To exclude such lobbyists would mean that the register would fail to achieve its objective of improving transparency and restoring public confidence.

7. We support the level of information that the Government proposes should be included in a statutory register, which is very similar to the information already provided on a voluntary basis by our 68 member consultancies (which is publicly available at www.appc.org.uk). We have been operating such a register for 17 years.

8. We think that the statutory register should be operated by an existing body, and funded by lobbyists themselves. Whichever body is chosen to hold the register should do so cost-effectively: we suggest that the APPC's membership subscriptions provide an appropriate benchmark. Indeed, the costs per registrant should be lower, since the introduction of a statutory requirement to register will deliver significant economies of scale.

9. The Committee asks a series of specific questions to which we respond below:

Does the Government's consultation paper represent a balanced approach to the idea of a statutory register?

10. We think that the level of information that the Government proposes should be included in a statutory register is appropriate. However, in our view the register should encompass all those who lobby on a

professional basis, not just public affairs consultancies who represent only a small proportion of professional lobbyists.

Does the paper present the evidence in a balanced way?

11. We think that the paper is right to emphasise the positive role of lobbying in the political process, providing it is conducted transparently. We do not think that the paper's proposal that registration should be confined to those lobbyists who are independent or work for multi-client consultancies would achieve the Government's aim of greater transparency and public confidence. We think that a statutory register needs to encompass all professional lobbyists. This means, as well registering lobbyists who work for multi-client agencies, the far larger number of lobbyists who work for law firms, management consultancies, planning consultancies, think tanks, trade associations, trade unions, NGOs, charities and in-house for businesses, should also be covered by the register, as comparable existing registers in Canada, the United States and the European Union already do. We think that the Government's expressed views on these issues reflects a lack of understanding of the role played by multi-client agencies and that it is therefore inevitable that some issues are presented in an unbalanced way. It is important to recognise that the principal role of lobbyists working for consultancies is to advise our clients on how best to make a case to government. In the vast majority of the cases, it is the clients themselves who are undertaking the lobbying, reflecting the view that they are their own best advocates. It is rare for a consultant to lobby on behalf of a client, not least because ministers and officials look to the clients to provide the front line evidence which can best inform better policy-making.

Are you confident that the issues covered are ones on which the Government has an open mind?

12. We fear that it is perhaps inevitable that, given what appears to be a limited understanding of how lobbying is organised and takes place, some issues properly raised by the Government are dismissed almost without discussion. For example, the lack of apparent understanding that the majority of lobbyists do not work for multi-client consultancies has led to some judgements being assumed which we would assert cannot be sustained in the face of the facts. We think that is unfortunate and that no legitimate issue should be excluded from the consultation. We are mindful that the introduction of a statutory register for lobbyists was included within the Coalition Agreement, and thus the fundamental policy has not been the subject of consultation. It is also worthy of note that the Cabinet Office did not hold consultation meetings with representatives of the industry—the APPC, PRCA and CIPR—before formulating its proposals, as would normally be the case.

Is the Government clear wherever it has a preference for a particular option, and is this preference in each case a reasonable one?

13. There is clarity on some options, but not others (eg whether the register should be based on a definition of lobbying or lobbyists and the status of trade unions and charities). On occasion where there is clarity (eg on the exclusion of in-house lobbyists) we see the Government's preference as unreasonable.

Does the consultation paper contain the right questions?

14. In broad terms, we think that it does and that it offers a useful opportunity for a public debate on the main issues and for Parliament, the public and affected stakeholders to give their views on the range of issues surrounding a statutory register for lobbyists.

Is each of the questions asked in a balanced way?

15. On the whole, we think that the questions are relatively balanced, though not always based on a full factual understanding of lobbying and who lobbies.

Are there any important questions that are not asked?

16. We think that the paper covers most of the important questions and are confident that respondents will raise all of the issues that they think are important. Our own response to the paper will be based on the principles outlined here, but offer more detail on implementation and, for example, on the issue of how a lobbyist covered by the register should be defined.

Which lobbying contacts are of greatest legitimate public interest?

17. In our view, all professional lobbying contacts (ie other than individual contacts between constituents and their MPs) are of legitimate public interest and so all professional lobbying should be covered by the register. We do not think that the legislation setting up the register can or should discriminate between one class of professional lobbyists and others. (Note that Members constituents are not "professional lobbyists" and we strongly support their not being caught by the proposed register.)

Does the consultation paper envisage the capture of appropriate information about these contacts, as opposed to other kinds of contact?

18. We agree with the level of information that the paper proposes should be disclosed but think that the Government's objectives on transparency and public confidence will only be achieved if the register encompasses all professional lobbyists (including in-house lobbyists) in the same way as existing registers in Canada, the United States and the European Union. We do not think that discrimination based either on the nature of the person conducting the lobbying on a professional basis or on the type of issue being advocated can be justified.

How should the Government deal in policy and practice with how it might be lobbied on the issue of a statutory register of lobbyists?

19. We think that it should deal with this consultation in the same way as it deals with all other consultations. It is right that any measure which impacts on a particular industry should be the subject of consultation and discussion with that industry, but equally that the industry's views should be assessed against the defined objectives of the Government's proposals.

How open should the Government be about such lobbying contacts?

20. It should be entirely open.

How should the Government analyse the consultation responses, and seek to balance the weight of opposing argument?

21. Thoughtfully, with an open mind and with a view to responding in a way which offers a relevant and proportionate set of proposals for a register that will deliver greater transparency and public confidence. We would hope that consultation responses will provide the Government with information and facts that it may hitherto lack and that the Government should reassess its proposals in the light of the information and arguments put to it. We believe that this is at the core of effective consultation.

Do you have any comments on how any proposals emerging from the consultation should be implemented?

22. There should be continuing dialogues on points of detail with all interested parties and adequate time for Parliamentary debate.

23. We are happy for our evidence to be made public and would welcome an opportunity to discuss our views with the Committee. We are currently finalising our submission to the consultation, and we would be pleased to share it with the Committee in due course.

February 2012

Written evidence submitted by the Chartered Institute of Public Relations (CIPR)

Does the Government's consultation paper present a balanced approach to the idea of a statutory register?

1. The Government has made it clear that it intends to introduce a statutory register of lobbyists. Whilst we have no problem with the aim of increasing the amount of information available about lobbyists, we maintain that this must be done in a way which does not damage their or commercial operations and does not have the effect of deterring others from entering this part of the democratic process. The paper, in our view, is not clear about the problem that it is aiming to solve. However, we applaud the intention made clear in the paper that the Government does not wish to introduce obstacles or burdens to those who engage in lobbying or who employ lobbyists. This would appear to us to be fundamentally sound approach to a statutory register. Our position on lobbying in general goes further than the Government's description of it as a legitimate activity[14] and we prefer to see it as a an essential part of the democratic process with an important relationship to freedom of speech. However, we also accept that influencing public policy is a sensitive issue and that ideally lobbying should be normalised—that is to say, open, understood and accepted. This is consistent with our view on professional standards in public affairs and we believe the provision of greater information in the public realm relating to lobbying activity will aid this objective.

Does the paper present the evidence in a balanced way?

2. The paper is perhaps somewhat light on evidence. The scope of the register, as the paper notes,[15] will be determined by the final definition of lobbying and lobbyists. The paper discusses international examples and the only domestic attempt (UKPAC) to set a definition,[16] which is dismissed as unsuitable. Whilst the paper offers little or no idea as to the Government's preferred definition, which is disappointing, it does present a positive opportunity for respondents to offer their own potential definitions. In our view, definitions should

14 "Introducing a Statutory Register of Lobbyists" p 9.

15 IBID p 12.

16 IBID.

centre on the activity of lobbying. Once the activity has been defined, it is a simple step to label all those who lobby as lobbyists, and all those who do so for remuneration as professional lobbyists—all of whom (in our view) should be covered by the scope of the statutory register.

Are you confident the issues covered are ones on which the Government has an open mind?

3. Yes, beyond the question of whether a register is necessary, or will achieve the Government's aims, they appear to have an open mind around the definition, level of disclosure and operation of a register and the sanctions that will meet non-compliance. We hope that this extends fully to the administration of the register and that the UKPAC will play part in their deliberations on who should run it.

Is the Government clear wherever it has a preference for a particular option, and is this preference in each case a reasonable one?

4. There is a clear initial preference for a register of those who lobby on behalf of third parties.[17] Although the argument presented in favour of this supports their preference for a register that increases the amount of information about lobbying in the public realm, it is unreasonable because it would place a disproportionate burden on the multi-client lobbying agencies and freelancers, and would ignore the significant role played in influencing public policy by in-house lobbyists.

5. This approach would also build loopholes into the register, which might be exploited by unscrupulous operators. Having a register which did not encompass three quarters of the industry would, in our view, be perverse—and possibly open to legal challenge. There is a clear initial preference for a register which requires a reasonable level of disclosure, which we support. There is a clear initial proposal for quarterly updates of the register, which would be a reasonable minimum to expect to keep the information current.

Does the consultation paper contain the right questions?

6. Broadly, the paper tackles the important issues that need to be addressed in the introduction of a statutory register. These include the definition of lobbyists/lobbying, the scope of the register, the information to be disclosed through the register, who should run the register and the cost of registration, and finally what sanctions should be in place in the event of non-compliance.

Is each of the questions asked in a balanced way?

7. One of the key questions asks whether the register should cover in-house lobbyists,[18] which we feel is not presented in a balanced way—as we have said above. The paper states that, since it is clear who in-house lobbyists represent, to register them would not provide additional transparency. This assumes a lack of transparency on the part of third party lobbyists which we believe is not the case. Whilst we accept that not all third party lobbyists are regulated by professional bodies such as the CIPR, PRCA or the APPC, the majority follow professional standards which require them to disclose on whose behalf they are lobbying. The guiding principles of the CIPR Code of Conduct require our members to "deal honestly and fairly in business with employers, employees, clients, fellow professionals, other professions and the public"[19] and to operate with "honest and responsible regard for the public interest".[20] Our understanding of good practice by third party lobbyists would be at least to disclose the party they are representing at any meeting or discussion through which they seek to influence public policy. For many in this sector, the client is the best advocate for their own cause, the role played by the third party lobbyist is to facilitate contact rather than to represent. On the specific point about the disclosure of information relating to previous employment in the Civil Service or any previous ministerial role, there is as much (and arguably more) reason to ask this of in-house lobbyists as there is of third party lobbyists.

Are there any important questions that are not asked?

8. No. The paper covers the important questions that arise from the introduction of a statutory register.

Which Lobbying contacts are of legitimate public interest?

9. In general, lobbying contacts, that is to say, where a person, group or organisation seeks to influence public policy, are of legitimate public interest. In this context, the usual relationship between a Member of Parliament and their constituents is not of legitimate public interest. We have also stated above that the proposed register should cover professional lobbyists, not individuals or groups campaigning over local issues which affect them or their neighbourhoods.

---

[17] IBID.
[18] IBID.
[19] CIPR Code of Conduct, Section A: "Principles". http://www.cipr.co.uk/content/code-conduct
[20] IBID Section A "Principles of Good Practice".

Does the consultation paper envisage the capture of appropriate information about these contacts, as opposed to other kinds of contact?

10. Yes. The amount of information to be disclosed would contribute to the compliance burden on lobbyists and should be kept to a reasonable minimum. The paper envisages a system that avoids duplication of information already collected elsewhere,[21] discloses relevant former employment and the clients of any third party lobbyist.[22] The paper asks sensible questions about whether information relating to commercial fees should be included.[23]

How should the Government deal in policy and practice with how it might be lobbied on the issue of statutory register of lobbyists?

11. The Government should seek the views of all interested parties through the consultation and through direct contact.

How open should the Government be about such lobbying contacts?

12. The Government should be "transparent" and disclose any representations they receive on a statutory register, either from interested parties, pressure groups or potential providers. It was notable that ministers were generally resistant to approaches before the consultation was published, which was not entirely helpful but was at least even handed.

How should the Government analyse the consultation responses, and seek to balance the weight of opposing argument?

13. The Government should be even handed as a rule in their analysis of the consultation responses. Perhaps, when considering the compliance burden that may accompany a register, the views of those working in the industry, particularly those who are freelance or from a small business, could be considered closely. Similarly, the sanctions recommended need to be realistic and enforceable as well as a fair.

Do you have any comments on how any proposals emerging from the consultation should be implemented?

14. We would like to see a statutory register implemented within a reasonable timeframe allowed by the legislative process and to allow the industry and profession to adjust to a new burden of compliance. The provider will also need to establish processes to handle the collection and representation of information on a publicly searchable basis but with due regard to issues including data protection. In this respect, our recommendation is that UKPAC, a body established by the industry to provide a model vehicle for a statutory register, should be considered as a potential provider, since it has experience and knowledge of creating a register of lobbyists on a voluntary basis. The CIPR, as a Royal Charter body with a strong track record in maintaining professional standards and in operating member databases, also stands ready to assist in the setting up and maintenance of the statutory register, bound by a strong code of conduct with disciplinary sanctions including expulsion from membership, if called upon to do so by government.

About the Chartered Institute of Public Relations

15. The Chartered Institute of Public Relations is the professional body for public relations practitioners in the UK. With 9,500 members involved in all aspects of public relations, it is the largest body of its kind in Europe. The CIPR advances the public relations profession in the UK by making its members accountable through a code of conduct, developing best practice, representing its members and raising standards through professional development. The CIPR, through the PR Academy, provides the CIPR Public Affairs Diploma, a professional qualification specific to lobbying.

16. The CIPR Public Affairs Group has nearly 700 members and meets regularly to discuss current issues in UK politics. It recently hosted the first industry meeting with Mark Harper MP, Minister for Political and Constitutional Reform, following the publication of the consultation paper.

February 2012

---

[21] "Introducing a Statutory Register of Lobbyists" p 14.

[22] IBID.

[23] IBID p 15.

Written evidence submitted by PRCA

INTRODUCTION

1. The PRCA welcomes the Government s proposal for a statutory register of lobbyists and the opportunity to contribute to the consultation process and the Political and Constitutional Reform Committee s inquiry.

2. The Association considers it to be an important step forward in increasing transparency of the public affairs industry. The questions put forward by the Committee have been answered in turn below.

3. Currently, the PRCA is in the process of consulting its members before responding to the Government s consultation document.

ABOUT THE PRCA AND A REGISTER OF LOBBYISTS

4. Founded in 1969, the PRCA is the professional body that represents UK PR consultancies, in-house communications teams, PR freelancers and individual PR practitioners. The PRCA promotes all aspects of public relations, public affairs and communications work, helping teams and individuals maximise the value they deliver to clients and organisations.

5. Members that conduct public affairs services are bound by a Public Affairs Code of Conduct and must submit details to a Public Affairs Register that is updated quarterly and posted to the PRCA website.

6. The register is retrospective, covering those who have conducted registrable public affairs activity in the three months prior to publishing, and includes the following details: an office address and contact information, a list of all staff that conduct public affairs services, and a client list (consultancies only).

7. The latest copy of the register can be found at www.prca.org.uk/paregister. At the time of writing, there are a total of 81 organisations represented on the most recent PRCA Public Affairs Register, including 946 individuals and 1,214 clients.

EXECUTIVE SUMMARY

8. The PRCA supports a statutory register of lobbyists that should be administered by an independent body that is credible with the Government, industry, and public alike.

9. The Association believes that any statutory register of lobbyists should be founded on a robust and universal definition of lobbying that ensures all professional lobbyists are included in the register.

10. A lobbyist is not defined by the specific profession of the person conducting the lobbying, but by the act of lobbying in a professional capacity itself.

11. This includes in-house communications teams, think tanks, trade unions, lawyers, management consultancies, and charities and other professional organisations.

12. The PRCA strongly disagrees with the Government s proposal to only include multi-client consultancies on the register, as it would mean that the register would fail its main aim of providing greater transparency of those who engage in lobbying activity.

13. The PRCA agrees with the information that should be submitted to the register. It notes this is similar to the information currently submitted to the PRCA s Public Affairs Register. The consultation is correct not to include financial information on the register due to its sensitive nature.

14. The purpose of a statutory register is to provide transparency, not to discriminate against different types of lobbyists. The PRCA believes the Government should not make a judgment that a certain type of lobbyist is of greater public interest than another.

15. The PRCA is concerned that the Impact Assessment does not provide enough information for there to be an accurate calculation regarding how much registration should cost each organisation or individual that is included.

16. The register should be updated quarterly, as is currently the case with the PRCA Public Affairs Register.

17. Statutory sanctions are a necessity if the register is to be credible in preventing non-compliance.

QUESTIONS FROM THE COMMITTEE

1. *Does the Government s consultation paper represent a balanced approach to the idea of a statutory register?*

— *Does the paper present the evidence in a balanced way?*

18. The PRCA has serious reservations in regards to the paper s evidence on who should be included in the register, which leads to imbalances. In particular, the PRCA is concerned that the paper does not sufficiently

take into account the nature and size of the in-house lobbying industry, which is according to the most recent evidence 80% of the public affairs industry.[24]

19. Equally the decision to only include multi-client agencies suggests a misunderstanding of their role within the wider public affairs industry. The consultation document presents the problem as an issue of not knowing who lobbying agencies represent in ministerial meetings. However, this is a problem that can be resolved in the declaration of ministerial meetings. The role of multi-client agencies is to facilitate meetings with the right minister, thus rarely do lobbyists meet government officials without their client. Therefore the PRCA believes focusing on this small issue, rather than the big picture of universal transparency of the lobbying industry, leads to an imbalance in the consultation s approach.

— *Are you confident that the issues covered are ones on which the Government has an open mind?*

20. The PRCA is confident that the Government has an open mind on the issues covered, but believes the paper is confused by the lack of a clear, robust definition of lobbying and lobbyists. For example, the paper s scope sets out that "A register should include those who lobby"[25] but limits its definition to "those who undertake lobbying activities on behalf of a third party client".[26] The consultation paper discusses other registers that include in-house lobbyists, so it is surprising that they are not included in the consultation s definition.

— *Is the Government clear wherever it has a preference for a particular option, and is this preference in each case a reasonable one?*

21. The Government is clear but unreasonable in its preference for a register that includes only multi-client agencies and excludes in-house lobbyists. A preference for only including one type of lobbyist means the register will not fulfil its main purpose in increasing transparency as it will not cover the entire industry.

22. The Government is unclear on its preference on whether trade-unions, think-tanks and charities should be included. The confusion arises from an acceptance that these organisations undertake lobbying activities but not necessarily through a multi-client consultancy.[27]It is our view that these organisations should be included in a statutory register.

2. *Does the consultation paper contain the right questions?*

— *Is each of the questions asked in a balanced way?*

23. The PRCA believes that the consultation paper asks the right questions that will result in a comprehensive understanding of the views and concerns of all relevant stakeholders, with one exception (see next question).

— *Are there any important questions that are not asked?*

24. In the Summary of Questions (Pages 18–19) there should be a specific question in relation to the inclusion of in-house lobbyists as this is one of the principal issues of contention in the consultation paper.

3. *Which lobbying contacts are of greatest legitimate public interest?*

25. It is vital that a statutory register does not make any political judgments regarding who is lobbying. All professional lobbyists should be treated equally under a register as they are of equal legitimate public interest. It must be emphasised that the purpose of the register is to provide greater transparency and public awareness, but not to directly comment on lobbying itself. Therefore a statutory register should not discriminate between different types of professional lobbyists.

— *Does the consultation paper envisage the capture of appropriate information about these contacts, as opposed to other kinds of contact?*

26. The PRCA agrees with the consultation regarding what information should be captured on the register.[28] The Association's current register captures identical information, with the exception of the requirement "whether those employees are former ministers or senior civil servants".[29] Law firms, management consultancies, and other organisations that represent third parties should also produce this information. In-house organisations do not need to produce client lists, but all other information will be applicable.

4. *How should the Government deal in policy and practice with how it might be lobbied on the issue of a statutory register of lobbyists?*

— *How open should the Government be about such lobbying contacts?*

27. The Government should not act any differently in this consultation process to how it normally interacts with lobbyists. Lobbyists seek to inform parliamentarians in the public policy process, and this will remain the

24 Karl Milner cited in Zetter, L. (2011) Lobbying: The Art of Political Persuasion London: Harriman House. Page 6.
25 Consultation Paper: Page 11.
26 Ibid.
27 Ibid., Page 13.
28 Ibid.; Page 10.
29 Ibid.

case for the consultation on a statutory register of lobbyists. The PRCA expects the entire process to be open, informative and productive.

5. *How should the Government analyse the consultation responses, and seek to balance the weight of opposing argument?*

28. The Government should take into account all responses equally in order that all issues are fairly covered and all relevant stakeholders have been heard. The PRCA expects that responses to the consultation will be highly informative in clarifying areas of the consultation where there appears to be confusion. In particular, the Government should examine responses to the definition of lobbyists/lobbying so that a robust definition can provide a more comprehensive and transparent register for the public affairs industry.

6. *Do you have any comments on how any proposals emerging from the consultation should be implemented?*

29. The Association is currently consulting with its members that conduct public affairs services, as well as other trade bodies, to ensure an industry-wide representation to the consultation. The PRCA looks forward to continuing its open discussions with the Government and the Political and Constitutional Reform Committee on how best to implement a statutory register of lobbyists.

February 2012

Written evidence submitted by NCVO

Do you have any comments on how any proposals emerging from the consultation should be implemented?

1. Charities, despite their disparate nature, are united by a vision of a better society.

2. Often, their experience of working with people on the ground gives them a unique insight into how public policy shapes our society. It is not surprising then that many charities wish to influence and shape public policy in order to help the causes they support.

3. We recognise that there is a need to regulate lobbying activity in order to prevent further ambiguity and mistrust in the political system.

4. NCVO has previously argued that "lobbyists" working for charities should be subject to the same rules and regulations as those working "in-house" or those working for multi-client consultancies. This is because of two key reasons:

- We believe in maintaining the high levels of public trust and confidence that the charity sector enjoys.
- We think that a two-tier system would be counter-productive, with the possibility of charities being used as a way round the system and ultimately damaging the charity brand as a whole.

5. However, it is important to remember that charities lobbying government are very different to businesses advancing private interests. Charities are already accountable to their board of trustees. Those above a certain income threshold are already regulated by the Charity Commission.

6. We remain concerned about the perception that charities are just lobbyists by another name. It is important to remember that whether we choose to lobby for a short period of time, no organisation in the charity sector is primarily a lobbying organisation (this is prevented by the Charity Commission rules on political activity).

7. We would also be particularly concerned if any system discouraged smaller organisations from engaging with the political system or presented an unreasonable administrative or financial burden on the sector.

8. This point cannot be stressed enough; many of NCVO's members are small charities or voluntary groups, who are already incredibly nervous about taking up their democratic right to engage with the political system. We are keen to ensure that any proposals do not create further confusion.

9. It remains important, that we do not discourage interaction with the political system as we believe the Government makes better decisions when it is informed by the knowledge and experience of organisations working on the ground.

10. NCVO sees the scope of the Government's proposals as too narrow.

11. Our view is that the Government has missed an opportunity to increase transparency, level the playing field between multi-client consultancies, in-house lobbyists and charities and to drive up standards across the board.

12. The purpose of the register seems to be to merely ensure transparency for multi client agencies. If this is the case, NCVO sees no reason for the inclusion of charities in the register that is currently proposed by government because such an action would add anything to overall transparency and accountability.

13. This register brings multi-client agencies up to the level of transparency, already exercised by charities and in-house lobbyist, by making clear who these agencies are representing. As a result, the proposals do not add anything additional for charities.

14. Through ministerial disclosure requirements, it is public knowledge that when charities meet with government ministers, it is on their own behalf. It is already common practice for charities to declare in their activities the details of who the minister has met with and the issue discussed.

15. An additional question is around whether the Government's objective of "increasing transparency" is a sufficient aim in itself. NCVO believes that the objective of this register should be to expose and eradicate bad practice. We remain concerned that the proposals do not seek to influence behaviour through a code of conduct; highlight the financial backing of different lobbies or enable the public to understand the impact lobbyists are having on the public policy process.

16. Therefore the key point of this exercise must be around the purpose of the register. If the purpose of the register is to inform the public of who is influencing policy, in-house lobbyists, including charities, should be included.

17. NCVO is currently consulting its members on this issue but we have identified four key areas which we believe would be particularly important for charities if the register was strengthened in this way:

(1) **Universality**—the system should apply to all lobbyists, regardless of sector. Crucially this includes in-house lobbyists as we strongly believe there should be parity between in-house lobbyists and charities.

(2) **Legislative footprint**—The most useful part of future legislation would be to identify the issues lobbied on. This would enable the public to understand how policy has evolved through discussion with external parties.

(3) **A code of conduct**—simply introducing an element of transparency is unlikely to impact on behaviour. A code of conduct, setting out acceptable professional conduct, alongside the register is essential to the proper working of the new system. It would set out clear expectations outlining how outside interests should interact with government. This would act as a powerful nudge, driving standards up across the board.

(4) **Proportionate**—Any system should be proportionate and easy to administer and, in these difficult times, should not present an additional financial burden to the charitable sector.

18. Lastly, NCVO believes that the Government can do more. More can be done to increase transparency and accountability from the Government's side. For example, if more detail was published more regularly on their meetings, it would be easier to see the influence on the public policy process. Too often the publication of details about ministerial meetings is neither timely nor clear.

February 2012

Written evidence submitted by the TUC

1. Introduction

1.1 The TUC welcomes this opportunity to make a submission to the Political and Constitutional Reform Select Committee inquiry into the Government's consultation *Introducing a Statutory Register of Lobbyists.*

1.2 The TUC is the umbrella body for Britain's trade unions. With more than 60 unions and over 6 million members we are Britain's largest voluntary body.

1.3 Before responding to the questions asked by the Committee in its call for evidence, we think it would provide useful context for our answers by setting out our view of the problem and providing more information about the work of the TUC and trade unions in seeking to influence government and policy makers.

2. *What is the problem?*

2.1 It is right that ministers and senior officials meet a wide range of people and consider all relevant views and interests before taking important decisions.

2.2 But there is a wide concern that there is inequality of access. Those with the resources to do so can employ professional lobbyists. Lobbyists have a perfectly reasonable role in helping their clients make their case effectively, but may also be able to achieve superior access to decision makers, whether ministers or senior officials, because of their connections and contacts.

2.3 This makes for a problem in a democracy. Those with the cash are not only able to buy assistance in making their arguments in the most effective way, but also get more opportunity to put their case. When everybody gets fair access, but no more, so that all views can be aired we have stakeholder engagement. When only some get to have their say—and access is based on resources and contacts—then we have unfair lobbying.

2.4 This is why the TUC supports more openness and transparency about the operation of lobbyists, and is in broad support of a register of their activities and clients.

2.5 However such a reform will be insufficient to deal with the problem we identify. Not all access to ministers and officials is arranged through lobbying companies. The recent concern about the excessive influence of News International companies was not due to the company's use of lobbying companies, but their close personal links with politicians of all parties. Sometimes this kind of access can be assisted by in-house lobbying staff, but their existence is not the root cause of this problem.

2.6 Transparency through a register can assist by providing information about the role of lobbyists. In particular it can deal with the specific problem that FoI requests only reveal which lobbyists have met ministers, not their clients. But while this is a genuine transparency gap it can only go some way in meeting public concerns about access to power and decision making. This is because there are two further major transparency gaps that we would identify.

— Real transparency comes from requiring those being lobbied to declare contacts. Whatever rules and disclosure requirements are set for lobbyists interest groups will seek ways round them. There are difficult definitional problems about who or who is not a lobbyist, particularly outside lobbying companies. But all their efforts are directed at decision-makers, and they are therefore in the best position to report on the activities—legitimate or otherwise—of those seeking to influence them. The formal meetings of ministers and special advisers are currently covered by FoI requirements, but so-called private or social contacts are not. This must change.

— There is a large group of organisations that are excluded from the consultation paper. To read it, one might think the only people who seek to influence government are professional lobbying companies, charities and trade unions. Yet trade unions and employer associations are already highly regulated and have to make comprehensive disclosures of their financial arrangements. The proposed register of lobbyists would introduce some requirements for professional lobbying companies and self-employed lobbyists. But this still leaves many other campaign organisations and think-tanks, whether registered charities or not, able to operate without revealing the sources of their income and other important information about their governance and activities. Of course many such organisations will choose to be transparent about their activities and publish such information—particularly those NGOs who rely on public fund-raising. But there are many secretive campaign organisations and think-tanks who do not publish details of their fund-raising and who would not be covered by the register. Some of these may be registered charities, but while this imposes some regulatory requirements, it does not compel the disclosure of major donors.

2.7 In this latter group we would single out what has become known as astroturfing groups. Wikipedia provides a useful definition:

> "Astroturfing is a form of advocacy in support of a political, organizational, or corporate agenda, designed to give the appearance of a "grassroots" movement. The goal of such campaigns is to disguise the efforts of a political or commercial entity as an independent public reaction to some political entity—a politician, political group, product, service or event. The term is a derivation of AstroTurf, a brand of synthetic carpeting designed to look like natural grass.
>
> Like other advocates, astroturfers attempt to manipulate public opinion by both overt (outreach awareness, etc.) and covert (disinformation) means. Astroturfing may be undertaken by an individual promoting a personal agenda, or by organized professional groups with money from large corporations, unions, non-profits, or activist organizations. Services may be provided by political consultants who also provide opposition research and other services. Beneficiaries are not "grass root" campaigners but the organizations that orchestrate such campaigns"

3. Unions and Lobbying

3.1 We do not think it is appropriate for unions to join a register of lobbyists. This is not because we have anything to hide, but because we already have to publish many details of our finance and activities. As we are mass membership organisations with a lively internal democracy much information is available about the activities of unions. We also think the onus should be on those who receive our representations to declare this as we—like many other organisations—often do not have easily defined lobbyists.

3.2 Unions are already some of the most regulated organisations in UK society. We have to make annual returns to the Certification Officer, and have to fund a wide range of campaign activities through a separate political fund.

3.3 The consultation document suggests that political funds exist for the direct support of political parties and election candidates. But there is a wider set of activities, other than such direct party support, that can only be funded from political funds. As well as direct support unions that wish to devote resources to

> *the production, publication or distribution of any literature, document, film, sound recording or advertisement the main purpose of which is to persuade people to vote for a political party or candidate or to persuade them not to vote for a political party or candidate. (S72 Trade Union and Labour Relations (Consolidation) Act 1992)*

need to set up a political fund from which members can opt-out. To set up such a fund they need a ballot of their members. This mandate must be renewed every ten years in a further ballot. Accounts for these must be returned to the Certification Officer.

3.4 There is a further argument that creates difficulties for unions and charities. The consultation concerns a register of *lobbyists*. Organisations such as unions may well employ parliamentary or public affairs officers who understand the power structures, processes and procedures of Westminster and Whitehall, but they will not be the only people who lobby. All of the TUC's senior officials are likely to be involved in meetings that could be described as lobbying. Any of our policy staff may from time to time be involved in representations covering their specialist policy areas. We are a campaigning organisation, not an organisation that employs lobbyists.

3.5 In addition it may be hard to define which meetings we have with ministers or officials count as lobbying. In recent months many meetings have been held as part of the process of seeking a negotiated settlement to the public sector pensions dispute. We would describe these as part of an industrial relations process, not a lobbying one.

3.6 But we would stress that our difficulties with including unions in the register should not be taken as opposition to openness and transparency in what we do. While we will naturally resent requirements based on any view that unions are inherently more suspect than other organisations, we are instinctively in favour of freedom of information about the political and decision making process.

4. The Committee's Questions

Does the paper present the evidence in a balanced way?

4.1 We have argued above that the consultation document extends the original focus on lobbying companies and self-employed lobbyists in an unbalanced way by including the work of charities and trade unions, but not the non-regulated campaign sector and in particular organisations that might legitimately be called Astroturf groups.

Are you confident that the issues covered are ones on which the Government has an open mind?

4.2 We note press reports such as that suggest some disagreement within government about the extension of the consultation's document to include trade unions and charities. These suggest that at least some ministers bring an agenda to this consultation document wider than the specific concern about the activity of paid lobbyists that spurred the original proposal for a register.

Is the Government clear wherever it has a preference for a particular option, and is this preference in each case a reasonable one?

4.3 If we confine ourselves to the procedures to register paid for lobbying companies and self-employed lobbyists, we accept that this is a reasonable consultation paper. Our problems are the arbitrary extension to include charities and trade unions and any claim that the proposals in the consultation paper provide a comprehensive solution to legitimate concerns about the lobbying process.

Does the consultation paper contain the right questions? Is each of the questions asked in a balanced way? Are there any important questions that are not asked?

4.4 As we say above if the paper is seen as a modest proposal to secure greater transparency about the work of paid for lobbyists, it takes a not unreasonable approach. However, we consider the extension of the consultation paper's remit to include unions, without considering other campaign groups to be biased. Nor does the paper ask whether its proposals are sufficient to meet public concern about lobbying. This would require the discussion of disclosure requirements on those being lobbied.

Which lobbying contacts are of greatest legitimate public interest? Does the consultation paper envisage the capture of appropriate information about these contacts, as opposed to other kinds of contact?

4.5 All kinds of lobbying contact are of potential public interest. Those which those being lobbied wish to keep confidential by describing them as private or social will, rightly or wrongly, cause the most suspicion. The exclusion of all such contacts—and the focus of the paper just on lobbyists, rather than the lobbied, is a fundamental weakness.

How should the Government deal in policy and practice with how it might be lobbied on the issue of a statutory register of lobbyists?

4.6 While it would be inappropriate to have a different set of rules of procedures for this issue, there is clearly a need for ministers and special advisers to be aware of the public interest in this issue. The limited nature of the proposals in the consultation document would not capture all such lobbying contacts and emphasises its limited scope.

How open should the Government be about such lobbying contacts?

4.7 As we argue, there should be a standard duty on the lobbied to disclose lobbying contacts.

How should the Government analyse the consultation responses, and seek to balance the weight of opposing argument?

4.8 The Government should treat this consultation in the same way that it should handle all consultations. This should include publishing an honest report on consultation responses, publishing it on the web and once the government has decided its course of action, explaining in detail why it has accepted or rejected the arguments made through the consultation.

Do you have any comments on how any proposals emerging from the consultation should be implemented?

4.9 We will set these out in our formal response, which we will be happy to share with the Committee.

February 2012

Written evidence submitted by the Law Society

Introduction

1. The Law Society is the representative body for more than 145,000 solicitors in England and Wales ("the Society"). The Society negotiates on behalf of the profession, and lobbies regulators, government and others.

Committee's Questions

1. *Does the Government's consultation paper represent a balanced approach to the idea of a statutory register?*

— *Does the paper present the evidence in a balanced way?*

— *Are you confident that the issues covered are ones on which the Government has an open mind?*

— *Is the Government clear wherever it has a preference for a particular option, and is this preference in each case a reasonable one?*

2. The Law Society will be commenting on the substance of the Government's proposals in the consultation paper in due course, and the Society remains optimistic that the Government will consider its concerns set out below.

2. *Does the consultation paper contain the right questions?*

— *Is each of the questions asked in a balanced way?*

— *Are there any important questions that are not asked?*

3. As presently drafted, the proposals are likely to capture some activities of law firms, accountancy firms, management consultancies, corporations and campaigning organizations within its scope. In the legal field a relatively small diffuse group of law firms in the UK currently offer "public affairs" services. These firms generally engage with a broad range of topics including monitoring of legislative developments, making submissions to government consultations, engaging with and influencing parliamentarians, politicians and civil servants, reputation management and crisis management.

4. While only a relatively small number of firms carry out what might be described as dedicated public affairs consultancy work, a larger number will routinely have discussions with government about, for example, proposals for legislation, without necessarily considering this to be general lobbying or public affairs work. A small number of firms also carry out parliamentary agency work, both promoting and opposing private legislation.

5. There are therefore specific issues engaging law firms that need to be addressed in the proposed legislation.

Mainstream legal work

6. The Society is currently consulting its members on whether a "de minimis" threshold would be appropriate to ensure that the register would not unnecessarily capture the more minimal activity conducted in the course of legal business as described above.

7. Regardless of such a provision, it will be important to ensure that the definition of lobbying does not (either deliberately or by unintended consequence) capture mainstream legal work within its scope. If firms are carrying out legal work for their clients in the normal fashion then this must remain robustly protected by client confidentiality as well as by legal professional privilege.

Confidentiality

8. If law firms are to be required to register, then ongoing legislative and regulatory structures should ensure a level playing field in the provision of such services between law firms and non-law firms.

9. Solicitors have to protect their client's confidentiality, including their identity, under the SRA Code. The Society has always acknowledged that a client may waive confidentiality so that a solicitor could continue to represent the lobbying client under a registration scheme. The Society has historically not endorsed voluntary registration schemes on the grounds that they would not provide a level playing field—those clients that did not want their identities revealed might simply move the work to other unregistered public affairs consultancies.

10. However, a statutory register would appear to level the playing field. All entities who take on lobbying activities would have to declare their clients and seek their authority to do so, to so act. Those clients who did not wish to do this would have no where else to go to engage such services. This would also resolve the issue with the SRA Code, as where a statutory register existed, disclosure would then be "required....by law" and would probably not therefore even require further statutory interference with the Code or rule changes by the SRA.

Legal professional privilege

11. It is to be hoped that the regulation of lobbyists in the UK will not undermine the principle of legal professional privilege. The Society would strongly oppose any attempt to undercut this important principle.

3. *Which lobbying contacts are of greatest legitimate public interest?*

— *Does the consultation paper envisage the capture of appropriate information about these contacts, as opposed to other kinds of contact?*

12. The Law Society believes lobbying is a vital part of the democratic process, helping to inform politicians and decision-makers of key issues and concerns and the potential outcomes of policies, actions and legislation. This is aided largely by the experience and expert knowledge possessed by many organisations seeking to influence the political process, including representative bodies, trade unions, businesses and interest groups. Their input equally helps to ensure that policy and legislation is made which is representative of the views of those who it may impact upon.

13. The Society therefore supports an open and inclusive approach towards lobbying, with adequate opportunity for individuals and organisations to have input into the decision-making and scrutiny processes.

14. The Society welcomes recent developments, including the expansion of pre-legislative scrutiny and the Public Bill Committee system, which have helped to enhance these opportunities. The Society believes that organisations should be able, if desired, to seek support and advice from commercial consultancies or in-house teams on how best to influence the political process.

15. The Society would however express concern if personal relationships between public affairs practitioners and politicians/decision-makers are exploited for commercial gain, for example, through the explicit sale of "access". In addition, the Society would strongly object to money being exchanged between clients or practitioners and politicians in return for sought action or influence.

4. *How should the Government deal in policy and practice with how it might be lobbied on the issue of a statutory register of lobbyists?*

— *How open should the Government be about such lobbying contacts?*

16. The Society's understanding is that the Minister did not meet with any interested parties prior to the publication of the Green Paper. The Society would expect subsequent external meetings to be declared in the usual way on the existing register.

5. *How should the Government analyse the consultation responses, and seek to balance the weight of opposing argument?*

17. The Society strongly supports a process of evidence-based policymaking.

18. The Society believes that it will frequently be the case that some organisations are in a position to provide more substantial and expert opinion on certain issues than others. For example, the Law Society possesses a number of specialist committees, made up of experienced and senior practitioners across various different areas of law. This means that the Society is able to offer authoritative, considered views on the practical implications of policies and legislation in many areas, such as housing, civil and family justice, criminal justice, immigration, companies and regulation.

19. It may therefore be the case that, as a general rule, where such expert opinion is available to politicians and decision-makers it will receive stronger attention. The Society does, however, support the view that where a range of views are communicated on a particular issue, all should be given equal consideration.

6. *Do you have any comments on how any proposals emerging from the consultation should be implemented?*

20. When the new register in the UK comes into force it will be important that there be a sufficient lead-in time for the issues raised above to be satisfactorily addressed.

21. It will be important that law firms not wishing to join the register be given sufficient time to address issues that this will give rise to with existing clients.

22. There should also be a clear procedure set out for de-registration if firms that have registered subsequently wish to withdraw from it, in the light of its continuing operation.

February 2012

Written evidence submitted by Dr John Hogan, College of Business, Dublin Institute of Technology, Professor Gary Murphy, School of Law and Government, Dublin City University and Dr Raj Chari, Department of Political Science, Trinity College Dublin

1. My colleagues Dr. Raj Chari, Professor Gary Murphy and I have gone over the Political and Constitutional Reform Committee's questions in relation to the introduction of a statutory register of lobbyists in the UK and we have developed responses to each. Hopefully, you might find these responses to be helpful as you examine this issue.

Does the Government's consultation paper represent a balanced approach to the idea of a statutory register?

2. A problem with the paper is that examples provided in Annex A concern lobbying regulations at the federal levels in the US, Canada and Australia. But, there is a lot of innovation going on in terms of lobbying regulations at the state and provincial levels in each of these countries as well. In our own research we found that states like Washington State in the US and Queensland in Australia were some ways ahead of their federal governments in terms of the rigour of the lobbying regulations they introduced. Given the size of the UK, it is probable that more will be learned from examining the type of lobbying regulations in place in a jurisdiction of similar economic size and population, such as the state of California, as opposed to Washington DC, which is capital to a vastly bigger country with a completely different structure—it being a federal republic. It may also be noted that several other regulatory regimes have recently been set up throughout the world, including Lithuania, Poland, Taiwan, Israel, France, and Slovenia. Please see www.regulatelobbying.com for the interactive map which will also allow one examine text of these and other country's legislation.

Does the paper present the evidence in a balanced way?

3. We think that the evidence could be presented in a more nuanced fashion. By this we mean that there are various types/categories of regulations in existence—low, medium and high (see Chari et al., 2010). Each of these categories of regulations contain certain pros and cons. Also, the reader should be made aware that the US and Canadian federal regulations, when initially introduced, were much weaker than they currently are. At the US federal level, the introduction of lobbying regulations has been a gradual iterative process from 1946, to 1995 and through to 2007. Each new law has been stronger than the past, as there is an institutional learning process in operation. As such, it is necessary to present to the reader the fact that there is no silver bullet in relation to lobbying transparency and that the legislation, once introduced, will by its very nature be subject to revisions as time passes. There is also the fact that other EU countries now have lobbying regulations—Germany, France, Poland, Lithuania. These examples could also be presented, as in the case of Poland and Lithuania, they like the UK, looked to the US and Canada when considering the introduction of lobbying regulations. So, there are probably experiential lessons to be learned from how these eastern EU states have found the process.

Are you confident that the issues covered are ones on which the Government has an open mind?

4. Yes we are confident that the present British Government has an open mind on the issues covered.

Is the Government clear wherever it has a preference for a particular option, and is this preference in each case a reasonable one?

5. In terms of defining what lobbying and what a lobbyists is, we think that the UK Government would do well to look to outside examples. As this is something which the UK has no experience of, but countries such as the US, Canada, Australia, Poland all do, then examining the various ways that they define lobbying and lobbyists will be of great assistance. In the case of the US, state governments have been regulating lobbying since the mid nineteenth century. Their approach has tended to be much more robust than that of the Federal Government. As such, the UK should be looking towards the regulations in place, as well as how they are

implemented, in states like Washington State, Kentucky, Connecticut and New York as opposed to simply looking to Washington DC.

6. Please also remember that in Australia, the lobbying regulations are based on codes of conduct not legislation, and this is something that the UK Government's discussion document omits. Further, in addition to excluding in-house lobbyists, Australian regulations also exclude accountants and lawyers. Many of the politicians we have spoken to in Australia, at both the federal and state levels, felt that this was an error that they were going to have to revisit and rectify as it has resulted in a large loophole in their regulations.

Does the consultation paper contain the right questions?

7. It generally seems to ask correct and relevant questions. But, considering that this is such a complex field, some more questions might be asked, such as those set out below.

Is each of the questions asked in a balanced way?

8. Most of the questions seem balanced and fair. We would just like to make the following observations:

9. In relation to the questions on sanctions: it seems obvious that non-compliance with the rules should warrant a penalty. In most jurisdictions there are clearly defined and proportionate penalties for lobbyists who engage in misconduct. The report highlights some of these penalties in Annex A. As such there are good examples to follow from both the US and Canada.

10. In relation to the questions on the Registrar's Operation: it might be well to ask about the level of independence the office will have from government, as well as the level of funding the Government intends to provide it with. International experience suggests that those countries which have Registrars who are structurally housed within part of an existing ministry (such as the case of Poland), inevitably have more political interference and thus lose their independence. It seems imperative that if a Registrar is to function effectively it must have institutional independence.

Are there any important questions that are not asked?

11. We would suggest that there are a number of other questions that should be asked:

11.1 Concerning lobbyist activity:

- How many days can a person be active as a lobbyist before they are required to register?
- Are lobbyists going to have to reveal on their registration from the subject matter or bill that their lobbying concerns?
- Is a lobbyist required to submit a photograph with registration?
- Is a lobbyist required to identify by name each of employer on the registration form?

11.2 Concerning lobbyist expenditure:

- Is a lobbyist required to file a spending report?
- Is spending on household members of public officials by a lobbyist required to be reported?
- Is a lobbyist required to disclose direct business associations with public officials, candidates or members of their households?
- Will the responsible agency/body provide overall totals for activity and spending throughout the year?

11.3 Concerning register location:

- Where will the register be located?
- How often will the details contained on the register be updated by the responsible body?
- Will the public have free electronic accesss to the register?

11.4 Concerning additional functions of the agency:

- Will this responsible agency/body have statutory authority to audit the lobbyists' returns?
- Will the agency have the power to conduct mandatory audits?

11.5 Concerning penalties:

- Will there be a statutory penalty for late filing of a lobby registration form?
- Will there be a statutory penalty for incomplete filing of a lobby registration form?
- Will the responsible agency publish lists of delinquent filers on their website?
- Will penalties follow the example set in the US by including fines as well as the possibility of imprisonment for very serious misconduct?

11.6 Concerning transparency:

- Will the responsible agency publish lists of lobbyists who have been struck off the register on their website?

11.7 Concerning former politicians who become lobbyists:

— Will there be a "cooling off" period required before former member of Parliament can register as lobbyists?

Which lobbying contacts are of greatest legitimate public interest?

12. Clients of lobbyists and the elected officials that are lobbied are the most important contacts. It is important to know who the lobbyists is acting as a conduit between.

— *Does the consultation paper envisage the capture of appropriate information about these contacts, as opposed to other kinds of contact?*

13. Yes this does seem to be the case.

How should the Government deal in policy and practice with how it might be lobbied on the issue of a statutory register of lobbyists?

14. The real value of such lobbying regulations comes from their implementation. The law itself can be very detailed and on paper look very strong, ensuring much greater transparency than previously. However, implementation is crucial in this case. It is vital that the Government, despite the recession, is ready and willing to provide the registrar with the necessary resources to police the industry as well as insuring its independence.

— *How open should the Government be about such lobbying contacts?*

15. In all regulatory systems where registration is mandatory, it is the lobbyist's responsibility to register. This allows the public to see with whom lobbyists are making contact when attempting to influence policy. Our research has shown that in many cases where this registration exists, politicians themselves will make it a point to know that the lobbyist is registered. Lobbying legislation, however, places very little responsibility on the politicians themselves to declare with whom they talk. But our research has shown that with a register, politicians themselves are open with whom they have talked.

How should the Government analyse the consultation responses, and seek to balance the weight of opposing argument?

16. The ultimate objective of this kind of legislation is to shine a light into the black box of policymaking. Any arguments made that would impede the sought after transparency, or provide certain groups, like lawyers or accountant (as in Australia) with exemptions from lobbying regulation, will need to be carefully considered. In Australia, many of the legislators we spoke with said that exempting lawyers and accountants had been a major mistake that they would have to rectify. Such regulations serve to make lobbying a more trusted and respectable industry. Something we found in Eastern Europe was that the word lobbyists ceased to be a fully pejorative term once a register was up and running. In that context it is well to remember that the work carried out by interest or lobby groups is a central and legitimate part of the democratic process within all liberal democratic systems. Although the term has often been associated with negative connotations, throughout the democratic world the work of lobbyists is essential when policy is formulated. Lobbyists are an accepted element within society, providing the necessary input and feedback into the political system, thereby helping to develop policy outputs which drive political and economic aspects of our daily lives.

17. The Government should not take too long in seeking to introduce the "perfect" lobbyist register. It should, taking its lessons from other jurisdictions, as well as the consultation process responses, seek to introduce a "good" register for the UK sooner rather than later. By "good", we mean one that is suited to the UK and its politics. Once the register is up and running there can be regular reviews as to how it is progressing, as well as comparative examinations as to how it measures up against similar registers in other countries. Further consultations can be held periodically in order to examine the function of the register and consider if additional amending legislations needs to be introduced, in order to tighten up any loopholes that might appear.

Do you have any comments on how any proposals emerging from the consultation should be implemented?

18. The implementation phase should, above all, be run by a Registrar that has complete independence and is free from partisan influence. The Registrar's office should, of course, report to Parliament on an annual or bi-annual basis.

February 2012

Written evidence submitted by Rob Mckinnon

Introduction

1. The Who's Lobbying project is an experiment to collate publicly available data on lobbying and public affairs.

2. Since Sept 2010 the Who's Lobbying project has run a publicly available website, containing information derived from government and Parliament reports, and other publicly available sources.

3. The Who's Lobbying website url is: http://whoslobbying.com/

4. Motivations for the Who's Lobbying project include:

— Public Transparency—to give us easy access on the Web to information about who is trying to influence government and public affairs.

— Government Policy—to inform the UK Government as to what information is and is not available, at a time when they are proposing to create a statutory register of lobbying activity.

— Government Implementation—to show government how to put this type of information on the web in an easy to browse, consistent format.

— Sustainability—to find a way to make the site financially sustainable (it survives on donated time and resources at present).

— Currently the website has separate pages on 8,458 entities that have been reported to either have met a minister, been a lobbying firm client, or given oral evidence to Parliament.

5. More information on the history and public data service offered by Who's Lobbying is contained in *Annex A: Who's Lobbying background.*

Departments in Breach of Ministerial Code

6. Who's Lobbying is extremely disappointed that departments have not released the last eight months worth of ministerial meeting reports.

7. Departments last published meeting reports for the period Apr-Jun 2011.

8. It is now 29 Feb 2012. Where are the last eight months worth of ministerial meeting reports?

9. To put this in perspective, it is now several months after the Liam Fox/Adam Werritty scandal. Yet the Ministry of Defence has still not published the complete ministerial meeting reports of who Liam Fox met in his last few months before resignation.

10. All ministers are in breach of the Ministerial Code May 2010's requirement that "Departments will publish, at least quarterly, details of Ministers' external meetings". - http://www..gov.uk/sites/default/files/resources/ministerial-code-may-2010.pdf

Question 1. *Does the Government's consultation paper represent a balanced approach to the idea of a statutory register? Does the paper present the evidence in a balanced way? Are you confident that the issues covered are ones on which the Government has an open mind? Is the Government clear wherever it has a preference for a particular option, and is this preference in each case a reasonable one?*

11. Very little "evidence" has been included in the Government's consultation entitled "Introducing a Statutory Register of Lobbyists".

PRCA withdrew from UKPAC

12. In the consultation's Annex A, the Government presents the UKPAC's combined voluntary register as if it was a successfully working register that is endorsed by the so-called "lobbying industry". This impression is a false one.

13. In December 2010, one of the three main lobbying industry bodies, PRCA, withdrew from the UKPAC stating:

> *"For the past 18 months, we have worked hard alongside our partners within UKPAC to find the best route forward for the public affairs industry. It is with regret that we have reluctantly concluded that UKPAC will not be able to deliver the statutory register that the Government has decided to introduce. Thanks to repeated delays and inaccuracies in its work, UKPAC simply lacks the credibility and competence to meet the Government's objectives." - http://www.prca.org.uk/UKPACresignation*

14. The UKPAC register website itself is flawed by design in that it does not have a history of registrations beyond the current period being reported.

15. In Nov 2011, the UKPAC register still only contained data covering the period Sep-Nov 2010. The data was a year out-of-date. Did the Cabinet Office delay the consultation in order to give UKPAC time to get more up-to-date data on its register before the consultation was released?

Justification for not proposing more rigorous disclosure requirements

16. In the consultation the Government fails to satisfactorily justify why it doesn't propose the more rigorous disclosure requirements of other jurisdictions.

17. There should have been at least consideration of requirements similar to that of USA law which requires all lobbyists to submit reports on their company (both for in-house and agency lobbyists), how much was spent, and what issues were being lobbied on for whom, including exactly which bills are being lobbied on, which public agencies were contacted, and whether the lobbyist had previous employment as a senior government official.

To reiterate statements from another submitter's evidence:

18. "Disclosure of ministerial meetings provides very little transparency and cannot be used as justification for limiting the scope of the register."

19. First, it is far from clear from the descriptions given in the ministerial meeting logs what issues are being discussed: of the 5,144 ministerial meetings recorded, over 1100 of these meetings are reported simply as "introductory meeting/introduction", general "catch-up" or "discussion". *[Who's Lobbying performed this analysis in January 2011.]*

20. Second, while the consultation underlines the requirement in the ministerial code to publish, at least quarterly, details of external meetings, disclosure is often delayed. For example, the last ministerial meetings logged by the Treasury, BIS, and Mark Harper's own department, Cabinet Office, are April-June 2011. *[No departments have published a report for a period past Apr-Jun 2011.]*

21. Third, it is not the case that all meetings between ministers and agencies are recorded. For example, it was recently revealed that Communities Secretary, Eric Pickles had accepted a dinner with lobbying group Bell Pottinger. Pickles said he was not required to register the dinner because he had attended in a "private" and not a "ministerial" capacity. - http://www.thebureauinvestigates.com/2011/10/22/gaping-hole-in-rules-lets-eric-pickles-keep-business-dinner-private/

22. Finally, the focus on face-to-face meetings with ministers shows a misunderstanding of the nature of lobbying. It excludes approaches made to countless other public officials, such as regulators, special advisers and civil servants.

23. Disclosure of ministerial meetings does nothing to address the lack of transparency in lobbying of other public officials."—http://www.publications.parliament.uk/pa/cm201012/cmselect/cmpolcon/writev/1809/mem01.htm

Question 2. *Does the consultation paper contain the right questions? Is each of the questions asked in a balanced way? Are there any important questions that are not asked?*

24. In the "How a register might work" section of the consultation the Government states: "A lobbying firm would be required to update the register quarterly".

25. Why do we have the concept of quarterly registry reports in the first place? Why do quarterly reports exist? They exist because before the Web it was easiest to collate information periodically for publication on paper.

26. The Web is not paper. When you have a new medium you need to rethink these things.

27. You need to think: how can this medium allow us more immediate connection with the world around us?

28. How can this medium allow us to work in a way that we can share what we're doing in a way that is transparent to the public?

Publish ministerial meetings weekly on register website

29. Most departments use the new medium of the Web to share frequent updates with the public via the photo website Flickr, and the social texting website Twitter.

30. At least 15 department's are paying staff to keep photostreams up-to-date on a weekly basis on the Flickr website (Annex B). The photos published include photos of *some* ministers' meetings.

31. At least 19 departments pay staff to provide daily updates on the Twitter social texting website (Annex C). The "tweets" published include mentions of *some* ministers' meetings.

32. Why not have these same staff keep a register website up-to-date with ministerial meetings with the same frequency as they post to Flickr and Twitter?

Publish lobbyists' employment histories on register website

33. About 500 out of the 1,000 lobbying agency staff list on APPC's public affairs register were found to have public LinkedIn profiles, based on research conducted by Who's Lobbying in 2010.

34. These public LinkedIn profiles contain employment histories, as well as the name, current title, and employer of each lobbyist.

35. It's likely that a large number of in-house lobbyists also have public LinkedIn profiles. Analysis of the LinkedIn profiles found being to current agency lobbyists, showed that there is a revolving door between employment at lobbying firms, thinktanks, and in-house public affairs positions.

36. Why not leverage this publicly available information when constructing a register?

37. Why not require all lobbyists on the register to provide details of their public LinkedIn profile if they have one? And give them the option to keep their employment details up-to-date there?

38. Software could be written to automatically keep this in sync with the register website. It may reduce the burden of compliance on the lobbyists, and ensure the register is kept more frequently up-to-date.

Public usability

39. There was no analysis of how a register should work for a member of the public.

40. Given we are in the 21st century, a register website that allows online updating, search, browsing, filtering by client organisation, by issue, by category of organisation would be a reasonable expectation by a member of the public.

Lobbying spend and lobbying issues and in-house lobbyists

41. Research by Who's Lobbying has identified 167 organisations with disclosed lobbying activity in both the UK and USA.

42. In the USA these 167 organisations have a ***combined disclosure of $3,499,731,804 total amount spent on lobbying and lobbying firms hired.***

43. Annex D lists organisations that have a declared US amount spent on lobbying of $10 million or more.

44. In the USA there is also disclosure of the issues and bills organisations have lobbied on. Some of this is shown in Annex D.

45. Through UK department ministerial meeting reports we know these 167 organisations have had at least 343 meetings with government.

46. However due to the vague meeting descriptions supplied by departments, there's inadequate information to determine the exact issues being lobbied on.

47. US data was taken from InfluenceExplorer.com. Figures are based on lobbying activity reported to the Senate Office of Public Records. Reported dollar amounts are required to be accurate to the nearest $20,000.

48. Given the amount of money disclosed by these organisations in the US, there is justification for legitimate public interest in requiring disclosure of the same information through legislation for a UK register of lobbyists.

49. The Government should have asked in the consultation whether the public want disclosure of financial spend, lobbying issues, bills being lobbied on, and those details for in-house in addition to agency lobbyists.

Question 3. *Which lobbying contacts are of greatest legitimate public interest? Does the consultation paper envisage the capture of appropriate information about these contacts, as opposed to other kinds of contact?*

50. The public are interested in the timely disclosure of who is lobbying government on what issues, on behalf of who, and how much is spent to do so.

51. Why not define the activity that has the greatest legitimate public interest, and ensure that is appropriately disclosed in a timely fashion?

52. Activity where there is a legitimate public interest includes the drafting of legislation, the drafting of procurement tenders, and the drafting of policy.

53. Any contacts involved in drafting or influencing the text written by drafters, should have their meetings, including phone conversations, with government disclosed, ideally within a week of them occurring.

54. Legislation and policy should not be drafted behind closed doors under the potential influence of external parties with privileged access to government.

Question 4. *How should the Government deal in policy and practice with how it might be lobbied on the issue of a statutory register of lobbyists? How open should the Government be about such lobbying contacts?*

55. Government departments have not disclosed who ministers have meet for the last 8 months. This is despite a promise in the Ministerial Code May 2010 that departments will publish at least quarterly ministers meetings with external interests.

56. The last period the Cabinet Office reported meetings for is Apr-May 2011.

57. In practice the Government should ensure it complies with the Ministerial Code and publish each quarter's meetings at the end of the quarter.

Question 5. *How should the Government analyse the consultation responses, and seek to balance the weight of opposing argument?*

58. That is for the Government to decide. But the Government should ensure the staff involved are reviewed for their impartiality.

59. It was of concern that civil servant Walsh Atkins, reportedly in charge of drafting the Government's register plans, tweeted on 22 December 2011: "I wish Unlock Democracy would die. I am prepared to help it along."

60. Hopefully after her resignation a more impartial civil servant was put into the role of Head of Constitutional Policy Branch at the Cabinet Office.

61. If the Cabinet Office meets organisations representing professional lobbyists, it also has a duty to meet organisations that are campaigning for greater transparency.

Question 6. *Do you have any comments on how any proposals emerging from the consultation should be implemented?*

62. The register should be a website operated on the Web, updated via the Web, with a separate page for the activity for each entity engaged in lobbying or public affairs activity. There should also be a separate page for each entity with in-house lobbyists.

63. "Free-text" organisation names are not unique enough for accurate reporting and onward analysis.

64. In collating data, Who's Lobbying has found at least 1,560 entities listed in different public documents under more than one variant of their name (eg under an acronym, name mis-spelling, trading name, previous name, or name variation or contraction).

65. Company numbers must be provided for every company mentioned, both clients and lobbying firms. This is similar to the manner in which company numbers are reported for companies declaring political donations via the Electoral Commission.

66. If an organisation is not registered in the UK, then its jurisdiction of registration should be supplied as well as its registration number in that jurisdiction.

67. Charity numbers should be provided for every charity mentioned, in addition to their company number if they have one.

68. The full text name of an organisation should be supplied separately from its acronym.

69. For example, the Ministry of Justice reported Kenneth Clarke, Lord Chancellor and Secretary of State for Justice, had a meeting with ICC in January 2011. This acronym is too ambiguous to match to a specific entity—is it the International Criminal Court, or International Chamber of Commerce, or one of the other scores of organisations with this acronym?

70. No umbrella names should be provided to obscure the actual identity of participants.

71. For example, in that same meeting reported by MOJ with Kenneth Clarke, there was a participant referred to as "MNCG". Research suggests that this is the so-called "Multinational Chairman's Group", an umbrella name to cover the identity of an unreported group of influential individuals. If they are representing themselves then they should be required to disclose their own names on a register, else to disclose the legal entities that they represent.

72. Conclusion

73. Who's Lobbying is available to provide further evidence to the Committee, or to generate reports from the data it has collated related to ministerial reports and other public affairs activity.

February 2012

Annex A

WHO'S LOBBYING BACKGROUND

The Who's Lobbying project was conceived after the release of the Public Administration Select Committee report on "Lobbying: Access and influence in Whitehall" in Dec 2008. http://www.publications.parliament.uk/pa/cm200809/cmselect/cmpubadm/36/3602.htm

Software code for a website was started at the end of October 2009, after the Labour Government's promise to publish quarterly ministerial meeting reports. Under the Labour Government no reports were forthcoming until after I sent an FOI request to each department in March 2010 requesting the meeting information.

Most departments refused disclosure, stating the Section 21 future publication exemption. Only some departments actually published reports before the election.

In the Ministerial Code May 2010 the coalition Government's ministers committed departments will publish at least quarterly ministerial meetings. Once again no reports were forthcoming until after I sent an FOI request to each department in July 2010 asking for reports for the Q1 and Q2 2010. Again, most departments refused disclosure, stating the Section 21 future publication exemption, and they also refused to give a date for when that publication was planned.

Since Sept 2010 the Who's Lobbying project has run a publicly available website: http://whoslobbying.com/

Currently the website has separate pages on 8,458 entities. Some summary statistics for those entities:

- Department ministerial meeting disclosures May 2010-June 2011 mention 5,543 entities.
- The 93 lobbying firms registered with APPC or PRCA in 2010–11 list 2,627 organisations as clients.
- At least 52 UK public authorities were listed as clients of lobbying firms in Jun-Aug 2011.
- More than 1,400 organisations had people providing oral evidence to parliament committees 2010–12.
- At least 1,560 entities were listed in different public documents under more than one variant of their name (eg under an acronym, name mis-spelling, trading name, previous name, or name variation or contraction).

On the Who's Lobbying website each entity is listed on its own page, alongside all its activity across ministerial meetings, lobbying firms hired, oral evidence given, and other information such as related Lords staff passes, and lobbying spend in the USA (where lobbying spend has been declared in the USA).

For example, BAE System's page is here: http://whoslobbying.com/uk/bae_systems—I welcome committee members to explore the website for themselves.

To find the same information without Who's Lobbying, you'd have to poke around through dense, difficult-to-navigate websites and hard to find PDF documents.

Ministerial meetings alone have been reported by departments in over 130 different files across 24 different department websites.

Annex B

DEPARTMENT PHOTOSTREAMS ON FLICKR

Department's have not released the last eight months worth of ministerial meeting reports, in breach of the Ministerial Code. The last reports were published for the period Apr-Jun 2011.

Yet at least 15 department's are paying staff to keep photostreams update on a weekly basis on the Flickr website. The photos published include photos of *some* ministers' meetings.

Government Flickr accounts include:

Prime Minister's Office photostream: http://www.flickr.com/photos/number10gov

Cabinet Office photostream: http://www.flickr.com/photos/cabinetoffice

Department for Business, Innovation and Skills photostream: http://www.flickr.com/photos/bisgovuk

Department for Communities and Local Government photostream: http://www.flickr.com/photos/communitiesuk

Department for Culture, Media and Sport photostream: http://www.flickr.com/photos/thedcms

Department for Education photostream: http://www.flickr.com/photos/educationgovuk

Department for International Development photostream: http://www.flickr.com/photos/dfid

Department for Transport photostream: http://www.flickr.com/photos/transportgovuk

Department of Energy and Climate Change photostream: http://www.flickr.com/photos/deccgovuk

Department of Health photostream: http://www.flickr.com/photos/departmentofhealth

Foreign and Commonwealth Office photostream: http://www.flickr.com/photos/foreignoffice

HM Treasury photostream: http://www.flickr.com/photos/hmtreasury

Home Office photostream: http://www.flickr.com/photos/49956354@N04

Ministry of Defence photostream: http://www.flickr.com/photos/defenceimages

Ministry of Justice photostream: http://www.flickr.com/photos/ministryofjustice

Annex C

DEPARTMENT TWITTER ACCOUNTS

Department's have not released the last eight months worth of ministerial meeting reports, in breach of the Ministerial Code. The last reports were published for the period Apr-Jun 2011.

Yet at least 19 departments pay staff to provide daily updates on the Twitter social texting website. The "tweets" published include mentions of *some* ministers' meetings.

Government Twitter accounts include:

http://twitter.com/Number10gov

http://twitter.com/DECCgovuk

http://twitter.com/DefenceHQ

http://twitter.com/Directgov

http://twitter.com/foreignoffice

http://twitter.com/DFID_UK

http://twitter.com/DHgovuk

http://twitter.com/CommunitiesUK

http://twitter.com/transportgovuk

http://twitter.com/cabinetofficeuk

http://twitter.com/educationgovuk

http://twitter.com/UKTI

http://twitter.com/DCMS

http://twitter.com/MoJGovUK

http://twitter.com/DefraGovUK

http://twitter.com/hmtreasury

http://twitter.com/COIgovuk

http://twitter.com/ukhomeoffice

http://twitter.com/bisgovuk

Annex D

USA LOBBYING DISCLOSURE BY ORGANISATIONS LOBBYING IN THE UK

The table below shows organisations with disclosed US lobbying spend over $10,000,000 that have also had disclosed UK based lobbying or public affairs activity in the UK.

US data is from InfluenceExplorer.com. Figures are based on lobbying activity reported to the Senate Office of Public Records. Reported dollar amounts are required to be accurate only to the nearest $20,000. For organizations that are not primarily lobbying firms, we display total amount spent on lobbying.

Organisation	US lobbying spend covers through to end of Q3 2011	US Most Frequently Disclosed Lobbying Issues	UK lobbying spend	UK Most Frequently Disclosed Lobbying Issues
US Chamber of Commerce	$544,505,445	Immigration, Taxes, Fed Budget & Appropriations, Law Enforcement & Crime, Trade	No UK requirement to disclose lobbying spend.	No UK requirement to disclose lobbying issues. Had at least 3 meetings with UK govt since May 2010.
Northrop Grumman	$163,518,093	Transportation, Trade, Government Issues, Energy & Nuclear Power, Aviation, Airlines & Airports	No UK requirement to disclose lobbying spend.	No UK requirement to disclose lobbying issues. Had at least 6 meetings with UK govt since May 2010 .
Exxon Mobil	$160,946,942	Fed Budget & Appropriations, Natural Resources, Government Issues, Consumer Product Safety, Chemical Industry	No UK requirement to disclose lobbying spend.	No UK requirement to disclose lobbying issues. Had at least 6 meetings with UK govt since May 2010 .
Boeing Co	$151,144,310	Taxes, Homeland Security, Foreign Relations, Labor, Antitrust & Workplace, Transportation	No UK requirement to disclose lobbying spend.	No UK requirement to disclose lobbying issues. Had at least 6 meetings with UK govt since May 2010 .
Lockheed Martin	$125,580,880	Homeland Security, Science & Technology, Energy & Nuclear Power, Taxes, Trade	No UK requirement to disclose lobbying spend.	No UK requirement to disclose lobbying issues. Had at least 8 meetings with UK govt since May 2010 .
General Motors	$117,371,000	Fed Budget & Appropriations, Trade, Finance, Transportation, Radio & TV Broadcasting	No UK requirement to disclose lobbying spend.	No UK requirement to disclose lobbying issues. Had at least 5 meetings with UK govt since May 2010 .
Pfizer Inc	$112,520,000	Pharmacy, Consumer Product Safety, Fed Budget & Appropriations, Agriculture, Torts	No UK requirement to disclose lobbying spend.	No UK requirement to disclose lobbying issues. Had at least 12 meetings with UK govt since May 2010 .

Organisation	*US lobbying spend covers through to end of Q3 2011*	*US Most Frequently Disclosed Lobbying Issues*	*UK lobbying spend*	*UK Most Frequently Disclosed Lobbying Issues*
Microsoft Corp	$100,585,000	Copyright, Patent & Trademark, Consumer Product Safety, Science & Technology, Labor, Antitrust & Workplace, Health Issues	No UK requirement to disclose lobbying spend.	No UK requirement to disclose lobbying issues. Had at least 16 meetings with UK govt since May 2010 .
ConocoPhillips	$78,182,717	Natural Resources, Foreign Relations, Clean Air & Water, Transportation, Marine, Boats & Fisheries	No UK requirement to disclose lobbying spend.	No UK requirement to disclose lobbying issues. Had at least 4 meetings with UK govt since May 2010 .
Royal Dutch Shell	$71,508,339	Natural Resources, Clean Air & Water, Trade, Chemical Industry, Foreign Relations	No UK requirement to disclose lobbying spend.	No UK requirement to disclose lobbying issues. Had at least 31 meetings with UK govt since May 2010 .
BP	$65,520,584	Foreign Relations, Clean Air & Water, Natural Resources, Transportation, Chemical Industry	No UK requirement to disclose lobbying spend.	No UK requirement to disclose lobbying issues. Had at least 21 meetings with UK govt since May 2010 .
JPMorgan Chase & Co	$62,759,775	Environment & Superfund, Copyright, Patent & Trademark, Education, Government Issues, Trade	No UK requirement to disclose lobbying spend.	No UK requirement to disclose lobbying issues. Had at least 11 meetings with UK govt since May 2010 .
Raytheon Co	$60,844,188	Science & Technology, Trade, Foreign Relations, Transportation, Aerospace	No UK requirement to disclose lobbying spend.	No UK requirement to disclose lobbying issues. Had at least 1 meeting with UK govt since May 2010 .
Bristol-Myers Squibb	$60,776,355	Pharmacy, Trade, Agriculture, Consumer Product Safety, Clean Air & Water	No UK requirement to disclose lobbying spend.	No UK requirement to disclose lobbying issues. Had at least 1 meeting with UK govt since May 2010 .
Abbott Laboratories	$53,296,000	Fed Budget & Appropriations, Agriculture, Food Industry, Pharmacy, Medical Research & Clin Labs	No UK requirement to disclose lobbying spend.	No UK requirement to disclose lobbying issues.

Organisation	US lobbying spend covers through to end of Q3 2011	US Most Frequently Disclosed Lobbying Issues	UK lobbying spend	UK Most Frequently Disclosed Lobbying Issues
Intel Corp	$52,530,779	Environment & Superfund, Telecommunications, Science & Technology, Immigration, Fed Budget & Appropriations	No UK requirement to disclose lobbying spend.	No UK requirement to disclose lobbying issues. Had at least 1 meeting with UK govt since May 2010 .
United Parcel Service	$45,311,216	Trade, Energy & Nuclear Power, Trucking & Shipping, Retirement, Fed Budget & Appropriations	No UK requirement to disclose lobbying spend.	No UK requirement to disclose lobbying issues. Had at least 1 meeting with UK govt since May 2010 .
MasterCard Inc	$44,185,000	Labor, Antitrust & Workplace, Computers & Information Tech, Copyright, Patent & Trademark, Gaming, Gambling & Casinos, Science & Technology	No UK requirement to disclose lobbying spend.	No UK requirement to disclose lobbying issues. Had at least 1 meeting with UK govt since May 2010 .
Qualcomm Inc	$43,632,100	Taxes, Transportation, Trucking & Shipping, Fed Budget & Appropriations, Education	No UK requirement to disclose lobbying spend.	No UK requirement to disclose lobbying issues. Had at least 1 meeting with UK govt since May 2010 .
Time Warner	$43,380,000	Trade, Postal, Consumer Product Safety, Computers & Information Tech, Advertising	No UK requirement to disclose lobbying spend.	No UK requirement to disclose lobbying issues. Had at least 2 meetings with UK govt since May 2010 .
DaimlerChrysler	$41,638,707	Defense, Health Issues, Transportation, Bankruptcy, Environment & Superfund	No UK requirement to disclose lobbying spend.	No UK requirement to disclose lobbying issues. Had at least 1 meeting with UK govt since May 2010 .

Organisation	*US lobbying spend covers through to end of Q3 2011*	*US Most Frequently Disclosed Lobbying Issues*	*UK lobbying spend*	*UK Most Frequently Disclosed Lobbying Issues*
Bayer Corp	$41,517,686	Fed Budget & Appropriations, Environment & Superfund, Energy & Nuclear Power, Pharmacy, Railroads	No UK requirement to disclose lobbying spend.	No UK requirement to disclose lobbying issues.
Visa Inc	$37,113,333	Taxes, Labor, Antitrust & Workplace, Government Issues, Gaming, Gambling & Casinos, Education	No UK requirement to disclose lobbying spend.	No UK requirement to disclose lobbying issues. Had at least 1 meeting with UK govt since May 2010 .
Siemens Corp	$36,190,223	Trade, Medicare & Medicaid, Telecommunications, Environment & Superfund, Copyright, Patent & Trademark	No UK requirement to disclose lobbying spend.	No UK requirement to disclose lobbying issues. Had at least 10 meetings with UK govt since May 2010 .
BAE Systems	$34,527,000	Taxes, Trade, Homeland Security, Aerospace, Law Enforcement & Crime	No UK requirement to disclose lobbying spend.	No UK requirement to disclose lobbying issues. Had at least 32 meetings with UK govt since May 2010 .
Blackstone Group	$34,032,314	Advertising, Finance, Trade, Automotive Industry, Health Issues	No UK requirement to disclose lobbying spend.	No UK requirement to disclose lobbying issues. Had at least 1 meeting with UK govt since May 2010 .
Accenture	$32,996,358	Homeland Security, Education, Finance, Veterans Affairs, Health Issues	No UK requirement to disclose lobbying spend.	No UK requirement to disclose lobbying issues. Had at least 6 meetings with UK govt since May 2010 .
Sony Corp	$32,972,000	Consumer Product Safety, Computers & Information Tech, Education, Science & Technology, Environment & Superfund	No UK requirement to disclose lobbying spend.	No UK requirement to disclose lobbying issues. Had at least 5 meetings with UK govt since May 2010 .
Coca-Cola Co	$32,721,775	Environment & Superfund, Agriculture, Labor, Antitrust & Workplace, Government Issues, Energy & Nuclear Power	No UK requirement to disclose lobbying spend.	No UK requirement to disclose lobbying issues.

Organisation	US lobbying spend covers through to end of Q3 2011	US Most Frequently Disclosed Lobbying Issues	UK lobbying spend	UK Most Frequently Disclosed Lobbying Issues
United Airlines	$32,305,732	Retirement, Taxes, Homeland Security, Environment & Superfund, Government Issues	No UK requirement to disclose lobbying spend.	No UK requirement to disclose lobbying issues. Had at least 1 meeting with UK govt since May 2010 .
Anheuser-Busch InBev	$31,870,406	Transportation, Agriculture, Alcohol & Drug Abuse, Fed Budget & Appropriations, Environment & Superfund	No UK requirement to disclose lobbying spend.	No UK requirement to disclose lobbying issues. Had at least 1 meeting with UK govt since May 2010 .
Baxter Healthcare	$31,140,209	Copyright, Patent & Trademark, Disaster & Emergency Planning, Agriculture, Medical Research & Clin Labs, Retirement	No UK requirement to disclose lobbying spend.	No UK requirement to disclose lobbying issues. Had at least 1 meeting with UK govt since May 2010 .
L-3 Communications	$31,050,356	Foreign Relations, Law Enforcement & Crime, Trade, Radio & TV Broadcasting, Labor, Antitrust & Workplace	No UK requirement to disclose lobbying spend.	No UK requirement to disclose lobbying issues. Had at least 1 meeting with UK govt since May 2010 .
American Express	$29,020,000	Bankruptcy, Copyright, Patent & Trademark, Labor, Antitrust & Workplace, Torts, Trade	No UK requirement to disclose lobbying spend.	No UK requirement to disclose lobbying issues. Had at least 1 meeting with UK govt since May 2010 .
Bank of America	$29,011,040	Housing, Trade, Consumer Product Safety, Education, Retirement	No UK requirement to disclose lobbying spend.	No UK requirement to disclose lobbying issues. Had at least 2 meetings with UK govt since May 2010 .
3M Co	$27,756,196	Environment & Superfund, Trade, Energy & Nuclear Power, Copyright, Patent & Trademark, Disaster & Emergency Planning	No UK requirement to disclose lobbying spend.	No UK requirement to disclose lobbying issues. Had at least 7 meetings with UK govt since May 2010 .
Genworth Financial	$27,280,000	Banking, Retirement, Medicare & Medicaid, Fed Budget & Appropriations, Medical Research & Clin Labs	No UK requirement to disclose lobbying spend.	No UK requirement to disclose lobbying issues.

Organisation	*US lobbying spend covers through to end of Q3 2011*	*US Most Frequently Disclosed Lobbying Issues*	*UK lobbying spend*	*UK Most Frequently Disclosed Lobbying Issues*
Nissan North America	$27,056,000	Finance, Labor, Antitrust & Workplace, Economics & Econ Development, Homeland Security, Consumer Product Safety	No UK requirement to disclose lobbying spend.	No UK requirement to disclose lobbying issues. Had at least 11 meetings with UK govt since May 2010 .
Clear Channel Communications	$27,019,576	Fed Budget & Appropriations, Law Enforcement & Crime, Arts & Entertainment, Media Information & Publishing, Finance	No UK requirement to disclose lobbying spend.	No UK requirement to disclose lobbying issues.
Goldman Sachs	$25,587,000	Trade, Retirement, Commodities, Copyright, Patent & Trademark, Agriculture	No UK requirement to disclose lobbying spend.	No UK requirement to disclose lobbying issues. Had at least 14 meetings with UK govt since May 2010 .
Genzyme Corp	$24,622,403	Medical Research & Clin Labs, Fed Budget & Appropriations, Insurance, Science & Technology, Food Industry	No UK requirement to disclose lobbying spend.	No UK requirement to disclose lobbying issues.
Hewlett-Packard	$24,396,727	Telecommunications, Immigration, Copyright, Patent & Trademark, Defense, Education	No UK requirement to disclose lobbying spend.	No UK requirement to disclose lobbying issues. Had at least 9 meetings with UK govt since May 2010 .
Amazon.com	$22,556,000	Labor, Antitrust & Workplace, Law Enforcement & Crime, Transportation, Banking, Computers & Information Tech	No UK requirement to disclose lobbying spend.	No UK requirement to disclose lobbying issues. Had at least 5 meetings with UK govt since May 2010 .
Google Inc	$20,790,000	Advertising, Computers & Information Tech, Science & Technology, Consumer Product Safety, Small Business	No UK requirement to disclose lobbying spend.	No UK requirement to disclose lobbying issues. Had at least 19 meetings with UK govt since May 2010 .
Motion Picture Assn of America	$20,499,220	Telecommunications, Education, Law Enforcement & Crime, Computers & Information Tech, Fed Budget & Appropriations	No UK requirement to disclose lobbying spend.	No UK requirement to disclose lobbying issues. Had at least 3 meetings with UK govt since May 2010 .

Organisation	*US lobbying spend covers through to end of Q3 2011*	*US Most Frequently Disclosed Lobbying Issues*	*UK lobbying spend*	*UK Most Frequently Disclosed Lobbying Issues*
SABMiller	$19,095,676	Clean Air & Water, Trucking & Shipping, Advertising, Food Industry, Immigration	No UK requirement to disclose lobbying spend.	No UK requirement to disclose lobbying issues. Had at least 1 meeting with UK govt since May 2010 .
ChevronTexaco	$17,459,296	Taxes, Environment & Superfund, Law Enforcement & Crime, Government Issues, Retirement	No UK requirement to disclose lobbying spend.	No UK requirement to disclose lobbying issues. Had at least 3 meetings with UK govt since May 2010 .
Universal Music Group	$16,880,000	Government Issues, Education, Homeland Security, Travel & Tourism, Computers & Information Tech	No UK requirement to disclose lobbying spend.	No UK requirement to disclose lobbying issues. Had at least 3 meetings with UK govt since May 2010 .
Diageo PLC	$16,854,000	Food Industry, Labor, Antitrust & Workplace, Small Business, Health Issues, Fed Budget & Appropriations	No UK requirement to disclose lobbying spend.	No UK requirement to disclose lobbying issues. Had at least 12 meetings with UK govt since May 2010 .
Emergent BioSolutions	$16,193,000	Medical Research & Clin Labs, Fed Budget & Appropriations, Government Issues, Pharmacy, Science & Technology	No UK requirement to disclose lobbying spend.	No UK requirement to disclose lobbying issues.
Continental Airlines	$15,878,895	Immigration, Postal, Trade, Bankruptcy, Insurance	No UK requirement to disclose lobbying spend.	No UK requirement to disclose lobbying issues.
eBay Inc	$15,205,700	Law Enforcement & Crime, Banking, Finance, Small Business, Immigration	No UK requirement to disclose lobbying spend.	No UK requirement to disclose lobbying issues. Had at least 1 meeting with UK govt since May 2010 .
Credit Suisse Group	$15,170,000	Housing, Health Issues, Fed Budget & Appropriations, Foreign Relations, Trade	No UK requirement to disclose lobbying spend.	No UK requirement to disclose lobbying issues.
Barclays	$15,020,000	Housing, Energy & Nuclear Power, Trade, Commodities, Bankruptcy	No UK requirement to disclose lobbying spend.	No UK requirement to disclose lobbying issues. Had at least 41 meetings with UK govt since May 2010 .

Organisation	*US lobbying spend covers through to end of Q3 2011*	*US Most Frequently Disclosed Lobbying Issues*	*UK lobbying spend*	*UK Most Frequently Disclosed Lobbying Issues*
Unisys Corp	$14,583,982	Taxes, Trade, Agriculture, Health Issues, Immigration	No UK requirement to disclose lobbying spend.	No UK requirement to disclose lobbying issues.
Boehringer Ingelheim Corp	$14,256,546	Trade, Environment & Superfund, Fed Budget & Appropriations, Agriculture, Animals	No UK requirement to disclose lobbying spend.	No UK requirement to disclose lobbying issues.
Syngenta Corp	$14,150,000	Trade, Government Issues, Taxes, Foreign Relations, Tariffs	No UK requirement to disclose lobbying spend.	No UK requirement to disclose lobbying issues. Had at least 1 meeting with UK govt since May 2010 .
Boston Scientific Corp	$13,690,000	Trade, Fed Budget & Appropriations, Science & Technology, Labor, Antitrust & Workplace, Finance	No UK requirement to disclose lobbying spend.	No UK requirement to disclose lobbying issues. Had at least 2 meetings with UK govt since May 2010 .
Sony Music Entertainment	$13,235,000	Arts & Entertainment, Labor, Antitrust & Workplace, Manufacturing, Media Information & Publishing, Science & Technology	No UK requirement to disclose lobbying spend.	No UK requirement to disclose lobbying issues. Had at least 2 meetings with UK govt since May 2010 .
Apple Inc	$12,703,008	Education, Environment & Superfund, Consumer Product Safety, Finance, Fed Budget & Appropriations	No UK requirement to disclose lobbying spend.	No UK requirement to disclose lobbying issues. Had at least 5 meetings with UK govt since May 2010 .
Capital One Financial	$12,428,000	Consumer Product Safety, Advertising, Labor, Antitrust & Workplace, Computers & Information Tech, Radio & TV Broadcasting	No UK requirement to disclose lobbying spend.	No UK requirement to disclose lobbying issues.
Toshiba Corp	$12,085,000	Copyright, Patent & Trademark, Computers & Information Tech, Science & Technology, Utilities, Finance	No UK requirement to disclose lobbying spend.	No UK requirement to disclose lobbying issues. Had at least 1 meeting with UK govt since May 2010 .
Unilever	$10,530,000	Fed Budget & Appropriations, Consumer Product Safety, Health Issues, Energy & Nuclear Power, Government Issues	No UK requirement to disclose lobbying spend.	No UK requirement to disclose lobbying issues. Had at least 3 meetings with UK govt since May 2010 .

Organisation	*US lobbying spend covers through to end of Q3 2011*	*US Most Frequently Disclosed Lobbying Issues*	*UK lobbying spend*	*UK Most Frequently Disclosed Lobbying Issues*
ING Group	$10,176,866	Banking, Torts, Government Issues, Environment & Superfund, Telecommunications	No UK requirement to disclose lobbying spend.	No UK requirement to disclose lobbying issues.
Rolls-Royce PLC	$10,132,386	Aerospace, Taxes, Transportation, Manufacturing, Trade	No UK requirement to disclose lobbying spend.	No UK requirement to disclose lobbying issues. Had at least 18 meetings with UK govt since May 2010 .

Written evidence submitted by Jeremy Heywood, Secretary to the Cabinet

1. Thank you for your letter of 30 April.[30]

2. The Government's commitment is to publish this information on a quarterly basis. In addition to information about ministers' meetings with external organisations, departments also publish a range of other information including, for ministers, information on gifts and hospitality received and overseas travel; for special advisers, information on gifts and hospitality received and meetings with senior representatives of media organisations; for permanent secretaries, information on meetings with external organisations, business expenses and hospitality received; and for the most senior civil servants details of their expenses.

3. This is a considerable amount of information published by departments and it does take time to collate and check the information. However, I do agree that this information should be published as quickly as practicably possible, and I have asked departments to continue to work to speed up the process.

May 2012

Printed in the United Kingdom by The Stationery Office Limited
07/2012 019994 19585

[30] See Q 402.

ISBN 978-0-215-04682-6
9 780215 046826
PEFC/16-33-622